D0762517

World population and the United Nations

Stanley P. Johnson

World population and the United Nations

Challenge and response

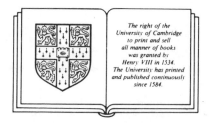

The right of the
University of Cambridge
to print and sell
all manner of books
was granted by
Henry VIII in 1534.
The University has printed
and published continuously
since 1584.

CAMBRIDGE UNIVERSITY PRESS

Cambridge

New York   Port Chester   Melbourne   Sydney

Published by the Press Syndicate of the University of Cambridge
The Pitt Building, Trumpington Street, Cambridge CB2 1RP
40 West 20th Street, New York, NY 10011, USA
10 Stamford Road, Oakleigh, Melbourne 3166, Australia

First published 1987
Reprinted 1990

Printed in Great Britain at
the Athenaeum Press Ltd, Newcastle upon Tyne

British Library Cataloguing in publication data
Johnson, Stanley, 1940-
World Population and the United Nations:
challenge and response.
1. United Nations   2. Population policy
I. Title
363.9   HB883.5

Library of Congress cataloguing in publication data
Johnson, Stanley, 1940-
World population and the United Nations.
Bibliography
Includes index.
1. United Nations-Population assistance.   2. Population policy.
3. Population   I. Title
HB884.5.J64   1987   363.9   87-5126

ISBN 0 521 32207 3 hard covers
ISBN 0 521 31104 7 paperback

US

This book is dedicated to the memory of Rafael M. Salas, Executive Director of the United Nations Fund for Population Activities, 1969–1987.

The ancient philosophers of Asia, in their wisdom, stressed the need for a balance and harmony between man and his world. Without a sane and orderly approach to the problems of population, there can be no balance and no harmony. (From Mr Salas' statement, as Executive Director of UNFPA, to the World Population Conference, Bucharest, Romania, 20 August 1974.)

Rapid population growth during the past three decades has led to the renewed perception that an equilibrium between population and life support systems has to be achieved.... Our goal is the stabilization of global population within the shortest period possible before the end of the next century. (From Mr Salas' statement, as Secretary General of the International Conference on Population, Mexico City, Mexico, 6 August 1984.)

Contents

List of Tables

List of Figures

Glossary of acronyms and initials

ACC	Administrative Committee on Coordination
AID	United States Agency for International Development
BEMFAM	Sociedade Civil Bem-estar Familiar do Brasil
BKKBN	National Family-Planning Co-ordinating Board, Indonesia
CAPMAS	Egyptian Central Agency for Public Mobilization and Statistics
CELADE	Centro Latinoamericano de Demografia
CIAP	Inter-American Committee of the Alliance for Progress
CONAPO	National Population Council of Mexico (Consejo Nacional de Población)
DAC	Development Assistance Committee of OECD (q.v.)
DTCD	United Nations Department of Technical Co-operation for Development
ECA	Economic Commission for Africa
ECAFE	Economic Commission for Asia and the Far East
ECE	Economic Commission for Europe
ECLA	Economic Commission for Latin America
ECOSOC	United Nations Economic and Social Council
EEC	European Economic Community
ESCAP	United Nations Economic and Social Commission for Asia and the Pacific
FP	Family Planning
FAO	Food and Agriculture Organization of the United Nations
GA	General Assembly (of the United Nations)
GOI	Government of India
GRR	Gross Reproduction Rate
IBRD	International Bank for Reconstruction and Development (or World Bank)
IDA	International Development Association, an affiliate of the World Bank
IEC	Information, Education and Communication programmes
IIED	International Institute for Environment and Development
IEP	International Encyclopaedia of Population
ILO	International Labour Organization
IPPF	International Planned Parenthood Federation
IUCN	International Union for the Conservation of Nature and Natural Resources
IUD	Intra-uterine contraceptive device

IUSSP	International Union for the Scientific Study of Population
JOICP	Japanese Organization for International Co-operation in Family Planning
LBKM	National Family Planning Institute, Indonesia
LDCs	Less-Developed Countries
MCH/FP	Maternal and Child Health/Family Planning
NGO	Non-Governmental Organization
NRR	Net Reproduction Rate
ODA	Overseas Development Administration, United Kingdom
PAHO	Pan American Health Organization
PD	Population Dynamics
PHN	Population, Health and Nutrition programmes
PPPO	Population Programme and Projects Office
PPO	Population Programme Officer
OECD	Organization for Economic Co-operation and Development
NIEO	New International Economic Order
SIDA	Swedish International Development Authority
TFR	Total Fertility Rate
UN	United Nations
UNCHE	United Nations Conference on the Human Environment
UNDP	United Nations Development Programme
UNEP	United Nations Environment Programme
UNESCO	United Nations Educational, Scientific and Cultural Organization
UNFPA	United Nations Fund for Population Activities
UNICEF	United Nations Children's Fund
UNTAB	United Nations Technical Assistance Board
UNA-USA	United Nations Association of the United States of America
USAID	United States Agency for International Development
WCS	World Conservation Strategy
WFS	World Fertility Survey
WHO	World Health Organization
WPC	World Population Conference
WPPA	World Population Plan of Action
WPY	World Population Year
WWF	World Wildlife Fund

A note on sources

Detailed references to the books, documents and papers consulted are given in the endnotes to each chapter. This short note indicates some of the most valuable sources.

The reports of the United Nations Population Commission, strictly the Population Commission of the United Nations Economic and Social Council, are published by the United Nations every two years, following the meetings of the Commission. The Population Division of the Department of Economic and Social Affairs, United Nations, has, since 1968, published a regular newsletter which, though it does not have the status of an official document, is informative and reliable. The *Population Bulletin of the United Nations* is published twice a year. The reports of the Belgrade, Bucharest and Mexico City World Population Conferences are published by the United Nations. The verbatim speeches given at the Bucharest Conference appear to exist only in the files of the Population Division in New York; the speeches delivered at Mexico have, however, been published, as noted in endnote 10.14, by the United Nations.

Concise reports on the World Population Situation in 1970, in 1970–5, in 1977, and in 1983, have been published by the United Nations covering demographic conditions, trends, prospects and policies. The *United Nations Demographic Yearbook* has appeared each year since 1948, and contains international and country figures on population, natality, infant and maternal mortality, general mortality, nuptiality and divorce.

UNFPA's *Annual Report* was first published in 1972 (covering the period 1969–72), and has been published annually since 1973. It now includes a State of the World Population Report, a summary of UNFPA activities, and a look at future plans and programmes. A series of Policy Statements provides the text of recent major policy statements and speeches delivered by the Executive Director. A series of Population Profiles either summarizes the population situation in a given country or provides an overview of a population-related topic. A series of *Policy Development Studies* is also published by UNFPA as well as a *Population Policy Compendium* which presents country-by-country information on population policy for the Member States of the United Nations and its specialized agencies. A series of *Needs Assessment Reports* covers the areas in which individual countries require assistance to achieve self-reliance in formulating and implementing population policies and programmes. A series of Evaluation Reports covers certain selected projects or programmes. UNFPA publishes a *Guide to Sources of International Population Assistance*, as well as an *Inventory of Population Projects in Developing Countries around the World*. An *Annual Review of Population Law* surveys national, regional and international developments which directly or indirectly affect population issues. UNFPA produces a quarterly journal, *Populi*, on population and development. Four books dealing specifically with the Fund have been cited in the endnotes. These are: *Population: The UNFPA Experience*, by Nafis Sadik, the Fund's current Executive Director; and (by Rafael Salas, UNFPA's late Executive Director) *Reflections on Population* (Pergamon, 1984), *People: An International Choice* (Pergamon, 1977), and *International Population Assistance: The First Decade* (Pergamon, 1979.) A two-volume *International Encyclopaedia of Population* was published in 1982 (The Free Press, New York).

The World Bank's *Annual Report* and its *Annual World Development Report* cover developments in that agency. The *World Development Report 1984* is, in particular, of outstanding interest for its coverage of demographic issues. The World Bank publishes a collection of *Staff Working Papers*, including a Population and Development Series. Major speeches given on population and development issues by the Bank's Presidents have been published by the Bank.

As far as the other United Nations specialized agencies with specific sectoral responsibilities are concerned (e.g. WHO, UNESCO, FAO, ILO, etc), apart from the reports and documents cited in the footnotes, reference should be made to the comprehensive *Bibliography of United Nations Publications on Population* published by UNFPA in 1979. This essential work of reference is over 250 pages long and obviously cannot be summarized here. In general, the Official Records of the World Health Organization contain a complete record of the documents, proceedings and decisions of the World Health Assembly, the decisions and resolutions of the Executive Board and the proposed annual Programme and Budget. The records of the UNESCO General Conference are published at the end of each session in three volumes comprising the *Proceedings*, *Resolutions* and *Index*. A published report containing a summary of the discussions is issued at the end of each session of the FAO Council and the FAO Conference. The main documents of the ILO Governing Body appear in final form in the *Minutes of the Governing Body*. The reports of the Executive Board of UNICEF appear as supplements to the Official Records of ECOSOC. Most of the specialized agencies publish regular periodicals, such as FAO's bimonthly *Ceres* or quarterly *Food and Nutrition*, UNESCO's *Courier* and WHO's *World Health*, which deal with population questions on an *ad hoc* basis. Some official publications of the agencies, such as FAO's *State of Food and Agriculture*, and UNICEF's *State of the World's Children* are of obvious interest. The United Nations Environment Programme (UNEP) has a co-ordinating and catalytic role in its field rather than substantive programme activities. The address of the Executive Director Mostafa K. Tolba to the International Population Conference in August 1984 contains some notable insights.

In the non-governmental sector, special mention must be made of the Population Council's *Population and Development Review* (PDR), the first issue of which appeared in September 1975. PDR has consistently reported and analysed developments in the field of population policy, including those involving the United Nations. IPPF's *Annual Report to Donors* provides a full account of the activities of the main private organization working in the field. IPPF has a significant publications programme, including the quarterly magazine, *People*, which reports on the world-wide effort to balance resources and population, to promote planned parenthood and to improve the human condition. The Worldwatch Institute, Washington DC, under the leadership of Lester Brown, has produced several influential papers on population, environment and development. For the last few years, the Worldwatch Institute has produced a 'State of the World Report' with regular coverage of the population situation. The Population Institute, also based in Washington, produces a monthly newsletter, *Popline*, which 'analyzes and evaluates facts and public policies relating to the problems of world overpopulation'. The (United States) National Research Council's Committee on Population and Demography has, since 1980, published a series of sc'entific reports on fertility in developing countries.

This is not the place for a general bibliography. A more exhaustive reading list on the subject of population, resources, development and environment would require a book in itself. A special mention here, however, for two books which seem somehow to have escaped citation in the endnotes: *World Population and Development*, edited by Philip M. Hauser (Syracuse University Press, 1979) and Paul and Anne Ehrlich's work on *Population, Resources, Environment* (second edition published by W. H. Freeman, San Francisco, 1972). In their own rather different ways both Dr Hauser and the Ehrlichs have made a large contribution towards a fuller understanding of the 'population problem'.

Finally, and not least important, the sources for this book included, as noted in the Introduction, a personal friendship or acquaintance with many of the actors in the cast and my own first-hand experiences as a contributor or participant in the studies and events described.

Acknowledgements

I could not have written this book without the help and co-operation of a large number of people extending sometimes over several years. Indeed, though I only began work on this project towards the end of 1984. I have been dealing with the subject matter on and off for over 20 years, and some of the people mentioned below will have helped me even though neither they nor I may have realized it at the time.

Towards the end of the Introduction I have said a few words about some of those to whom I owe a special debt of gratitude including, in particular, the late Rafael Salas, the former Executive Director of the United Nations Fund for Population Activities to whom the book is dedicated, the late Dr Bernard Berelson, President of the Population Council, the late William Clark, Vice-President of the World Bank, the late John D. Rockefeller 3rd, Chairman of the UNA–USA National Policy Panel on World Population, Professor Richard Gardner of Columbia University, Oscar Harkavy of the Ford Foundation, Professor Richard Symonds of St Anthony's College, Oxford and Professor William Brass, the President of the International Union for the Scientific Study of Population.

I should also like to thank many other friends, colleagues and helpers. Taking the United Nations system first, I am especially grateful to the staff of UNFPA for the co-operation they have given me, and, in particular, to Halvor Gille, Hans Janitschek, John Keppel, Ed Kerner, Dr A. Laquian (in charge of UNFPA operations in China), Mr S. Rao, David P. Rose, Dr Nafis Safik now Executive Director of UNFPA, Jyoti Singh, S. L. Tan, A. Thavarajah and Jack Voelpel. I must also thank Stephen Viederman, formerly of UNFPA, now Executive Director of the Jessie Smith Noyes Foundation, Tarzie Vittachi, formerly Executive Secretary for World Population Year, now Deputy Executive-Director of UNICEF; Milos Macura and Leon Tabah, both former directors of the United Nations Population Division, and Madame E. Sauterot, former librarian of the Population Division; Alex Graham of UNESCO; Kailas Doctor of ILO; the late W. Schulte of FAO; Dr Fred Sai, Dr K. Kanagaratnam, John North, Nancy Birdsall, Christopher Willoughby, and Bernard Chadenet of the World Bank.

As far as the world of non-governmental organizations is concerned, I owe a special debt to IPPF, and in particular to Julia Henderson and Carl Wahren, both former Secretary Generals of that organization, as well as to Mrs Frances Dennis, Mrs Joan Swingler, Mr Bernard Aluvihari, Mr George Cadbury, Susan Perl, Sunetra Puri, Teresa Farrelly, Mrs A. Wadia and Don Lubin.

I should like to take this opportunity of thanking other representatives of the 'non-governmental sector', particularly my old friend Brian Johnson, Senior Fellow of the International Institute for Environment and Development; Professor Nicholas Polunin, Editor of Biological Conservation; the Maharajah of Baroda; John Davoll, Director of the Conservation Society; Professors Paul and Anne Ehrlich of Stanford University; Porter McKeever and Elmore Jackson, formerly of the United Nations Association of the USA; the late Dr Frank Notestein; Robert Rhodes James, MP, formerly of Sussex University; Sir Peter Scott, CH; the late Barbara Ward; Mrs E. Laquian, of the *New York Times* office in Beijing and Akio Matsumura, Executive Director of the Global Committee of Parliamentarians on Population and Development.

I pay tribute also to Ernst Michanek, former head of the Swedish International Development Authority (SIDA), to Sir Crispin Tickell, former head of the United Kingdom's Overseas Development Administration, now Britain's ambassador to the United Nations, and to Ambassador Richard Benedick of the United States – all of whom have contributed in important ways to this book and to the subject of this study.

Sharon Livingstone of All-Hours Word Processing has done most of the typing; I am grateful, too, to Anne Crosley for help given in her off-duty hours.

Finally, I would like to thank my wife, Jennifer, for her support and encouragement. I am sure she would have preferred me to have given her more help with two small children instead of writing a long book about population and birth-control but she kindly refrained from saying so at the time!

Introduction

In 1969, U Thant, then Secretary-General of the United Nations, made the following statement:

> I do not wish to seem over-dramatic, but I can only conclude from the information that is available to me as Secretary-General that the Members of the United Nations have perhaps 10 years left in which to subordinate their ancient quarrels and launch a global partnership to curb the arms race, to improve the human environment, to defuse the population explosion and to supply the required momentum to development efforts. If such a global partnership is not forged within the next decade, then I very much fear that the problems I have mentioned will have reached such staggering proportions that they will be beyond our capacity to control.

Today, U Thant's remarks can be seen as some kind of a watershed. They came at a time when the involvement of the United Nations with at least one of the global issues alluded to by the Secretary-General, namely population growth, had reached a critical stage. The key questions in 1969 were: Was the United Nations after a long – some would have said an excessively long – courtship finally about to move to a new level of engagement with the population problem? Would it now seek not merely to respond to population trends through economic and social programmes, but also to influence those trends by direct and deliberate action?

The answer to those questions in that pivotal year of 1969 was by no means clear. Though it may seem, as one looks back, that there was a slow but steady evolution towards the present-day position, that was not necessarily how it appeared at the time.

This book is an account of 40 years of United Nations involvement with population questions, with particular emphasis on the period since 1969.

I had three main reasons for writing it. The first was that, as far as I know, no other book has been written about these recent developments. Professor Richard Symonds' and Michael Carder's scholarly volume: *The United Nations and the Population Question* was published as long ago as 1973 and has not been updated.[1]

The second was my own personal interest in the subject and the fact that I have had the good fortune to have participated in one capacity or another in many of the events described, including the Bucharest and Mexico Conferences.

The third reason is the intrinsic importance of the subject itself. For about as long as I can remember, certainly since my undergraduate days at Oxford, I have regarded the population question as the dominant issue of our time. To me therefore it is by no means surprising that a detailed examination of the United Nations record in this field reveals a story of intense political and human interest – a stage on which the action and commitment of certain key individuals have sometimes had as much influence as the policies of nations, where the sound of clashing ideologies has sometimes, but not always, drowned the cries of human suffering, where both religion and prejudice have played a role, not always constructively, and where the final outcome, seen in terms of the attempt, as U Thant put it, to 'defuse the population explosion' still hangs in the balance.

If the Secretary-General of the United Nations, sitting in his office on the 38th floor, had been looking not at the gleaming skyscrapers of Manhattan but at an image of the United Nations' involvement with the population question, what would he have seen? A landscape, surely, where, in the background, there are some imposing and clearly discernible structures; a middleground where there are one or two important landmarks but also a good deal of jumble and confusion as though the architects and city planners were not quite sure what they were trying to achieve; and nearer at hand, in the foreground, signs that the foundations were being laid of some new building which might, just possibly, o'er top all the rest.

This imagined panorama contains, of course, an element of caricature. Yet it is not too fanciful to see the creation in 1946 of the United Nations Population Commission as the major element in the background of this particular landscape. The work of the Population Commission and of the Population Division, established at United Nations Headquarters (both of them building on the statistical and demographic work of the defunct League of Nations), was absolutely crucial in laying the groundwork for subsequent United Nations action. Professor Richard Gardner, who himself was to play an important role in the early 1960s as a United States delegate to the General Assembly, sums it up admirably in his essay 'Toward a World Population Programme'[2].

The significance of these UN activities should not be underestimated. When the Population Commission met for the first time in 1947, demographic statistics, including census and vital statistics, were so incomplete that it was hardly possible to speak of world population problems. Without the devoted labours of the population and statistical sections of the UN Secretariat operating under the Population and Statistical Commissions, one might not be able to discern even now the outlines of the world population problem or the problems of the major regions. Moreover, the UN played a major role in encouraging and assisting Member Governments to obtain factual information on the size, composition, and trends of their populations and on the interaction between population growth and economic development. It helped train nationals of less developed countries in census-taking and demography. Slowly but surely it helped alert the new leaders of the developing nations to the dangers of too rapid population growth. The UN system was not yet ready to face the issue of family planning; but the basis for a breakthrough was being laid.

This intellectual contribution was not, of course, confined to the work of the Population Commission and the Population Division within the United Nations Secretariat, or to the regional economic commissions and demographic centres. Economists, demographers and development planners, inside and outside the United Nations, pointed out the relationships between population and economic growth. The United Nations' specialized agencies came increasingly to appreciate the sectoral implications – for employment, for health, for food and agriculture, for education. Thus, Julian Huxley, UNESCO's first Director-General, emphasized in his second annual report in 1948 that over-population could drastically affect the type of civilization possible and its rate of advance. The Sixth Session of the FAO Conference which took place in 1951 expressed concern that food production 'was not keeping pace with population growth'. And David Morse, Director-General of ILO, in his report to the Organization's Second Asian Regional Conference, held in Ceylon (now Sri Lanka) in 1950, argued that 'only if population growth can be checked will the workers in Asian countries be able to obtain substantial and lasting gains from programmes of economic and social development', a reflection which was welcomed by the representative of Ceylon though predictably criticized by the delegate of France[3].

It was in the World Health Organization that the most vigorous debate took place in those early years. The practical result of the controversy which took place within the organization in the early 1950s was to put a stop to any expansion of WHO's work into family-planning activities, though it could be argued that the emphasis WHO placed on the training of doctors and the strengthening of national health services helped, as Richard Gardner puts it, 'to create an infrastructure essential to the implementation of family planning programmes'.

This, then, is the rather murky middle-distance view which anyone looking back at the UN's record must have seen. There are some outstanding personalities in the picture, such as Frank Notestein who was an early Director of the United Nations demographic work; B. R. Sen, FAO's Director-General, who did much to move his organization towards a more mature understanding of the food–population relationship; Dr

Evang of Norway who fought long, often lonely battles in the attempt to broaden WHO's mandate; John D. Rockefeller 3rd who, in 1952, set up the Population Council of New York which, together with organizations like the International Planned Parenthood Federation and the Ford Foundation, was and has remained a magnificent example of the way in which the non-governmental sector has worked together with, and sometimes ahead of, the United Nations in the population field.

Yet, for all their eminence and dedication, these men and institutions were not enough. The canvas at this point lacks both focus and direction. There are plenty of white knights riding around on chargers, engaging in the occasional skirmish; there are, as has been indicated, some outstanding personalities. But, looking at the 1950s as a whole, it cannot truly be said that the United Nations system was ready to grasp and grapple with the population issue. The remark made by President Eisenhower in 1959 that he could not 'imagine anything more emphatically a subject that is not a proper political or governmental activity or function or responsibility' cannot, unfortunately, be said to be wholly uncharacteristic of the tenor of the decade.

In 1961, Eisenhower's successor, President John F. Kennedy, invited the General Assembly to designate the 1960s as the United Nations Development Decade, thus reflecting the growing consensus that, of all the economic and social objectives of the United Nations, development of the Third World was now of paramount importance. The United Nations, as it had emerged from the San Francisco Conference, was essentially an organization with a heavily 'Western' orientation. The United Nations at the beginning of the 1960s, its membership swollen by the addition of some 50 new States, most of them newly independent nations, was a very different affair: a forum where the concerns of the developing countries were increasingly voiced and where, for both political and moral reasons, there was growing pressure on the rich industrialized nations to respond.

If there was indeed one single factor which contributed to the 'breakthrough' in the United Nations, it was the presence of so many developing countries on the membership roll of this new United Nations. The old guard, particularly the Catholic countries of Western Europe, had over the previous decades (if we count in the period of the League as well) done its best to delay any effective UN response to this most pressing of social problems. But finally, even the old guard had to recognize the overwhelming pressure which was building up in Africa, in Latin America and above all in Asia, where the governments of newly independent countries had, for the first time, to confront the ineluctible fact that their best endeavours for development might founder and be rendered null and void unless they could find ways of dealing with their demographic problems. That they should turn to the United Nations for assistance was understandable and, truth to tell, the United Nations in this area seemed to have much to offer. It was non-political; it was non-racial; it had already – with the network of specialized agencies and the creation of the United Nations Development Programme – a proven track-record in delivering development assistance; above all, it offered the hope that population programmes could be integrated with development programmes since both, as it was increasingly recognized, were sides of the same coin.

So it was countries like India and Pakistan and Ceylon, aided by the more enlightened Western nations, such as Sweden and the United States, who pushed through the crucial resolution in the General Assembly in December 1966. Paragraph 4 of the resolution (GA resolution 2211(XXI) on Population Growth and Economic Development):

> ... called upon the Economic and Social Council, the Population Commission, the Regional Economic Commissions, the United Nations Economic and Social Office in Beirut and the specialised agencies concerned to assist, when requested, in further developing and strengthening national and regional facilities for training, research, information and advisory services in the field of population bearing in mind the different character of population problems in each country and region and the needs arising therefrom.

Philippe de Seynes, Under-Secretary-General for Economic and Social Affairs, commented that the 1966 General Assembly resolution expressed:

> ... the consensus of Member States in recognition of the seriousness of population problems, the need for a proper understanding of these problems and their effect on economic and social development; it also emphasized the necessity for accelerated action to implement the expanded programme recommended by the Population Commission.

So the focus shifts to the foreground of this historical canvas. How was the 'accelerated action' of which Philippe de Seynes spoke to be achieved? The mandates of the United Nations and of the specialized agencies to deal with population questions, including through direct support of population activities, had slowly and laboriously been worked out. The World Bank, itself a specialized agency of the United Nations, was under President Eugene Black, George Woods and, from April 1 1968, Robert McNamara, giving clear indications that it was not only concerned by the impact of rapid population growth on development prospects, but also that it wished to help countries take appropriate actions. But how was the gap between words and deeds to be bridged? In the real world, and where money is concerned, the real world is never far away, it was obvious that a straightforward diversion of resources from development programmes to population programmes was neither achievable nor desirable. Nothing would kill the fragile plant quicker than the impression, erroneous or otherwise, that population assistance was somehow an alternative to, or a substitute for, 'conventional' development assistance. The solution lay in a new United Nations initiative – the creation of a Trust Fund for population.

In opening ECOSOC's 43rd session, which took place in the summer of 1967, U Thant stated:

> I have decided to establish a Trust Fund to which I hope Governments and institutions will pledge voluntary contributions. This will help us to lay the ground for training centres as well as for pilot experiments which will assist the less developed countries in establishing and expanding their own administration and programmes.

As Richard Gardner commented in the essay already quoted:

> ... the Trust Fund opened in the summer of 1967 could be the first step towards a World Population Programme and toward a really effective response by the UN to the challenge of population growth. At least one earnestly hopes so. In the long run this might prove to be the Organization's most vital contribution to human welfare second only to keeping the peace. In a matter of such transcendent importance to humanity as a whole the United Nations belongs at the very centre of the picture.

The creation of the Trust Fund in 1967 was an event of major importance. And the process of transforming the Trust Fund of the Secretary-General into the United Nations Fund for Population Activities, a process which took place over the next two years, must be seen as the crucial factor in the subsequent spectacular growth of the United Nations involvement with the population question. As the Secretary-General of the United Nations looked about him in 1969, he must have felt justified in concluding that the foundations of the building in the very foreground of the canvas had been properly laid. He had by then agreed that the United Nations Development Programme would be entrusted with the administration of the Fund, now renamed the United Nations Fund for Population Activities. He had seen, as a consequence, the first substantial increases in the resources devoted to the Fund with $US 15 million being pledged for 1970; he had enthusiastically welcomed Paul Hoffman's, the Administrator of UNDP, inspired choice of Rafael Salas, a former Executive Secretary of the Philippines and a prime instigator of the Philippines's own 'rice revolution', as the first Executive Director of UNFPA; he had personally initiated the United Nations first training programme for population programme officers, a body of men and women who would, at the request of developing countries, be located in the field to help those countries prepare requests for assistance in the population field, including family planning, from the United Nations and its agencies.

But could U Thant have foreseen, as he made those famous remarks in 1969, in precisely what way the United Nations would in the future measure up to the challenge of world population? Could he have looked ahead to that other canvas on which, even as he spoke, new patterns were being traced and new directions charted? Since prescience is not a normal characteristic of human beings, not even of Secretaries-General of the United Nations, the odds are against it. Yet in their own way the next 15 years of United Nations involvement with population are as fascinating and as revealing as the first 25.

What we have seen is an example of the way in which the creation of an institution – in this case the United Nations Fund for Population Activities – at the right moment and with the right management, exerted a catalytic effect in a large number of areas, some of them going considerably beyond the field of activities with which that institution was principally concerned. In the summer of 1969, men first stepped on the moon. That same summer saw the first burgeoning of United Nations activities in the field of population, including programming missions to major countries such as Iran and Pakistan. Which of these events will ultimately be of more significance to mankind is hard to say with certainty, but, on present showing, the odds lie heavily with the latter.

It has become a conventional image to describe world population growth as an aeroplane lifting from the ground after a very long take-off and quickly changing into a rocket accelerating precipitously towards the stratosphere. The same kind of imagery can be applied to the population activities of the United Nations. They took off slowly, but when they did finally leave the ground things moved very quickly indeed. In fact, when Salas addressed the World Population Conference in Bucharest in August 1974, he was able to refer to a 'Population Fund explosion'.

> So far the Fund has supported population activities in some 90 developing countries and areas of almost all of the developing world. We have financed, or helped to finance, more than 900 projects covering such diversified fields as census-taking, improvement of vital statistics, registration, maternal and child health programmes, family-planning services, communication and education, studies on law and population and training of personnel and institutional building in many different areas.

In five years, Salas said, donors had made available nearly $US 175 million to the Fund. But he estimated, somewhat to the surprise of the delegates, that about $US 500 million would be needed for the period 1974–77 to respond to the most urgent requirements of the developing countries for the Fund's support. This rapid expansion of demand on the Fund, while presenting a financial challenge, was also satisfying in that it testified to the viability of the multilateral approach in this most sensitive of all matters and to the acceptability of the Fund's own procedures. A momentum had been generated and an atmosphere had been created in which it was possible to think in terms of solutions to problems which at one time seemed insoluble. Salas asked: 'will that momentum and that atmosphere be maintained?'

The World Population Conference, which took place in Bucharest in August 1974, was not without its tensions and even moments of drama. The 1972 resolution of the United Nations Economic and Social Council that had called for the formulation of a draft World Population Plan of Action with the assistance of an Advisory Committee of Experts on Global Population Strategy had also urged Member States to co-operate in exploring the possibility of setting targets for reducing population growth rates in countries that considered their rates too high.

The process of preparing for the Conference had led many to expect that a consensus would readily be reached both on the importance of the population factor for development and also on the need for policies to restrain rates of population growth. In the event, the course of the 1974 World Population Conference did not run entirely smoothly. One group of participants which included industrialized countries such as the United States, the United Kingdom, Canada and the Federal Republic of Germany, urged the Conference to focus its attention on population, particularly population growth, as an obstacle to social and economic development of the quality of life. They emphasized family planning as a human right – recognized as such in the Final Act of the International Conference on Human Rights which had been held in Teheran, Iran, in 1968 – and regarded it as an appropriate and effective means to reduce fertility where it was too high. On the whole, they supported 'targets', at the global and the national levels, for both mortality and fertility.

A second larger group of participants, mindful of the fact that the United Nations was engaged in a debate on the New International Economic Order, argued that high rates of population growth were more a symptom than a cause of underdevelopment, that development would itself lead to declines in fertility and that the rich countries should be urged therefore to provide increased levels of assistance to the development programmes of the LDC's while opening up their markets to trade from the Third World.

Out of these somewhat antithetical positions, an uneasy compromise at last emerged. The World Population Plan of Action adopted at Bucharest left out any specific references to 'targets', whether at the global or national level. Instead, countries which considered that their present or expected rates of population growth hampered their goals of promoting human welfare were invited, if they had not done so, 'to consider adopting population policies, within the framework of socio–economic development, which are consistent with basic human rights and national goals and values'. Because the 'per capita use of world resources was so much higher in the developed than in the developing countries', the developed countries were urged to adopt appropriate policies in population, consumption and investment, 'bearing in mind the need for fundamental improvement in international equity'.

In its own way, Bucharest 1974 was a major landmark on the path towards the acceptance by the nations of the world that the population problem was of real and vital concern and that it was a legitimate subject for concerted action at all appropriate levels ranging from the humblest village hut with barefoot doctor at the door to the loftiest podium of the United Nations. Though, as noted, there was in some quarters a reticence about various aspects of the World Population Plan of Action, what finally precipitated Bucharest's general consensus was the sense that something had to be done and that institutions, such as the United Nations, could not be seen to falter before a challenge which many who were in Bucharest recognized as important, if not vital, for the development aspirations of a large proportion of the world. The story of the next ten years, 1974 to 1984, is one in which we see develop a still greater awareness of the population–development relationship, while at the same time new per-spectives were introduced which served both to enrich and deepen understanding of the nature of the population problem. To the classic themes of population and development or population and human rights other concerns were added, in particular the implications of population growth and distribution for resources and the environment, for the role of women in developing countries and – last but not least – for the maintenance of world peace itself, a task which could indeed be seen as the United Nations' primary mandate. Some account of these developments is given in Chapter 9.

Most important of all, the decade which followed Bucharest saw what the official demographers of the United Nations, cautious men and women at the best of times, have referred to as a 'spectacular decline' in fertility in both the developed and developing world. In my view the fall in birth-rates which has occurred over the last 15 or 20 years is possibly the single most important trend of our time. I have found it useful, even essential, to examine the record of population and family planning programmes in some key countries of the developing world – for example: China, India, Indonesia, Mexico, Colombia – where such declines have occurred.

There is still, of course, a very long way to go. In parts of Asia (particularly the 'highland' and South Western regions); in much of tropical South America and the Middle East; and in virtually all of Sub-

Saharan Africa we have not yet witnessed the full – or sometimes even the first – onset of fertility decline.

That is why the International Conference on Population, held in Mexico City in August 1984, which is the subject of a later chapter of this book, was of such importance. In spite of the quixotic position of the United States (long the leading proponent of international co-operation in the field of population, the United States in Mexico advocated the adoption of a 'free-market' approach to family planning), the Mexico Conference succeeded in providing an important impetus to national and international efforts in the population field.

The Conference noted that experience with population policies in recent years had been encouraging. Since Bucharest the global population growth rate had declined from 2.03 to 1.67 per cent per year. Mortality and mortality rates had been lowered, although not to the desired extent. Family-planning programmes had been successful in reducing fertility at relatively low cost.

The Conference recommended that countries which considered that their population growth rate hindered their national development plans should adopt appropriate population policies and programmes and that timely action could avoid the accentuation of problems such as overpopulation, unemployment, food shortages and environmental degradation. Unwanted high fertility adversely affected the health and welfare of individuals and families, especially among the poor, and seriously impeded social and economic progress in many countries. Although considerable progress had been made since Bucharest, millions of people still lacked access to safe and effective family-planning methods. By the year 2000 some 1.6 billion women would be of child-bearing age, 1.3 billion of them in developing countries. 'Major efforts must be made now to ensure that all couples and individuals can exercise their basic human right to decide freely, responsibly, and without coercion, the number and spacing of their children, and to have the information, education and means to do so.'

The Conference also noted that rapid urbanization would continue to be a salient feature and that by the end of the century almost half the world's population might live in cities, frequently very large cities. It noted that the volume and nature of international migratory movements continued to undergo rapid changes. Illegal or undocumented migration and refugee movements had gained particular importance and these too were not unrelated to population pressures.

As far as environmental problems were concerned, the Conference urged Governments, in the context of overall development policies, to adopt and implement specific policies, including population policies, that would contribute to redressing such imbalances and promote improved methods of identifying, extracting, renewing, utilizing, and conserving natural resources. Efforts should be made to accelerate the transition from traditional to new and renewable sources of energy while at the same time maintaining the integrity of the environment. Governments should also implement appropriate policy measures to avoid the further destruction of the ecological equilibria and take measures to restore them.

The years since Bucharest had shown that international co-operation in the field of population was essential for the implementation of recommendations agreed upon by the international community and could be notably successful. Adequate and substantial international support and assistance would greatly facilitate the efforts of Governments. The Conference stressed that the United Nations family 'should continue to perform its vital responsibilities', and urged that 'in view of the leading role of the United Nations Fund for Population Activities in population matters, the Fund should be strengthened further, so as to ensure the more effective delivery of population assistance, taking into account, the growing needs in this field'.

In his own speech to the Conference, Salas – speaking as Secretary-General of the Conference as well as Executive Director of UNFPA, stated:

> ... our goal is the stabilization of global population within the shortest period possible before the end of the next century.

The goal of stabilization for the world's population within the shortest period possible was not explicitly retained by the Mexico Conference either in its Declaration or in the recommendations it made for the further implementation of the World Population Plan of Action adopted at Bucharest ten years earlier. However, the Mexico Conference did reconfirm that 'countries which consider that their population growth rates hinder the attainment of national goals are invited to consider pursuing relevant demographic policies, within the framework of socio–economic development. Such policies should respect human rights, the religious beliefs, philosophical convictions, cultural values and fundamental rights of each individual and couple to determine the size of its own family'. And the tenor of the general debate itself which took place in Mexico City left some observers, including myself, in no doubt that world population stabilization was now a realistic, though necessarily, distant goal. In the Mexico Chapter, as in the Bucharest Chapter, I have made use of quotations wherever possible. The 'politics of population' emerge most clearly from the verbatims and in this story the political dimension – how different nations or groups have perceived that their own interests are affected by demographic factors – is an important underlying theme if only for the way in which it has influenced the posture of countries in international fora.

This book covers these and other highlights of what is, therefore, a momentous story. We can see how, sometimes slowly, sometimes painfully, but often with tenacity and wisdom, the world's major, indeed only, international system, namely the United Nations and its network of agencies, has come to grips with the world's foremost problem.

Today, as noted, we can state with confidence that some important declines in population growth rates cases have already been achieved. And success in lowering fertility rates through government intervention has been demonstrated, for example, in China, Cuba, Fiji, Indonesia, Mexico, and Singapore. But time alone will tell to what extent projections of further fertility declines (the 'medium' variant, as opposed to the 'high' variant, or the 'low' variant as opposed to the 'medium') are realized in practice. And, no doubt, scholars will be able to conclude with greater certainty than is possible at present the part that has been played by population and family-planning programmes in fertility declines; the relevance of international assistance to such declines; and in particular of assistance provided by the United Nations.

The evidence is not yet in for a comprehensive and authoritative statement on this subject to be made. It is, however, a reasonable supposition that the contribution of the United Nations has been not only important but crucial. Numerous studies have indicated that increased access to sources of contraceptive supply results in an increase in contraceptive use and a decrease in fertility. (The literature is admirably summarized in a World Bank Staff working paper published in May 1985 entitled 'The effects of Family Planning Programs on Fertility in the Developing World'[4].) Roughly 50 per cent of all spending on population and family programmes in developing countries is financed through external assistance (which at present amounts to around $500 million per annum). Of this figure, more than a quarter is provided by or through the United Nations and its agencies and the proportion is even more significant if World Bank lending for population, health and nutrition (currently running at around $250 million a year) is counted in, though it is not always easy to identify precisely the 'population' component of PHN projects.

But even if matters appear to be progressing in the right direction, we are certainly not out of the woods yet. The declines in fertility which have so far been achieved, though important, are – as I have already suggested – only the first steps on the long and difficult road towards population stabilization and, in any case, China's success in lowering her population growth rate bulks so large in the global perspective that any optimism must at best be cautious. When you are talking of a nation of over one billion people, the quantitative impact in terms of global human numbers of even modest falls in the Chinese birth-rate can be enormous. But, by the same token, a reversal of trends in China (a shift in political priorities, a change of regime, public pressures?) could have a major effect on global rates and totals.

The other principal reason for tempering optimism with caution lies in the present attitude of the United States. Having given advance notice of its intentions at the Mexico City conference, the United States administration announced in September 1985 that it would not pay $10 million of its pledged contribution of $46 million to UNFPA because of the alleged participation of UNFPA in the 'management' of China's population programme which in the judgement of the US included coercive abortion.

UNFPA argued for its part that this allegation was contradicted by the facts. It was a matter of public record that the Fund did not support any abortion programme anywhere in the world. Nor did the Fund 'manage' programmes in assisted countries, management being the sole prerogative of recipient governments. The Fund pointed out that the charges that led to the withholding of the $10 million were refuted by AID itself, when in a careful review of UNFPA assistance to China in April, 1984 and in March, 1985, the Agency had cleared UNFPA of any involvement in coercive family planning programmes or in abortion activities. The Government of this People's Republic of China had furthermore categorically stated that no UNFPA assistance had been utilized for any abortion-related activities, a fact which was doubly affirmed by the Fund's records.

Since, up to the present time, the United States has been the single largest contributor to the Fund, providing about 25 per cent of its budget, it can be seen that the situation is serious both for UNFPA's future and for the future of all United Nations work on population. Up till now, UNFPA has been relatively immune to the financial crises which have periodically wracked the United Nations. But the resolve of donors (other than the US) will now be tested where it most counts, i.e. in pledges and contributions. At the time of writing this Introduction, it seems that these other donors have indeed risen nobly to the challenge. Even without the United States contribution, UNFPA has – for 1987 – funds amounting to some US $150 million at its disposal, either in pledges or in actual contributions. This substantial sum, however, has to be seen in the context of the growing volume of requests for UNFPA assistance, particularly from the countries of Sub-Saharan Africa, an area which – as I indicate in Chapter 8 – has to be considered a priority among priorities.

In the longer run, it is clear that the return of the United States to the donors' camp is absolutely crucial. At the moment it is still too early to predict the outcome of the dispute between the United States, the United Nations and China, the details of which are given in Chapter 11. Negotiations and *pour parlers* are still proceeding. But when the time comes, ten years from now, to complete the story of half a century of United Nations involvement with population, we shall probably know whether or not this particular tale had a happy ending.

My own fervent hope is that we shall not look back on the decade of the 1980s as the time when the era of multilateral population assistance reached its zenith but, on the contrary, at a time when the international commitment to the goal of World Population Stabilization was established on a solid and substantial basis. The publication, on April 27, 1987, on the Report of the World Commission on Environment and Development, under the leadership of Mrs Gro Brundtland Prime Minister of Norway, can be seen as a hopeful sign. Though the Brundtland recommendations, at time of going to press, still had to be considered by governments, and by the General Assembly of the United Nations under whose auspices the World Commission had been established, the initial reception appeared to be favourable, not least because of the integrated view the Commission took of the issues of population, development and environment.

I end this Introduction on a personal note. If I have had the chance to study the record of the United Nations in the population field, and the motivation to do so, it is to a large extent as a result of the contact which I have had over the years with a number of people whose interest in demography or the United Nations or both has been a source of inspiration. Many of them, of course, are mentioned in these pages because, as well as being personal friends, they are *dramatis personae* in their own right. Nevertheless, I take advantage of this opportunity to mention the names of some of those individuals who, at least as far as I am concerned, occupy a special place.

The first of these is Dr Bernard ('Barnie') Berelson who was running the Population Council in New York at the time when I was a young staffer at the World Bank in the latter part of the 1960s. Berelson had an overwhelming intellectual curiosity and an ability to inspire friendship at both the personal and professional level. Because this book is centred on the United Nations rather than on the non-governmental movement, the work of the Population Council, and Berelson's part in it, is not perhaps given the full treatment it deserves. But there is no doubt about the measure of his contribution. He is sorely missed.

Next I want to pay tribute to William Clark, former Vice-President of the World Bank, who encouraged me to write this book and died before it was completed. No man had more friends. Those who crowded into St James, Piccadilly, to attend his memorial service early this year represented, as it were, only the tip of the iceberg. As far as population is concerned, Clark's influence on the World Bank was of particular interest. The powerful series of speeches on population and development which Mr Robert McNamara gave during his time as President of the World Bank owed much to William's intellectual insights and his gift for words. A classic example was the address MacNamara delivered at Notre Dame University on May 1, 1969 which laid out in the clearest terms before a potentially hostile audience the implications of continued rapid population growth for developing countries and the role which the World Bank could play in this field.

After I left the World Bank, I went to work for the United Nations Association of the United States of America as the Project Director of the UNA–USA's National Policy Panel on World Population. The Chairman of the Panel was John D. Rockefeller 3rd, whose quiet guidance and encouragement I greatly valued throughout that fascinating year in New York. I last met Mr Rockefeller in Bucharest in August 1974 at the time of the World Population Conference. The talk he gave on that occasion – at the so-called NGO Forum – surprised many people. While the 'official' conference was, as I have indicated, split between the 'developers' and the 'birth-controllers', Rockefeller argued forcefully that these were false alternatives and that the only hope lay in a combination of both approaches.

As we look back, this may seem like conventional wisdom, but at the time Rockefeller's message had a considerable impact on international attitudes. That impact, of course, continues today not only through Mr Rockefeller's widow and other members of his family, but through the network of foundations and charitable activities with which the Rockefeller name is associated.

Other members of the UNA–USA Panel also merit my thanks. Professor Richard Gardner, Henry L. Moses Professor of International Relations at Columbia University, had an enviable ability to grasp and explain the intricacies of the UN system and the difference between one set of initials and another. Oscar ('Bud') Harkavy, who was in charge of the Ford Foundation's Population programmes, knew as much about the substance of the subject as anyone and later arranged for me to acquire at least a rudimentary knowledge of demography as a student in the MSc course run by Professor David Glass at the London School of Economics.

My thanks also to Dr William Brass, at the London School of Hygiene and Tropical Medicine who, like William Clark, encouraged me to write this book. And to Professor Richard Symonds, formerly of Sussex University, now of St Anthony's Oxford, whose own report on the involvement of the United Nations in the population question was a pioneering work.

Professor Symonds' incisive comments on the early drafts of this book enabled me to reduce it to what are, I hope, now manageable proportions and he was also good enough to correct numerous errors of fact or interpretation.

Finally, I must record a special debt to Mr Rafael Salas, whose sad death at the age of 58, occurred in March 1987 as this book was in press. If Salas' name occurs in these pages more frequently than anyone else's, it is because for the last 18 years he has occupied a central place on this particular stage. I first met him in New York in 1969, soon after he had been appointed head of the fledgling UNFPA. It was immediately clear that Paul Hoffman, then the Administrator of UNDP, and U Thant, then Secretary-General of the United Nations, had together selected precisely the right man for the job. Salas was a Catholic; he was from the Third World; and he had a proven record as an innovator and as an administrator in his previous work in the Philippines.

That first meeting took place in the cramped temporary offices which UNDP had provided for the Fund in the old Alcoa building. As I recall, there were no more than two or three permanent staff at the time – Salas was still recruiting his team. I realized then that he regarded his new assignment as a enormous challenge. UNFPA's birth had not been without trauma; there were institutional problems to sort out – the Fund's relationship with the United Nations itself, particularly the Population Division, and the Specialized Agencies. There were political problems of considerable magnitude – population and family planning was a controversial subject and there were still people around who believed, with President Eisenhower, that the state and, by extension, international organizations, had no business in the bedroom.

Nor, at a more technical level, was it clear what UNFPA's mandate ought to cover. Where did population activities begin? Where did they end? What should be the balance in the Fund's financing between, say, demographic statistics on the one hand and family planning on the other?

Salas confronted all these questions head-on. I was privileged to work with him in the preparations for the World Population Conference which took place in Bucharest in August 1984 and to be present, ten years later, in August 1984, at the International Conference on Population held in Mexico City, where as noted he served as the Conference's Secretary-General. During that time he became, in a real sense, 'Mr Population'. Without Salas' dynamism and diplomacy, without the leadership he provided to worldwide population efforts, we would certainly not be where we are.

Rafael Salas had the gift of combining professional with personal friendships. He didn't live his life in watertight compartments. He wrote

xxxvi

poems on planes on his way to meetings and he sent them to his friends later in the form of a small beautifully produced collection. I met him over the years in different parts of the globe – Colombo, Bucharest, Vienna, Rome, to name a few of the places – and as often as not we had a meal together and talked about anything under the sun. He was painstaking, in the literal sense, in his relationships. Once, when I was a Member of the European Parliament, he came to Strasbourg (not the easiest place to get to), met Madame Simone Veil, who was the Parliament's President at the time and then – instead of rushing back to Geneva – sat in the gallery of a sparsely attended chamber to hear me make a speech about the import of fruit juices into the EEC! He was that kind of man.

The Salas era is over. If he had not died, perhaps – after 17 exhausting years as head of UNFPA – he would have moved on. There were other challenges inside the United Nations and there was always the pull of the Philippines, the country where he had first made his name, which was now under new and perhaps more congenial management. All that, of course, is speculation. As I write these words, I am at least certain of this: that Rafael Salas was a good man and a great man. I count myself fortunate to have been numbered among his friends. We miss him.

Dr Nafis Sadik has now succeeded Mr Salas as the new Executive Director of the United Nations Fund for Population Activities. Anyone who struggles through to the end of this book, and particularly through the long Chapter 8, which records the progress of population and family-planning programmes in the different regions of the world, will find frequent references to Dr Sadik's work, first as the Head of Pakistan's national family-planning programme and later as the Fund's Assistant Executive Director. Her book on United Nations' population programme activities, which I have cited in the Note on Sources and extensively in the footnotes, was an invaluable work of reference. I first had the pleasure of encountering Dr Sadik in Pakistan in 1968, when I was working as Project Director of the UNA-USA Panel on World Population. Members of the panel were anxious to have reports on the progress family-planning programmes, and the Pakistan programme under Dr Sadik's direction was given a high rating. She has kept her deft touch and I am quite sure that Salas' legacy and the institution which he did so much to build are in safe hands.

I have been conscious, as I wrote this book, of the need to remain objective in spite of, or possibly because of, my friendship with some of the personalities involved. Even if I personally was not bothered about the bubble reputation, my publishers as an academic press of renown could hardly afford to ignore the requirements of scholarship. Dr Robin Pellew, Cambridge University Press's Senior Editor for Biological Sciences and a tower of strength to the faltering author, has – as the saying goes – been polite but firm on this point. So I have tried not to let my enthusiasm for the subject get the better of me.

But I am not sure, in the end, that I have succeeded in being wholly objective. The truth of the matter is that I seem to be one of that dwindling band of men and women ('we few, we happy few, we band of brothers') who still actually, amazingly, incredibly believe in the United Nations and in what it is doing or trying to do. And since I judge the record of the United Nations, as I hope this book makes clear, to be some kind of success story in the population field at least, it's hard not to let that show. As Walter Cronkite used to say when he was anchoring the CBS news: 'That's the way it is.'

Brussels
May 1, 1987

1

The rise of concern

The demographic background

Present generations stand on the shoulders of those who have preceded them. In demography, the past determines the future. The historical perspective is useful and sometimes essential. It seems sensible, therefore, at the beginning of a book such as this, which seeks to be global in scope, to say a few words about the evolution of the world's population. In fact, little is known about world population before the Christian era. The development of ancient city-centred civilizations in the Old World, with the accumulations of relatively large and dense agricultural populations that they required, suggests[1] that the third millenium before Christ may have been a period of comparatively large growth in the population of Asia and North Africa if not of the world as a whole.

During the first millenium of the Christian era, the indications are that the pendulum swung again towards slower growth or stagnation. In spite of uncertainties in the estimates, some demographers take the view that population made relatively little gain, if it did not suffer a loss between AD 0 and 1000 in China, Europe, North Africa and South-west Asia. Population may have increased substantially during the first Christian millenium in Japan, South-east Asia, Tropical Africa and America, but increases in the relatively small populations of these regions would not have carried much weight in the global trend.

Between AD 1000 and 1750, it is clear that a much larger growth in the world population occurred than in the previous 1000 years. Populations expanded between AD 1000 and 1300 in China and Europe and this process continued after the setbacks of the 14th century. (The loss of life which occurred in Europe and neighbouring regions as a result of the Black Death and its sequel of plague epidemics was probably paralleled in Central Asia, China and India.)

By the year 1750, total world population – which had stood at around 250 million at the beginning of the Christian era – had grown to approximately 730 million distributed roughly as follows: China – 207 million; India–Pakistan–Bangladesh – 100 million; South-western Asia – 13 million; Japan – 26 million; remainder of Asia – 32 million; Europe, excluding USSR – 102 million; USSR – 34 million; Africa – 100 million; North America – 2 million; Middle and South America – 13 million; Oceania – 2 million.

Around the middle of the 19th century world population passed the 1000 million mark, a milestone whose significance was almost certainly not appreciated at the time. If it took all of history, recorded or unrecorded, to reach that first 1000 million (or billion), it took less than 100 years to reach the second (achieved around 1930); about 30 years to reach the third and only 15 years to reach the fourth. Table 1.1 indicates that world population in 1975 stood at around 3,967 millions, with China – at 839 millions – accounting for 21 per cent, followed by India–Pakistan–Bangladesh with 745 millions (19 per cent), and America (North, Middle and South) with 561 millions (14 per cent). It is of interest to note that the relative dominance of China in the world total has declined considerably over the last two or three centuries *vis à vis* that of the Indian subcontinent and other parts of Asia and Latin America, though in absolute terms China remains – of course – of great importance.

Political attitudes

It is against this demographic background, summarily described, that the events recorded in this book must be set. We are concerned with the role of the United Nations in relation to population, with particular emphasis on the period since 1969 which has seen the active involvement of the United Nations in the attempt to influence the demographic trends whose broad historical thrust has been described above. But no account of the developments of recent years can ignore the more distant past. The political framework of the 1960s and 1970s which enabled crucial decisions to be taken by the United Nations and its agencies was at least to some extent formed as a result of past demographic experience in different countries and regions, and especially the events of the previous several decades.

As noted in the Introduction, any account of these historical antecedents must be heavily indebted to Professor Richard Symonds & Michael Carder's earlier work: *The United Nations and the Population Question*[2]. Symonds & Carder outline attitudes towards population in numerous countries, attitudes which in one form or another resurface on many occasions along the long and often difficult road which lay ahead. One man or woman's view of the population question is seldom just that. More often, it is an amalgam of historical experience and political motivation garnished as appropriate with a dash of morality or prejudice.

Thus Symonds and Carder, on France, write:

> At first the slow rate of growth was considered an advantage, and it was not until the Second Empire that the low level of fertility began to arouse concern. The defeat of France by Prussia in 1870 transformed the situation. Defeat was attributed to the relative decline of France's population in comparison with that of Germany. In the years which followed, pro-natalist agitation stressed the military and political implications of a stationary population. Victory in 1918 afforded no more than a temporary reassurance and pressure for 'demographic rearmament' recommenced with renewed vigour after Hitler's seizure of power in Germany[3].

France created in 1919 a 'Conseil Supérieur de la Natalité', attached to the Ministry of Health; the following year saw the passage of a law which prohibited the dissemination of contraceptive knowledge and in 1923 further measures against abortion were adopted. Family allowances came to be seen as an important element of pro-natalist policy.

France was not the only European country to express fears of population decline. Belgium had similar preoccupations and both Italy and Germany were, as Symonds and Carder put it, 'attached by their ideologies to a young and growing population'. Sweden, in 1935, set up a Royal Commission which laid down the framework of the generally enlightened policy on matters of population which that country has subsequently pursued. Incentives to child-bearing were introduced but no repressive measures against birth-control or abortion were adopted. Similarly, the Soviet Union's attitudes towards population in the 1930s reflected the Marxist's scepticism about neo-Malthusianism, while the government sought to provide free abortion (later limited to cases where pregnancy endangered the health of the mother).

In Britain, in the early years of the century, Malthusian thinking tended to dominate and the vigorous growth of the birth-control movement was due as much to concern with demographic factors as for individual health and well-being.

In North America the population continued to grow more rapidly than in Europe during the 19th century. It was not until 1924 that the higher fertility of immigrants caused alarm and controls on immigration were imposed.

Table 1.1. *Population estimates for world regions since the time of Christ, according to Clark (figures in millions, letter codes denote grades of reliability)*

Region	AD 14	1000	1200	1500	1750	1900	1975
World total	256	280	384	427	731	1,668	3,967
China*a*	73 B	60 B	123 B	100 C	207 B	500 C	839 B
India-Pakistan-Bangladesh	70 D	70 D	75 D	79 D	100 C	283 A	745 A
Southwestern Asia, total	34	22	21	15	13	38*g*C	118 B
Asia Minor, Syria, and Cyprus*b*	14 C	10 D	10 D	8 D	7 D	–	
Other Southwestern Asia*c*	20 D	12 D	11 D	7 D	6 D	–	
Japan	2 D	10 C	12 C	16 C	26 A	44 A	111 A
Remainder of Asia, exc. USSR	5 D	10 D	11 D	15 D	32 D	120*g*B	440 B
Europe. exc. USSR, total	37	32	45	62	102	284 A	476 A
Southern Europe*d*	32 C	24 C	33 C	39 C	60 B	–	–
Northern Europe	5 D	8 C	12 C	23 C	42 B	–	–
USSR, total	8	12	12	12	34	127	255 A
European part	3*h*D	7 D	6 D	6 C	28 B	110*g*A	–
Asian part	5 C	5 D	6 D	6 D	6 D	17*g*B	–
Africa, total	23	50	61	85	100	122	401
Northern Africa*c*	11 C	4 D	4 D	6 D	5 D	27*g*B	80 A
Remainder of Africa	12 D	46 D	57 D	79 D	95 D	95*g*C	321 B
America, total	3 D	13 D	23 D	41	15	144	561
Northern America*f*	–	–	–	1 D	2 B	81 A	237 A
Middle and South America	–	–	–	40 D	13 C	63 B	324 A
Oceania	1 D	1 D	1 D	2 D	2 C	6 A	21 A

Source: Article by John D. Durand entitled: 'Historical Estimates of World Population: an Evaluation', published in *Population and Development Review*. Vol. 3, No. 3. September 1977.

AD 14–1900, except as noted: Clark (1968), Tables III.1 (p. 64) and III.15 (p. 108).

1975: United Nations *Demographic Yearbook*, 1975.

Notes: [a] Present area, including Manchuria, Inner Mongolia, Sinkiang, Tsinghai, Tibet, and Taiwan, as well as historic China Proper.

[b] Asian sector of the Roman Empire in AD 14.

[c] Iran, Iraq, Arabian countries, and other parts of southwestern Asia outside the borders of the Roman Empire in AD 14 (excluding the European part of Turkey).

[d] Total of estimates for areas corresponding approximately to the territories of the Roman Empire in Europe in AD 14 (France, Belgium, Netherlands, Spain, Portugal, Italy, Greece, and the 'Rest of SE Europe' in the nomenclature of Clark's Table), including the European part of Turkey.

[e] Egypt, Libya, Tunisia, Algeria, and Morocco.

[f] United States, Canada, Greenland, Bermuda, and St. Pierre and Miquelon.

[g] Estimates for regions not shown separately in Clark's tabulation, derived from other sources in such a way as to agree with Clark's totals for broader regions.

[h] In Clark's total estimate of 4 million for Russia in Europe, 'Poland, Czechoslovakia, etc,' and Hungary, 3 million are allocated to Russia in order to complete the regional classification in the form given here.

In the developing world, the level of 'demographic awareness' on the part of the ruling colonial classes was relatively low. In India, for example, Symonds and Carder suggest that British policy towards the promotion of social change was influenced by memories of the Indian mutiny of 1857 and by fears that advocacy of birth-control would bring accusations of genocide. Nevertheless, there was a substantial degree of enlightenment among many sections of the Indian educated classes. The Congress National Planning Committee, set up in 1935 to prepare for independence, convened a special sub-committee to investigate family planning and population policy and recommended: 'in the interests of social economy, family happiness and national planning, family planning and the limitation of children are essential, and the State should adopt a policy to encourage these'. This forthright statement can be seen as a precursor of the 'policy commitments' which would serve not only as the basis of India's population and family-planning efforts, but also as the model for other newly independent countries anxious to follow a similar path.

In so far as the educated 'native' in India or elsewhere received external support in the attempt to come to terms with the country's population problems, this was more likely to be provided through the non-governmental sector, for example, the Birth Control International Centre in England, than through official channels. The colonial regime in much of the world helped to 'trigger' the population explosion (in the sense that the provision of medicine and relatively stable government both contributed to demographic expansion). But the colonial regimes of Asia, Africa and Latin America singularly failed to provide the necessary counterbalance in the sense of the 'promotion of demographic awareness' (to use a now-favoured phrase) or the provision of contraceptive information and supplies. It will emerge later in this book that a substantial part of the impetus behind the United Nations' efforts in the field of population has been provided by those who were once the servants, not the masters. It is the countries who have suffered most from the effects of high fertility who have been most ready to press for effective national and international action. Similarly, it was the *non-governmental* organizations who expanded on their early involvement to perform – particularly in the post-war decades – a crucial role not only in providing direct assistance to developing countries in the field of family planning but also in generating the climate of opinion which later made governmental responses and decisions both necessary and possible.

Of course the 'old guard' – particularly those countries of Europe who were pursuing pro-natalist policies – did their best to apply the brakes and indeed succeeded in delaying an effective international response to this most pressing of problems to a late hour. The record of the League of Nations' involvement with the population issue illustrates this.

1 The rise of concern

The League of Nations

In 1927, at the initiative of Margaret Sanger, a World Population Conference was held in Geneva. Though Sir Eric Drummond, the Secretary-General of the League of Nations and a Roman Catholic, insisted that the League of Nations could not be represented since the conference would be concerned with questions 'which arouse the strongest national feelings and which were of a delicate character'[4], League officials attended in their private capacity and the League's Health Division gave considerable encouragement to the organizers[5]. The League's Economic Section published a Statistical Year Book which included information on population size, birth- and death-rates, age structure, occupation and migratory movements for a number of countries. At the policy level the League was more concerned with removing barriers to migration – at a time of growing international distrust and tension – than it was with population growth as such. However, in 1938, the Assembly adopted a resolution requesting the Council to set up 'a special committee of experts to study demographic problems and especially their connection with the economic, financial and social situation and to submit a report on the subject which may be of value to governments in the determination of policy'. The Committee was established in 1939 and included among its members Sir Alexander Carr-Saunders, the British demographer, as well as experts from India, Egypt, Argentina, Brazil and Poland. The Committee met only once before the outbreak of war.

As far as the issue of birth-control was concerned, the League's involvement was at best uneasy. In 1923, an International Conference was held (under the auspices of the League) on the Suppression of the Circulation of and Traffic in Obscene Publications, at which some delegates argued that the provision of contraceptive information was merely a cloak for obscenity. In 1932, the Second Committee of the Assembly debated a report of a committee set up by the Health Organization which included references to 'Abortion and Birth Control'. The Assembly returned to the subject inconclusively in the following year. As Symonds and Carder remark: 'It is notable that in the League period its Health Organization took a more advanced position regarding the League's involvement in population and birth control questions than did the Assembly and Secretary-General. In the United Nations period the converse was to be the case. In the 1960s the Secretary-General and ECOSOC were ahead of the World Health Organization in advocating involvement of international organizations in family planning and population questions'[6].

Symonds and Carder argue plausibly that the League Health Organization had no political independence: it was subject to the Secretary-General and the Assembly of the League; Health Organization officials not having a direct political constituency (unlike the World Health Organization later with its governmental membership) could perhaps take a less cautious attitude than their counterparts in the League Secretariat. There, as noted above, the 'old guard' tended to dominate, the old Catholic countries of Europe accounting for a far higher proportion of total membership than was the case with the League's successor organization.

The United Nations – early days

The Conference held at San Francisco in 1945 which established the United Nations authorized the Economic and Social Council to set up 'such commissions as may be required for the performance of its functions'. On 3 October, 1946, the Population Commission was created, on the basis of a joint Anglo–American resolution and over the opposition of the USSR and Yugoslavia. After some protracted debates, it was agreed at the third session of the Economic and Social Council in May 1948 that the Commission was 'to arrange for studies and advise the Council on:

(a) the size and structure of population and the changes therein;

(b) the interplay of demographic factors and economic and social factors;

(c) policies designed to influence the size and structure of population and the changes therein;

(d) any other demographic questions on which either the principal or the subsidiary organs of the United Nations or the Specialized Agencies may seek advice'[7].

Part of this mandate was uncontroversial in the sense that the Population Commission would be continuing with the statistical tasks already begun by the League of Nations. But there were more contentious aspects as well including the extent to which the Population Commission should concern itself with policy issues. At the Commission's first session, for example, the Soviet member disagreed with the use of the term 'optimum population'; the Chinese member called for a study of areas where the pressure of resources on population presented a major obstacle to the improvement of public health and the attainment of higher standards of living; and the Ukranian member objected to activities (e.g. population control) which he said would be 'contrary to the humanitarian aims of the United Nations'.

In spite of these differences of opinion, the Population Commission was able to decide on a programme of work and the establishment within the United Nations of a Population Division (whose first head was Frank

8

Notestein, the former Director of the Princeton Office of Population Research) enabled the United Nations to develop the series of studies and publications on demographic trends, their causes and consequences, which were to prove such vital tools in increasing understanding of the population question. For example, the *Demographic Year Book* which was first published in 1948 was rapidly recognized as a central work of reference and has not ceased to be regarded as such over the intervening years. Though the relative slowness of the United Nations' involvement in action programmes can be and has been criticized, the importance of the intellectual contribution made by the United Nations in those early years can hardly be overestimated. In fact it is doubtful if the basis of action would have existed at all if the groundwork had not been so carefully prepared. It is hard to think of any other area of scientific activity where the intellectual contribution of the United Nations has been so pre-eminent.

I have already quoted in the Introduction Professor Richard Gardner's comment in his essay 'Toward a World Population Program'[8] but it is worth repeating that comment here in an expanded context:

When the Population Commission met for the first time in 1947, demographic statistics, including census and vital statistics, were so incomplete that it was hardly possible to speak of world population trends or of world population problems. Without the devoted labors of the population and statistical sections of the UN Secretariat, operating under the Population and Statistical Commissions, one might not be able to discern even now the outlines of the world population problem or the problems of the major regions. Moreover, the UN played a major role in encouraging and assisting Member governments to obtain factual information on the size, composition, and trends of their populations and on the interrelation between population growth and economic development. It helped train nationals of less developed countries in census-taking and demography. Slowly but surely it helped alert the new leaders of the developing nations to the dangers of too rapid population growth. The UN system was not yet ready to face the issue of family planning; but the basis for a breakthrough was being laid.

This intellectual contribution was not, of course, confined to the work of the Population Commission and the Population Division within the United Nations Secretariat, or to the regional economic commissions and demographic centres. Economists, demographers and development planners – inside and outside the United Nations – pointed out the relationships between population and economic growth and the United Nations Specialized Agencies – even in those early years – did not fail to appreciate the sectoral implications – for employment, for health, for food and agriculture, for education. Thus, Julian Huxley, UNESCO's first Director-

9

General, emphasized in his second Annual Report in 1948 that overpopulation could drastically affect the type of civilization possible and its rate of advance. Huxley was not supported with any great enthusiasm by the UNESCO Conference but at least a number of studies were undertaken on the population-resource theme. Sir John Boyd-Orr, FAO's first Director-General, appears to have believed, at least during his time of office that 'modern science (had) the answer to Malthus'[9] but by the early 1950s, with the increase of population growth in the less-developed countries, there was a certain lessening of confidence. The Sixth Session of the FAO Conference which took place in 1951 expressed concern that food production 'was not keeping pace with population growth'. And in his introduction to the FAO's survey of the State of Food and Agriculture which appeared in the same year, the Director-General commented that a combination of factors, including population growth, had 'limited actual progress to much less than had been hoped'.

David Morse, Director-General of ILO, in his report to the organization's second Asian Regional Conference, held in Ceylon in 1950, argued that 'only if population growth can be checked will the workers in Asian countries be able to obtain substantial and lasting gains from programmes of economic and social development', a reflection which was welcomed by the representative of Ceylon though (predictably) criticized by the delegate of France.

It was in the World Health Organization that the most vigorous debate took place in these early years of the 1950s. Men like Dr Brock Chisholm, WHO's first Director-General, were ready to point out that the preamble to WHO's Constitution defined the objective of the organization as 'complete mental and physical well-being'. If a government judged that population growth constituted a health problem and applied to WHO for assistance, then WHO had a duty to respond. On the other hand, Chisholm was reluctant to plunge the organization into controversy. In 1950, WHO's Regional Committee for South-East Asia, meeting in Kandy, Ceylon (now Sri Lanka) passed a resolution recommending that 'the Regional Director, in cooperation with the other international agencies dealing with the problem of over-population and its effect on employment, food production, and the standard of living, should obtain from Member States of the region all possible demographic data, which should thereafter be circulated to member governments for any action which the governments may consider necessary'[10]. The debate was broadened at the fifth World Health Assembly in May 1952. Dr Evang of Norway urged that the 1953 programme of work should provide for the setting up of an expert committee on the health aspects of population, a proposal which sparked an intense debate. A rival resolution was promoted by Italy and the Lebanon which affirmed that 'from a medical standpoint population problems (did) not require any particular action on the part of WHO'[11]. In the event, both resolutions were withdrawn and an uneasy truce ensued during which countries such as India, Ceylon and the UAR continued to insist on the relevance of the 'population explosion' to the work of WHO, while the majority of members opposed any involvement by WHO in family planning activities. In practical terms, the effect of the controversy was to put a stop to any expansion of WHO's work in this area. When Dr Candau of Brazil succeeded Chisholm in 1953, governments who applied to WHO for assistance in this field were informed that the relevant activities did not fall within WHO's mandate.

Any judgement on WHO's early record in population and family planning need not – and should not – be wholly negative. If it is true that successful programmes of disease eradication – through control of malaria[12], smallpox, cholera, yaws and trachoma – resulted in an unprecedented measure of 'death control' (which unaccompanied by action on birth control aggravated the demographic imbalance at least in the short and medium term), it is also true that the emphasis WHO placed on the training of doctors and the strengthening of national health services, as Richard Gardner puts it, 'helped to create an infrastructure essential to the implementation of family planning programmes'[13]. And in the long term it can be argued, as we shall see, that lasting declines in fertility are to be associated with an improvement in the levels of social and economic development, which in turn must be linked to improving standards of health and nutrition.

World Population Conference, 1954

When Julian Huxley, during his brief tenure as Director-General of UNESCO at the end of the 1940s, proposed the holding of a World Population Conference, the Population Commission shelved the idea, ostensibly on the grounds that it would be better to wait for the results of the 1950 round of censuses. In practice, some members of the Commission were suspicious of Huxley's motives and anxious to avoid any suggestion that a World Population Conference might be used as a forum for birth-control propaganda. At its sixth session in 1951, the Commission affirmed its belief in the 'scientific' value of holding a Conference, and, in June 1952, the Economic and Social Council decided that the Conference would be held in 1954 under the auspices of the UN and in collaboration with the International Union for the Scientific Study of Population (IUSSP) and interested Specialized Agencies. Thus the 1954 World Population Conference was from the start different from the 1927 Conference. In 1927, as we have seen, the League of Nations took a highly circumspect view of what had begun as a private initiative of Margaret Sanger. In 1954, the United Nations had moved to the centre of the stage. Though the World Population Conference was to be confined to 'scientific' themes, the fact that it was to be held under UN auspices with the active participation of the Specialized Agencies (except for WHO which was still suffering its own internal crisis over its involvement with population matters) was a powerful demonstration that the world body had staked out a dominant position in the field.

In the event, the 'birth controllers' were not wholly excluded from the deliberations of the Conference. Twelve associates of the newly formed International Planned Parenthood Federation (IPPF) attended the Conference as participants, and nine presented papers. IPPF was invited to send two observers. Altogether 400 delegates from 80 countries and colonies attended the Conference which took place in Rome from 31 August until 10 September, 1954. Thirty working sessions were held and over 400 papers presented. The Conference was received by the Pope who commended the participants for their concern with a pressing problem and called on them not to ignore its moral and human aspects.

Though largely scientific in the sense that the main emphasis was on demographic research, case studies and the identification of gaps in knowledge, the first World Population Conference did nevertheless provide a platform for the airing of wider concerns. As Symonds and Carder put it[14]:

> Speakers, notably from India, Egypt and Japan, described efforts that were being made in their countries to spread birth control. The respectful attention with which their contributions were received was an indication of the changing climate of opinion with respect to the gravity of the world population situation.

By the end of the 1950s there was a growing recognition that the United Nations could not confine itself to research and studies however valuable these might be. At its tenth session in 1959, the Population Commission for the first time recognized that population growth could jeopardize hopes for economic progress. In its Report, the Commission says:

> the question must frankly be raised as to whether, in certain of these nations (the less developed countries), population growth has reached such a point as to make economic development more difficult or slower in its progress, or to make it dependent on special kinds of measures[15].

12

Though it was 'not the task of the Population Commission to suggest policies that any Government of any member state should pursue', the report nevertheless emphasized that each government should study the interrelations between population growth and economic and social progress as fully as possible and should take them into account when formulating and implementing its policies.

Thus, slowly but surely, the groundwork was laid by the end of the 1950s for the breakthrough which came in the early 1960s. In practice, this breakthrough can be ascribed to the continuing evolution in attitudes to the population question among the rich industrialized countries (whose resources would be needed in support of action programmes) together with the steady pressure of certain developing countries, a pressure which could itself be seen as their own (partial) response to the ineluctible demographic facts with which they were confronted.

2

The breakthrough in the United Nations

Build-up

In 1961 President John F. Kennedy invited the General Assembly to designate the 1960s as the United Nations Development Decade (UNDD). In its resolution on the subject the General Assembly set as its goal the attainment by the developing countries of 'a minimum annual rate of growth of aggregate national income of 5 per cent at the end of the Decade'[1]. It expressed the hope that the flow of international assistance and capital to developing countries 'should be substantially increased, so that it might reach as soon as possible approximately 1 per cent of the combined national incomes of the economically advanced countries'[2].

The General Assembly's designation of the (first) United Nations Development Decade was a reflection of the growing consensus that, of all the economic and social objectives of the United Nations, the development of the Third World was now the overwhelming objective. The United Nations, as it emerged from the San Francisco Conference, was essentially an organization with a heavily western orientation. The original 51 Member States included eight European States enjoying traditional democratic structures; four old British Commonwealth States; 20 Latin American countries who, by and large, maintained strong links with the United States; seven States from the Middle East who had intellectual, commercial and to some extent political ties with the west; as well as the United States and Canada. There were only three Asian countries – China, India and the Philippines – and only two African states – Ethiopia and Liberia. The Eastern bloc was represented by the Soviet Union (and two of its constituent republics), Czechoslovakia, Poland and Yugoslavia.

Only nine new members were admitted to the UN during the nine years from 1946 to 1954: two developed countries from Western Europe (Ireland and Sweden); six developing countries from the Middle East and Asia (Afghanistan, Thailand, Pakistan, Yemen, Burma, and Indonesia);

14

and Israel. As Walter M. Kotschnig put it in his Essay: 'The United Nations as an Instrument of Economic and Social Development'[3]

> these accessions, while slightly increasing the voting strength of the developing countries and providing a somewhat larger audience for Soviet speeches on colonialism and the new economic imperialism of the United States, did not substantially change the power constellation in bodies such as ECOSOC or their preoccupations'.

Kotschnig argues, for example, that the United States initiative in 1949 proposing a greatly enlarged programme of technical assistance (the Expanded Program of Technical Assistance (EPTA)) was largely a self-generated expression of practical American idealism as formulated by President Harry S. Truman in his second inaugural address.

In 1955, 16 new members were admitted to the United Nations, including four developing countries from Asia, one Middle Eastern nation; and Libya, the first African country admitted since 1945. Though only seven new members were admitted between 1956 and 1959 (all, with the exception of Japan, newly emerging States from Africa), in 1960 17 new States were accepted for membership, all, with the exception of Cyprus, from Africa and between that date and 1966, another 22 achieved membership (13 from Africa, plus Mongolia, Jamaica, Trinidad and Tobago, Kuwait, Malta, the Maldive Islands, Singapore, Barbados and Guyana).

In other words, during the early 1960s the United Nations changed from being essentially a Western-type (and largely Western-dominated) organization into a forum where the concerns of the developing countries were increasingly voiced and where, for both political and moral reasons, there was growing pressure on the rich industrialized nations to respond.

In 1959, a Presidential Committee on the American foreign aid programme, chaired by General William Draper Jr recommended that the US government should 'assist ... countries ... on request in the formulation of ... plans designed to deal with the problem of rapid population growth' and that it should support research, within the United Nations and elsewhere, on the question. But President Dwight D. Eisenhower had repudiated this recommendation: 'I cannot imagine anything more emphatically a subject that is not a proper political or governmental activity or function or responsibility'[4]. But only a couple of years later, attitudes in the United States were beginning to change rapidly. For the United States, like other industrialized countries, had subscribed to the goals and objectives of the Development Decades and could not therefore ignore the implications for development which were being posed by rapid rates of population growth in the developing countries. Nor, even if the Administration had wanted to ignore the issue, would it have found it easy to do so. The non-governmental bodies involved with family planning, particularly those associated with the International Planned Parenthood Federation, carried considerable political weight inside as well as outside America. And the great American Foundations – such as Ford and Rockefeller – had throughout the 1950s been steadily increasing their support of population and family-planning activities. The Population Council of New York was set up in 1952 as a result of an initiative by John D. Rockefeller 3rd. In addition to supporting training and research it became closely involved in the elaboration of policies and programmes. The influence of these bodies extended not just to the developing countries to whom they were tendering assistance but was felt also in the industrialized countries – and particularly the United States – where the new democratic administration of John Kennedy seemed particularly open to the advice profferred by the East Coast 'foreign policy establishment' among whom men like John D. Rockefeller 3rd were most certainly to be counted.

Equally important was the influence on the US Government and on other key donor governments brought to bear by the developing countries themselves. Committed as they were on their side to the goals of the Development Decade, several developing countries had, by the early 1960s, already introduced or strengthened population or family planning policies or programmes.

In 1959, for example, the Indian government declared its support for all methods of family limitation, including sterilization. The Third Five Year Plan declared that the 'objective of stabilizing population growth over a reasonable period ... must be at the very centre of planned development'. With the death rate declining from 27.4 per thousand to 22.8 between 1951 and 1961, and with the birth-rate somewhere over 40, India's population grew from 360 million to 439 million, an increase of 78 million or 21.5 per cent over the decade[5].

Developments in Pakistan to some extent paralleled those in India. The population enumerated in the area now constituting Pakistan increased from 45 million at the beginning of the century to about 76 million at the time of the 1951 census. In 1958 a group of public-spirited people founded the Family Planning Association of Pakistan and family planning clinics were opened in a few cities. There was no official policy, either for family planning or for population control. The government gave no financial support and the staff involved generally worked on an unpaid part-time basis.

In the first five-year plan, 1955–60, the Government became more conscious of the urgency of the problem. The plan stated:

16

The opinion of the educated classes, particularly of medical men, economists and social workers, is strongly in favour of extension of family planning facilities .... The country must appreciate that population growth is a rock on which all hopes of improved conditions of living may founder. It admits of no approach except that the rates of growth must be low.

Notwithstanding this declaration of intent, there was no family-planning organization and no programme during the first plan. With the accession to power of Ayub Khan, after the October Revolution of 1958, the declaration of intent was elaborated into a more formal population policy. In a speech in March 1959, Ayub Khan announced that he had impressed upon the Minister of Finance 'the need for allocating more and more funds for the movement of family planning'. As the second five-year plan, 1960–5, put it:

Since population growth can threaten to wipe out the gains of development, the Plan clearly recognizes the paramount need for a conscious population policy and its implementation. A population policy, however, must take into account many implications of population growth for other aspects of planning. The existing pressure of population leads to an intense struggle for the means of life at subsistence levels. Inadequate diet results in a prevalent malnutrition that cannot be cured by public health measures alone. Apathy is the companion of malnutrition and ignorance. Under these conditions people have meagre reserves of energy to strive for wider understanding and improvement ....

A gradual decrease in the rate of population growth, with the consequent lightening of the burden on family earnings, and a shrinkage in the amount of unemployment, will have an encouraging effect on the rate of industrialization. An over-plentiful supply of cheap labour leads to its wasteful utilization by employers, high turnover and an apathetic response to factory discipline and organization of productive skills ...[6].

Nor were these pressures limited to the Indian subcontinent. In Japan, for example, the Cabinet made a definite decision in November 1951 to promote contraception. The Eugenic Protection Law, passed in 1948, took a broad liberal approach to induced abortion. Together these measures helped to achieve the Japanese 'demographic miracle'. In the early 1920s birth-rates in Japan were as high as 33–6 per thousand. Mortality had begun to decline and stood at a level of 21–5. Since there was no sizeable international migration, the rate of natural increase was the gap between birth- and death-rates, i.e. around 12 per thousand, or 1.2 per cent. In 1948, with declines in the death-rate, natural increase stood at 2.2 per cent per annum. But in the 1950s the birth-rate began to decline (with perhaps 70 per cent of the decline being due to induced abortion and 30 per cent to family planning)[7]. The net result was that the birth-rate during

17

the 1950s declined sharply, as did the rate of natural increase. An awareness of Japan's 'demographic miracle' – the sense that dramatic falls in fertility could be achieved (even if the emphasis on induced abortion was not something to be publicly applauded) – was undoubtedly a factor in the minds of those who had to decide whether the United Nations could or should move from studies to action.

Elsewhere in Asia, particularly in city states like Hong Kong and Singapore or island economies like Taiwan, the basis of policy was also being laid – implicitly or explicitly.

In Hong Kong, for example, the population had grown in the course of the century (from 1891 to 1941) from 4000 to 1.6 million. The combined effects of immigration and natural increase brought the population up to 2 million in 1951 and to over 3 million (according to the census) in 1961 which implied a density of over 9000 per square mile of the colony (or some 63,000 people per square mile if the habitable area is regarded as around 60 square miles). With the tacit encouragement of the Hong Kong authorities, the Hong Kong Family Planning Association had – by the end of 1957 – opened 14 clinics and by the end of 1964 the number had risen to 51.

Even in non-Asian countries there was in the late 1950s a stirring of concern which could be readily discerned by those who had an ear for these things. Small island states of the Caribbean and the Pacific who had joined the United Nations in increasing numbers since the war (and who exercised a voting power within the United Nations which was quite disproportional to their size) were beginning to experience the 'limits to growth' in all their painful reality. In Barbados, for example, a Parliamentary committee was set up in 1952 'to examine the question of over-population and to make recommendations for dealing with this problem'.

In summary, it is fair to say that these developments among Third World countries were crucial not merely in persuading powerful donor countries like the United States that the time was ripe for more vigorous and concerted international action on the population question, but also in ensuring that the proponents of action could muster the necessary votes in the General Assembly and elsewhere to counter the Catholic countries of Latin America and Western Europe.

The decisive debate

At the 15th Session of the General Assembly, Mrs Lindstrom of Sweden indicated that it was her Government's intention that the population question should be put on the agenda of the Assembly. In February 1961, the Population Commission embarked on a review of the United Nations' work in the population field and reported that, while it was 'the responsibility of each government to decide its own policies and devise its own programmes of action ... it was in the interests of the UN that decisions on national policy should be planned in the light of knowledge of the relevant facts and that the programme should be adequate to assure satisfactory economic and social progress'. The report continued: 'it is also considered appropriate for the UN to give technical assistance as requested by Governments for national projects of research, experimentation and action for dealing with the problems of population'.

In August 1961, Sweden and Norway's Permanent Representatives at the United Nations formally requested that the item 'Population growth and economic development' be placed on the agenda of the 16th Session of the General Assembly. Subsequently, the two countries obtained the support of Ghana, Greece, Pakistan and Tunisia for the tabling of a draft resolution.

The General Assembly did not finally debate and vote upon the Swedish initiative until December 1962. Support for the draft resolution came notably from India, Tunisia, Syria, Pakistan and Greece. Richard Gardner, who at the time was serving as Deputy Assistant Secretary of State for International Organization Affairs, stated – in the course of a speech which had been cleared by President Kennedy – that his government believed 'that obstacles should not be placed in the way of other governments which sought solutions to their population problems'. He indicated that the United States government was willing to help these countries 'in their search for information and assistance on ways and means of dealing with this problem'.

In the course of the debate in the Second Committee of the General Assembly, amendments were tabled by France with the support of Lebanon, Liberia, Spain and Gabon, for the deletion of that part of the resolution which dealt with the provision of technical assistance and for the addition of a section calling on the United Nations to undertake an enquiry among governments 'on the problems confronting them as a result of the reciprocal action of economic development and population change'. The sponsors of the resolution accepted the proposal for an enquiry but not the deletion of the clause relating to the provision of technical assistance. In the ensuing vote, the amendment was defeated by 32 votes (against deletion) to 30 votes (for deletion) with 35 abstentions. Fourteen countries voted against the resolution as a whole in the Second Committee. These were Argentina, Austria, Belgium, Colombia, France, Ireland, Italy, Lebanon, Liberia, Luxembourg, Peru, Portugal, Spain and Uruguay.

When later the resolution as adopted by the Second Committee came before the General Assembly, the debate was to a large extent repeated. Mr Viaud of France pressed for a separate vote on the last part of paragraph 6 which referred to the provision of technical assistance. This time the voting was 34 in favour with 34 against and 32 abstentions. Lacking the necessary two-thirds majority, the clause fell. The final resolution, without the contentious paragraph 6, was adopted by 69 votes to nil with 27 abstentions.

In his own account of this affair, Richard Gardner writes

> it was of enormous importance that this resolution was carried without any negative votes .... A number of countries that voted in Committee for the resolution as a whole with the technical assistance section included abstained in the separate vote on the section. The United States was one of these, but it took pains to emphasize that the elimination of the paragraph would in no way detract from the existing authority of the UN to grant technical assistance upon request to the Member governments.

Professor Gardner adds:

> Abstention on the controversial section – and its consequent defeat – was the price that had to be paid for achieving a broad consensus among the membership. It was also the price the United States and some other Members had to pay for this first big step forward on population, given the uncertain state of domestic opinion.[8]

Gardner argues that the elimination of the paragraph relating to technical assistance made possible affirmative votes on the resolution by many countries who, though conceding the existence of population problems in some areas, felt that UN action should be deferred pending further study. It also made possible abstentions by other countries who would otherwise have voted against – including Soviet bloc states who expounded the traditional Communist position that Western discussions of the population problem were based on 'neo-Malthusian fallacies' and that population problems would cease to exist under Communism.

The full text of the Resolution adopted at the 1197th Plenary meeting of the General Assembly on 18th December 1962 is set out in Annex A. Examined almost a quarter of a century later, this Resolution must appear to the more passionate devotees of UN involvement as a fairly bland statement. But in fact the operative paragraphs of the resolution, cautiously worded though they were, served to establish the main signposts which would guide UN activity in the population field over the next decade and more.

Under paragraph 3 of the Resolution, the Secretary-General was requested 'to conduct an enquiry among the Governments of State

Members of the United Nations and members of the specialized agencies concerning the particular problems confronting them as a result of the reciprocal action of economic development and population changes'.

In paragraph 4, the General Assembly recommended that the Economic and Social Council, in co-operation with the specialized agencies, the regional economic commissions and the Population Commission, and taking into account the results of the enquiry referred to in paragraph 3, should:

> intensify its studies and research on the interrelationship of population growth and economic and social development, with particular reference to the needs of the developing countries for investment in health and educational facilities within the framework of their general development programmes.

The fifth paragraph 'further recommended' that the Economic and Social Council should report on its findings to the General Assembly not later than at its nineteenth session. This was important. As Richard Gardner comments: 'this laid the basis for the Assembly's next leap forward in 1966'. As we shall see the 1966 Resolution of the General Assembly compensated for the inadequacies of the earlier version by an explicit reference to the provision of technical assistance.

The sixth paragraph endorsed the view of the Population Commission that the United Nations should encourage and assist governments, especially those of the less developed countries, in obtaining basic data and in carrying out essential studies of the demographic aspects, as well as other aspects, of their economic and social development problems.

Finally, the General Assembly Resolution recommended that the Second World Population Conference (which would be held in 1965) 'should pay special attention to the interrelationship of population growth and economic and social development, particularly in the less-developed countries, and that efforts should be made to obtain the fullest possible participation in the Conference by experts from such countries'.

1962 to 1966

Several factors were important in bridging the gap between 1962 and 1966. Though Richard Gardner as the US delegate at the 17th session of the General Assembly had observed that the UN already had the necessary authority to provide technical assistance to governments in the formulation and execution of population policies (a remark which to Professor Symonds and Michael Carder appeared to be legally sound)[9], other countries – particularly those who were opposed to birth control for religious reasons – took the view that the language of paragraph 6 of

21

Resolution 1838 (XVIII) in fact precluded the United Nations from carrying out such activities. It was the impetus provided by the United Nations regional bodies, and by the results of the enquiry on population and development which the Secretary-General had been asked to undertake under the General Assembly Resolution, which helped to nudge the ship onward through the water.

In 1963, the Economic Commission for Asia and the Far East (ECAFE) held an Asian Population Conference. It met in New Delhi in December of that year; lasted ten days and was attended by over 200 participants from 14 Asian countries and five members of ECAFE from outside the region. A resolution adopted by the Conference recommended that the UN and its specialized agencies should expand the scope of the technical assistance which they were prepared to give on the request of governments on statistics, research, experimentation and action programmes. Governments in the region were 'invited to take account of the urgency of adopting a positive population policy related to their individual needs and the general needs of the region'[10].

Similarly, the UN Economic Commission for Latin America (ECLA) published a survey that indicated that the people of Latin American countries were ahead of their leaders in respect to population control[11]. The report cited the example of Chile as the first Latin American country to initiate family planning through its national health service, largely as a result of concern over the increasing number of illegal abortions. Similar concerns were being felt in other countries of the region.

Results of the enquiry
on population and economic development

Fifty-three governments and the Vatican had replied to the Secretary-General's Enquiry on Population and Economic Development at the time when this item appeared on the agenda of ECOSOC in July 1964. Twenty-eight of these replies were from governments of less-developed countries. It was clear that many governments viewed the current rate of population growth with concern, although only six African and six Latin American countries responded. Symonds & Carder comment 'Significantly, many of the governments which had opposed the original draft resolution in 1962 failed to reply, including Argentina, Brazil, Peru and nearly all the French-speaking African countries'[12].

Following the lead given by Japan's representative in the Council's Economic Committee, three Asian countries, Japan, India and Iran, introduced a draft resolution noting the 'serious concern' expressed by many governments of less developed countries in their replies to the enquiry; and called on the General Assembly, the regional economic commissions and the Population Commission to examine the replies and 'to make recommendations with a view to intensifying the work of the UN in assisting ... governments ... to deal with the population problems confronting them'. This resolution was adopted in substance by the Council at its last meeting[13].

Within the United Nations Secretariat itself, steps were taken to respond to the growing pressure for UN action even in advance of formal endorsement by the General Assembly of an expanded mandate. In January 1965, the UN Technical Assistance Board, at the request of the Indian Government, sent a team led by Sir Colville Deverell, the Secretary-General of the IPPF, to review India's family planning programme and to make recommendations for its intensification – this was the first such mission ever sent by the UN. In February of the following year, the UN's Population Branch was upgraded to the level of a division. Its head, John Durand, resigned and was replaced by the Yugoslavian Milos Macura.

World Population Conference, Belgrade, 1965

The holding of the second World Population Conference in Belgrade, Yugoslavia, from 30 August to 10 September 1965 was another important stimulus to action. Though, like the Rome Conference which took place a decade earlier, the Belgrade meeting was not a gathering of official governmental representatives but rather a technical and scientific assembly, the Conference provided a forum where experts could examine population trends in different parts of the world and assess their implications.

While no consensus of views was attempted, certain main themes emerged which can be summarized:

(a) In many countries with high fertility rates, attempts to achieve economic development were being offset by growing populations. However, current high birth rates might not continue long into the future. As countries progressed economically, it was suggested, people with better education and higher income would produce fewer children. Even so, an immediate drop in the birth-rate would not affect population growth for some 30–40 years, when women already born would have passed the child-bearing age.

(b) Recent gains in disease control might be offset by increased death-rates due to malnutrition and hunger. Some expert papers showed that food output per person was declining and that an increasing proportion of new populations in developing countries was being sustained by outside food shipments.

(c) The shift of populations from rural to urban areas posed special problems, including those linked to crime and disease.

(d) The two most potentially useful methods of birth-control were described as the oral contraceptive and the intra-uterine contraceptive device (IUD), from which there appeared to be no serious side-effects. Male sterilization and legal abortion were other potentially effective control methods, if acceptable to the society concerned.

(e) If the UN system was to emerge as the essential, if not indispensable, framework for both national and supranational action, population studies had to extend far beyond the traditional demographic, clinical and biological topics[14].

Speaking in an opening statement to the participants, Philippe de Seynes, the United Nations Under-Secretary for Economic and Social Affairs, asked 'What is it then that makes us feel in opening this Conference – ostensibly a technical conference – that we are taking part in an exceptional occurrence, with a political dimension'[15]. He declared that the UN was ready to respond to all requests for assistance from any country which had decided to embark on a population programme or to explore its possibilities. And Julia Henderson, Head of the Bureau of Social Affairs (and subsequently to become Secretary-General of IPPF), added, when opening the session on fertility, that 'although prescribing solutions for population problems is not part of the terms of reference of this assembly of experts', it was hoped that the discussions would shed 'light on the paths of policy and action'.

The 1966 General Assembly Resolution

These then, were some of the elements in the background when the General Assembly met in 1966. In addition to the resolutions from the UN's regional bodies, the results of the enquiry into population and economic development, and the impact of the World Population Conference which had taken place the previous year, the General Assembly was aware that the World Health Assembly had, in May 1966, confirmed the right of WHO to give advisory services on the medical aspects of family planning, and the General Conference of UNESCO had adopted a resolution authorizing studies of the effect of population growth on education. According to the 1967 Report on the World Social Situation, the number of governments with official policies aimed at moderating the rate of population growth had grown to 14, while at least ten other countries

24

were actively supporting family-planning activities. On Human Rights Day – 9 December – 1966, 12 Heads of States issued a Declaration[16] drawing attention to the effects of rapid population growth on hopes for a better life and called on Heads of State everywhere to recognize family planning as a vital interest both to the family and the nation.

Welcoming that statement, Secretary-General U Thant said:

in my view, we must accord the right of parents to determine the numbers of their children a place of importance at this moment in man's history. For, as one of the consequences of backwardness, rates of population growth are very much higher in the poor two-thirds of the world than they are among the more privileged countries and it is being increasingly realized that, over the two or three decades immediately ahead, when present world-wide efforts to raise food production will not have yielded the fullest results, the problem of growing food shortage cannot be solved without, in many cases, a simultaneous effort to moderate population growth.

A draft resolution on Population Growth and Economic Development was sponsored by 25 countries, including the United States, the United Kingdom and several Latin American countries. It was unanimously approved in the Second Committee and adopted – also unanimously – by the Assembly at its 1497th Plenary Meeting on 17th December, 1966.

Though there were still some who would have preferred a more explicit text, there was no doubt in most observers' minds that the 1966 General Assembly Resolution represented a net advance by the United Nations in its attempts to come to grips with the population issue, when compared with the General Assembly Resolution adopted four years earlier. What principally distinguished the 1966 Resolution from its predecessor was its operative Paragraphs 3 and 4.

Paragraph 3 requested the Secretary-General:

(a) to pursue, within the limits of available resources, the implementation of the work programme covering training, research, information and advisory services in the field of population in the light of the recommendations of the Population Commission contained in the report on its thirteenth session, as endorsed by the Economic and Social Council in its Resolution 1084 (XXXIX) and of the considerations set forth in the preamble of the present resolution:

(b) to continue his consultations with the specialized agencies concerned, in order to ensure that the activities of the United Nations system of organizations in the field of population are effectively co-ordinated;

(c) to present to the Population Commission at its 14th session, as envisaged in Economic and Social Council Resolution 1084 (XXXIX), proposals with regard to the priorities of work over periods of two and five years, within the framework of the long-range programme of work in the field of population.

Paragraph 4 of the General Assembly Resolution called upon the Economic and Social Council, the Population Commission, the Regional Economic Commissions, the United Nations Economic and Social Office in Beirut and the specialized agencies concerned to assist, when requested, in further developing and strengthening national and regional facilities for training, research, information and advisory services in the field of population, bearing in mind the different character of population problems in each country and region and the needs arising therefrom.

The reference, in Paragraph 3(a), to the preamble to the Resolution was not a purely formal one. One preambular paragraph in particular was dear to the delegates of some countries who might otherwise have opposed the Resolution. This was the sentence which 'recognized the sovereignty of nations in formulating and promoting their own population policies, with due regard to the principle that the size of the family should be according to the free choice of each individual family'. It is not an exaggeration to say that this dual concept of the sovereign right of nations to decide on population policy in the broad sense, allied to the sovereign right of families to make their own individual choices as to family size, has always received the fullest recognition in all UN doctrine. To what extent these 'sovereign' rights have been or may be limited or modified in practice is an issue which will be touched on later in this book. 'Sovereign' or 'inalienable' rights, which fit very well into preambular paragraphs, do not always accord so neatly with the realities of a shrinking world. (The full text of General Assembly Resolution 2211 (XXI) – Population growth and economic development of 17 December 1966 is given in Annex B.)

Philippe de Seynes commented that the 1966 General Assembly Resolution on population growth and economic development expressed:

the consensus of Member States in recognition of the seriousness of population problems, the need for a proper understanding of these problems and their effect on economic and social development; it also emphasized the necessity for accelerated action to implement the expanded programme recommended by the Population Commission[17].

The creation of the trust fund

In his State of the Union Address to Congress in January 1965, President Johnson said: 'I will seek new ways to use our knowledge to help deal with the explosion in world population and the growing scarcity in world resources. In December of that year, a Committee on Population[18] which had been formed as part of President Johnson's National Citizen's Commission to offer recommendations to the United States Government during International Cooperation Year proposed:

> That the US Government be prepared to make available upon request up to $100 million a year over the next three years to help other countries implement programmes of family planning and strengthen national health and social services necessary for the support of family planning programmes.
>
> That US assistance to other countries in all of these areas be related to the maximum possible extent to the work of multilateral agencies, particularly the relevant agencies of the United Nations, including the World Health Organization, the United Nations Children's Fund and the United Nations Development Programme.

In the spring of 1967, Senator J. William Fulbright, with 18 co-sponsors, introduced a bill to authorize an appropriation of US $50 million per year for three years, plus available United States-owned foreign currencies, for use in support of voluntary family planning programmes in friendly foreign nations. It was all a far cry from the days when President Eisenhower made his famous disclaimer[19].

The passage of the General Assembly Resolution – taken together with these indications of support by the major donor nation – was sufficient to persuade the Secretary-General that the time was ripe for a new United Nations initiative – the creation of a Trust Fund for Population. Though many members of the United Nations had a general policy against establishing new voluntary programmes within the United Nations, the Secretary-General recognized that, in the case of population (which, in spite of all the progress of recent years, remained a controversial topic), a voluntary programme under which nations who wished to give aid for this purpose joined together in mutual cooperation with nations who wished to receive such aid, stood the best chance of success.

In opening ECOSOC's 43rd session in July–August 1967, U Thant stated:

> On the strength of a historic General Assembly resolution, the United Nations can now embark on a bolder and more effective programme of action in this field. With its Population Commission, Population Division and its regional units, with the demographic centres already linked to the Organization, and with the cooperation of the World Health Organization, the United Nations Children's Fund and other interested agencies, the United Nations has now at its

disposal an institutional infrastructure which, given some additional means, could be put to much more effective use in support of large scale programmes.

He then went on to announce:

I have decided to establish a trust fund to which I hope governments and institutions will pledge voluntary contributions. This would help us to lay the ground for training centres as well as for pilot experiments which will assist the less developed countries in establishing and expanding their own administration and programmes[20].

By mid-July 1968 the resources of the Trust Fund exceeded US \$1 million. This included \$500,000 which the USA had pledged for the specific purpose of project stimulation, \$200,000 from Sweden, and \$100,000 from Denmark and £100,000 from the United Kingdom. The United States had announced that it had submitted to Congress a request for a further \$2.5 million as a new contribution on the understanding that these funds would be administered by UNDP.

As Richard Gardner commented[21]:

The trust fund opened in the summer of 1967 could be the first step towards a World Population Program and toward a really effective response by the UN to the challenge of population growth. At least one earnestly hopes so. In the long run this might prove to be the Organization's most vital contribution to human welfare, second only to keeping the peace. In a matter of such transcendent importance to humanity as a whole, the United Nations belongs at the very centre of the picture.

With hindsight, it is impossible not to agree with Professor Gardner. The creation of the Trust Fund marked the beginning of the new more active phase of United Nations involvement in population questions; the United Nations Fund for Population Activities (whose actions will be described in subsequent chapters) grew out of the Trust Fund, though as we shall see, there were important qualitative as well as quantitative changes in its manner of operation. As for Professor Gardner's comment that UN activity in this field may prove to be 'the Organization's most vital contribution to human welfare second only to keeping the peace', this too – with the benefit of hindsight – seems to be a justifiable statement. Indeed, at the end of the period with which this book is concerned, serious consideration was being given by both academics and politicians to the links and correlations between population trends and pressures and the outbreak of violence, including both internal conflict and external aggression. Thus, population planning was beginning to be seen in itself as a form of peacekeeping activity, and therefore as a part of the United Nations' primary mandate.

Family planning as a human right

In these years of the late 1960s, international attention focussed not merely on the relationships between population growth and economic development, but also on the relevance of activities connected with population, especially family planning, to the promotion and protection of human rights. 1968 was celebrated as International Year for Human Rights. When the General Assembly requested UNESCO, amongst others, to devote the year 1968 'to intensified efforts and undertakings in the field of human rights', the question of the extent to which family planning was a human right in the accepted sense of the term was inevitably raised.

The right to family planning is not explicitly mentioned in the United Nations Universal Declaration of Human Rights, 1948, nor in the Draft Covenants on Civil and Political Rights, and Economic, Social and Cultural Rights, nor in the Covenant on Civil and Political Rights, 1966. However, the concept of a family planning right can, some commentators have claimed, be inferred from the rights to privacy, conscience, health and well-being set forth in various conventions and declarations of the United Nations and bodies such as UNESCO, ILO and WHO. For example, a statement by the Secretary-General issued in 1967[22] included the following specific references to family planning in the context of human rights:

> There are important links between population growth and the implementation of the rights and freedom proclaimed in the Universal Declaration of Human Rights ... population planning is seen not only as an integral part of national efforts for economic and social development, but also as a way to human progress in modern society.
>
> The Universal Declaration of Human Rights describes the family as the natural and fundamental unit of society. It follows that any choice and decision with regard to the size of the family must inevitably rest with the family itself, and cannot be made by anyone else. But this right of parents to free choice will remain illusory unless they are aware of the alternatives open to them. Hence, the right of every family to information and the availability of services in the field is increasingly considered as a basic human right and as an indispensable ingredient of human dignity.

In May 1968, the International Conference on Human Rights, held in Teheran under the auspices of the United Nations, took a step towards the more explicit recognition of family planning as a human right. In its resolution XVIII on the human rights aspects of family planning, the Conference observed that

> the present rapid rate of population growth in some areas of the world hampers the struggle against hunger and poverty, and in particular reduces the possibilities of rapidly achieving adequate standards of living, including food, clothing,

housing, medical care, social security, education and social services, thereby impairing the full realization of human rights.

The Conference recalled General Assembly Resolution 2211 (XXI) of 17 December 1966[23] which recognized the sovereignty of nations 'in formulating and promoting their own population policies, with due regard to the principle that the size of the family should be the free choice of each individual family'. It also recalled UNESCO Resolution 3.252, the World Health Assembly's Resolution WHA 20.41 and the conclusions of the 1965 World Population Conference on the subject of family planning – and believed it was timely to draw attention to the connection between population growth and human rights.

So far, so unsurprising. Where the Resolution added to the corpus of doctrine was in going on to recognize that 'moderation of the present rate of population growth would enhance the conditions for offering greater opportunities for the enjoyment of human rights and the improvement of living conditions'; it considered that 'couples have a basic human right to decide freely and responsibly on the number and spacing of their children and a right to adequate education and information in this respect'; and urged Member States and United Nations bodies and agencies concerned to give close attention to the implications of population increase for the exercise of human rights.

In presenting the draft resolution to the plenary meeting for approval, the Rapporteur emphasized that family planning must be based on the free and responsible decision of each couple, and stated that the resolution said 'yes' to planning *by* the family and 'no' to planning *for* the family.

Forty-nine countries, including the Holy See, voted in favour of the resolution which was introduced by the UAR on behalf also of Chile, Finland, India, Morocco, Pakistan, Sweden, Tunisia, Turkey, UK and Yugoslavia.

The International Conference on Human Rights concluded its session with the unanimous adoption on 13 May, 1968, of the Proclamation of Teheran. In the Proclamation, the Conference 'solemnly proclaims', among other things, that:

The protection of the family and of the child remains the concern of the international community. Parents have a basic human right to determine freely and responsibly the number and spacing of their children.

The inclusion of these references to family planning as a human right in the results of the International Conference on Human Rights was, as Symonds and Carder point out[24], seized on by the family-planning movement and its supporters among member governments.

They had argued for many years not only that all children should be wanted children, but also, by implication, that governments had an obligation to accept responsibility for the provision of family planning advice and services in order to enable couples to plan the size of their families.

However, the fact that the representative of the Holy See felt able to vote for the Teheran Resolution was a clear enough indication that not all the participants at the Conference saw things in the same light. If the Vatican could approve of the idea of family planning as an individual human right, it did so – at least in part – in order to make clear that this was certainly *not* a responsibility of the State. A few months later the publication of the Encyclical *Humanae Vitae* would spell out with great clarity precisely where the Vatican stood on this issue – and the news was not encouraging for the birth-controllers. For even though *Humanae Vitae* recognized that there might in certain circumstances be a case for contraception, the methods to be used were severely limited (essentially the 'rhythm' method was the only one to receive any kind of official approval) while the notion of a state population policy intended to limit births remained anathema.

In fact, as one looks back at the first 40 years of United Nations involvement with the population question, it is hard not to see the Papal Encyclical of July 29, 1968, as a deadly torpedo launched at the UN's frail vessel when it was barely off the slipway.

The 45th session of ECOSOC, for example, which was concerned with preparations for the Second Development Decade (launched by the General Assembly in 1970), was hardly able to ignore the link between population and development. The United Nations' Secretary-General pointed out that the population increase in the 1970s would probably exceed that of the 1960s by one-third, reaching a total of 626 million new people during the decade, with a yearly increase of 54 million persons and a rapid increase in the younger age groups. Yet the resolution with ECOSOC adopted on 30 July, 1968[25], the day after the Encyclical *Humanae Vitae* had been issued, was approved only by 12 votes to 7 with 4 abstentions.

Though the author now regrets the somewhat intemperate language he used in an earlier reference to *Humanae Vitae*[26], he nevertheless believes that the long-term effect of the Encyclical taken together with the pronouncements of subsequent Popes – in particular John–Paul II – has been severe. If the Roman Catholic Church had taken a different position on population and family planning (as once seemed possible), we might have seen a far more rapid evolution of attitudes and policies, particularly in Latin America. Such an evolution could have had a dramatic effect on population trends.

Because the resolution cited above was another milestone in the United Nations progress towards full engagement with the population question, it is worthwhile looking at it in some detail. The crucial third paragraph recommended

> that the United Nations Development Programme give due consideration to applications submitted for financing projects designed to assist developing countries in dealing with population problems, primarily in the fields of economic and social development, including both national and regional projects.

This reference to the role of UNDP in population matters was interesting and important in that it prefigured decisions which would be taken the following year as far as the administration of the Secretary-General's Trust Fund was concerned. The fourth paragraph of the ECOSOC Resolution, however, reflecting the still unresolved nature of the institutional issues, requested the Secretary-General, within the approved programme of work to:

> (a) pursue a programme of work covering training, research, information and advisory services in the fields of fertility, natality and morbidity, internal migration and urbanization and demographic aspects of economic and social development, in accordance with Council Resolution 1084 (XXXIX) of 30 July, 1965, and General Assembly Resolution 2211 (XXI);
>
> (b) give special attention to further developing those aspects of work in population fields, within the context of economic, social and health policies, and where appropriate, religious and cultural considerations;
>
> (c) submit to the General Assembly biennially a concise report on the world population situation, including an assessment of current and prospective population trends;
>
> (d) bring promptly up to date the study *Determinants and Consequences of Population Trends*[27]

Status of Women

One other strand which emerged at the 1968 meetings of ECOSOC – and which would be of continuing importance in succeeding years – was the link between population and family planning and the status of women. On the recommendation of the United Nations Commission on the Status of Women, one of the six functional Commissions originally established under the Economic and Social Council, ECOSOC adopted on 31 May 1968 resolution 1326 (XLIV) on family planning and the status of women. The Commission had considered an interim report of the Secretary-General relating to the status of women and family planning[28] which outlined relevant background information, including recent policy of the United Nations and its agencies in the fields of population and family planning, and indicated a number of factors which appeared to be relevant to the further study of the relationship between the status of women and family planning.

In its resolution the Council requested the Secretary-General to transmit the interim report to State Members and to the specialized agencies concerned as well as to interested non-governmental organizations, and invited interested Governments:

> to undertake national surveys or case studies on the status of women and family planning, taking into account such factors as the implication for the status of women of the effects of population growth on economic and social development, factors affecting fertility that relate directly to the status of women, the implications of family size for maternal and child welfare, the scope of existing family planning programmes in relation to the status of women, and current trends in population growth and family size and the protection of human rights, in particular the rights of women.

This bland and bureaucratic language, a feature of so many United Nations resolutions in this field as in most others, tends to mask the intrinsic importance of the subject at issue. By the end of the period which is the subject of this study, improvements in the status of women – including such questions as the access of women to education, equal pay for equal work, and the status of women under laws dealing with the family and with property rights (the traditional preoccupation of bodies such as the Commission on the Status of Women) – were generally recognized as being crucial to the 'deliverability' of family planning programmes and to the achievements of lasting declines in fertility. In the summer of 1985, the United Nations held a conference in Nairobi to mark the end of the United Nations Women's Decade. The final resolutions and declarations of that conference laid special stress on the links between the status of women in all its manifold aspects and on the broad questions of natality and fertility.[29]

3

The role of the agencies

When the Secretary-General of the United Nations stated in July 1967 at the 43rd session of ECOSOC that 'the United Nations has now at its disposal an institutional infrastructure which, given some additional means, could be put to much more effective use in support of large-scale (population) programmes[1], he was undoubtedly engaging in a degree of wishful thinking. As the Project Director of the Policy Panel on World Population and the United Nations, set up by the United Nations Association of the United States of America under the Chairmanship of John D. Rockefeller 3rd, the author had the opportunity to visit during the course of 1968 most of the elements of the United Nations system which were actually or potentially concerned with population and family planning and to discuss the possibilities for progress with a wide variety of people, both inside and outside the international bodies.

From one point of view, the results of that series of visits and discussions were encouraging. Whereas in the past it had been possible for certain of the agencies to argue that they 'had no mandate' to engage in population activities, most of the questions of constitutional and institutional propriety seemed either resolved or well on the way to being so.

The World Health Organisation (WHO)

For example, the World Health Organisation had by then, in theory at least, recovered from the agonizing debates of the early 1950s[2]. In the World Health Assembly's debates of 1963 and 1964 support for WHO involvement in population policies was expressed by – amongst others – the representatives of Jamaica, Thailand, Indonesia and Korea (India, Ceylon and the UAR had remained perennially faithful to the cause throughout the doldrum years).

34

In 1965, the tide began to turn. WHO carried out and published various studies of human reproduction. And at the 1966 World Health Assembly 17 countries put forward a draft resolution urging that WHO should extend its activities to include the provision of expert advice on the planning, execution and evaluation of family-planning programmes. However, the Director-General (still Dr Candau of Brazil) made what has been considered a decisive intervention, and a less radical resolution was passed confirming that WHO could give advice on request to members 'in the development of activities in family planning, as part of an organized health service'. In 1967, a unanimous resolution again confirmed existing policy. At the same time, however, it authorized the Director-General to assist governments on request in securing the training of teachers and professional staff for family-planning activities. It also drew attention to the serious health problem created in many countries by high abortion rates.

In April 1968 the Director-General submitted a report to the World Health Assembly entitled the 'Health Aspects of Population Dynamics'. He stressed that family-planning activities should be included as part of the health services, particularly of their maternal and child health component, and that family-planning services, where introduced, should not impair the normal preventive and curative function of health services. WHO did not endorse or promote any particular population policy, recognized that the problem of human reproduction involved a family unit as well as society, and that the size of the family was the free choice of each individual in the family.

WHO's role was therefore, by the end of 1968, sufficiently well defined to permit the Organization to play its part in the upgraded effort to which U Thant had referred.

Food and Agricultural Organization (FAO)

The same could be said about the Food and Agriculture Organization (FAO). In fact, the most vigorous initiative on population by any head of a UN agency came from Dr B. R. Sen, a former Indian government official, who was from 1956 to 1967 Director-General of FAO. At the International Eucharistic Congress in Bombay in 1964, after indicating that food production was not keeping up with the growth of population, Dr Sen asked 'can we any more turn our faces away from the concept of family planning when the alternative is starvation and death'? Subsequently he entered into a dialogue with the Vatican and in March 1967, when Pope Paul issued an Encyclical on the 'Development of People' which contained an ambiguous statement on 'demography', Dr Sen called a press conference to express the gratitude of FAO for the Encyclical in general and described the passage as of tremendous significance.

In his 1967 report on the 'State of Food and Agriculture' Dr Sen noted that unless there was a radical change in the agricultural production of developing countries, their food import needs might be expected to continue to increase in line with their rapidly increasing population. He called *inter alia* for steps to be taken to control population growth in order that the developing countries might have time in which to make a sufficient increase in their agricultural production.

No specific resolution on family planning was adopted at the 1967 conference of the FAO. However, the report of the Conference shows that it took the problem into consideration (but in a very cautious manner). The Conference officially approved a programme of work for 1968 and 1969 which included a budgetary allocation of $91,600 for the staffing of a unit on 'Better Family Living'. In making this allocation, the Conference recognized the need to help families achieve, through appropriate policies and programmes, conditions that would increase well-being and would contribute to national development. It also recognized that established extension programmes, specialized programmes for women and youth, and applied nutrition programmes provided excellent channels through which to reach the family. It agreed that education and training activities which supported national programmes to improve the levels of family living through better utilization of resources and improved nutrition were within the competence of FAO. The Conference stressed the need to collaborate with the UN and its Specialized Agencies and with non-governmental bodies whose governing bodies had adopted policies and programmes in the field of population stabilization.

It also recommended that, on governmental request, FAO be prepared to provide assistance in the organization of educational programmes aimed at helping people in their search for a balanced family life.

In a declaration connected with the International Year for Human Rights (1968) the Conference noted, *inter alia*, the need for developing countries to mobilize their internal resources to establish a stable balance between food production and population growth.

United Nations Educational Scientific and Cultural Organization (UNESCO)

In 1946 the UNESCO General Conference had agreed to a study of problems caused by population increase in relation to tensions leading to war and, as indicated earlier, UNESCO's first Director-General, Julian

Huxley, in his 1948 annual report emphasized that over-population could drastically affect the type of civilization possible and its rate of advance. He was particularly concerned by the undernourishment of much of the world's population and with the problems of erosion and possible exhaustion of mineral resources. However, the member states expressed little interest in his preoccupations and it was only in 1966 that there was a further debate on population in the UNESCO General Conference. At that Conference, Sweden proposed that an advisory committee be set up to advise the Director-General about UNESCO's responsibilities in the population field.

The committee reported in July 1967 making two general recommendations: (i) That UNESCO undertake those activities in the population field that were truly distinctive to its own special character. The committee recognized that several activities were currently being undertaken by other members of the United Nations family, e.g. the Population Division – WHO, UNICEF, FAO, ILO, regional commissions like ECAFE and others – as well as by a number of voluntary, non-profit organizations with international programmes. It stressed that there was a particular role for UNESCO within this range of activities, that UNESCO was well qualified to play an important collaborative part in this field in view of its educational character etc; (ii) that UNESCO should continue and where possible expand its efforts to promote literacy, education, science and communication throughout the developing world. These were absolute goods in advancing the human condition and hence needed no further justification. But the committee believed they were additionally valuable in that they would have an indirect effect in lowering fertility, and hence whatever could be done in this regard would contribute not only directly to human welfare but also indirectly in lessening the impact of population growth.

The Executive Board of UNESCO endorsed the broad perspectives of the Committee's recommendations, and these were in turn confirmed by the General Conference in 1968[3].

International Labour Organization (ILO)

Albert Thomas, ILO's Director, had supported the holding of the 1927 World Population Conference and, as an organization, ILO had a deep and long-standing interest in all aspects of migration which, together with births and deaths, made up the three basic demographic variables. The ILO moved towards a more central position, as far as the subject matter of this book is concerned, when in June 1967 the International Labour

Conference unanimously adopted a resolution asking the Organization to study the consequences of rapid population growth on the training, employment and welfare of workers, particularly in developing countries, and to consider how the ILO might, in co-operation with the United Nations and other organizations, undertake further action.

This was the first time the ILO's tripartite constituency – the representatives of governments, employers and workers – had jointly raised this issue at the world level. Mr D. Morse, the Director-General, had explained this new departure for ILO quite simply:

> Vast population increases are diverting resources to consumption that might otherwise be used for investment to promote more rapid economic and social development, higher per capita income and more employment opportunities. In this way, population increases are slowing down considerably, if not nullifying completely, the efforts of the ILO (and of other organizations engaged in promoting economic and social development) to create conditions in which men and women everywhere can live in prosperity and dignity. Measures to combat and overcome these population problems are an essential precondition for the success of ILO's world-wide mission.

Mr Morse had in several forums outlined the contribution ILO might make to this effort of moderating population growth. While ILO had no direct responsibility for family planning, he had suggested that there were several ways in which it could back up the activities of other organisations more directly involved. Its contact with trade unions and employers' organizations, for example, and its activities for workers' education and co-operative development in the developing countries, should enable it to acquaint workers throughout the world with the immense problems created by population pressure, as well as the prospects of improving the living standards and the quality of life of individual families through family planning.

ILO might provide audio–visual means of information or handbooks for use within trade unions and by employers to underline the need to curb the population growth and to provide family planning information. At the same time, ILO could help to ensure that family planning would not be prohibitive in cost to the worker by encouraging governments to provide adequate benefits for this purpose under their social security schemes. Or again, ILO could promote professional family planning advice, supplies and supervision through institutions which it was helping to create throughout the world such as medical services at places of employment, or through similar services operated by social security institutions, trade unions or co-operatives.

United Nations (International) Children's (Emergency) Fund
(UNICEF)

Progress on population questions had also been registered by the United Nations Children's Fund. UNICEF provided equipment, supplies and training facilities for programmes to meet the needs of children, taking the professional advice of the UN or the appropriate Specialized Agencies in developing its projects. On several occasions in the past, individual members of its Executive Board had urged that an important contribution which UNICEF could make would be to help in ensuring that families were so spaced as to give all children a better chance of survival and well-being. It was only in 1965, however, on the proposal of the USA, that the Executive Director (Mr H. Labouisse – a US national) was asked by the Board to prepare proposals and authorized to submit to the Board one or two requests from governments for assistance in family planning.

In May 1966 the Executive Director presented to the Board a document which argued the case on economic, social and medical grounds for UNICEF assistance in family planning, the most cogent argument being that in many countries the rate of population growth was seriously outstripping the ability of the governments to provide services for children, and that too often the early arrival of a younger brother or sister had a disastrous effect on the state of health and nutrition of an older child and its mother. He also presented requests for assistance from India and Pakistan.

The debate in the UNICEF Executive Board in June 1966 was almost as impassioned as that in the World Health Assembly in 1952. The opposition was led by Switzerland who argued that UNICEF must not get ahead of WHO. Belgium suggested that the proposals might endanger the organization's very existence and that if they were carried by a majority a number of members would 'doubtless consider themselves released from their obligations'. This line of argument was stated even more bluntly by the chairman of the Irish National Committee for UNICEF who said he would be reluctant to 'hand the private contributions raised in his country over to UNICEF if they were to be used to prevent children from being born'. The USSR considered that UNICEF participation would be 'contrary to the spirit and letter to its mandate'. The Latin American countries were all opposed, Brazil arguing that other projects ought to have a higher priority than family planning. Ethiopia and Senegal were also opposed.

The most eloquent support came from India and Pakistan: the latter declared, in response to arguments that family planning should be postponed because of inadequate medical knowledge, that 'Pakistan could not afford to wait'. Among the principal contributors, the USA, UK and Sweden were firmly behind the proposals, as was France although with reservations. There were general Asian support. Nigeria was in favour and Morocco indecisive.

Eventually it was agreed that the whole matter should be referred to the UNICEF/WHO joint committee on health policy. This committee met in February 1967 and recommended that UNICEF assistance should be given to requesting governments for the development of maternal and child health services, including family planning: thus the provision of clinical equipment, transport and the organization of training would be authorized; but the provision of contraceptive supplies or manufacturing equipment would be precluded. These recommendations were approved by the WHO and UNICEF Executive Boards in June 1967. UNICEF's mandate, as it stood after those decisions, permitted it to assist family planning as part of a maternal and child health service, if so requested by a government and subject in each case to the technical approval of WHO.

The World Bank

Last, but certainly not least, the *World Bank* (like the International Monetary Fund a rather special Specialized Agency of the United Nations) was – at the end of 1968 – ready, or so it seemed, to play a much larger part in the population field.

On September 30, 1968 Mr Robert McNamara who had succeeded Mr George Woods as President of the World Bank in April of that year, in addressing the Board of Governors at its annual meeting, announced that he had proposed 'a programme of greatly increased activity by the World Bank Group', to inject new momentum into the global economic development effort. He stated that as a result of a survey of the potential for future Bank operations, 'we have concluded that ... the Bank Group should during the next five years lend twice as much as during the past five years'. He referred to the assistance given during the 1960s – the United Nations Development Decade – which was felt to be too little, and referred also to the shadow cast over the scene by 'the mushrooming cloud of the population explosion'. 'If we take this into account', he said, 'and look at the progress for human beings rather than nations, the growth figures appear even less acceptable'.

The President outlined the major new directions for the Bank's lending, with dramatic changes foreseen not only in geographic shifts to Latin America and Africa, as well as the continuation of substantial aid to Asia, but also among sectors of investment. Great increases would occur in the sectors of education and agriculture, and there is 'yet another area where the Bank needs to take new initiatives – the control of population growth'.

He stated further: 'This is a thorny subject which it would be very much more convenient to leave alone. But I cannot, because the World Bank is concerned above all with economic development, and the rapid growth of population is one of the greatest barriers to the economic growth and social well-being of our member states.' He continued as follows:

As a development planner, I wish to deal only with the hard facts of population impact on economic growth. Recent studies show the crippling effect of a high rate of population increase on economic growth in any developing country. For example, take two typical developing countries with similar standards of living, each with a birth rate of 40 per 1000 (this is the actual rate in India and Mexico) and estimate what would happen if the birth rate in one of those countries, in a period of 25 years, were to be halved to 20 per 1000, a rate still well above that in most developed countries. The country which lowered its population growth would raise its standard of living 40% above the other country in a single generation.

He declared that:

In terms of the gap between rich countries and poor, these studies show that more than anything else it is the population explosion which, by holding back the advancement of the poor, is blowing apart the rich and the poor and widening the already dangerous gap between them.

He emphasized that the studies show 'this drag of excessive population growth' as being quite independent of the density of population, and stated:

It is a false claim that some countries need more population to fill their land or accelerate their economic growth. There are no vacant lands equipped with roads, schools, houses, and the tools of agricultural or industrial employment. Therefore, the people who are to fill those lands, before they can live at even the current low standard of living, must first eat up a portion of the present scarce supply of capital – it is this burden which defeats a nation's efforts to raise its standard of living by increasing its population.

The President proposed three courses of action by the World Bank 'to lift this burden from the backs of many of our members':

First: to let the developing nations know the extent to which rapid population growth slows down their potential development, and that, in consequence, the optimum employment of the world's scarce development funds requires attention to this problem.

Second: to seek opportunities to finance facilities required by our member countries to carry out family planning programmes.

Third: to join others in programmes of research to determine the most effective methods of family planning and of national administration of population control programmes.

'With these three proposals for immediate action', he stated, 'I hope we may contribute to the success of the UN system which is already working in this field, and to the well-being of the developing nations'.

The system's shortcomings

This then was the situation among the principal UN agencies – WHO, FAO, UNESCO, ILO and the World Bank – as the author found it during the enquiries he conducted in the course of 1968. Superficially, the progress seemed to be encouraging. The mandates were adequate, sometimes more than adequate. There was no lack of good intentions, if the spoken or printed word was anything to go by. There had already been some significant programme activities.

But there were also some glaring shortcomings. Interagency rivalry was as acute in the population field as in any other. WHO, for example, whose mandate was clearly limited to family planning, was deeply suspicious that 'population activities' undertaken by other elements of the UN System, for example technical assistance provided through the United Nations itself, might trespass on what it regarded as its own exclusive territory. This did not imply that WHO was eager to boost its own efforts; it simply meant it did not wish to see others undertake activities which it saw as being its own responsibility even though it was not doing much in practical terms about it.

The role of the United Nations

Another problem was the confusion that existed with the United Nations itself. As a functional Commission reporting to the Economic and Social Council, the Population Commission had been active since 1946. The Commission's mandate covered studies and advice on the size and structure of population and on policies designed to influence it; the interplay of demographic factors and economic and social factors; and other demographic questions on which the organs of the United Nations and the specialized agencies might seek advice. In addition to demographic statistics and demographic research, other activities had been added gradually, in particular, training, information services and technical cooperation centred around advisory services.

The Population Division was the arm, within the Secretariat, of the Population Commission. The Population Commission's work programme for the next five years provided for expanded research in fertility, mortality and morbidity, internal migration and urbanization, demographic aspects of social development and demographic aspects of economic development, which were the five priority areas established by the Economic and Social Council. The aspect of the Population Division's work that was directly concerned with population growth was its programme in fertility and family planning.

In 1965 the UN sent a team to review India's family planning programme and make suggestions for its intensification[4] and early in 1968, at the request of the Government of Pakistan, a joint United Nations/World Health Organization's Advisory Mission visited that country from January to March 1968, to review and evaluate the family-planning programme launched by the Government in 1965, its progress and effectiveness, and to advise the government on modifications required in the effort to accomplish its target of reducing the birth-rate from about 50 per 1000 population to about 40 per 1000 by 1970.

A Programming Mission on Population visited a number of countries in Africa from March to May 1968 to make an assessment, at regional and country levels, of (a) the present status and the requirements for the development of training, research and operational activities in the population field, and (b) the steps needed to establish a regional infrastructure for the expansion of work in this field.

Finally, the United Nations participated in a consultative six-weeks' mission to Colombia on maternal and child health and family planning, requested by the government, which began in mid-March 1968. It was a joint project with the Pan-American Health Organization, led by the PAHO representative, to study the possibility of assisting the government in initiating a demonstration project in maternal and child health and family planning which would encompass statistical evaluation, and the demographic, social, family welfare, clinical and medical and public health aspects of a family planning programme in its broad sociological, cultural and educational contexts. The mission was also requested to assist in defining the organizational and substantive components needed for the project.

These more recent activities symbolized a genuine effort by the Population Division to broaden the base of its activities in accordance with its mandate, to include – besides its most important demographic work – a kind of 'action capability' in the sense of giving governments advice about population policies, evaluating family-planning programmes and even preparing population projects. The establishment of the Trust Fund[5] had probably helped in achieving this change of emphasis. The Programming Mission to Africa, for example, was financed from it. But there was real uncertainty in the United Nations about how far the expansion of population activities beyond the traditional realm of demographic studies and research should be allowed to go.

So far, the expenditures by the United Nations in the field of population had been relatively small and concentrated on headquarters activities. Gross expenditures (i.e. including staff assessment) increased from $1.2 million in 1955 to $1.6 million for 1966 and $1.7 million for 1967. This was around 5 per cent of the UN's expenditures in the Economic and Social field. In December 1966 Philippe de Seynes, the Under-Secretary-General for Economic and Social Affairs stated that family-planning activities were only 6 per cent of all assistance in the population field in 1965 and 6.8 per cent in 1966.

The number of established posts in the Population Division had risen from 19 in 1966 to 22 in 1968.

The Regional Commissions

The same dilemma, *mutatis mutandis*, was felt by the Regional Commissions. The situation as far as these were concerned may be summarized as follows:

In April 1967, the *Economic Commission for Asia and the Far East* – ECAFE – welcoming the General Assembly Resolution of December 1966 which recommended that ECAFE assist, when requested, in further developing national and regional facilities for training, research, information, advisory services in the field of population – requested its Executive Secretary:

> (a) to take appropriate steps to expand the regional population programme, with a view to providing for the analysis and consideration in depth of the region's population problems and for the application of the most effective means of solving them through regional and national cooperative efforts;
> (b) to assign primary emphasis to existing priority areas and to emerging needs of governments for assistance in the field of population through an expanded programme of training, research, information and advisory services, making full and economical use of regional and national resources.

Following that request, the ECAFE Secretariat had prepared 'Proposals for an Asian Population Program', covering the main areas in which regional cooperation in the field of population needed to be intensified.

The *Economic Commission for Latin America* – ECLA – collaborated in the establishment of the Latin American Centre for Population Studies (CELADE) in Santiago, Chile but did not directly control its activities. ECLA tended to refer population questions to CELADE but its Secretariat prepared the very prestigious annual economic survey of Latin America, which went deeply into questions of economic planning and development. This survey had, up to the current time, dealt cautiously with the effects of the area's fast population growth rate on Latin American development. The last annual report of ECLA showed that the Commission was becoming more explicitly aware of the implications of fast population growth. In particular, it pointed out its implications for employment and investment.

CELADE itself was founded in August 1957 as a result of a resolution adopted in 1955 by the ECOSOC, requesting the Secretary-General to explore possibilities of establishing in the underdeveloped regions of the world centres for the study of population problems and the training of personnel in techniques of demographic analysis.

CELADE's work programme was almost exclusively oriented towards demographic research and teaching. Within those limits, however, it had – like ECLA itself – valuable influence on Latin American governmental thinking.

The *Economic Commission for Africa* – ECA – had taken a more backward position on the whole population question than either ECAFE or ECLA. The Programming Mission on Population which visited 12 African countries and after due consultation prepared suggestions and recommendations for the expansion of population programmes, appeared to have done its work without the active co-operation of ECA.

This reserve stemmed perhaps from the widespread belief that much of Africa did not have a population problem. Nevertheless ECA did have two population officers on its staff and there was a North African demographic and training centre under the ECA, located in Cairo.

The *Economic Commission for Europe* – ECE – worked on European demographic issues.

Summary

The basic issue, as it appeared to the author in 1968, could be summarized as follows. FAO, UNESCO, and ILO had important parts to play in this business of bringing down birth-rates particularly through programmes which could have an indirect effect on fertility. WHO, on the other hand, had the potential to fulfil a role of outstanding importance where programmes leading directly to fertility reduction were concerned. However, the World Health Organization seemed to be unable or unwilling to move beyond traditional health-oriented services including family planning (and, as we have seen, it had been quite a struggle to arrive even at this point).

On the other hand, since the United Nations units both at headquarters and in the regions had real hesitations about moving beyond demography towards support of population activities directly linked to influencing demographic variables, in particular fertility, there would inevitably remain in the middle a huge unfilled area of unmet need. The people who suffered would not of course be the bureaucrats at the headquarters of the international agencies. It would be the millions, even the billions, of poor people in the Third World who were stretching out their hands for assistance and finding none on offer.

Could the gap be met by the expanded programme of lending for population by the World Bank of which Mr McNamara had spoken? Superficially, the idea was attractive. The Bank's reputation for delivering effective development assistance was second to none. There was no reason to suppose that population projects would be ultimately any less amenable to the techniques of project appraisal that the Bank had perfected than projects for, say, electricity or roads. Interest in population policy and projects had been expressed by the Bank's staff as well as its President. For example, a paper produced early in 1968 within the Projects Department under the joint authorship of Bernard Chadenet and Bernard Bell entitled 'New Directions in Bank–IDA Lending' called for the expansions of the Bank's activities in the population field some months before Mr McNamara's first address to the Board of Governors. (As a Young Professional then working in the Bank the author was privileged to contribute some insights to the paper.)

But in spite of these developments, there were real questions about how far and how fast the Bank could expand in this unfamiliar territory. Apart from the IDA countries (i.e. a group of low income countries who qualified for credits made on concessionary terms through the Bank's sister body, the International Development Association), Bank support for population projects would have to take place on normal Bank terms, i.e. through interest-bearing repayable loans. It was by no means clear (whatever the theoretic calculations about economic rates of return might suggest) that countries would be ready to incur (and repay) loans made in hard currencies, even though the Bank's repayment periods were long (often 20 years or more) and the rates of interest relatively favourable.

In short the Bank would have an important role both at the project level and at the level of policy formulation (this latter could be of particular importance given the intellectual prestige and political weight of the Bank's Country Economic Reports). But it was fanciful to believe that the Bank could by itself fill the gap.

If the United Nations system was to accomplish the high mission which the Secretary-General had outlined for it at the 43rd session of ECOSOC, it was clear that some new impetus was necessary. Such an impetus would have to involve not only the injection of substantial funds but also the creation of some new co-ordinating and catalytic force which could ensure that such funds were spent to best effect. Indeed it was likely that the issues of funding and management would prove inseparable. There have over the years been numerous attempts within the United Nations System to create new institutions or new funds for one purpose or another. Many of these attempts have foundered, often sooner rather than later. Indeed, the foreshore of this particular landscape is littered with the wreckage of good, and sometimes not so good, intentions – the principal cause of death or decay being, of course, the unwillingness of major donors to fund bodies whose purposes, structure or management did not appeal to them.

Could a United Nations population agency avoid a similar fate? If so, what shape should it take? Under what rules should it operate? At the end of 1968, the answer to these questions was by no means clear. Four reports, appearing at the end of the decade of the 1960s, provided the critical stimulus and led in a more or less direct fashion to the birth of UNFPA.

4

Four reports

The Symonds report

In May 1968 Professor Richard Symonds from the Institute of Development Studies at the University of Sussex was appointed as a Senior Consultant to the Population Division of the United Nations on a four months assignment to advise on the acceleration of population programmes in implementation of General Assembly resolution 2211 (XXII)[1]. Symonds, who had previously served as Resident Representative of UNTAB/UNDP in Ceylon and Yugoslavia, and as Regional Representative in Europe, East Africa and South East Africa, was asked to give particular attention to the relationship of UN programmes to those of UN agencies, bilateral programmes and programmes of foundations. His recommendations were to include the programming and administrative machinery required in the United Nations and assistance in establishing this machinery.

The Symonds report, as Symonds and Carder comment in their book[2], recommended that the Trust Fund whose establishment has been described in Chapter 2, be expanded to support programmes of the Specialised Agencies and UNICEF, as well as of the UN itself, at an annual level of $5 million in the first year, $10 million in the second and $20 million in the third[3]. The Fund should be used to finance not only technical assistance but research, transport and equipment; it should also be more flexible than other UN technical assistance programmes in financing local costs and using local institutions to carry out research. Whilst not rejecting the ultimate establishment of a UN population agency, the report proposed as an immediate measure the appointment of a UN Commissioner for Population Programmes, with a staff drawn from all the UN agencies concerned, who would co-ordinate the programme and whose status would enable him to attend the ACC meetings of the Executive Heads of

48

Agencies which took place within the framework of the Administrative Committee on Co-ordination (ACC).

The Symonds report was of immense importance because it addressed itself unflinchingly to institutional questions at a time when, as we have seen, there was a good deal of mutual suspicion among the agencies concerned and susceptibilities were easily aroused. Symonds worded his description of the Population Commissioner with the idea that Sir David Owen, the Co-Administrator of UNDP, could have taken on the job while retaining his existing status. Thus he recognized, implicitly if not explicitly, that a UNDP-style arrangement was likely to play an important part in any resolution of the United Nations institutional problems in the field of population.

The UNA–USA report

Another report, which appeared at the same time as the Symonds study, also endorsed the idea of a UN Commissioner for Population, while suggesting in very clear terms that both the Commissioner and the management of the Trust Fund should be placed firmly within the ambit of the United Nations Development Programme. The membership of the National Policy Panel on World Population established by the United Nations Association of the United States of America was impressive. Its Chairman was John D. Rockefeller 3rd, Chairman of the Board of the Rockefeller Foundation and also Chairman of the Population Council. Its Vice-Chairman was George D. Woods, the former President of the World Bank. Members included David Bell, Vice-President of the Ford Foundation and a former director of the Budget and of USAID; Ansley Coale, Director of the Office of Population Research at Princeton University; Frank Notestein, President Emeritus of the Population Council and a former head of the United Nations Population Division; Oscar Harkavy, the programme officer in charge of population at the Ford Foundation; Gilbert White, Professor of Geography at the University of Chicago and Richard Gardner, whose name has already appeared in these pages, a former Deputy Assistant Secretary of State for International Organization Affairs. The author, a former official of the World Bank, served as the Project Director of the UNA Panel.

The full title of the panel's report was World Population: A challenge to the United Nations and its system of Agencies.

After reviewing the mandates and performance of the United Nations and its specialized agencies, the panel concluded that:

49

No institution or group of institutions has more reason to be involved with population than the United Nations and its system of agencies. It is a truly global problem; the United Nations is mankind's global agency.

High fertility affects individual rights. This is a matter of concern to the United Nations whose members undertook 'to reaffirm faith in fundamental rights, in the dignity and worth of the human person'.

High rates of population growth jeopardize national goals. This, too, is a matter of concern to the United Nations whose members determined to 'promote social progress and better standards of life' for all people, established international machinery to that end and, over the years, have devoted an increasing volume of resources to the cause of economic development through the medium of multilateral agencies.

Population growth threatens international stability. The United Nations, above all, is concerned with peace. It is also charged with finding solutions to 'international economic, social, health and related problems'. Its call for an international conference in 1972 on the Human Environment reflects its increasing sensitivity to the deteriorating quality of man's habitat.

Because the United Nations is the world's highest authority, it can appropriately take the lead in dealing with one of the world's most serious problems. And, because the majority of its members are from the developing world, it can do so without arousing the fear that family planning is a device of the rich nations to avoid their obligations to the poor.

There was another key reason for UN system involvement in population activities. Its structure permitted it to see population planning as part and parcel of the whole process of economic development. Assistance in the field of population was not a 'bargain basement substitute for development aid'; population planning and 'orthodox' economic and social programmes were 'two sides of the same coin'. Without a reduction in the rate of population growth, economic development might be impossible; at the same time, without economic development a reduction in the rate of population growth would not solve the problem of poverty.

Understandably, given the inadequacy of current efforts, the emphasis of the report was on increasing the amount of UN system assistance to the population programmes of member governments. But an increase in all forms of economic assistance remained a paramount goal. The United Nations system, taken as a whole, was in a position to make increased emphasis on population part of a total programme of increased aid.

Successful family planning programmes require the involvement of many different groups of people – economists and planners, demographers, health personnel, social workers, etc. This can be best achieved by the formulation of a national population policy as an integral part of the development plan, and by the involvement of the whole governmental apparatus in support of a national family planning programme. The relationships established between the various UN agencies and the different organs of government (e.g. Planning Boards,

Ministries of Health, Education, etc) offer unique possibilities for achieving this 'total involvement' of government. The FAO expert on agricultural production or the World Bank advisor on fiscal policies are as much concerned as the WHO advisor on child health. Improvements in the social and economic environment will make the successful conduct of family planning programmes easier. More specifically, certain conventional development programmes, e.g. in health, education and agriculture, may be formulated in such a way as to achieve maximum demographic impact, or to show the need to supplement them with population efforts if their goals are to be achieved. Here, too, the concern of the UN system with all aspects of development planning may lead to a wider concept of population planning.

The Panel believed that the precondition for successful UN system action was radical upgrading in the priority accorded to population activities by the agencies involved and that this could be achieved through a series of feasible and realistic programmes.

The panel had five recommendations to make in this connection:

1. That a Commissioner for Population be appointed within the United Nations Development Programme, and a high-calibre staff recruited; that the Commissioner – acting with the agreement of the Administrator of UNDP – have the central role in planning and co-ordinating UN system assistance to the population programmes of member governments; and that, in this work, he report to the Governing Council of the UNDP.

2. That the Commissioner for Population be responsible for handling the Population Trust Fund recently established by the Secretary-General; that all decisions concerning budgets and work programmes financed from the Population Trust Fund be made by the Commissioner with the approval of a Special Population Committee of the UNDP Governing Council, the membership of which Committee would be drawn from those countries which have made contributions to the Population Trust Fund and from those countries which wish to receive assistance from it; and that the Commissioner – with similar approval of the Special Population Committee – have authority to allocate funds to UN agencies, other bodies outside the UN system or directly to governments.

3. That the Commissioner for Population have responsibility for the implementation and expediting of projects financed from the Population Trust Fund as well as population projects financed from the regular resources of the UNDP.

4. That provided this system of strong central co-ordination and direction is working successfully, the Population Trust Fund be expanded from its present level of $1.5 million to $100 million a year by

the end of a three-year period, thus permitting a meaningful multilateral commitment in the population field and providing a real incentive to the governments assisted to develop effective and imaginative projects.

5. That the Commissioner for Population serve as principal representative of the UN in those intergovernmental forums where population policies and programmes are or should be under discussion, such as meetings of the UN and its Specialised Agencies, the World Bank's Consortia and Consultative Groups, the Inter-American Committee of the Alliance for Progress (CIAP), the Development Assistance Committee (DAC) of OECD, the Regional Development Banks and the Regional Economic Commissions.

The report of the UNA–USA Panel was well received. The *New York Times* ran a front-page story. President Nixon himself (having taken office as a Republican President on January 1, 1969) endorsed its conclusions in a message on population which he sent to Congress on July 18, 1969.

> It is our belief that the United Nations, its specialised agencies, and other international bodies should take the leadership in responding to world population growth. The United States will co-operate fully with their programmes. I would note in this connection that I am most impressed by the scope and thrust of the recent report of the panel of the United Nations Association, chaired by John D. Rockefeller 3rd. The report stresses the need for expanded action and greater co-ordination, concerns which should be high on the agenda of the United Nations.

In his message to Congress, President Nixon coupled his remarks about the need for population control in the Third World with concern for the effects of continued population growth within the United States itself. He proposed the creation by Congress of a Commission on Population Growth and the American Future[4]. This was an astute move. However fanciful it might seem to an impartial observer, it was still being argued in certain quarters that the readiness of the industrialised world to promote family planning in the Third World was simply a disguised form of genocide. The fact that President Nixon chose so deliberately to link population policy for 'them' with population policy for 'us' was certainly helpful. His term of office cannot be said to have ended in a blaze of glory, but in one respect at least it began well.

The Pearson Commission

On October 27, 1967, in a context of increasing concern about the future of international co-operation for economic development, the then President of the World Bank, Mr George Woods, suggested a 'grand assize' in which an international group of 'stature and experience' would meet together, study the consequences of 20 years of development assistance, assess the results, clarify the errors and propose the policies which would work better in the future.

On August 19, 1968, the Right Honourable Lester B. Pearson, former Prime Minister of Canada, accepted an invitation from the World Bank's President, Robert S. McNamara (who had succeeded Mr Woods on April 1, 1968) to form a Commission to undertake such a study. Mr Pearson invited several colleagues from different countries in their individual capacities. They were: Sir Edward Boyle (United Kingdom), Roberto de Olivera Campos (Brazil), C. Douglas Dillon (United States), Dr Wilfried Guth (Federal Republic of Germany), Professor W. Arthur Lewis (Jamaica), Dr Robert E. Marjolin (France) and M. Saburo Okita (Japan).

The Commission concluded its work in time for the Annual Meeting of the Board of Governors of the World Bank in October 1969. Like its successor, the Brandt Commission which reported 12 years later[5], the Pearson report had a considerable impact both on public opinion at large and among policy-makers concerned with aid, trade and development. Its recommendations for action were addressed to the developing countries, to the industrialized countries, and to international organizations. The Commission looked first at the overall framework of the international economy and then proceeded to the measures to be taken in the field of foreign aid.

As far as population was concerned, the Pearson report commented starkly:

No other phenomenon casts a darker shadow over the prospects for international development than the staggering growth of population. It is evident that it is a major cause of the large discrepancy between the rates of economic improvement in rich and poor countries.

After a review of the nature of the problem, Pearson concluded.

Whether or not a deliberate policy on population should be adopted is a decision which each individual country itself must face. We are well aware of the controversial nature of the matter which, until very recently, placed family planning behind a wall of silence in the industrialized countries themselves. But it is clear that there can be no serious social and economic planning unless the ominous implications of uncontrolled population growth are understood and acted upon.

The Report recommended that 'developing countries identify their population problem, if they have not already done so, recognize the relevance of population growth to their social and economic planning, and adopt appropriate programmes'.

Turning to the role of the aid-givers, Pearson recommended that 'bilateral and international agencies press in aid negotiations for adequate analysis of population problems and of the bearing of these problems on development programmes'.

However, Pearson suggested that it would be unwise for aid-givers to insist on the adoption of population policies by other countries as a condition for aid, believing that only a genuine conviction on the part of governments in developing countries could produce the strong political support and the determined leadership which experience had shown that family-planning programmes and population policy required. Pearson believed, moreover, that the governments of the aid-giving countries should be in a position to practise what they preached and should bring their legislation and social policy into line with the practice of family planning among their own populations.

Looking at the performance of the international bodies in the population fields, Pearson commented:

> the passivity and hesitancy of international bodies has to a large extent reflected the ambivalence and confusion of the industrialized member countries. It seems particularly wrong for countries which themselves have so far been spared the acute need for population policy to refuse international organizations the right or the means to help countries which request assistance in this field.

Turning to the financial requirements, the Pearson report had this to say:

> The financial requirements of family-planning programmes are not very large compared to other development expenditures. Budgets in developing countries, however, are often so strained and foreign exchange shortages so acute that programmes are held up by bottle-necks which can be broken by relatively modest amounts of aid. Such aid is now provided by some bilateral donors, notably the United States and Sweden, and on a modest scale by international organizations. For aid suppliers who hesitate to build up specialised machinery for this kind of assistance, the use of special trust funds administered by international organizations should commend itself. In 1967, a Trust Fund for Population Activities was established in the United Nations, with the purpose of supporting activities in the population field. We believe that this fund could expect far more generous support than it has so far received if prospective donors could be assured that good projects are, in fact, available, and that UN activities in the population field are satisfactorily co-ordinated.

Pearson followed both the Symonds and the UNA–USA reports in endorsing the creation of a United Nations Commissioner for Population. Without explicitly locating the Commissioner within the framework of UNDP (as the UNA–USA report had done), he nevertheless stated that the task of the United Nations Commissioner for Population 'should be to obtain and maintain an overall view of the needs of the developing countries in the population field, to have principal responsibility for the allocation of the Trust Fund, and to head up machinery to co-ordinate the population activities of UN agencies'. Pearson concluded: 'It is necessary to take far-reaching but practicable actions if the great opportunities for international assistance in this area are to be utilized.'

The Jackson Report

Anyone who seeks to chronicle the birth of the United Nations Fund for Population Activities must accord due credit to the favourable concatenation of events which took place in 1969. There was not only the Symonds, UNA–USA and Pearson reports. There was also, crucially, the work (begun in 1968 and continuing into 1969) of Sir Robert Jackson in his Study of the Capacity of the UN Development System.

The Jackson Report, like other enquiries such as the Pearson Commission and the Tinbergen Committee on the Second Development Decade, owed its origin in part at least to the sense that all was not well with the state of aid and development. Jackson in particular, commissioned by the UNDP to produce a study on the capacity of the United Nations system to meet the needs of developing countries, focussed on one simple question, the reform of the UN structure to enable it to play a fresh, more effective role in designing development programmes and channelling aid. As Lord Balogh wrote:

> The Jackson report provides a definitive textbook on the role of the UN organization .... Its proposals, which would effectively integrate development planning on the multilateral plane, are as much to the point as they are bound to arouse the rage of the great feudal chieftains of the UN bureaucracy. They have slid into a position of virtual independence on the backs of the specialized ministries composing their governing bodies and the votes of recipient ministries now in a vast majority in their membership. Their unregulated and unarticulated Parkinsonian triumph was completed through the divisive impact of the cold war which prevented collaboration between the superpowers and their partisans[6].

The Jackson Report referred to the United Nations and its bodies as 'a system without a brain'. It described a situation where the agencies, often with overlapping mandates, competed for resources; where the principle of negative competencies prevailed ('this is my job even if I don't do much about it') and where there was inadequate co-ordination and programming both among the agencies and at the country level. Symonds & Carder describe the Jackson Report as 'the most vivid, and indeed brilliant, critical account of the UN agencies' approach to development ever to appear as an official UN document'. More prosaically, the United Nations itself comments that Sir Robert Jackson 'proposed a number of steps to overhaul the system and suggested the restructuring of UNDP as a strong central co-ordinating organization, having a primary role in relation to the field apparatus of the Specialised Agencies carrying out UNDP-aided projects'. A 'country programming' approach was central to the changes proposed[7].

Under the new arrangements, which were scheduled to go into effect in January 1971, the existing system, in which projects were generally proposed and acted upon individually, was to be replaced by the country programming method. Under this method, the Government of each country, in co-operation with the UNDP Resident Director, would formulate a programme based on national development plans and objectives for which UNDP assistance might be available. The country programme was to be worked out within the framework of indicative planning figures constituting an advance estimate of the share of UNDP resources which each individual country might anticipate receiving over a period of years. Every effort was to be made to co-ordinate all sources of assistance within the United Nations system with a view to achieving integration of the assistance at the country level.

Under the new system, at least 82 per cent of the resources available each year was to be set aside for country programmes and a maximum of 18 per cent for regional, interregional or global undertakings.

The preparation and publication (in late 1969) of the Jackson report with its emphasis of the role of UNDP in providing the necessary 'brain' for the UN system, together with effective machinery for programming assistance at the country level, built around the strengthened role of the Resident Representative ('Res Rep'), was an important element in determining the institutional choices which were made in the course of 1969 about the future course of the United Nations' population activities.

5

UNFPA: the early days

Under new management

On 14 January 1969, the Secretary-General of the United Nations, U Thant, made an historic statement at the opening ceremony of the United Nations Population Programme Officers' orientation course (ten persons of varied background and experience had been selected and appointed to serve in the developing world to help prepare population policies and programmes[1]):

> In answer to the call from many quarters for United Nations leadership in this field, I have considered it appropriate to extend our Population programme, and have established in July 1967 a United Nations Trust Fund for Population Activities to supplement the resources provided under regular budget and the United Nations Development Programme. Not only have the activities so far undertaken under the aegis of the Fund proved encouraging, but I hope that the resources available to the Fund will be rapidly increased to an extent which will allow the United Nations family to broaden its work in this field, and to include types of assistance not so far provided. I should add that it is my intention that the managerial experience of the United Nations Development Programme (UNDP) be utilized to the full, and, further, that projects in the population field executed by the Specialised Agencies and the United Nations Children's Fund may draw on the Trust Fund's resources. In view of the significant step forward in our work taken today, I would like on this occasion to renew my invitation to governments, non-governmental organizations and individuals to contribute to the Fund.

In June 1969 in his statement 'A time to plan, a time to work' to the Eighth Session of the UNDP Governing Council, Paul G. Hoffman, the Administrator of UNDP said:

> At the request of the Secretary-General, I have entered into an agreement under which the UNDP will be entrusted with the administration of the United Nations Fund for Population Activities. Under this important new programme,

arrangements have been made to utilize the UNDP field establishment and the specific capacity and machinery of the UN and the Specialised Agencies concerned with various aspects of population programmes including that of family planning.

This was not, of course, by any means the first time that Paul Hoffman had referred to population and family planning within the context of UNDP's activities.

In May 1967 UNDP Resident Representatives had been instructed to assist governments to formulate requests in this field and Hoffman himself, in the same year, had remarked during the course of a panel discussion at UN headquarters:

A major responsibility of the United Nations Development Programme is to help the poorer countries raise per capita incomes; and per capita income, of course, depends on several factors. One is population growth; another is the gross national product. In the First Development Decade, there has been a fairly good increase in gross national products, averaging a little over 4% a year. This is not bad; but population growth has been 3%, which means only 1% actual increase in per capita income. I believe it is possible to achieve a 6% average growth rate in gross national product in the developing countries. If population growth were reduced to 2%, it would mean 4% increase in per capita income. Compare 4% growth per year with 1%. That spells the difference between a safe world and a very unsafe world[2].

But perhaps Paul Hoffman's greatest single contribution to the population activities of the United Nations system was his appointment in May 1969 in consultation with the Secretary-General, of Mr Rafael Salas as the first Executive Director of the United Nations Fund for Population Activities (UNFPA).

At the time when the author was still serving as the Project Director of the UNA–USA Panel[3], he recalls having an interview with Paul Hoffman in which the Administrator of UNDP, confronted with the transfer of administrative responsibility for the Population Trust Fund from the United Nations to UNDP, discussed several possible candidates for the job of Executive Director of UNFPA but indicated, without naming names, that he had one person particularly in mind as an ideal choice. Some weeks later he announced that he had invited Mr Salas to take on the assignment and that Mr Salas had accepted.

It was an inspired choice. Mr Salas already had an international reputation as the man who had helped the Philippines towards self-sufficiency in rice. Most recently he had held the position of Executive Secretary of the Philippines cabinet, the highest government post next to that of the President. He had served as his country's representative to ECAFE and to the UNDP Governing Council. He was a Catholic, yet he had been instrumental in developing the Philippines' own population policy and programme. Perhaps most important of all Salas' managerial ability – of both men and money – would be crucial in enabling the Fund to develop into an effective entity on the international stage – and this was something that Paul Hoffman (who as former President of the automobile manufacturing firm Studebaker, and former Administrator of the Marshall Fund, was no stranger to management issues) had been able to recognize at an early date[4].

Good management is something which, when it is there, people tend to take for granted. But the absence of good management can turn success into failure more surely, perhaps, than any other single factor. No amount of resolutions of the General Assembly or of ECOSOC could, in the last analysis, help any institution of the UN system deliver the goods in accordance with its mandate if the basic management structures were inadequate. In UNFPA's case because the institution had been created *ex novo*, and so many of the paths were uncharted, management was even more crucial. Salas brought to the international stage centred upon New York the techniques and philosophy of management which he had perfected under an Asian sky, the other side of the world. In his own book *People* he described his approach – one which relied to a large extent on delegation, on discussion and consensus, on an understanding of people, while retaining the responsibility for key decisions firmly in the Executive Director's hand[5]. (The title Executive Director was eventually chosen instead of Population Commissioner. Given the susceptibilities of the agencies at the time who were understandably suspicious that UNFPA might turn out to be a cuckoo in the nest, Executive Director was deemed to be a less aggressive, more modest description of the functions of the new head of UNFPA though his essential job did not differ markedly from that assigned to the 'UN Commissioner for Population' in the Symonds and UNA–USA reports. There was also the danger that confusion might arise between the Population Commissioner and the Population Commission, a body which continued to function under its existing mandate regardless of the institutional charges under way. To avoid such confusion the UNA–USA report had suggested that the title of the Population Commission be changed to Demographic Commission, and that the Population Division to Demographic Division.)

In his own account of his arrival in New York in July 1969 to take over the management of the United Nations Fund for Population Activities, Salas is engagingly frank about some of the difficulties he encountered. The transfer of the Fund from the United Nations to the UNDP had the support of major donors, recipients and the agencies. Hoffman was known to be a good fund-raiser; UNDP was accustomed to working with the agencies; population assistance could be seen as an integral pattern of development assistance. In practice, numerous hurdles still had to be cleared before the transfer was fully achieved. Though the resources of the Trust Fund, for example, stood in 1969 at less than $3 million, Salas' own control over those resources was severely circumscribed. Initially, despite responsibility for the administration of the Fund having been transferred to UNDP, responsibility for the technical appraisal of projects was to be retained by the Department of Economic and Social Affairs. (As Salas charitably comments 'During the period 1967 to 1969 (Milos) Macura (a Yugoslav demographer who directed the United Nations Population Division in the Department of Economic and Social Affairs) laid the groundwork within the United Nations Secretariat for an expanded population programme. Macura, Leon Tabah (the French demographer who now heads the Division) and the other able men and women who have worked there deserve recognition for the very substantial and fundamental contribution they have made.'[6])

It was not in fact until January 1970 that arrangements were finally completed for the transfer of the administration of UNFPA to the UNDP, following an agreement between U Thant and Paul Hoffman.

Staff

As far as staff was concerned, Salas who had been responsible for a rather massive programme during his previous jobs in the Philippines, found that he had more or less to start from scratch. His first colleague was an American called John Keppel who had been recruited to take charge of a small unit set up within UNDP's Bureau of Operations and Programming to help with Fund affairs. Keppel had served with the US foreign service; had a degree in the history of fine arts and a fellowship in international relations, both from Harvard. He had also studied population at Johns Hopkins University.

Keppel joined Salas immediately and suggested that the staff potentialities of the Population programme and projects office (PPPO) which the United Nations Population Division had founded when it expected to continue to administer the trust fund be explored. They were successful in persuading Halvor Gille, Associate Director of the Population Division and Chief of the PPO Programme to join the Fund. Gille, an economist from the university of Copenhagen, had worked for some years with the Swedish and Danish governments and had also undertaken a research programme at the London School of Economics. Since 1950 he had been associated with the United Nations Social Affairs and Population Divisions and, apart from a short spell with the Danish Social Research Institute in Copenhagen, had held a number of key posts in these Divisions in New York, Bangkok and Geneva. As Salas comments 'Getting Gille transferred to the fund to serve as Deputy Executive Director was politically important. It also gave the fund an experienced population specialist'[7].

Building an institution – particularly one which relies on voluntary contributions – needs not only qualified staff but also, where possible, staff at appropriate levels who have links with the donor community. Gille qualified admirably on both counts.

A third recruit, who joined the Fund in its early days, was Dr Nafis Sadik from Pakistan. Before coming to New York Dr Sadik had played a leading role in Pakistan's family planning programme where she was responsible for the overall administration of an organized effort which at that time was one of the largest in the world. Sadik's personal drive, efficiency and organisational ability complemented admirably Gille's skills in demography and his long experience of the sometimes arcane workings of the UN system.

Principles and procedures

Besides acquiring the nucleus of key personnel, around which the organization could grow, it was also important to have an authoritative statement of UNFPA principles and procedures. As Salas puts it: 'a separate unit with a high degree of operational freedom was essential if a programme was to be developed vigorously and quickly, if donors were to be convinced that the matter was being handled seriously, if the lessons already learned by others in the population field were to be mastered, and if adequate coordination with other organizations providing assistance to population programmes was to be maintained'[8].

UNDP Resident Representatives were to be the field representatives of the Fund and were to be assisted by the Population Programme officers. (The PPOs, who had originally been an outgrowth of the UN's Population Division programme in the pre-transfer days, would subsequently be absorbed into the body of UNFPA 'co-ordinators' working on population programmes at the country level). By insisting that the UNFPA representative should work under the UNDP Res Rep, Salas sought to establish the principle that population projects and programmes, multifaceted and interdisciplinary in nature (like the overall development programmes of countries), had to be handled and co-ordinated at the central level. Right from the start he was anxious to avoid the situation where one of the specialized agencies sought to establish its own privileged relationship with some client department of government, to the detriment of the balance and execution of the programme as a whole. It was, of course, fortunate from this point of view that the agencies had so few population activities funded out of their regular budgets – a consequence of the relative slowness with which they had acquired the necessary mandates and of the fact that the concept of central funding of UN development activities had been steadily gaining strength in recent years. Salas possessed, therefore, the leverage of the purse in his search for effective co-ordination at headquarter and country level – and within the United Nations system, as in most other organizations, no leverage is more effective.

It was also an astute move to insist in the Principles and Procedures draft paper that while 'the Administrator will normally choose the participating and executing agency for a project from among the United Nations or Agencies related to it', he might 'choose an agency outside the United Nations system if it seems advisable to do so'. This was, of course, something that others had advocated, e.g. the Symonds and UNA–USA reports. The notion that UN agencies had somehow a prescriptive right to spend the funds raised by UNDP was firmly entrenched – especially in the minds of the agencies – and by analogy many assumed that the same principle and practices would apply in the case of funds raised (and spent) by UNFPA. The transfer of the administration of the Fund to UNDP had only served to strengthen this presumption. It was therefore salutary to spell out clearly the principle of fair and free competition as far as the choice of executing agencies was concerned, if only to keep the UN agencies up to the mark with the hint (or threat) that projects might go elsewhere if they did not live up to their promises.

But there was another reason as well. There were some elements in population programmes which the UN agencies were not necessarily best equipped to supply, but where other bodies, for example, national private or non-governmental bodies often working with an international private or non-governmental bodies, had already developed expertise and facilities. It might be more appropriate to use these bodies, either because they responded more to the perceived need or because the government preferred not to take an official responsibility (e.g. for family planning activities), than, say, to use the Ministry of Health or the Ministry of Education (via WHO and UNESCO).

In specifying that non-UN bodies might be used, the principles and procedures paper also foreshadowed the time when increasing amounts of UNFPA resources would be devoted to direct support of country programmes and projects without the mediation of a UN executing agency in the traditional sense. This development, as we shall see, was something strongly recommended by the Michanek Review Committee[9].

Salas comments on this aspect of the Principles and Procedures paper[10]:

This was an important divergence from UNDP practice at that time, under which all projects were executed on UNDP's behalf by the various United Nations offices and the Specialized Agencies. Had we accepted the principle that only United Nations organizations could execute projects, it would have meant that the Agencies and not the recipient countries would have had the stronger voice in determining the nature of requests to the Fund:

While the Draft stated that UNFPA could go beyond the United Nations system in choosing an organization to provide technical assistance, it also made it clear that the Fund did not regard itself as an executing agency in the usual sense of the term. That is, it did not propose to build up its own staff to the point where it would be in direct competition with the Agencies in providing technical assistance within the terms of their respective mandates. It would have been a rash act to do so. In one stroke the Fund would have lost the experience, competence, and support of the organizations in the United Nations system and perhaps, in some cases, governmental approval as well.

The draft also provided for the possibility of the Fund's giving assistance with local and recurrent costs not ordinarily borne by United Nations organizations. Effective population programmes might, through their very nature, involve a higher proportion of local and recurrent costs, than, say, the construction of a large hydro-electric dam. Again, the benefits of population control are on the whole not of the short term variety though they are not all for the distant future (primary education needs, for example, may be influenced in the relatively near term by changes in demographic trends). As Salas put it:

Although political leaders and planners may be convinced of the need for moderation of population growth rates, when it comes to the agonizing business of allocating scarce resources among competitive demands, programmes which promise short-term benefits are likely to get preference over the usually long-term population undertakings. A judicious use of external funds in local cost financing might increase the priority given to population programmes of long duration[11].

Mandate of the Fund

One aspect of the draft Principles and Procedures paper was of special importance: the mandate of the Fund. A main reason for the transfer of the Fund from the United Nations to the UNDP had been the perceived need to broaden the scope of population activities from classic demographic studies (at which, as we have seen, the United Nations had proved itself to be highly competent) towards actions more specifically aimed at influencing population trends, whether directly or indirectly. It was essential therefore that UNFPA's mandate, while respecting any broad direction already laid down by the General Assembly and by ECOSOC, be broad and encompassing.

This is not to say that the support of demographic analysis would be unimportant for the Fund. As Salas notes[12] 'there were still many countries which had only the vaguest notion of their demographic situation and had little concept of the need for population data in their economic planning'. Financing demographic work was also a way of ensuring the participation in 'population activities' of governments who as yet might be reluctant to launch into family planning programmes. Within its first few years, the Fund helped 15 African countries to conduct censuses for the first time in their history and some of those countries would subsequently come to recognize the value of family planning for the health and well-being of their citizens.

But the Fund's terms of reference were expanded to cover

the entire range of population activities, including advice in the formulation of population policies, assistance in demographic studies, in applied and basic research, in education and training and support for family planning projects[13].

Salas[14] referring to the decision to give assistance to countries with family-planning programmes says:

in retrospect this seemed an obvious move, but, at that time, little assistance had been given to countries with family planning programmes. Moreover, no United Nations organization had a legislative mandate that permitted it to supply contraceptives. I reasoned, however, that a population fund which could not help requesting countries with family planning would be no population fund at all. Furthermore, a fund which did help countries to do what they wanted would be respected even by countries not themselves in favour of government-sponsored family planning programmes. Virtually every government I spoke to was, happily, of this opinion. Anxious to move in this direction, we decided, as our first major project, to respond to an urgent request from the Egyptian Government to finance a large supply of contraceptives for its family planning programme.

In his statement to the Fifteenth Session of the Population Commission on 10 November 1969, the Executive Director of UNFPA indicated that it was 'the underlying premise of the UNFPA programme that assistance from the Fund shall be given only to countries which request such assistance'. This was to remain a fundamental principle. Coercion, even if this were possible, was excluded as a mode of operation.

Salas indicated that the role of the United Nations and specialized agencies would differ considerably from country to country, depending on each country's level of development and population patterns. Broadly, it could be envisaged in stages as:

(a) to assist governments in determining the size of populations and to assess population trends;

(b) to assist governments in understanding the consequences of population trends in relation to economic and social development;

(c) to assist governments in formulating population policies, taking into account all factors which affect fertility;

(d) to assist governments which adopt population policies in carrying out and evaluating measures to control fertility, including assistance in organization of family planning programmes and in training for an evaluation of such programmes;

(e) to assist governments in preparing requests for assistance in the form of projects.

The approach to the programme would be interdisciplinary and would be made in close co-operation with the United Nations and the specialized agencies in accordance with the mandates which they had received from their governing bodies. Salas told the Commission in surprisingly unequivocal terms:

> In future years, it is expected that the main volume of requests to the Fund will be for international assistance in controlling the expansion of population. Nevertheless, no population policy, and indeed no serious economic and social plans, can be formulated unless they are based on sound demographic and statistical foundations. For this reason, the Fund is available to finance activities over the entire population field. This is a point which may not be sufficiently understood by governments.

Given the circumstances, this was a felicitous choice of words. The representatives of the 19 members of the Population Commission who attended its 15th session in Geneva from 3 to 14 November 1969 were on the whole demographers. By choosing his words carefully, Salas was able to reassure them that, whatever other developments might take place, UNFPA would always be ready and willing to finance basic demographic work, not just as the precursor to family-planning activities (though that could never be an irrelevant consideration) but because censuses and surveys and demographic analysis of one kind or another (the language of demography was full of colourful terms like pyramids and cohorts) were of value in their own right.

Funding

In November 1969 some $4.9 million had been contributed to the Fund of which $2.9 million had been obligated, with valid requests being processed to permit the allocation of the balance of $2 million. Donor countries included the United States, Sweden, Norway, Denmark, the United Kingdom, Finland, The Netherlands, Trinidad and Tobago and Pakistan. (Right from the start, Salas sought to enlarge his number of donors as much as possible. This included seeking contributions from the developing countries themselves, often of nominal amounts, on the grounds that this would help demonstrate the truly multinational (non-racist, politically neutral) character of the Fund while leading, he hoped, to a greater feeling of participation in the programme of UNFPA by 'recipients' who were also 'donors'.)

Two years later, at the Sixteenth Session of the Population Commission, Salas reported that 31 governments had pledged voluntary contributions of a total amount exceeding $24 million which assured that the Fund's estimated needs for 1971 (around $25 million) would be met. However, based on realistic estimates in terms of the absorptive capacities of the developing countries concerned and the agencies, he foresaw a need for contributions amounting to at least $40 million in 1972 to cover priority activities and urgent requests.

Status and accountability

Looking back it is probably true to say that no other United Nations programme has seen so rapid a growth in its resources and responsibilities. UNFPA was, by the end of 1971, involved in spending relatively large sums of money on a wide range of projects in all regions of the world – and there was every prospect that the trend would accelerate. The Fund had developed its own principles and procedures paper, as we have seen; it had competent and responsible staff, including an Executive-Director who commanded increasing respect among donor and recipient governments alike and whose untiring travels had done as much to put the Fund on the map, to 'get it known', as more formal decisions taken in international fora. But by the end of 1971 a real question had arisen as to the 'accountability' of the Fund – a question which seemed the more urgent and important as the resources which governments were willing to devote to UNFPA increased. Freedom of action, as Salas was the first to recognize, could be a two-edged sword. There comes a time when a prudent operator, however independent he may be in his day-to-day judgements and actions, knows the usefulness, indeed the necessity, of the political umbrella.

UNFPA's birth had been an untidy business. The transfer of its administration from the UN to the UNDP had left it something of a bastard institution. It was not really clear where the lines and responsibility and accountability lay. It is to his credit that Salas saw the dangers, as well as the advantages, in this situation, and pushed for a degree of institutionalization of the Fund which has subsequently ensured that UNFPA has been able to operate in a more-or-less conventional manner as far as the norms of international institutions are concerned, while retaining those precious characteristics of independence and non-bureaucratic behaviour which were so much the hall-marks of the early years.

In December 1971, the General Assembly[15] passed a resolution noting that the Fund had become a 'viable entity in the United Nations System' and stating its conviction 'that the fund should play a leading role in the United Nations system in promoting population programmes – consistent with the decisions of the General Assembly and the Economic and Social Council ...'. It 'recognised the need for the executing agencies of the Fund to implement with dispatch, in close cooperation with the Fund, population programmes requested by developing countries in order that such programmes may have the desired impact.' The operative paragraphs of the resolution read as follows:

1. (The General Assembly) invites Governments which are in a position to do so and whose policies would allow it to make voluntary contributions to the United Nations Fund for Population Activities.

2. Requests the Secretary-General in consultation with the Administrator of the United Nations Development Programme and the Executive Director of the United Nations Fund for Population Activities, to take the necessary steps to achieve the desired improvements in the administrative machinery of the Fund aimed at the efficient and expeditious delivery of population programmes, including measures to quicken the pace of recruiting the experts and personnel required to cope with the increasing volume of requests, as well as to consider the training of experts and personnel in the developing countries;

3. Further requests the Secretary-General to inform the Economic and Social Council at its fifty-third session and the General Assembly at its twenty-seventh session of the steps he has taken in the implementation of the present resolution and of any recommendations he may wish to make in this regard.

Salas commented:

Since the words of intergovernmental bodies, specially those of ECOSOC and the General Assembly, make a difference and open many doors in the United Nations System, this represented a major advance for the Fund. It also went part way toward according the Fund the clearly recognized legal status which I felt that it had to have. But more was still needed[16].

The second operative paragraph of the General Assembly Resolution provided the opportunity.

The Michanek Review

On 26 January 1970, the Secretary-General of the United Nations had inaugurated – at UN headquarters – the first meeting of UNFPA's Advisory Board. Since UNFPA, as a Trust Fund of the Secretary-General, lacked an intergovernmental board, U Thant, Hoffman and Salas had decided that it would be important for the Fund to explain its policies and operations to influential people in various regions of the world for the dual purpose of obtaining their advice and guidance and of enlisting their aid in making the Fund better known in their countries.

Members of the Board included distinguished individuals, invited to serve in their personal capacity by the Secretary-General, as well as the heads of the regional economic commissions and the United Nations Economic and Social office in Beirut.

Dr Alberto Lleras Camargo, the former President of Colombia who had on several occasions expressed strong opinions about the impact of population growth on his own country, was elected Chairman and, taking the membership as a whole, there was no doubt that it was a blue-riband panel. Some of the names – such as those of John D. Rockefeller 3rd and B. R. Sen – have already been mentioned in this account. Others, such as Lord Caradon who would lead UNFPA's first population mission to Iran in November 1971, or Maurice Strong, who would serve in June 1972 as the Secretary-General of the United Conference on the Human Environment, or Carmen Miro, Director of CELADE who would receive the United Nations Population Award in Mexico City in August 1985 for her work over several decades, would have a continuing impact on UN population affairs.

In welcoming them that day U Thant said:

All of us are anxious to make use of our lives, and of our talents, to help our fellow men realize more fully the great potential they have as human beings. I know of no field more important to this end, and in which I am sure a more real contribution can be made, than helping individuals and societies to understand the relationship between human numbers and human opportunity, and to have the best possible means to realize their own wishes in this matter. ... Along with our efforts to ensure that technology serves man, rather than destroy him, the efforts to see that population numbers and their rate of growth are in balance with the quest for development lies at the very heart of the task facing the world.

In the event UNFPA's Advisory Board had a somewhat short-lived existence because, in response to GA Resolution 2815, it established a Review Committee under the Chairmanship of Ernst Michanek, the Director-General of the Swedish International Development Authority (SIDA), to make recommendations on the following points:

1. Planning and programming procedures of the UNFPA including collaboration on the utilization of its resources with the United Nations, its specialized agencies and interested non-governmental organizations;

2. the capacity of the UNFPA and the collaborating organizations in the United Nations system to execute effectively programmes and projects including the possibility of project implementation as appropriate by UNFPA and non-governmental bodies;

3. ways of ensuring the effective execution of the regional and field responsibilities of UNFPA;

4. study of the role of the Fund in relation to UNDP country programming;

5. the decision-making process within the UNFPA, including the functions of the Programme Consultative Committee and the possible use of *ad hoc* advisory groups;

6. the role of the UNFPA in support of programmes to increase the availability of qualified experts and personnel in less developed countries;

7. the responsibilities of UNFPA with regard to financial and personnel matters.

Perhaps even more important than the above was the statement that the Review Committee might also consider and make recommendations on the way in which UNFPA could effectively discharge its responsibilities for leadership within the United Nations system and promote a focus for co-ordinated international efforts to deal with population problems. Behind this last injunction could be detected Salas' concern to ensure that the Review Committee did not duck the issue of finding (or indeed inventing one if they had to) an appropriate intergovernmental body for UNFPA.

The other members of the Review Committee, in addition to Ernst Michanek, were Dr Albert Lleras Camargo, Lord Caradon, Soleiman Huzayyin, John D. Rockefeller 3rd and B. R. Sen. The Committee was to report to the meeting of UNFPA's Advisory Board scheduled for September 1972, so that the Secretary-General could in turn inform the 53rd session of the Economic or Social Council and the 27th Session of the General Assembly of the steps he had taken.

It was a tight schedule. Independent consultants served as the Committee's staff, headed by Dr George Brown of the Canadian-sponsored International Development Research Centre (where he was chief of the Population and Health Sciences Division). Another Canadian, Wendy Dobson (Marson) – who would later act at Bucharest, in August 1974, as the Rapporteur for the World Population Plan for Action – came with him. The author was also a member of the staff of the review, as were Altan Unver of Turkey and Edward Trainer of the United States.

In the event, the Review Committee was able to keep to schedule though the final result was not perhaps everything that Salas had hoped for. The Committee made a number of recommendations which on the whole tended to reflect the view that, while in its formative years it had been right and proper for the Fund to work almost exclusively through the agencies, the time was now ripe for a different emphasis which would stress the real potential which the Fund could develop if it sought more direct contact with the developing countries, including where appropriate direct funding of programmes and projects. This meant that the Fund should rapidly develop its own field staff and that, wherever feasible and appropriate, countries themselves should be able to manage directly the project components of country programmes financed by the Fund. Countries should have available to them as wide a choice of potential participating organizations, whether inside or outside the United Nations system, as possible; and the Fund should have a collective guarantee by donor governments of a certain volume of future programming commitments.

Many of these recommendations were taken up by UNFPA and eventually embodied in ECOSOC resolution 1763 (LIV) of 18 May 1973 which will be discussed below[17]. Where, however, the need for UNFPA to have an intergovernmental body was concerned, the Review Committee was less than clear. It is the author's recollection that this particular point led to sharp debate within the Committee and its staff. Though some, including the author, argued that the logic behind the transfer of the administration of the Fund to the UNDP; the overriding necessity – as Paul Hoffman had insisted at the first meeting to the UNFPA Advisory Board – to see population and development as 'sides of the same coin' implied, indeed demanded, that the UNDP Governing Council should also function as UNFPA's intergovernmental body, the final recommendation of the Review Committee attempted uneasily to straddle all horses at once. UNFPA, Michanek recommended, should remain as a Secretary-General's Trust Fund and 'report annually to the Governing Council of the UNDP and to the Secretary-General for further reporting to the Economic and

Social Council .... The Secretary-General should reconstitute a UNFPA Board composed of individuals selected for the contribution they can make in giving guidance for the leadership of the Fund'. As Salas commented, 'this could have led to the Fund still being without intergovernmental supervision'.

He summed up the situation in this way:

> Total independence was in principle attractive, but I doubted if it was really available. The choice seemed to be between being in the orbit of UNDP or in that of the United Nations Secretariat. Undoubtedly our affinities were more with the UNDP. It was important that population assistance should be clearly related to other economic and social development assistance, most of which in the United Nations system was already under the supervision of the UNDP Governing Council. Moreover, it was very advantageous for UNFPA to continue to avail itself of the services of the UNDP Resident Representatives in the field and to maintain close operational and policy coordination with UNDP. It might have been hard to do this if the Fund were to have a different governing body from UNDP. After much thought and discussion with Fund staff members and with the strong support of some of the major donors, I suggested to the Secretary-General that he might wish to recommend that the Fund be put under the UNDP Governing Council[18].

The outcome was that the Secretary-General, after careful considera-tion, recommended to the General Assembly that the UNFPA should be placed under the supervision of the UNDP Governing Council. The developing countries, some of whom had reservations because they felt closer to ECOSOC than the Governing Council where they occasionally complained about donor domination, accepted the Secretary-General's recommendation but made their point about the overall policy control of ECOSOC very explicit in the General Assembly's decision.

General Assembly resolution of 5 December 1972

At the 1509th meeting of the Second Committee of the General Assembly, on 5 December 1972, a draft resolution entitled 'United Nations Fund for Population Activities' was introduced by the representative of the Philip-pines, sponsored by Indonesia, The Netherlands, Norway, the Philippines, Sweden and the United States of America, and joined also by Japan, Malaysia and Uganda. At the 1511th meeting, on 6 December, a revised draft resolution on this subject was introduced by the representative of Norway on behalf of the above sponsors joined by Iran, Sri Lanka and also by Thailand. After a number of oral amendments by Argentina, Brazil,

Chile, Cuba and Kenya, the Second Committee in a recorded vote at that meeting adopted the revised text[19].

With this resolution of the General Assembly, the institutionalization of the UNFPA was almost complete. It remained for ECOSOC to respond to the invitation of the General Assembly to establish any conditions which might qualify the exercise of the UNDP Governing Council of its new mandate as UNFPA's Governing Body.

ECOSOC resolution of 18 May 1973

At its 1858 plenary meeting on 18 May 1973, the Council adopted resolution 1763 (LIV) on the United Nations Fund for Population Activities, on the recommendation of the Economic committee, by 22 votes to none, with five abstentions. The draft resolution which was put forward by Malaysia used the language of the Michanek Review Committee as its basis and was co-sponsored by what Salas describes as 'an unusually strong and representative group of countries: Ghana, Haiti, Indonesia, Madagascar, Malaysia, Mali, the Philippines, Romania, Sri Lanka, Turkey and Uganda'. As a result of that vote for the first time the Fund had terms of reference approved by an authoritative intergovernmental body. Since almost 14 years later these remain the formal terms of reference of the Fund, they are worth printing in full.

The Economic and Social Council stated, in its first operative paragraph, that:

> the aims and purposes of the United Nations Fund for Population Activities are:
> (a) to build up, on an international basis, with the assistance of the competent bodies of the United Nations system, the knowledge and the capacity to respond to national, regional, interregional and global needs in the population and family planning fields; to promote co-ordination in planning and programming, and to co-operate with all concerned;
> (b) to promote awareness, both in developed and in developing countries, of the social economic and environmental implications of national and international population problems; of the human rights aspects of family planning; and of possible strategies to deal with them, in accordance with the plans and priorities of each country;
> (c) to extend systematic and sustained assistance to developing countries at their request in dealing with their population problems; such assistance to be afforded in forms and by means requested by the recipient countries and best suited to meet the individual country's needs;
> (d) to play a leading role in the United Nations system in promoting population programmes and to co-ordinate projects supported by the Fund.

Taken together, GA resolution 3019 (XXVII) of 18 December 1972 and ECOSOC resolution 1763 (XXVI) of 18 May 1973 established UNFPA's constitutional position within the UN system rather clearly. It remained to be seen, of course, in precisely what manner the UNDP Governing Council would discharge its function as UNFPA's Governing body; also whether the bold claim that UNFPA was 'to play a leading role in the United Nations system in promoting population programmes ...' would be justified in practice. But the fact of the matter is that without these attempts to clarify UNFPA's mandate and terms of reference, and the lines of authority under which it was to operate, there was every likelihood that the Fund, in spite of the evident interest of both donors and recipients, might have failed to develop beyond the embryonic stage. Boring and bureaucratic though these United Nations resolutions must sometimes seem to those who have to draft them or vote upon them (or read about them) they are ultimately essential – the test of legitimacy; and in the population field, perhaps more than in other fields, legitimacy is important. This is an area of activity open to challenge on many grounds – religious, political, practical. Pieces of paper with the right words written on them count for something.

This was perhaps especially true of the second operative paragraph of ECOSOC resolution 1763 (LIV). UNFPA was, as noted above, anxious to establish that the task of carrying out population programmes and projects lay with countries themselves who should look wherever they could for the most appropriate form of assistance. Now ECOSOC confirmed this approach by '*Deciding* that the United Nations Fund for population activities should invite countries to utilize the most appropriate implementing agents for their programmes, recognizing that the primary responsibility for implementing rests with the countries themselves'.

It was clear from this language that though UNFPA was to play a leading role in the United Nations system in promoting population programmes, countries would also be free to use the funds UNFPA provided either to implement projects themselves directly or to turn to other forms of external assistance, outside the UN system itself. In practice the countries who received support from UNFPA tended increasingly to avail themselves of the flexibility provided for under UNFPA's mandate. Whereas in the early years of the Fund's operations, the lion's share of UNFPA resources were allocated to countries via the UN agencies (except for the proportion retained for regional or interregional projects) by the end of the period under consideration – over 40 per cent of country-spending was allocated direct (sometimes with the UNFPA itself being indicated as Executing Agency).

As a result of these resolutions of the General Assembly and ECOSOC, UNFPA's Advisory Board became redundant. By setting up the Michanek Review Committee it had, as it were, set in motion the process which would result in its own demise. Some members of the Advisory Board had clearly expected to perform their functions longer than was in fact the case, but on the whole the political necessity of the new arrangements was apparent.

Salas commented:

The arrangements made by the General Assembly, ECOSOC and the Governing Council late in 1972 and in 1973, establishing the Fund's new position and the means by which it was to be supervised by ECOSOC and the Governing Council, still left the Fund a wide operating margin. The hard work, good will, and understanding that went into formulating these arrangements on the part of many officials in home governments and office staffs of the permanent missions of the United Nations were impressive and should be noted by those who sometimes doubt the United Nations' ability to act constructively ... [20].

First report to the Governing Council

Reporting to the UNDP Governing Council for the first time in January 1973, Salas presented a factual account of the Fund's overall position.

He reassured the members of the Governing Council that UNFPA was 'entirely separate' from UNDP programming. There had never been a hint from UNFPA or UNDP that UNFPA population programmes might be promoted at the expense of UNDP's economic and social assistance. (In the short term, this was no doubt true, but over a longer time period the very substantial levels of funding which UNFPA would attain would raise the question in some quarters as to whether or not population assistance was in some sense in competition with other forms of assistance, or whether it could truly be regarded as 'additional' finance which would not otherwise be available for development.)

Secondly, he assured the Governing Council that the Fund never sought to urge any particular population policy or programmes on any country. It was 'neutral with respect to policy'. It had, for example, responded to requests to assist countries with problems of sub-fertility or sterility as well as those with problems of high fertility rates. (The Fund's 'neutrality' with respect to policy did not imply that the Fund was unable to develop certain priorities for population assistance as we shall see later[21].)

Third, Salas defined what he understood by 'population' or 'population activities'. This was important. None of the official resolutions of the General Assembly attempted such a definition; yet the terms 'population', 'population programmes' or 'population activities' were freely used in the context of UNFPA's role. The staff of UNFPA had, of course, several working definitions including those given in the Principles and Procedures

74

paper of April 1970 but in spelling out the concepts for the benefit of the Governing Council Salas was performing a useful service.

In the United Nations the words 'population' or 'population activities', he told the Governing Council, are broadly understood to include: population censuses, vital statistics, sample surveys on population, economic and social statistics related to population, related research projects, training facilities required, demographic aspects of development planning, family-planning delivery systems, techniques of fertility regulation, planning and management of family-planning programmes, support communications, population and family-life education in schools and in out-of-school education, activity connected with the World Population Year 1974[22], documentation centres and clearing houses on population matters, and interdisciplinary population training.

In arriving at this inventory, Salas (and UNFPA) benefited greatly from the work begun by Halvor Gille before he left the United Nations Department of Economic and Social Affairs. Gille's project was to prepare a report for the United Nations Advisory Committee on the Application of Science and Technology to Development which from its inception had been concerned with the need for more knowledge and intensified research and application of technology in the field of population. The report of the Committee was published by the United Nations Department of Economic and Social Affairs in January 1971, under the title 'Human Fertility and National Development: A Challenge to Science and Technology'. It described in a clear and concise manner which has largely remained valid to the present time the scope and potential of population policies and programmes in the different regions of the world[23].

Thus, the Committee recognized that in Asia, a number of countries needed, and were likely to request, assistance on a large scale for implementing an effective population programme, including family planning. This would include setting up local training schemes, obtaining supplies, fellowships, transport and other equipment, including educational materials and mass media equipment, and direct support to operational activities. There might also be a considerable demand for expert advice in the evaluation of such programmes and for assistance with the manufacture of contraceptives.

In Africa, the main need in the majority of countries in the immediate future was the creation of awareness and understanding of population problems and their economic and social implications. Countries which did not now recognize the need for a population policy might in the near future require experts and training facilities at home and abroad to assist in the planning, execution and analysis of censuses and sample surveys as well as in the training of demographers, economists, sociologists, etc.

However, the Committee noted, an interest was beginning to show itself in a number of countries, either with or without a national programme and policy, for assistance in regard to various aspects of family planning activities.

In Latin America, an increasing number of governments were interested in assistance for family planning through health services by means of advice and for financing of training in the country or abroad. The need for international aid of this and other kinds was likely to increase rapidly.

In his remarks to the Governing Council in January 1973, Salas repeated the information about Fund allocations which he had given to the Population Commission a few weeks earlier: The Fund was preparing to respond favourably to requests for assistance with censuses from 20 African countries, 17 of which had never had a population census and three of which had not taken censuses in many years. It was preparing to expand its assistance in demographic data gathering and interpretation to other areas, such as Latin America, in response to interest shown by countries there. Twenty-eight per cent of Fund resources had been dedicated to wholly demographic projects.

As far as family planning was concerned, Salas confirmed that in response to requests from many countries, by no means confined to Asia, the Fund had provided assistance to family-planning programmes and to support communications and had devoted some 56 per cent of its resources to this purpose. 'Some of the family planning programmes we have supported have demographic goals; other do not and are conceived entirely as measures of individual and family welfare under the direction and supervision of the Ministry of Health'[24].

Country programmes

Behind the statistics lay a new trend in the Fund's financing. The Fund's first country agreement for a comprehensive population programme was worked out with the Government of Pakistan. The objectives of the agreement, signed in August 1970, were to support the goals of the family planning programme and in particular the Government's aim of reducing the birth rate in Pakistan from 43 to 33.2 per 1000 population. $1.7 million was to be provided by the Fund over the first 12 months of a five-year programme, with further financing to follow.

The second country agreement was made with Mauritius, when in late 1970 the Government of Mauritius and UNFPA signed an agreement for UNFPA assistance of $600,000 over a three-year period to the National

Family Planning Programme of Mauritius. (At the time, the population of Mauritius was 800,000 and a continuation of current trends would have led to a doubling of the population by the year 2000.)

Other major country projects supported by UNFPA at the time Mr Salas made his first report to the UNDP Governing Council included: Egypt, where under an agreement operative since 1971 the Fund was providing $1.25 million for the first year of a five-year programme of support for public information, education, study of population trends, research, fellowships and the supply of contraceptives through UNICEF; India, where the Fund was contributing $1 million for an innovative vasectomy campaign; Indonesia, where under an agreement signed in April 1972 the Fund was participating with the World Bank and the Government of Indonesia in a major project designed primarily to expand and upgrade a network of maternal and child health/family-planning centres in East Java, Bali and Jakarta (UNFPA's contribution, like the Bank's was $13.2 million); Iran, where the Fund had agreed in 1971 to provide $1.6 million in aid of the Iranian family planning programme; Thailand, where under an agreement signed in November 1971, UNFPA was providing $3.3 million over three years – also for family planning; the Philippines, where under a 1972 agreement, UNFPA was providing $3.3 million to cover on-going and planned projects following the passage into law of the Philippines Population Act of August 15, 1971; and Chile, the first Latin American country to sign an agreement with the Fund, under which the Fund was to supply $3 million over a four-year period in support of Chile's family health and population programme.

More will be said in a later chapter about the programming of population assistance and the impact in these (and other) countries of United Nations involvement, through UNFPA, and the executing agencies, in population activities. At the time Mr Salas made his first speech to the UNDP Governing Council in January 1973, it was already clear that the UN's involvement varied in both qualitative and quantitative terms. There was no single model, no single preferred solution. If flexibility was the keynote of those early years of UN response to the population challenge, and if flexibility has remained a dominant characteristic (in spite of the inevitable tendencies towards institutionalization and bureaucratization which are experienced whenever an organization reaches a certain maturity or grows beyond a certain size) the reason is precisely because those who ran the Fund understood that the population question appears in different forms in different countries, or at different times within a country. It is protean, changes shape before it can be grasped and only finally surrenders to an approach based on a combination of persistence, vision, luck and – necessarily – money.

Money

In his final closing remarks to the Governing Council, Mr Salas turned to the financial question. He pointed to the gap which was already beginning to open up between the needs of countries for financing and the available resources and asked the Council to permit the Fund to adopt the principles of annual funding as a means of improving planning, programming and implementation. (This meant that the Fund was able to abandon full funding principles under which all project commitments for future years had to be held against current resources[25].)

Even when the Council granted this request – its first authoritative action in relation to the Fund – it was clear that the battle to obtain adequate resources would be a continual one and, moreover, that it could never be won. For successful funding operations by themselves would generate more requests for funds. The Fund's senior staff, and in particular its Executive Director, discovered very soon that governmental contributions do not grow on trees, waiting for someone to come along and gently rattle the branches, so they can drop off in a nice generous shower. They have to be worked for; earned, begged; cajoled. It may not sound very grand; it may not always be very dignified, but, if UNFPA has succeeded where other voluntary funds have failed, at least part of the reason is that Salas and his advisers took the business of fund-raising with deadly seriousness, asked dedicated enthusiasts like General Draper to help them, knew whom to approach and whom to leave strictly alone; were, in the end, convincing because they knew – or at least sincerely believed – they had a decent product to sell.

6

The World Population Conference,

Bucharest, 1974:

preparations and general debate

The Conference process

With the passage of the General Assembly Resolution of 5 December 1972,
and the ECOSOC Resolution of 18 May 1973, it could be argued that a
UN population agency had at last been created. It had been an unusual
process. New UN bodies are often produced as a result of what is
sometimes referred to as 'the Conference process'. Typically, an intergovernmental meeting is called some months or even years in advance of
the date on which the gathering is to take place. Draft agenda are
prepared, as well as background papers and plans of action. When
delegates at last meet, almost invariably one of the papers that confronts
them is entitled 'International Institutional Implications'; they are invited
to agree – if they can agree on nothing else – on the establishment of some
new unit (to which will be attributed a 'small high-calibre' staff) which will
carry the good work forward. Thus, the mammoth United Nations
Conference on the Human Environment (UNCHE), which had been held
in Stockholm in June 1972, had – besides approving a Declaration and
Plan of Action on the Environment – led to the setting up of the United
Nations Environment Programme. The 'Conference process', ably orches-
trated by UNCHE's Secretary-General, Mr Maurice Strong, had arrived at
a consensus and that consensus had in turn allowed the appropriate
institutional decisions to be taken.

Such was the world-wide publicity that, as far as UNEP was concerned,
we were all, so to speak, in at the birth. The author, who attended the
United Nations Conference on the Human Environment as a delegate for
IPPF, remembers those two weeks spent in Stockholm in the high summer

of 1972, as a heady time. As Barbara Ward and Rene Dubos reminded us there was 'Only One Earth' and we were busy making a terrible mess of it[1]. The Save the Planet signs were out in force; UNEP was to be one of the tools, if not *the* tool, for the job.

Because UNFPA was created under the circumstances described in the previous chapters, the publicity which heralded its arrival on the international stage was of an altogether different order. It could hardly be said that the key General Assembly and ECOSOC resolutions had been the reflection of a broad and public consensus of the kind that had led to the World Environment Plan of Action and, as part of that Plan, to the setting up of UNEP. When UNFPA was born, no trumpets had sounded from the steep.

So the World Population Conference, which was to be held in Bucharest in August 1974, could be seen as an ideal occasion to make up for the deficiencies: a kind of post-natal celebration. Such a conference should, so its proponents believed, proclaim an international consensus on population questions, endorse a world plan of action and, last but not least, legitimize the infant UNFPA. But did such an international consensus truly exist?

Early decisions

Plans for a World Population Conference had in fact been afoot for some time. As early as 1969 a consultative group of experts, which included the ubiquitous General Draper, had been convened at UN headquarters with the object of informing the Secretary-General on the advisability of holding another World Population Conference. In its Resolution 1484 (XLVIII), of 3 April 1970, the Economic and Social Council approved the proposal that a world population conference should convene in 1974 under the auspices of the United Nations, with representatives of governments (members of the UN and of specialized agencies), their technical advisors, and other selected specialists as participants. ECOSOC decided that 'the conference shall be devoted to consideration of basic demographic problems, their relationship with economic and social development and population policies and action programmes needed to promote welfare and development'.

In a parallel resolution 1485 (XLVIII), the Council recommended that the General Assembly designate 1974, the year in which the third World Population Conference would be held as 'World Population Year'. ECOSOC expressed its conviction that 'an appropriate way of intensifying the activities of lasting nature is to devote the year 1974 to extensive national and international efforts and undertakings in the field of population, and also to an international review of the achievements in the field'. It authorized the Secretary-General to undertake a programme of measures and activities by the United Nations, by member states and by the interested organizations of the United Nations system during the year 1974.

These decisions taken by ECOSOC in April 1970 were of great significance for the development of UN activities in the field of population. Though two World Population Conferences had been held before under the auspices of the United Nations and with the close collaboration of the IUSSP and interested specialized agencies – the first in Rome in 1954, the second in Belgrade in 1965[2] – the Third World Population Conference to be held in 1974 was the first which would be an official governmental conference. The resolutions or decisions coming out of that conference would have to be seen in an altogether different light from the resolutions emerging from Rome and Belgrade which in the final analysis committed no-one except, perhaps, the individual participants themselves. The positions taken at Bucharest by States Members of the United Nations would be of considerable interest and would certainly indicate the degree to which newly created institutions like UNFPA were likely to grow and prosper.

By the same token, in declaring 1974 World Population Year – in spite of the considerable scepticism which the designation of 'Years' of any sort frequently incites – ECOSOC showed its willingness to recognize that population was a field where the generation of widespread public interest, from the highest levels of government down to the parish pump, was of crucial importance.

When it met for its 16th session (1 to 12 November 1971) the Population Commission had before it the report of the Preparatory Committee referred to in ECOSOC resolution 1484 (XLVIII). The Commission in its own report noted that scientifically established knowledge on population trends and structure and related economic and social matters, as well as a thorough examination of national experience, would be provided by the technical advisors and other experts, and through documentation for the Conference, and that the Regional Population Conferences which were to be held before the World Population Conference would make a significant contribution towards the objective appreciation of the specific situations prevailing in various parts of the world. On that basis the conference could synthesize the basic issues of the contemporary world related to population and its evolution in different economic, social, cultural and political settings. It should aim at improvement of understanding of the crucial role of population in the development process, particularly in such crucial areas as the relationship between population change and economic development, environment, family and individual health and human welfare, including human rights. Because of the marked diversity of economic, social and demographic situations, emphasis should be placed on the understanding of the dynamic role of population in different circumstances, and on the types of policies that might be applied.

The Commission felt that the conference must take account of the implications of unprecedented rates of growth implicit in recent population trends, but that it should not be exclusively devoted to reduction of growth rates. Proper attention should be given to the need for scientific examination of population structure and trends and the social–economic interrelationships, on the one hand, and to the consideration of diverse policy and action programmes in keeping with the observed diversity of national circumstances and values on the other.

This bland language, almost inevitable in the official reports of a United Nations body such as the Population Commission, nonetheless contained some interesting features. For example, by recognizing that the Conference should not be exclusively devoted to reduction of growth rates, the Population Commission was implicitly accepting that the question of lowering fertility would and should occupy the attentions of delegates at least some of their time.

The Commission 'recommended that a study on global population strategy be undertaken through the Secretary-General of the United Nations with the assistance of a high-calibre expert committee to highlight the world-wide implications of population growth and of national population policies ... it was suggested that possibilities of achieving a population growth of 1% by the end of the century be explored, together with the possibilities of adopting a world-wide objective in this regard'.

For those who wished to see some hard-hitting language emerge eventually from Bucharest, this was encouraging.

The Population Commission also reviewed the document presented to it by the Secretary-General entitled 'proposed programmes of measures and activities for the World Population Year, 1974'[4]. The Commission was of the view that the measures and activities to be undertaken for the World Population Year by all concerned – local, national and international bodies as well as voluntary organizations – should aim at the following five major objectives: (a) improved knowledge of and information on the facts concerning population trends and prospects, and the relevant associated factors; (b) sharpened awareness and heightened appreciation of population problems and their implications by individual governments, non-governmental organizations, and scientific institutions; (c) effective education on population, family life and reproductive functions through

82

formal and other educational systems; (d) the discussion of alternative policies, the promotion of demographic considerations in development planning and the development of policies and programmes in population fields which individual governments might wish to undertake; (e) the expansion of international co-operation in the population field and the supply of increased and suitable assistance to countries desiring it, and in accordance with their needs[5].

Because the programme was concerned with radical improvement in thinking and action, its measures and activities were by no means limited to one year. Rather, it should be an extended effort by governments, voluntary organizations, individuals and the world community to focus world-wide attention on population, to stimulate thought and energy towards raising the scope and quality of knowledge about population and to direct that knowledge into action towards improving human life. Activities of the Year should begin at once, progressively increase up to the high peak of the designated Year, and continue thereafter, conceivably throughout the Second United Nations Development Decade.

The Commission recognized that, while the programme for World Population Year outlined a number of national measures which might be undertaken by Member States to achieve the specified objectives, there was no suggestion that all the measures were of equal relevance to every country; countries would naturally choose those appropriate to their stage of economic, social and demographic evolution and their own aspirations for future development.

The report of the 16th session of the Population Commission went before the Economic and Social Council's 52nd session. On June 2, 1972, ECOSOC passed a comprehensive resolution on Population and Development[3]. The resolution urged all Member States:

(a) to give full attention to their demographic objectives and measures during the biennial review and appraisal of the implementation of the Second United Nations Development Decade, and to take such steps as may be necessary to improve demographic statistics, research and planning machinery needed for development of population policies and programmes;

(b) to co-operate in achieving a substantial reduction of the rate of population growth in those countries which considered that their present rate of growth is too high and in exploring the possibility for the setting of targets for such reduction in those countries;

(c) to ensure, in accordance with their national population policies and needs, that information and education about family planning, as well as the means to effectively practise family planning, are made available to all individuals by the end of the Second United Nations Development Decade.

In the same resolution, ECOSOC dealt in detail with arrangements for the World Population Conference and the World Population Year. It endorsed in principle the draft programme and arrangements for the World Population Conference, 1974, as approved by the Population Commission at its 16th session; it decided to assign to the Population Commission amongst its functions that of the intergovernmental preparatory body for the World Population Conference and the World Population Year. It called upon States Members of the United Nations or members of the specialized agencies or the International Atomic Energy Agency to take part in the World Population Conference and urged interested Member States to report on the actions they had undertaken in developing their population policies, programmes and activities.

Most important of all it decided to place on the agenda of the World Population Conference a draft World Population Plan of Action and requested the Secretary-General to elaborate such a draft with the assistance of the Advisory Committee of Experts on Global Population Strategy which had been decided upon at the 16th session of the Population Commission.

Thus for the first time a United Nations gathering would be seized of a document which set out to propose not merely further demographic studies, important though these would be, but also a series of actions to be taken by the world community. Just what those proposed actions would entail remained to be seen. But the auguries were good.

ECOSOC also requested the Secretary-General, with the financial assistance of the United Nations Fund for Population Activities:

(a) to announce the World Population Year and World Population Conference at an early date and commend those programmes to the urgent attention of Governments of all Member States in order to emphasize that high priority should be given to the preparation for the Conference and the Year, and take such other steps as may be desirable for the attainment of the basic objectives of the Conference and the Year;

(b) to appoint, within the Department of Economic and Social Affairs and at the Assistant Secretary-General level, a Secretary-General for the World Population Conference and those World Population Year activities specifically related to the Conference, among them the symposia on population and development, human rights and the environment, equipped with the necessary secretariat resources, by drawing particularly upon the expertise and competence of the United Nations' system as well as the Advisory Committee of Experts on Global Population Strategy;

(c) to designate the Executive Director of the United Nations Fund for Population Activities as having responsibility for preparations for the World Population Year and to request him to take the necessary steps, having regard to the sources available, to establish a secretariat from within the Fund and to work closely with the Population Division, the Centre for Economic and Social Information, the specialized agencies and the relevant non-governmental organizations.

ECOSOC also urged the Secretary-General of the Conference and the Executive Director of the Fund to co-operate to the extent necessary to ensure that preparations for the World Population Conference and the World Population Year proceeded smoothly, bearing in mind the complementary nature of the activities of the Year and the Conference.

The ECOSOC resolution, stressing the roles both of the Population Division and of the United Nations Fund for Population Activities, was in its way *de facto* recognition of the now bi-polar nature of the United Nations' population work. Traditionally, the Population Division had been in the lead, particularly at events like the World Population Conference. Yet it was clear that the Fund was gaining in importance and visibility. It could not be left on the side-lines. There was an obvious need to link the Fund closely with the planning for 1974. Salas himself commented that the ECOSOC resolution introduced

> a curious division of labour; the United Nations in designating previous 'years' and their accompanying conferences had entrusted the management of both events to one specific body. Normally this was a special secretariat. But in 1972 the Fund already had world-wide visibility, and many participants in the Preparatory Committees thought it should be given a more definitive part in the celebration. Stanley Johnson, the IPPF representative, persuaded his government's representative to propose an active role for UFPA. What came out in the final ECOSOC resolution was an ingenious device of not giving the total responsibility either to the Fund or to the Population Division. The responsibility for the WPY was given to the Executive-Director of UNFPA and the responsibility for the Conference to a Secretary-General staffed by the Population Division. A very unusual arrangement somehow obscured by the agreement that the World Population Conference was to be the highlight of the Year[6].

On 20 September 1972, in a special press conference held at UN headquarters, the Secretary-General of the United Nations followed the advice of ECOSOC and proclaimed 1974 as World Population Year and announced the convening of a World Population Conference in that year.

In opening his remarks, the Secretary-General stated:

It is impossible to think of solution to the major problems confronting the world – economic development, pollution of the environment, improvement in the quality of life, even disarmament – without some reference to population trends ... it is my hope that the World Population Year and Conference will rank in the history of the United Nations among the great events of the 70s and that they will bring us appreciably closer to the day when the world can say that the demographic problems facing us are understood, and actions to solve them are under way.

The Secretary-General told his audience that

each year 127 million children are born, each year 95 million come of school age and each year 19 million reach the age 65. These totals are likely to rise steeply in the years ahead as more young adults swell the ranks of potential parents and improved medical care advances life expectancy. At two per cent a year the rate of world population growth is now more than double the rate in 1940. It may still rise. Each nation, each community, each family must assess in detail how these trends effect their hopes for higher living standards, better education and greater health and happiness.

He announced that the overall preparations for the World Population Year in 1974

are in good hands: those of Mr Rafael Salas, Executive Director of the United Nations Fund for Population Activities. Mr Salas came to the United Nations after serving as a member of the Philippine Government for many years and is an outstanding administrator, who has built the Fund into an effective international body in a very short time.

The Secretary-General also announced 'with great pleasure' that Dr Antonio Carrillo Flores of Mexico had agreed to serve as Secretary-General of the World Population Conference.

Dr Carrillo Flores has served for many years in the Government of Mexico as Minister for Finance and Minister for Foreign Affairs. He is another example of the good fortune of the United Nations in securing the services of distinguished and experienced persons to carry out important and demanding tasks.

Four symposia

With the passage of the ECOSOC resolution of June 1972, and the Secretary-General's announcement of September of that year, the preparations for the events of 1974 switched into a higher gear.

Three symposia were held in the course of 1973 to prepare for the Conference. The subjects covered were, in turn, population and development; population and the family; and population, resources and the environment. A fourth symposium, on population and human rights, was held in early 1974. The reports of these symposia formed part of the background documentation for the conference and were also used for the preparation of the draft World Population Plan of Action. They were important because they reflected the intellectual basis for action and were part of the consensus-building process.

The participants in the symposia were present in their personal rather than official capacities. To that extent the conclusions which were reached (for example, that very high rates of population growth are usually an obstacle to development, or that in some countries resource and environmental problems were acute because of rapid population growth) could not be said to represent fully-fledged intergovernmental positions and therefore had to be regarded more as pointers to policy than policy itself.

Second population enquiry

More significant, from the latter point of view, was the report of the Second Enquiry among governments on population and development which had been requested by the Population Commission at its 16th session for completion in 1972/3. The questionnaire was sent out to States Members of the United Nations under cover of a letter from the Secretary-General dated 26 October 1972. Governments were asked to reply not later than 31 January 1973 in order to give the Secretariat time to prepare an analytic report for presentation to the World Population Conference, 1974.

By the end of 1973 the United Nations had received replies from 80 governments, including six responses in which the Government regretted not being in a position to deal with the questionnaire. The 74 positive replies included 21 from the ECE region, 15 from ECAFE region, 15 from the ECA region, ten from the ECLA region, eight from the ECWA region and five which had not been allocated by region.

Summarizing the replies, the UN Secretariat took the view that only very cautious conclusions could be drawn:

1. It seemed warranted to state that governments on the Asian Continent, which comprised half of mankind, had recognized that continued population growth could be a burden on the economy and they were increasing their efforts to achieve a rate of growth which would render the persistent efforts of economic and social development more manageable.

2. Although some changes in the population policies in Africa and Latin America were taking place, differences of national approach among countries in these regions were quite apparent.

3. Most of Europe, North America and Oceania had already achieved low rates of population growth. The moderate acceleration of growth rates which were the targets of some European countries would probably be counteracted by further declines in other countries, so that an even lower rate of population growth was apt to result in these regions combined.

The UN Secretariat also reached some broad conclusions as far as the spread of family-planning activities was concerned.

1. The most advanced family-planning activities organized by Government agencies could be found in Asia and Northern Africa. On the other hand, Europe and Northern America were perhaps the continents where family planning was most widely practised by the population even though these measures were not usually on a Government policy level.

2. The situation clearly indicated a tendency towards spreading and improving family-planning activities and making them become an integral part of health and welfare concerns.

Population Commission discusses draft World Population Plan of Action (WPPA)

At its 17th regular session (held between 29 October and 9 November 1973), the Population Commission met also in its capacity as the intergovernmental preparatory body for the World Population Conference, 1974, and the World Population Year, 1974, a role which had been assigned to it by the Economic and Social Council[7]. The Commission therefore had before it the draft World Population Plan of Action prepared by the United Nations Population Division within the UN Secretariat taking into account guidelines produced by the Advisory Committee of Experts on the World Population Plan of Action at its second meeting[8].

The report of the Commission on its 17th session makes it clear that there was by no means a consensus of view about the recommendations which should be contained in the draft Plan. Paragraph 175, for example, summarized the Commission's debate on the vexed question of targets – should the world be aiming at some global target of population growth? If so, what should that target be?[9]

It was maintained by some members that the apprehension certain people had of the present rates of population growth in the world as a whole, and particularly in developing countries, was generally based on the false assumption that population would continue to grow exponentially for a long time in the future. Such an assumption, it was indicated, was unwarranted since the present exponential growth might well be the middle phase of a logistic trend. It was suggested that the world capacity for supporting more people was far from being exhausted and that, consequently, the argument of impending shortage of space or of natural resource should be rejected. It was pointed out, on the other hand, that while a shortage of space in the absolute sense was not impending, the world had reached a stage, where, in many parts, there is a shortage of space for decent and civilized living. It was pointed out, furthermore, that while impending shortages might be fictitious, the rate at which population was growing was unprecedented in history and should, itself, be the subject of major concerns; in this regard, bold action to moderate the present rate of growth of world population was called for. The view was expressed that the World Population Conference should give particular attention to means of conserving resources and that it should not accept the premise that population growth was the cause of under-development but only that development and population should be planned in a harmonious way. One member noted that the population growth targets in the present draft of the plan were the summation of national targets and hence not an imposition of the international community on national Governments. Some members pointed out that the structure of the document dealing with recommendations on the questions of population policy should be based on the demographic variables – mortality, fertility and migration – and suggested, therefore, that the section on demographic growth be deleted. Some also warned against the utilisation of growth targets which were internationally set and hence implied such an imposition. It was further pointed out that some countries already had low or replacement levels of fertility or even negative population growth rates and that their problems should also be dealt with in the Plan. Several delegations, finally, were of the opinion that quantitative population goals and targets should be included in the draft World Population Plan of Action. Other members were against the inclusion of quantified targets.

Paragraph 176 foreshadowed the controversy which would emerge later as a key theme of the Bucharest conference. Assuming birth-rates had to come down, would this best be achieved as a result of programmes of economic and social development, or should direct action be taken, for example, through organized family planning programmes, to influence the 'fertility variable'?

The Commission emphasized the importance of economic development and social modernization in determining fertility levels but it was also pointed out by some members that the effect of economic and social development upon fertility might only come about with a delay of many decades. The Plan of Action should emphasize those social and economic measures that could be utilised by countries wishing to regulate fertility. Furthermore, the plan should encourage research in this field, both at the micro and macro levels. At the same time, it was a fundamental human right that all persons had the necessary information and the means to control fertility, and family planning should be viewed in this perspective. While some members considered the relative emphasis on family planning in the present draft of the Plan quite justified, others maintained that it was not warranted. In many developing countries, it was noted, the shortage of medical and para-medical family personnel acted together with other factors as a limit to the expansion and effectiveness of national planning programmes. At any rate it was agreed that family-planning programmes should emphasize the protection and well-being of children, mothers and the family and should involve, in particular, the active participation of women in their formulation and execution. The recommendation in the present draft of the plan for restricting the minimum age of marriage for women to seventeen years was questioned by some members.

Since not all the delegations to the Population Commission had had the opportunity to study the draft thoroughly, members were invited to submit detailed suggestions relating to the different aspects of the draft Plan to the Secretariat. These would be brought to the attention of the Advisory Committee and taken into account by the Secretariat for the purposes of redrafting the Plan.

The regional consultations

The WPPA was also considered at five regional consultations held with Governments as part of the preparatory arrangements for the conference. It was considered that these consultations could assist Governments in their preparations for the Conference, as well as giving them an opportunity to express their preliminary views on the basic conference documents. The meetings took place in San Jose, Costa Rica; Bangkok, Thailand; Addis Ababa, Ethiopia; Damascus, Syrian Arab Republic; and Geneva, Switzerland, over the period April to June 1974. Though, for practical reasons, none of the amendments to the WPPA proposed at the regional consultations could be reflected in the draft as it was put before the conference the views of the Governments as expressed in the course of the regional consultations would, it was assumed, be reflected later on, at Bucharest itself[10].

By the time the process of regional consultation was over only two months remained before the opening of the Conference. In spite of the differences of view that had emerged in the course of the preparatory process, particularly in the context of the Population Commission's discussion of the draft WPPA, the organizers of the Conference believed that the necessary consensus existed to permit the adoption of the World Population Plan of Action more or less in the form in which it was presented to delegates on the opening day of the Conference. In particular, the regional consultations, at which governments had been represented, had given the organizers ground for optimism. There had, admittedly, been some straws in the wind which might have given them pause. For example, the countries of the ECA region who attended the meeting held in Addis Ababa in May 1974 had recommended that in Section 1, the Background to the Plan, reference be made, among the International Strategies cited, to the Declaration on the Establishment of a New International Economic Order (NIEO) and its related Plan of Action which emerged from the Sixth Special Session of the General Assembly[11]. This was known to be a sensitive issue as far as certain other countries were concerned, particularly the United States, which was firmly opposed to all mention of the NIEO. On the other hand, the Asian countries who attended the meeting held in Bangkok wanted to toughen the references to fertility reduction contained in the draft plan, recommending that countries with very high birth rates should reduce these rates by 10 per 1000 before 1985 and 'endeavour to attain replacement levels of fertility in two or three decades or as soon as practicable'.

But these straws in the winds, significant though they might be, were not deemed to be of the kind capable of breaking the camel's back. The draft World Population Plan of Action presented to the Conference for discussion under item 11 of the provisional agenda carried with it the hopes of many who believed not only in the importance of the population problem, and in the need for action, but also in the role the United Nations and its system of agencies could play in this field.

In the event, the deliberations which took place in Bucharest in those two weeks of August 1974 turned out to be full of passion and controversy. The author attended the Conference as the representative of the Commission of the European Economic Community and it was clear to him, as to many others, that whatever might be the state of play by the end of the Conference – and that remained to be seen – there was no way in which it could be said on the opening day that a global consensus existed already on the question of population and in particular on the draft WPPA. The high officials of the United Nations who spoke at the inaugural session may indeed have believed – or been led to believe – that such a consensus existed but the course of the debate was soon to show them to be wrong.

The opening of the World Population Conference

The United Nations World Population Conference was held at Bucharest, Rumania from 19 to 30 August 1974. The representatives of 136 states invited in accordance with Economic and Social Council Resolution 1672b (LII) took part[12].

The Conference was attended by representatives from the United Nations bodies with an interest in population and development, as well as representatives from ILO, FAO, UNESCO, WHO and the World Bank. Observers from 11 inter-governmental organizations participated in the Conference as well as representatives of 109 international non-governmental organizations.

The Conference was opened by the Secretary-General of the United Nations. He recalled that at the special session of the General Assembly in April 1974 he had identified six issues which demanded immediate attention by the international community. These were mass poverty, food supplies, the utilization of energy, military expenditures, the world monetary system and the unprecedented rate of population growth.

> Beyond the compelling evidence that they are interconnected, these problems have increasingly come to display an international character, leaping over boundaries drawn on maps, much as the separate nations themselves have become increasingly interconnected through evermore complex international arrangements. It is a situation that consequently gives rise to new and complex demands on the United Nations system. Where else can the nations of the world turn, especially those on the road to development? Events have written a scenario in which the United Nations must take the centre of the stage.

Mr Waldheim went on to refer to the Draft World Population Plan of Action.

> There should be no question that the Plan emphatically recognises the prerogatives of national sovereignty and is respectful of fundamental rights. Although it addresses itself to problems associated with rapid population growth and therefore speaks to nations concerned about this matter, the Plan also deals with those other demographic matters that nations perceive as problems – mortality and morbidity, especially infant mortality, subfecundity, internal and international migration, family formation and the status of women. It suggests that nations might be well served by taking population factors into account throughout their planning processes and by formulating explicit population policy suited to particular national needs and circumstances. It anticipates that the expansion of population policy will result in ever greater demands on the resources available through international assistance. It calls, finally, for improved and expanded data collection and analysis and more intensive efforts in demographic research.

Mr Waldheim was at pains to point out that the adoption of a population strategy by the international community could never be the whole answer.

> It must be borne in mind that this is a Population Conference, with the Plan in consequence inevitably limited in scope. Its approach to the interconnected set

of problems which confront us is but one part of a broad set of strategies directed toward improving the quality of life. No-one would assert today that economic and social development can be achieved solely through measures that have demographic effects, for while such actions may have a profound impact on developmental processes, they must be accompanied by other measures which are directly productive of developmental goals. .... Population policy, whatever forms it may take in the separate nations, should be viewed as one element in a complex policy structure formulated for the achievement of a full set of national goals.

The Secretary-General's closing remarks encapsulated the challenge which confronted the Conference:

Demographic change ultimately depends on the accumulated decisions of individuals. Because they involve the most intimate areas of life, it is a matter that has been sensitive and controversial, and to take political decisions in population matters has seemed to be a course fraught with peril. Nonetheless, demographic matters have intruded roughly on our attention, demanding action and solutions that the world now seems prepared to undertake and strive for. This Conference, indeed, marks a turning point of attitudes to this important subject. We are now ready to discuss population policy because we have come to understand that the effects of population change pervade many aspects of our lives, and we are ready to deal with it not from any exceptional predilection for numbers but because we are interested in human well-being and social justice.

Mr Waldheim's optimistic view of the forthcoming proceedings was echoed by the Secretary-General of the Conference, Antonio Carrillo-Flores. The United Nations official biography described Dr Carrillo-Flores as a 'diplomat, jurist and scholar of wide experience'. His career as a professor of law, author, administrator, Minister in the Mexican Government and international representative of his country, had spanned four decades. Sixty-five years old at the time of the Bucharest Conference, his ministerial posts had included finance and foreign affairs; he had been ambassador to Washington, Director-General of the National Financing Corporation, Director of the Bureau of Credit of the Ministry of Finance and Judge of the Federal Fiscal Tribunal. Perhaps as important as Dr Carrillo-Flores' personal achievements, was the fact that he came from Mexico, a country which, while so far resisting a policy to curb population growth, had in 1972 began a programme to bring family-planning information and services to all its citizens. Carrillo-Flores had commented in a recent paper:

It is, however, quite obvious that this programme developed in support of human rights may well moderate the growth of Mexico's population and bring it more into line with the number of new jobs which the country's favourable rate of economic growth can be expected to assure.

There was no doubt that Carrillo-Flores' position as a Mexican, and Mexico's position as one of the leading countries in Latin America, might be expected to encourage certain Latin nations to adopt a warmer attitude towards the Conference and its deliberations, than they might otherwise have done.

Dr Carrillo-Flores recalled that 'during the past two decades there has been resistance in the United Nations to dealing with the problems of population, except on a purely statistical or scientific basis. This,' he suggested, 'was due to the misgivings many states had that under the auspices of our organisation population policies might be defined or implemented that were incompatible with the dignity of a human being and with the diversity of social and cultural values which differentiate contemporary societies'. However, he believed that the favourable reception given the World Plan of Action at the five regional consultations indicated 'that a consensus is possible despite the great diversity of the situations'. Anticipating, perhaps somewhat unwisely, on the outcome of the Conference, he went on to say:

> 'Although concrete suggestions for modification were made in all the regions, the consensus was possible because, fortunately, the most important measures through which a population policy can be implemented have their own justification from a human point of view.'

He referred to the fact of, or need for, consensus yet again when he stated that:

> This Conference will be more effective if it can approve, by consensus, recommendations to facilitate political action in areas where it is necessary. ... In a world preoccupied with worries not only of today, but of tomorrow, it is not easy to mobilise public opinion to support population policies, the effect of which can only be seen over very long periods. That is the difficulty which population policies face nationally and internationally. Nevertheless, the slower and the more difficult the path, the more urgent it is to start on it.

The Secretary-General of the Conference concluded his remarks by expressing his conviction that the Conference would

> be remembered as one of the noblest initiatives of the United Nations, since it is inspired by desire for social justice towards women, children and those men who have the least on earth – as I understood the duties entrusted to me by Secretary-General Waldheim. We have come to the illustrious city of Bucharest for love of life, not for fear of it.

The third of the triumvirate to speak at the opening session in Bucharest's Great Hall of the Republic (*Sala Palatuloui Republicii*) was President Nicolae Ceausescu of Rumania whose remarks in some sense prefigured the controversy which would develop over the course of the meeting. He extended, on behalf of the State Council, the Government and himself, cordial greetings to all the participants. He went on to call for a new international economic order, saying that it was evident that population questions and development prospects were directly linked to the abolition of the imperialist, colonialist world.

> More than ever before firm actions are necessary for basing international relations on new principles of equality, respect for national independence and sovereignty, non-interference in internal affairs, on the observance of every people's right to develop freely in keeping with its aspirations.
>
> The population question is closely linked to the setting up of a new international economic order, to establishing economic relations on the principles of mutual advantage, to attaining a correct ratio between the prices of industrial products and of raw materials favouring a more rapid development of the countries lagging behind.

The President dismissed as pessimistic the argument that a general food shortage would result from present rates of population and growth and the depletion of resources. 'Science will reveal new food resources and also increase soil fertility on the earth's surface which will allow for bigger quantities of additional plant and animal output for consumption.'

President Ceausescu suggested that the conditions of under-development in many countries had been caused by insufficient use of material and human resources. There must be a more judicious distribution of wealth and access by all to contemporary science and technology.

> The problem of the population is, therefore, primarily linked to the multi-lateral, progressive development of human society, to a correct distribution of a national product and to equitable social relations, both on a national and international plane.

In making the New International Economic Order the key-note of his address, President Ceausescu of Rumania possibly disappointed those who had hoped that the location of the world population conference in Rumania, a Marxist country, would demonstrate that population was no longer a major ideological issue. On the contrary, by urging in his key-note address that population be considered in the context of a New International Economic Order, he in some sense set the tone for the subsequent deliberations. Nevertheless, Rumania as the host country was committed to the success of the Conference, qua conference, and worked behind the scenes to achieve that outcome[13].

At its first plenary meeting on 19 August 1974, the Conference elected by acclamation Mr George Macovescu as President of the Conference. The official biography noted that Mr Macovescu, who had been Minister of

Foreign Affairs of Rumania since October 1972, had been a member of the Rumanian Communist Party since 1936 and, since 1949, a Professor at Bucharest University, specialising in the theory of literature. At its second plenary meeting, held on the same day, the Conference elected 31 vice-presidents as well as the chairman, vice-chairman and rapporteurs of the three Committees and of the working group on the World Population Plan of Action. The appointment of the Algerian delegate, Mr Oubouzar Ali, as Chairman of the working group was some surprise. The position had been the subject of intense debate in the pre-conference meetings, and Ghana and Kenya had been tipped as the most likely candidates. The election of Mr Oubouzar Ali would not be without its importance over the coming days as the debate on the WPPA continued.

China attacks

One of the most intriguing questions, as the Conference opened, was the attitude which would be taken by China. Though China had joined the United Nations a few years earlier and had been in favour of the ECOSOC resolution calling for a World Population Conference to be held in 1974, China had not been present at the regional consultations nor had it given any preliminary indications of the view it was likely to adopt on the draft Plan. Now, as delegates and observers gathered in Bucharest, it requested the UN to delete all references to the Chinese population from the official documents submitted to the conference on the grounds that, so UN secretariat officials understood, the Chinese Government preferred to publish population details itself rather than through the world body. This request was turned down by the United Nations, the documents having all been printed and distributed to delegates.

This little squabble was an augury of worse to come. When the head of the delegation of The People's Republic of China, Mr Huang Shu-Tse – the Vice-Minister for Health, addressed the Conference, he launched a blistering attack on the two superpowers (the United States of America and the Soviet Union), in general and on their views on population in particular.

> One superpower asserts outright that there is a 'population explosion' in Asia, Africa and Latin America and that a 'catastrophe to mankind' is imminent. The other superpower, pretending at some Conferences to be against Malthusianism, makes the propaganda blast that 'rapid population growth is a mill-stone around the neck of the developing countries'. Singing a duet, the two super-powers energetically try to describe the Third World's population growth as a great evil. If this fallacy is not refuted, there will be no correct point of departure in any discussion on the world population.

The Chinese delegate then proceeded to refute the fallacy in inimitable language.

Of all things in the world, people are the most precious. Once the people take their destiny into their own hands, they will be able to perform miracles. Man as worker, as creator and user of tools, is the decisive factor in the social production forces. ... After prolonged and heroic struggles waged by the people in Asia, Africa and Latin America, a large number of countries in these regions have successively won political independence and achieved marked progress in developing their national economy and culture as compared with the past. Along with this development, the population has grown rather quickly. This is not at all a bad thing but a good thing. In the situation of 'great disorder under heaven', in which the broad masses of the population are increasingly awakening, the large population of the Third World constitutes an important condition for strengthening the struggle against imperialism and hegemonism and accelerating social and economic development. ... Today, the world population has more than trebled since Malthus' time, but there has been much greater increase in the material wealth of society, thanks to the efforts of the broad masses of the people in surmounting numerous obstacles. In the twenty-odd years since the founding of the People's Republic, China has increased her products manyfold. The creative power of the people is boundless, and, so is man's ability to exploit and utilize natural resources[14].

The Chinese delegate concluded his rapid review of current attitudes to the world population problem in a typically caustic way:

The pessimistic views spoken by the Superpowers are utterly groundless and are being propagated with ulterior motives.

The Chinese delegate then went on to deal with the true cause of the population problem, as he saw it.

The claim that 'overpopulation is the reason the have-not countries are poor' is a worn-out tune of the Superpowers. What a mass of figures they have calculated in order to prove that the population is too large, the food supply too small and natural resources insufficient! But they never calculate the amount of natural resources they have plundered, the social wealth they have grabbed and the super-profits they have extorted from Asia, Africa and Latin America. Should an account be made of their exploitation, the truth with regard to the population problem will at once be out.

As for the solution, he had only to turn to the Chinese experience:

The deplorable conditions of unemployment and poverty in Old China are universally known. Under the leadership of Chairman Mao Tse-tung and the Chinese Communist Party, the Chinese people, through a long struggle, overthrew imperialism, feudalism and bureaucrat-capitalism which weighed on them like three big mountains, and has since carried out socialist revolution and socialist construction and in a relatively short time succeeded in abolishing unemployment left over from Old China. In the twenty-odd years since the founding of the People's Republic, China's population has increased nearly 60%, from about five hundred million to nearly eight hundred million. Yet in the same period, annual grain output has more than doubled, rising from 110 million to over 250 million tons, ... at present the living standard of our people is still rather low, yet everyone is assured of employment, food and clothing and the livelihood of the people is steadily improving. The broad masses of the Chinese people have never displayed such a high degree of initiative and creativeness. In building socialism, China's vast manpower resources are being used in a planned and rational way. Facts of China's history have completely exploded the various fallacies spread by the Superpowers with regard to the population problem and fully borne out the truth that revolution plus production can solve the problem of feeding the population as set forth by Chairman Mao Tse-tung.

With these few paragraphs of his speech pungently delivered within hours of the opening of the Conference, the Chinese delegate punched a sizeable hole in the notion that a consensus already existed and all the meeting had to do was dot the is and cross the ts. There was no way China could be ignored; no way the speech could be discussed as being merely ritual posturing. In terms of sheer numbers of inhabitants, China was super-preponderant, accounting at the time for some 800 million out of the total world population of around 4000 million. (It was estimated that the four-billion mark could be passed around the time of the Conference itself.)

Moreover, China, in 1974, was a new member of the United Nations. As far as population matters were concerned, this was in a sense her maiden speech. What she said now could influence not only the outcome of the Conference but, over the longer term, the ability of the United Nations as a whole to come to grips with the population question.

Having destroyed from the outset all possible myths, while putting the Superpowers firmly in their allotted place in the dust-bin of history, Mr Huang Shu-Tse to the visible relief of the same delegates who had visions of a Conference shipwrecked on its opening day went on to devote the remainder of his speech to what he described as 'the formulation and implementation of a population policy'.

Our emphasis on combating Imperialism and Hegemonism and developing the national economy and culture as the primary way of solving the population problem does not imply that in our view population policies are of no consequence. ... After overthrowing the rule of the Imperialists and their lackeys, we in China secured the pre-requisites for the planned development of the national economy as well as the planned regulation of the rate of population growth. On the basis of energetically developing production and raising the living standard of the people, China has developed medical and health services throughout the cities and countryside, strengthened the work of maternity and child care, and, while reducing mortality on the one hand, practised birth planning on the other to regulate the birth rate. Our birth planning is not merely birth control as some people understand it to be, but comprises different measures for different circumstances. In densely populated areas, late marriage and birth control are encouraged on the basis of voluntariness, while active treatment is given in cases of sterility....

The Chinese delegate pointed out that in national minority areas and other sparsely populated areas, appropriate measures were taken to facilitate population growth, while birth control advice and help were given to those parents who had too many children and desired birth-control.

Such a policy of planned population growth is in the interest of the thorough emancipation of women and the proper bringing up of future generations as well as of national construction and prosperity.

He admitted that these were

but initial achievements. We have not yet acquired adequate experience in the work of birth planning, and we must continue our efforts.

Of special interest, particularly to those who favoured an active role for the United Nations in population matters, were the Chinese views on the role of international assistance.

Any international technical co-operation and assistance in population matters must follow the principles of complete voluntariness of the parties concerned, strict respect for state sovereignty, absence of any strings attached and promotion of the self-reliance of the recipient countries. We are firmly opposed to the Superpowers intervening by any means in the population policy of other countries on the pretext of what they call 'population explosion' or 'over-population'. We are firmly opposed to the attempt of some international organisations to infringe on the sovereignty of recipient countries by conditioning aid on restricting their population growth rate.

As far as his last remark was concerned, the Chinese delegate did not specify which international organizations he had in mind. Certainly, none of the agencies represented at Bucharest – such as the World Bank or the United Nations Development Programme – would have accepted any suggestion that their aid was conditional on the adoption and implementation of population policies by the receiving countries. They might, however, have felt the need to assure themselves of the existence of a sound basis for development in those countries and to that extent, of course, population would have been a factor.

Argentina joins in the attack

If China had sounded several warning notes at an early stage, Argentina went considerably further. Argentina had not been present at the regional consultation of Latin American countries which was held before Bucharest. Unfettered, therefore, by any previous commitment to the substance of the draft Plan, the head of Argentina's delegation, Ambassador Juan C. Beltramino made a speech to the Plenary in which he indicated that, while some countries had emphasised the accelerated growth of population and pressure on resources, Argentina's problem stemmed rather from a low density of population in relation to resources. He questioned whether it was population growth or the lack of proper utilisation of resources that was the main problem for developing countries. In a well-balanced system population growth would be an asset.

Poor countries could not be expected to restrict their fertility for the benefit of developed countries.

He told the Conference that, 'while Argentina supported the work of international organisations in education and social justice, it believed that the efforts of international family planning organisations must be suppressed because they are negative and not in keeping with ecumenical teachings'.

The Argentine delegation backed up its stance by tabling no less than 68 amendments to the World Plan of Action, including the deletion of the plan's aim to give 'all who so desire' the information and means to practise family planning by 1985. Explaining his stand in the Working Group on the Plan, the Argentine delegate said it was impossible to accept the approach that population should be treated in a 'peculiar and singular manner'.

Both Brazil and the USSR gave early indications that they sympathized with the Argentine amendments. So did Peru. Appearing in military uniform before a dwindling audience at the end of the day, the Deputy Prime Minister Mr Grao de Brigada Enrique Falconi, told the Plenary that it was true that developing countries shared the problem of rapid population growth. But the cause lay in the conditions of poverty and the lack of social justice. Peru had come to the Conference table in a constructive spirit but countries must be allowed to decide these issues for themselves. There could be no generalization at the world level.

Mexico's position was more ambiguous. In a long speech delivered to the Plenary on 21 August 1974, Dr Mario Moya Pelencia, *Secretario de Gobernacion y jefe de la Delegacion*, described Mexico's attempts to achieve economic and social development and the need to place this in its international context of 'greater equity'. However, towards the end of his remarks, he informed the gathering that: *'La politica demographica Mexicana*

100

esta en marcha'. Services of mother and child health were being reinforced and they were already in operation in 700 urban and rural clinics which were serving more than a million women.

The Mexican delegate recognised that there was a role for international assistance but 'it should not be conditioned in any way on the adoption of specific policies, or on the intervention of foreign organisations or transnational firms, less still on the fixing of quantitative targets of a demographic character'.

The incrementalists' position

It can be seen from this account of some of the statements made early on to the Conference that those who believed the draft Plan should be adopted without amendment, were unlikely to get what they wanted. The 'incrementalist position' could be principally identified with a group of Western powers, including the United States, the United Kingdom, Canada and Germany, who felt that rapid population growth was a serious impediment to development[15]. From their perspective, a principal objective of the Bucharest Conference was to build on the statements and resolutions of earlier international gatherings to *increase* the commitment of governments and international agencies to carry out population and family planning programmes. The draft Plan, as presented to the Conference, though not perfect, served this purpose well enough. Thus, the American Secretary for Health Education and Welfare, Mr Caspar Weinberger, addressing the afternoon session of the Plenary on 20 August, indicated that the United States intended to carry out the Plan and to help other countries to do so by providing aid to the development of health services including family planning. Medical diagnosis by satellite, now at an experimental stage, might be extended to other health services and family planning. He offered to get together with other agencies to seek ways of providing additional funds for population programmes. 'It is very possible that our Congress will respond favourably.'

Mr Weinberger also said that the Plan must be strengthened by setting national goals to achieve a replacement level of population by the year 2000. If steps could be taken now the total population by the turn of the century might be 5900 million instead of 6400 million, and 8200 million by the year 2050 instead of the projected 11 million. However, no amendment to this effect was put to the vote in the Working Group on the Plan.

Similarly, Lord Shepherd – the Minister who represented the United Kingdom at Bucharest – affirmed: 'Here we have a basis for a Plan of Action which can commend general support'.

The Scandinavian countries, long-time practitioners of international population assistance, were also firmly behind the draft Plan although, because of their other interests in aid and development, they were more ready to see references to the New International Economic Order included in it than was the United States.

France was more equivocal. Michel Durafour, France's Minister of Labour, made a long and cautious speech to the Plenary in which he rejected any notion of global demographic targets.

> In our eyes there cannot be either today or in the foreseeable future any world population policy, but only the aggregation of the individual policies of nations.

France did not believe that birth-control policies could be pursued as an end in themselves. World population growth, whose risks so many chose to proclaim, would only be a handicap if it meant that the exploitation and distribution of the world's resources was impeded. In any case, the human rights aspects of the question were pre-eminent – above all, the right of couples to decide freely and responsibly on the number and spacing of their children.

Mr Durafour accepted the need for international co-operation as far as demographic research was concerned while being studiously vague about other more direct interventions by the United Nations or other international agencies.

As might be expected from a country where 'co-operation for development' was an important objective of foreign policy, France laid much stress on the need for other wider measures to be taken ... the fight against social evils, progress in the field of health and education, exploitation of resources, including marine resources, the protection of the environment and the recovery of waste, the improvement of the terms of trade between rich and poor countries – all these, in France's eyes, were the fundamental objectives to which efforts should be directed. The World Population Plan of Action had to be looked at within the whole complex of national and international strategies intended to promote economic development and an improvement in the quality of life.

The Third World holds the ring

In this situation, the Third World effectively held the ring. It was clear that if a World Population Plan of Action was to be adopted at Bucharest, changes would have to be made to the draft, but could those changes be acceptable to all?

Several Third World countries held positions similar to that of the 'incrementalist' group of nations. They would have regarded the deletion of all references to the need for a reduction in population growth rates or the spread of family planning as totally unacceptable. A good example was provided by the speech of the delegate from Bangladesh, a country which was to be found among the poorest of the poor. 'I come from that region of the world' the Bangladesh delegate told the Conference

which is experiencing unprecedented population explosion. But nowhere is it more acute and critical than in Bangladesh – a country with 76 million poverty-stricken people compressed in an area of only 55 thousand square miles of land subject to natural calamities like cyclones and floods. As I am speaking here, millions of people are watching helplessly as the fruits of their labour are being washed away by floods described as the worst in twenty years. But even otherwise floods are now occurring with a frequency not experienced before. It is believed that the pressure of increasing population on available land has led to deforestation of river basins causing more erosion, more silting and a creeping ecological imbalance characterised by a pattern of almost annual flooding.

He informed the gathering that the estimated population of Bangladesh had grown from 40.7 million in 1941 to 74.0 million in 1974. The estimated rate of population growth was now 3 per cent. With the prospect of a gradual decline in mortality, together with an unfavourable age structure of the population, Bangladesh might reach an average density of about 2600 people per square mile by the end of the century, as compared with 1350 at the present time.

Our demographic situation leaves us with no alternative but to try to contain and curb our population growth by all possible means and as quickly as possible. Under the leadership of Prime Minister Shaik Mujibur Rahman and with such favourable factors as the willing participation of the people, the homogeneity of our population and compactness of area, we have been able to undertake a sizeable action programme in the field of population. Our nationwide family planning programme is field-oriented and has been integrated with the health services to bring information, services and supplies to the doorsteps of the people.

Another Asian country, Indonesia, took a similar stance by referring in clear and unambiguous terms to the Government's efforts 'to check its rate of population growth in order not to hamper the nation's development and nullify the gains derived from our development efforts'. Professor Soenawar Sakowati, Minister of State for People's Welfare, told the Conference that

Indonesia has given high priority to population problems in its development efforts ... the National Family Planning Co-ordinating Board was established with a view to co-ordinating and expediting family planning activities. The need

103

is felt for an integrated national population policy; the recently established National Commission of Population is at this stage actively engaged in its formulation. To increase the awareness of the importance of population problems several activities have been undertaken in Indonesia within the framework of the World Population Year.... We fully admit that the primary responsibility for solving population problems lies with national governments. At the same time we hold the view that concomitant international measures are still required to complement our own efforts in this field.

Dr Sokowati expressed his gratitude for the assistance given by the World Bank, UNFPA and other agencies to Indonesia's National Family-Planning Programme.

Even in Sub-Saharan Africa, the region of the world where population policies were least developed, there was at least one country ready to argue the case that development without population control was unthinkable. Dr James Mbogo Gekonyo, Senior Deputy Director of Kenya's Ministry of Health told the Conference:

> Our great leader, Mzee Jomo Kenyatta, the President of the Republic of Kenya, has always placed a great importance on all measures, social, economic or political, be they Governmental or voluntary, which are directed towards the overall welfare of each citizen of our country; and indeed towards the welfare of all mankind.... In Kenya's spirit of 'Harambee' or 'working together', it is realised that the destiny of our country lies in the able hands of each one of the people.... The Government of Kenya, after passing through its own school of experience in earlier Development Plans, has evolved further national strategies for the well-being of its people, which among other fundamental decisions now includes defined population programmes.

The delegate from Kenya summarized his country's demographic background. The recorded total population of Kenya at the time of the first national census in 1948 was 5.4 million. In the censuses of 1962 and 1969, the total population had risen to 8.6 and 10.9 million respectively. The total population had therefore approximately doubled in 21 years. The crude death-rate which was estimated at 25 per thousand in 1948 had by 1969 fallen to 17 per thousand. The crude birth-rate, on the other hand, had remained relatively constant at 40 per thousand over the same period. The rate of population growth had risen from 2.5 per cent in 1948 to 3.3 per cent in 1969. The 1969 census showed that approximately 48 per cent of the total population was under 15 years.

Assuming no change in age-specific fertility rates, the population of Kenya would rise from approximately 11 million in 1970 to 34 million in the year 2000. Assuming a decline in age-specific fertility from seven or six in 1969 to four in the year 2000, the total population would still be expected to exceed 28 million.

Dr Gekonyo quoted the following passage from Kenya's Development
Plan for 1974–8:

> In a country already suffering from high unemployment, a high population
> growth rate has only adverse economic effects. First, it will increase the
> proportion of total income that is consumed, thus diminishing the level of
> domestic savings available for investment.
>
> Second, the new population requires more capital, schools, houses, hospitals,
> roads and machines. Only after the new population is provided for will there be a
> net increase in these amenities per person.
>
> Third, when the dependency ratio is increasing, more people will be employed
> simply providing for the new people without increasing new income per person.
> Fourth, the pressure of people on land and capital will reduce the productivity of
> labour.

He then told the Conference about Kenya's family-planning efforts.

> In the past family planning has been carried out in Kenya on an *ad hoc* basis,
> mainly through inadequate Government agencies, voluntary organisations and
> individuals. There have been no targets set for attainment. The Government has
> decided to intensify family planning through a definite programme with set
> targets. It is planned to recruit 640,000 new acceptors in the 1974–1978 plan
> period, thereby helping to avert about 150,000 births and reducing the rate of
> population growth from 3.3% in 1974 to 3.0% in 1978.

If Bangladesh and Kenya were, in their different ways, representative of
those countries who wished to see some tough language about population
control and family planning retained in the Plan, there were others who
regarded any such emphasis as misplaced.

Ambassador Ibrahim Boye of Senegal told the Plenary that questions of
demographic policy were premature. He noted that in Africa only six out of
50 countries had population densities higher than 50 inhabitants per
square kilometre, while 18 had densities lower than 10 inhabitants per
square kilometre. Africa, he said, was not like Asia where population
densities often exceeded 100 per square kilometre.

Senegal's population was very young, in fact people of under 20
constituted 52 per cent of the population, while the over 60s accounted for
only 6 per cent. He admitted that obstacles to development were aggravated by the rapid growth of population but he asked, nevertheless: 'Is it
possible or even desirable to actually limit the Senegalese population? The
Government of Senegal thinks that in the present socio–economic situation, it is not even desirable to limit births.'

Ambassador Boye admitted that certain private initiatives regarding
family planning were taking place in his country, including the provision
of actual family planning services, and these would continue '*là où les*

besoins s'en font réellement sentir'. But, in his view, *'la meilleure pillule, c'est le développement'*. The best pill was development.

So he pleaded with the Conference not to give too great attention, in the World Plan of Action, to achieving a fall in fertility rates. This would only lead to a further diversion of resources away from development.

> Our profound conviction is that today Africa must choose development – eonomic, social and cultural; and tomorrow, perhaps, 'the pill'.

The middle way

If a compromise eventually emerged at Bucharest, it was because a large number of countries from the developing world saw the need for a middle way. It was not a question of presenting population policy and family planning as an alternative to development. Nor was it enough to state that all problems would be solved by economic and social development (and the implementation of the New International Economic Order) and that there was therefore no need for population policy and family planning. What was needed, they argued, was a combination of both approaches though each individual country had, of course, its own ideas as to the precise balance which would be appropriate.

Thus Dr Karen Singh, India's Minister of Health and Family Planning, made it clear that, even though India had been trying to reduce fertility for over two decades, fertility levels could

> be effectively lowered only if family planning became an integral part of a broader strategy to deal with the problems of poverty and under-development.

He recognized that, even with the use of the most advanced technology,

> we cannot go on raising the population in a finite world indefinitely.

However, the real question was more complex:

> How should policy designed to regulate population growth be effectively woven into plans for economic development and social transformation? ... We would, therefore, urge that the main question before this Conference should be how to integrate at the international level those instruments of co-operation and common action which aim at promoting development on a global scale, so that those countries which wish to reduce their fertility levels are enabled to do so effectively.

And Dr Ismail Sapri-Abdalla, Egypt's Minister of Planning, told the Plenary on 23 August:

We agree that each country should have a population policy *définie souverainment* with the double aim of accelerating development and ensuring voluntary parenthood. Egypt has known its demographic crises. After half a century of growth oscillating around 1.7%, the maximum rate of 2.54% was attained in 1965 as a result of the fall in mortality from 29 to 14.5 per thousand and above all as a result of the fall in infant mortality from 153 to 116, a figure which even so remains high. With this situation our country has since the revolution of 1952 followed a firm policy of economic and social development without at the same time neglecting family planning. We believe with conviction that a development policy without family planning runs the risk of meeting serious difficulties but a family planning programme without a development policy will certainly run into the sand.

The Egyptian delegate went on to illustrate this double approach: an economic growth rate which had attained 6.7 per cent over the period of 1956 to 1966, though reduced 'after the Israeli aggression of 1967 and resulting military expenditure' to less than 5 per cent in recent years; an industrial policy which had permitted industrial production to increase by 400 per cent in 22 years; progress in agriculture and the countryside thanks to agrarian reform, the Aswan High Dam, electrification of villages etc; the spread of education – 80 per cent of children between 6 and 12 years in school, a quarter of a million students at university, 3000 engineers and 2000 doctors graduating each year; important steps taken towards the emancipation of women – all the above being measures which would have a direct or indirect effect on the structure of the family.

At the same time the Government had created a 'Population and Family Planning Council' whose task was to mobilize public opinion, counteract superstitions which still prevailed about the voluntary control of births and to see to it that the necessary information and services relating to contraception were provided.

Dr Abdalla noted with satisfaction that the birth-rates had declined one per 1000 per year since 1967 and stood at 2.24 per cent in 1972. By the end of the decade he was persuaded that the rate would fall below 2 per cent.

Egypt's population policy, which is integrated in our National Plan for Economic and Social Development, is aimed to ensure an annual fall in natality of 1 per thousand per year between now and 1982, so that our population would not exceed 41 million on that date instead of the 49 millions which a simple projection of present rates of growth would lead us to expect.

Among the other delegates from North Africa who spoke at the Conference, the remarks of the representative of Morocco were particularly interesting. Dr Abdul Kader Laraqi, Secretary-General of the Ministry of Public Health in Morocco, told the Conference that his Government had established a 'Commission Superieure de la Population', as well as regional commissions at the prefectoral or provincial level, to draw up and co-ordinate a Governmental policy as far as population growth was concerned, and to supervise the implementation and execution of that policy. In Morocco, population density was 37 inhabitants per square kilometre in 1973, but the distribution was very uneven with nine-tenths living in the north-western half of the country along the Atlantic or Mediterranean coasts and in certain large urban centres in the interior. In 1971 a census had been held which indicated that Morocco had over 15 million inhabitants, that the birth-rate was around 50 per thousand and the death-rate around 17 per thousand, having fallen from 35 at the beginning of the century. The annual average rate of population growth between 1960 and 1971 was estimated at 2.7 per cent.

Like other speakers, Dr Laraqi emphasized the need to set family planning within the framework of other programmes of social and economic development, particularly the fight against illiteracy and programmes aimed at improving the status of women. However, he pointed out that:

> We have too often linked the problem of family planning purely to the question of the emancipation of women. I would like to recall that the man also plays a role of the first importance *'dans l'application de toute politique de régulation d'equilibre de foyer'*. An effort to educate and inform men about their role should be undertaken alongside efforts to educate and motivate women.

He also pointed out the urgent need to reduce infant mortality:

> One of the major obstacles lying in the path of family planning programmes is the high rate of infant mortality which we encounter in most parts of the Third World. How can we ask a couple to limit the number of their children if no reasonable guarantee can be given them about the chance of those children's survival?... It seems to me to be vain to hope for any change in attitude and behaviour as far as procreation is concerned if the fundamental reasons for such behaviour remain unchanged. And among these reasons – and there are many – infant mortality occupies a special place.

Dr Laraqi had some thoughtful remarks to make about the administration and organisation of family-planning programmes.

> The fair distribution of the budget, the evaluation of costs, a proper study of the needs in terms of personnel, of equipment, of contraceptive supplies and educational material; the training of qualified people, the retraining of people already in place, statistical evaluation of the results of the programme, the conduct of studies and research, the publication and distribution of documents ... these are all important factors in a planned population policy.

He called for an avoidance of excessive propaganda, an emphasis on methods of *'vulgarisation et motivation'* which were 'as agreeable as possible'.

Dr Laraqi also raised an issue which was of a moral nature and in its way fundamental to the population debate. He believed that, from the moral point of view, three principles were important:

–recognition of the sovereign right of governments to adopt the demographic policy of their choice;

–whatever measures were adopted to influence demographic variables should be founded on internationally recognized principles and based on respect for the fundamental rights of man without distinction of race, sex, language or religion;

–absolute respect for liberty, that is to say the possibility of choice: for nations to choose their own policies and for a couple to choose the size of its family.

Dr Laraqi drew the attention of the Conference to the possible inconsistency between national policy and personal choice. What if the sum of the choices of the individual families did not square with the demographic policy of the nation? If one admitted that the state had a role to play, how far could one go?

The delegate from Morocco raised these questions but did not, of course, answer them within the compass of his short speech. For some delegates these were matters of genuine concern. They believed, as President Eisenhower had – at least at one point – believed, that 'the State had no business in the bedroom'. For others, the issue seemed largely academic. There was so much distance still to be covered if all unmet needs for family planning services were to be filled, that the problem of too many 'wanted' children seemed hardly to arise. That there was no obvious way, either theoretically or practically, of ensuring that the sum of individual choices regarding family size added up to an optimum choice for a nation, or that the choices of nations added up to the optimum policy taking the world as a whole, was therefore a matter of secondary concern.

The position of the Vatican

If China's statement to the Plenary had been awaited with considerable interest, so too was that of the Representative of the Holy See. Six years earlier Pope Paul VI had launched his encyclical *Humanae Vitae* on a shocked world. Would the Vatican's position have changed in the meantime and, if so, in what direction?

On the whole, the Vatican's remarks to the World Population Conference were a discouragement to those who had hoped that the Catholic Church might be moving towards a more liberal view of population and family planning programmes. The Vatican's representative stressed above all the need for economic and social progress.

> The first thing which the people have a right to expect from our Conference is, therefore, an energetic appeal, backed up by suitable recommendations, for the inauguration of a new order in development, called for by Paul VI in his letter to the Secretary-General of the United Nations on the occasion of the Special Session of the General Assembly last April. Would the developed world accept the invitation to bring a remedy to the formidable 'social inequality' of today – that of individuals and that of whole peoples which is still more striking? The egoism of the rich plays a larger part in this than the fertility of the poor.

Like some other delegates, the representative of the Vatican saw the call for increased international development efforts not merely in terms of a transfer of resources from rich to poor countries but also – as a necessary consequence – in terms of changed patterns of life and consumption in the developed world.

In this sense, the text of the draft World Population Plan of Action represented only a segment of the problem.

> As we understand it a genuine population policy will seek to establish the equitable sharing of resources and dwelling spaces; the contribution of different age groups and classes to the national and international life of today and of tomorrow; the responsibility and tasks of States and of the World Community with regard to populations already in existence and those yet to come.

Having said that, the delegate of the Holy See told the conference that he thought the Plan was one-sided in paying too great attention to the problem of demographic variables....

> We fear that to concentrate exclusively on demographic growth, to make it a privileged subject in campaigns on development, to channel huge resources into the solution of this one problem, is to upset the perspectives and only to prepare for mankind new frustrations.

And he had an interesting comment on the frequent reference to the right of married couples to freedom of choice.

> This principle is repeated all through the draft Plan but is interpreted only as a right to 'the limitation of birth'. The intention of those who were the first to insert this in international texts was, above all else, to protect the freedom of the married couples against the intrusion of an indiscreet policy for the reduction of fertility.

Finally, the Vatican's delegate turned to the question of contraception.

110

We will not pass over the fact that the passages of the Plan relative to contraception and the methods of preventing birth are not acceptable to us. They are not acceptable in what concerns contraceptives, in regard to which the Catholic Church has already made her position clear, and is aware of the need to reaffirm and maintain her teaching without ambiguity. Nor are these passages acceptable because we have no guarantee that those who have recourse to abortion and to its legalisation will not appeal to them.

The abortion issue did not dominate the discussions in Bucharest in any sense, but the remarks of the Vatican both in the Plenary and in the Committee on this subject were intended to ensure, lest there be any doubt, that the topic could never be ignored. As we shall see ten years later, at the International Conference on Population held in Mexico, the links between abortion and family planning, particularly in the context of the Chinese experience, had a much more dramatic impact on the proceedings and, to some extent, on the whole direction of international assistance in the population field[16].

7

The World Population Plan of Action

A historic moment

The adoption by the World Population Conference in August 1974 of a World Population Plan of Action has to be seen as one of the high points of the United Nations' endeavours in this, or indeed in any other, field of activity. Admittedly the event was not attended by the emotional fervour which had been felt two years earlier as the United Nations Conference on the Human Environment wound up its deliberations in Stockholm. But the achievement was nonetheless real and important. Indeed, it could be argued that if anything the accomplishment was greater than Stockholm's. There the overwhelming problem had been to persuade the developing countries that the new enthusiasm of the rich countries for environmental policy was not simply a device to hold back the Third World on its path to development. With population, the problems of acceptance were more varied and sometimes more difficult. Though the goal of both Conferences was the same, namely a World Plan of Action adopted by consensus, the World Population Conference had to cover a considerably greater distance, and over rockier terrain, to reach the same point.

Changes to the draft plan

As the Conference entered its second week, the opinions which had been expressed in the Plenary found their counterpart in amendments discussed, and voted, in the committees and in particular in the Working Group on the draft Plan. According to *Planet*, the conference's daily journal, the first Chapter of the World Population Plan of Action 'had been systematically stripped of all references to the need to curb population growth, as a result of amendments adopted by the working group over the weekend.' Major changes had been made to six of the first 12 paragraphs and numerous word changes had been approved. Five amendments were put to a vote and on one occasion a roll call vote was taken[1].

The main effect of the changes to Chapter 1 – the section of the Plan which set out the Background – was to give greater emphasis to social and economic development, reduce the role of population growth as an influence on development, and aid the General Assembly's call for a new international economic order. Some Asian countries were plainly upset by the turn of events.

Our part of the world is sinking under the weight of population,

pleaded Mr A. A. Choudhuri, of Bangladesh.

Our growth rate is 3%. We are short of food, short of educational facilities, short of everything. Every flood sinks us. The Plan must be for everyone, not just for some countries.

Another plea came from Indonesia, a warning not to change the focus of the Conference to cover all economic and social development but to keep a balance between development and population.

In the developing countries we are still fighting hard to focus on population.

Altogether the Working Group spent nearly 20 hours debating the first 12 paragraphs of the 93 paragraph text. Most of the amendments to Chapter 1 were proposed jointly by Argentina, Egypt, Ethiopia, India, Italy, Lesotho, Liberia and Yugoslavia following informal consultations to reach a compromise on separate proposals.

Background

Some of the major changes to Chapter 1 were the following (italic type indicates the language finally adopted by the Conference and appearing in the World Population Plan of Action)[2]:

The draft Plan began by stating: 'The promotion of economic development and the quality of life requires co-ordination of action in all major socio-economic fields, including the field of population.' In the text as it emerged from the Working Group, the words, *'which is the inexhaustible source of creativity and a determining factor of progress'* were tacked on at the end of the sentence after 'population'. The beginning of the fourth sentence of the first paragraph which had read in the draft 'The explicit aim of the World Population Plan of Action is to affect population variables', was changed to read '*The explicit aim of the World Population Plan of Action is to help co-ordinate population trends and the trends of economic and social development,*' thus omitting the aim 'to affect population variables'.

A proposal from ten Socialist countries added two new sentences before the final sentence in paragraph one:

> The basis for an effective solution of population problems is, above all, socio-economic transformation. A population policy may have a certain success if it constitutes an integral part of socio-economic development; its contribution to the solution of world development problems is hence only partial, as is the case with the other sectoral strategies.

There was bitter debate over a move by the Argentine group to amend the second sentence of paragraph two in the draft Plan, which read: 'Where trends of population growth, distribution and structure are out of balance with social, economic and environmental factors, they can constitute serious barriers to the achievement of sustained development.' A number of developing countries spoke against amendment, but on a vote 31 countries approved the new sentence with 21 against. It read:

> Where trends of population growth, distribution and structure are out of balance with social, economic and environmental factors, they can at certain stages of development create additional difficulties for the achievement of sustained development.

The United States lost by 51 votes to one with 15 abstentions its attempt to reject an amendment by the Argentine group providing for an inclusion of a reference to the establishment of the New International Economic Order and the programme of action to achieve it, adopted by the Sixth Special Session of the United Nations General Assembly.

There was also sharp controversy over the Argentine group's proposal to delete the final sentence of paragraph 3, which drew attention to efforts already being made to reduce population growth as a matter of urgency. By 38 votes to 35, with seven abstentions, the sentence was deleted.

A final paragraph in the Background section of the draft Plan had discussed the phenomenon of demographic inertia:

> Because of the relatively high proportions of children and youth in the populations of less developed countries, declines in fertility levels in these countries will not be fully reflected in declines in population growth rates until some decades later. To illustrate this demographic inertia, it may be noted that, for less developed countries, even if replacement levels of fertility – approximately two children per completed family – had been achieved in 1970 and maintained thereafter, their total population would still grow from a 1970 total of 2.5 billion to about 4.4 billion before it would stabilise during the second half of the 21st century. In these circumstances, the population of the world as a whole would grow from 3.6 billion to 5.8 billion. This example of demographic

inertia demonstrates that whatever the fertility policy formulated, socio-economic development, particularly in less developed countries, must continue to respond to growing population for many decades to come. It also demonstrates that countries wishing to affect their population growth must anticipate future demographic trends and take appropriate decisions and actions well in advance.

After a vigorous debate in the Working Group, the last sentences of paragraph 12 were finally amended to read:

> *This example of demographic inertia, which will lead to a growth of population for many decades to come, demonstrates that whatever population policies may be formulated, socio-economic development must be accelerated in order to provide for significant increase in levels of living. Efforts made by developing countries to speed up economic growth must be viewed by the entire international community as a global endeavour to improve the quality of life for all people of the world, supported by just utilisation of the world's wealth, resources and technology in the spirit of the new international economic order. It also demonstrates that countries wishing to affect their population growth must anticipate future demographic trends and take appropriate decisions and actions in their plans for economic and social development well in advance.*

The amended paragraph 12 was adopted by 41 votes to 31 with 16 abstentions[3].

From the 'incrementalists' point of view this latter amendment was particularly significant. The language of the draft Plan implied that population policy should not merely aim at the attainment of replacement levels of fertility; it should, because of the phenomenon of 'demographic inertia, in a sense 'aim off' so as to anticipate and avoid future population growth. In the text as adopted the emphasis was changed to the need to accommodate future population growth through economic and social development.

Principles and objectives

The next chapter of the Plan dealt with its Principles and Objectives. A preambular paragraph (13 in the draft, 14 in the Plan as adopted) was amended to stress the point that the formulation and implementation of population policies was

> *the sovereign right of each nation. This right is to be exercised in accordance with national objectives and needs and without external interference, taking into account universal solidarity in order to improve the quality of life of the peoples of the world. The main responsibility for national population policies and programme lies with national authorities.*

The new paragraph went on to recognize, however, that '*international co-operation should play an important role in accordance with the principles of the United Nations charter*'.

This chapter of the Plan was also influenced, as indeed were all other sections of the Plan, by the countries who pressed for a 'redistribution of wealth'. A new paragraph (13j) was included as follows:

> *In the democratic formulation of national population goals and policies, consideration must be given, together with other economic and social factors, to the supplies and characteristics of natural resources and to the quality of the environment and particularly to all aspects of food supply including productivity of rural areas. The demand for vital resources increases not only with growing population but also growing per capita consumption; attention must be directed to the just distribution of resources and to the minimization of wasteful aspects of their use throughout the world.*

Finally, it must be said that this chapter of the Plan contained four new principles (new in the sense that they were not in the draft) which reflected the regional consultations held before Bucharest. Two were especially important. Their inclusion to some extent compensated the incrementalists for battles they had lost earlier. Paragraph 14(f) stated:

> *All couples and individuals have the basic right to decide freely and responsibly the number and spacing of their children and to have the information, education and means to do so; the responsibility of couples and individuals in the exercise of this right takes into account the needs of their living and future children, and their responsibilities towards the community;*

An amendment by the representative of Brazil to delete the second part of the sentence beginning with the words 'the responsibility of couples' was rejected by 70 votes to seven, with ten abstentions. Following a procedural question, the chairman ruled that he would put to a vote the word 'couples' and the words 'couples and individuals' to determine the preference of the Working Group. Forty-one were in favour of the word 'couples' and 48 were in favour of the words 'couples and individuals' with six abstentions. The Chairman therefore interpreted that the words 'couples and individuals' were the preference of the Working Group and declared them adopted.

The inclusion of the word 'individuals' in the text of the Plan, even though linked with 'couples', was not achieved easily. Though a small enough matter in itself, the reluctance of some delegates, for example, the representative of Ireland, to admit that contraceptives might be available even outside the context of marriage was a nice illustration of the way in which points of considerable substance might lie behind the technicalities of drafting.

Paragraph 14(h) dealt with the status of women:

Women have the right to complete integration in the development process particularly by means of an equal access to education and equal participation in social, economic, cultural and political life. In addition, the necessary measures should be taken to facilitate this integration with family responsibilities which should be fully shared by both partners.

Both in the Conference meeting rooms and outside the formal proceedings, the question of women's rights and the way in which these rights should be reflected in the outcome of the Conference was a matter of considerable interest. Luminaries of the women's movement, such as Margaret Mead and Germaine Greer, were in evidence in Bucharest throughout the Conference. If any delegates were unaware of the relevance of 'status of women' issues to the matters under discussion before they came to Bucharest, they could hardly have remained in ignorance after their arrival. Paragraph 14(h) is only one example of the way in which the draft Plan was strengthened so as to give greater emphasis to the role of women.

Population growth targets

It was in the discussions on the third section of the Plan – Recommendations for Action – that the political differences seemed to be at their sharpest. Paragraph 15 of the draft Plan had noted that, if governments which had population objectives were successful in achieving these objectives, population growth in the less-developed countries would decline from the present annual rate of 2.4 per cent to about 2.0 per cent by 1985, would remain largely unchanged at less than 0.9 per cent in the more developed countries and would, therefore, decline in the world as a whole from 2.0 per cent to about 1.7 per cent. 'These rates', the draft had proposed 'which must be revised as new national targets are set, should be used in the review and appraisal of this Plan.' In other words, in cautious and roundabout language, the draft did in fact suggest some overall demographic goals. The Working Group would have none of it. By 72 votes to 18 with ten abstentions, it deleted the final sentence. The representatives of Sweden and the United States made reservations.

And where the draft Plan indicated that 'countries which consider that their present or expected rates of population growth hamper their goals of promoting human welfare are invited, if they have not done so, to consider setting quantitative population growth targets', the Plan as it emerged from the Working Group (Paragraph 17) merely invited countries to *'consider adopting population policies, within the framework of socio-economic . development...'.*

Family planning

From the incrementalists' point of view, as well as from the standpoint of those developing countries who saw the urgent need for it, another key issue was the extent to which references to the importance of family planning would be retained in the final text. On August 27, working under pressure of time, the Working Group rejected by 58 votes to 42 the proposal contained in paragraph 27(b) of the draft Plan to: 'make available, to all persons who so desire, if possible by the end of the Second United Nations Development Decade, but not later than 1985, the necessary information and education about family planning and the means to practise family planning effectively and in accordance with their cultural values.'

The alternative text which the Working Group adopted merely talked of the need to *'encourage appropriate education concerning responsible parenthood and make available to persons who so desire advice on the means of achieving it'*. Like so many other amendments whose effect was to pull some of the teeth from the draft Plan, the new sub-paragraph was proposed by Argentina.

Yugoslavia, Mexico and the United States made public protests at the decision. Mr Philander P. Claxton, the American delegate, maintained that it was a step back from the position already taken by the UN through resolutions of the Economic and Social Council. 'It will hurt women and children most', he said. Miss Julia Henderson, Secretary-General of the International Planned Parenthood Federation, also expressed dismay that the decision removed all sense of urgency from the provision of family-planning services. 'It virtually amounts to no plan, no action', she said.

Another Argentine amendment had the effect of filleting paragraph 25 which stated: 'While no universal family size norm is recommended, it is recognised that the majority of the people of the world lives in countries that wish to reduce present fertility levels, and a larger majority lives in countries that favour small family-size norms.' The text as adopted by the Working Group, and subsequently by the Conference, merely stated: *'This Plan of Action recognises the variety of national goals with regard to fertility and does not recommend any world family-size norm.'* (WPPA Para 27).

However, some important paragraphs in the draft Plan survived almost intact in the final version. Para 28 of the draft invited governments 'to consider integrating or coordinating family planning programmes with health and other programmes designed to raise the quality of family life'. In the text as approved by the Conference this became:

> *Governments which have family planning programmes are invited to consider integrating and co-ordinating those services with health and other services designed to raise the quality of family life, including family allowances and maternity benefits, and to consider including family planning services in their official health social insurance systems.* (WPPA Paragraph 30).

Reduction on fertility levels

Most importantly, the main thrust of Paragraph 34 of the draft which reintroduced, if in an oblique way, the notion of targets, was retained.
Paragraph 34 of the draft read:

> The achievement of the population growth and mortality objectives for 1985 ... implies an average crude birth-rate of around 30 per 1000 in the less developed regions. This compares with the present average of about 38 per 1000 which, according to United Nations' projections, would decline to about 34 per 1000 in 1985. Therefore, if the above growth and mortality objectives are to be reached in 1985, substantial national and international efforts would need to be expended urgently to reduce fertility levels in less developed countries that wish to reduce these levels.

The text adopted by the Working Group for this paragraph (*WPPA Paragraph 36*) read:

> *The projections in para 16 of future declines in rates of population growth, and those in para 22 concerning increased expectations of life, are consistent with declines in the birth-rate of the developing countries as a whole from the present level of 38 per 1000 to 30 per 1000 by 1985; in these projections, birth-rates in the developed countries remain in the region of 15 per 1000. To achieve by 1985 these levels of fertility would require substantial national efforts, by those countries concerned, in the field of socio-economic development and population policies, supported upon request, by adequate international assistance. Such efforts would also be required to achieve the increase in expectation of life.*

Thus, the notion of targets for fertility reduction was retained in the WPPA if only as the mathematical consequence of other assumptions about mortality and population growth rates.

However, in the concertina process of negotiation, a further note of caution was struck in the draft's Paragraph 35 which followed.

The draft Plan had stated in clear and positive language:

119

countries which have a very high birth-rate may consider taking action compatible with the principles and objectives of the Plan (including paragraph 16 above) to reduce these rates by about 5 to 10 per 1000 before 1985.

The Working Group rejected by 43 votes to 40, with eight abstentions, an amendment to delete the words 'by 1985' and also rejected by 39 votes to 38 with 14 abstentions, a further amendment to add at the end of the paragraph, the sentence 'in view of the different circumstances in each country the formulation of goals for population growth is undesirable'. The Working Group finally adopted, by 57 votes to 19, with 10 abstentions, a text which read:

> *In the light of the principles of this Plan of Action countries which consider their birth-rates detrimental to their national purposes are invited to consider setting quantitative goals and implementing policies that may lead to the attainment of such goals by 1985. Nothing herein should interfere with the Sovereignty of any Government to adopt or not to adopt such quantitative goals.* (WPPA Paragraph 37)

These discussions about rates and targets were among the warmest of the Conference and the outcome often hung in the balance. For example, the Chinese delegate argued strongly that the text of draft Paragraph 34 failed to take into account those countries who wished to increase their populations or who had no population growth problems. Africa, for example, needed – so he asserted – more people to make up for losses during the days of the slave trade. A spokesman for Brazil argued that the implication that it was desirable to reduce the birth-rates of developing countries was quite unacceptable, while the Algerian delegate thought any target would be restricting even for interested countries – because of the danger that it could not be achieved.

The Philippines and Indonesia spoke out in favour of the new text (WPPA Paragraph 36). Miss Jean Thompson of the United Kingdom pleaded for an understanding of the great effort that had been made to achieve neutrality and to avoid making a judgement on any country. The proposed Chinese amendment, she said, would have deleted any reference to achieving 'future decline in rates of population growth or to target dates'.

In the event the Chinese amendment was rejected by 49 votes to 36, with 6 abstentions.

Draft Paragraph 35 was even more controversial since it proposed quantitative goals and the implementation of the policies to achieve them by 1985. Algeria, proposing deletion of the goals, found support from Tanzania, who feared that limited resources and the risk of failure would make governments reluctant to fix targets for fertility reduction. But the Algerian motion failed by 43 to 40.

China countered with a proposal to state that uniformity of goals for population growth was undesirable. Cuba and Tanzania came to China's support, but the Philippines delegate, Miss Mercedes Concepcion, quickly pointed out that the wording already covered the possibility of countries seeking to increase rather than decrease their population. China lost by the narrowest vote of the Conference, 39 to 38 with 14 abstentions.

Recommendations for implementation

The fourth chapter of the draft Plan was entitled: 'Recommendations for Implementation'. Section A dealt with the role of national governments. Even though the Working Group was by this time showing signs of fatigue, some important changes between draft and final version can still be noticed. For example, Paragraph 81 of the draft Plan stated: 'The success of this Plan of Action will largely depend on the actions undertaken by national Governments. The major burden of development of a country will continue to fall on the country itself.' By 35 votes to 32 with 15 abstentions, the Working Group adopted an amendment to add the words, '*and governments are urged to utilise fully the support of the inter-governmental and non-governmental organisations*'. This amendment was significant in that it sought to establish the legitimacy of international assistance. Of special interest was the reference to the role of non-governmental organizations. As we have noted earlier, the work of the NGOs in the field of population and family planning has been particularly vital. The fact that this was recognized at Bucharest was a considerable achievement since many of the delegates came from countries where the role of the NGO was often either not well understood or not appreciated.

The other three paragraphs relating to the role of national governments survived unamended in the final version. They read as follows:

97. *This Plan of Action recognises the responsibility of each Government to decide on its own policies and to devise its own programmes of action for dealing with the problems of population and economic and social progress. Recommendations, insofar as they relate to national Governments, are made with due regard to the need for variety and flexibility in the hope that they may be responsive to major needs in the population field as perceived and interpreted by national Governments. However, national policies should be formulated and implemented without violating, and with due promotion of, universally accepted standards of human rights.*

98. *An important role of Governments with regard to the Plan of Action is to determine and assess the population problems and needs of their countries in the light of their political, social, cultural, religious and economic conditions; such an undertaking should be carried out systematically and periodically so as to promote informed, rational and dynamic decision-making in matters of population and development.*

99. The effect of national action or inaction in the fields of population may, in certain circumstances, extend beyond natural boundaries; such international implications are particularly evident with regard to aspects of morbidity, population concentration and international migration, but may also apply to other aspects of population concern.

This last paragraph – and in particular the last few words '... may also apply to other aspects of population concern' – was of some interest in that it attempted to establish, however hesitantly, some qualification to the principle that nations are entirely sovereign in matters of population. Two years earlier, at the United Nations Conference on the Human Environment, the nations of the world had adopted Principle 21 of the Declaration on the Human Environment which, while recognizing that States had 'the Sovereign right to exploit their own resources pursuant to their own environmental policies', also recognized that they had 'the responsibility to ensure that activities within their jurisdiction or control do not cause damage to the environment of other States or of areas beyond the limits of national jurisdiction'. Now the same idea was being expressed in more hesitant and tortured language as far as population was concerned. One nation's population growth might be another nation's social problem or even threaten the 'global commons'.

Role of international assistance

The second section of the chapter of the Plan entitled 'Recommendations for Implementation' dealt with the role of international co-operation. To those who had followed the steady evolution of international assistance in the field of population, and in particular United Nations action in this area, the outcome of the debate on this section was of course of special interest. In the event, it survived unscathed. Though, inevitably, certain amendments were adopted aiming at increasing total flows of development assistance, as opposed to specifically population assistance, the final language was consistent with, and complementary, to the corpus of texts which had over the years established the locus of international assistance in the population field and, more particularly, the role of the United Nations.

100. International co-operation, based on the peaceful co-existence of States having different social systems, should play a supportive role in achieving the roles of the Plan of Action. This supportive role could take the form of direct assistance, technical or financial, in response to national and regional requests and be additional to economic development assistance or the form of other activities, such as monitoring progress, undertaking comparative research in the area of population, resources and consumption, and furthering the exchange among countries of information and policy experiences in the field of population and consumption. Assistance should be provided on the basis of respect for Sovereignty of the recipient country and its national policy.

101. The General Assembly of the United Nations, the Economic and Social Council, the Governing Council of the United Nations Development Programme/ United Nations Fund for Population Activities and other competent legislative and policy-making bodies of the Specialised Agencies and the various inter-governmental organisations are urged to give careful consideration to this Plan of Action and to ensure an appropriate response to it....

102. Countries sharing similar population conditions and problems are invited to consider jointly this Plan of Action, exchange experiences in relevant fields and elaborate those aspects of the Plan that are of particular relevance to them. The United Nations regional economic commissions and other regional bodies of the United Nations system should play an important role towards this end.

103. There is a special need for training in the field of population. The United Nations system, Governments and, as appropriate, non-governmental organisations are urged to give recognition to that need and priority to the measures necessary to meet it, including information, education and services for family planning.

104. Developed countries, and other countries able to assist, are urged to increase their assistance to developing countries in accordance with the goals of the Second United Nations Development Decade and, together with international organisations, make that assistance available in accordance with the national priorities of receiving countries. In this respect, it is recognised, in view of the magnitude of the problems and the consequent national requirements for funds, that considerable expansion of international assistance in the population field is required for the proper implementation of this plan of action.

One small, but significant, amendment occurred on the next paragraph where the co-ordinating role of the United Nations Fund for population activities was stressed. Paragraph 105 read as follows:

105. It is suggested that the expanding, but still insufficient, international assistance in population and developing matters requires increased co-operation; the United Nations Fund for Population Activities is urged, in co-operation with all organisations responsible for national population assistance, to produce a guide for international assistance in population matters which would be made available to recipient countries and institutions and be revised periodically.[4]

The final paragraph of this section dealt with international non-governmental organisations, and could be seen as a rather unusual (though wholly merited) tribute by governments to the work of the private sector, in particular bodies like the International Planned Parenthood Federation.

106. International non-governmental organisations are urged to respond to the goals and policies of the Plan of Action by co-ordinating their activities with those of other non-governmental organisations, and with the relevant bi-lateral and multi-lateral organisations, by expanding their support for national institutions and organisations dealing with population questions, and by co-operating in the promotion of widespread knowledge of the goals and policies of the Plan of Action and, when requested, by supporting national and private institutions and organisations dealing with population questions.

In purely literary or artistic terms, the six paragraphs on the role of international co-operations (100–106) could have been better expressed. They were certainly as long-winded as any others in the document. But the lack of art was less important than the fact that these paragraphs were approved by the Working Group and in turn by the Plenary. There is no doubt that those who first called for an inter-governmental conference on population did so not merely because the exchange of views and information would be important (as it was) but also in the hope that the conclusions of the conference would give the necessary impetus to increased international collaboration, and – more particularly – would help the process of co-ordinating and directing the work of multifarious bodies active in the field of population under the banner of the United Nations.

It was an exercise that was not without its attendant risks. As Finkle and Crane comment: 'A failure to reach consensus at Bucharest would have brought into question the legitimacy of these international population activities and weakened the political support essential to their effectiveness'[5].

In retrospect, the result was worthwhile. In spite of the (sometimes painful) compromises that had to be made along the way, the Bucharest World Population Conference did indeed serve to move the United Nations, and in particular the still new United Nations Fund for Population Activities (UNFPA) to the centre of the stage. Though the Population Commission, and the Population Division, had borne the brunt of the preparations for the Conference, Mr Salas as Executive-Director of UNFPA had been – as we have seen – charged with the responsibilities for World Population Year; moreover, it was clear that countries which had come to Bucharest looking for assistance for their population activities – whether it was census-taking or full scale family-planning programmes – were aware that, realistically speaking, UNFPA was the best, and possibly only, source of support, a role that was confirmed in the WPPA.

In the margin of the Conference, Cuba and UNFPA signed a $3.8 million agreement under which UNFPA was to provide material and technical support for Cuba's population programme. This was the 17th long-term agreement concluded by UNFPA (the first with a socialist country). With the blessing of the Conference being given in clear, if not ringing tones, there seemed to be no reason why the pace of international assistance in population should not accelerate.

In his own speech to the Conference Mr Salas discussed in some detail the new role of the UNFPA.

If there is a need for caution and for extreme sensitivity at a national level, for example, in dealings between official government agencies and individual families, this must be equally true of the dealings between external agencies and the government of people of any particular country. The cardinal principle which has governed UNFPA's activities over the last five years is that the Fund should respond to countries' own assessments of their needs and priorities.

Of course, external aid should be used at the point and in the form where the effect it produces will be of the greatest benefit to the recipient country. There is, therefore, inevitably a creative dialogue between donor and recipient. Sometimes, perhaps, we should call it 'creative tension'. But I think it is fair to say so far the Fund's programme has been agreed to in an atmosphere of full confidence and mutual trust.

Towards the end of his speech, Mr Salas turned to the question of the Fund's resources:

Perhaps the word 'explosion' is overworked, particularly at population meetings. But we can truly say in all modesty, that these last five years have indeed seen an explosion within UNFPA, both in terms of activities and resources.

So far, the Fund has supported population activities in some 90 developing countries and areas or almost all of the developing world. We have financed, or helped to finance 900 projects covering such diversified fields as census-taking, improvement of vital statistics, registration, maternal and child health programmes, family planning services, communication and education, studies on law and population, and training of personnel and institutional building in many different areas. The largest programme, amounting to US $40 million over 5 years has very recently been formulated and agreed upon with the Government of India. That our approach is also acceptable to the donors is clear from the fact that they have increased in numbers from 5 to 67 – most of them developing countries – in a brief span of 5 years and have made available in support of the Fund's activities nearly US $175 million over the same period.

If you consider that the Fund in 1969 had less than US $3 million, you will I am sure agree that I am justified in speaking of the 'Population Fund Explosion'.

Mr Salas was, however, careful not to give the impression that the Fund's coffers were bursting. Indeed, the very reverse was the case. Current trends showed a steadily increasing demand for the Fund's services – he estimated that about US $500 million would be needed for the period 1974 to 1977 to respond to the most urgent requirements of the developing countries for the Fund's support. This rapid expansion of demand on the Fund testified to the viability of the multilateral approach in this most sensitive of all matters, and to the acceptability of the Fund's own procedures, developed as they had been in co-operation with the countries.

125

Out of this co-operation, a momentum has been generated, and an atmosphere has been created in which it is possible to think in terms of solutions to problems which at one time seemed insoluble. The question we put to you today is this: Will that momentum and that atmosphere be maintained?

Mr Salas ended his speech by referring to the World Population Plan of Action which, he said, could be a milestone of the greatest importance.

It could guide and re-inforce the activities of the Fund and at the same time the Fund could play an important role in the realisation of the Plan. The Plan will, of course, only take on its full meaning when it is translated into actual programme at the international and national levels – programmes appropriate to the needs.... The UNFPA, with the co-operation of the United Nations system and other intergovernmental and non-governmental bodies, is ready to offer every possible assistance to enable countries to solve these problems themselves in the long run. We need hardly add that the UNFPA can only discharge this historic task if those members of the international community who have supported us so generously in the past continue to support us even more generously in the future.

The last paragraph of Mr Salas's address to the World Population Conference in Bucharest was a model of eloquence.

I do not believe that it is possible to underestimate the challenge and the significance of this moment. To solve the population problems of countries will require more from us in a shorter time than ever before in the history of mankind. It will require a long-sustained effort without any guarantee that the final aim will be achieved. Yet without the effort, can there be any prospect for a just and peaceful world in the future? The ancient philosophers of Asia in their wisdom, stressed the need for a balance and harmony between man and his world. Without a sane and orderly approach to the problems of population, there can be no balance and no harmony.

Adoption of the World Population Plan of Action

The Working Group completed its review of the 93 paragraphs of the draft World Population Plan of Action on 28 August 1974 at 21.30 hours and approved it for transmission to the full Conference. After a marathon 15 sessions and, as one delegate put it, 'no hot meals for eight days' broad agreement was reached on a whole range of controversial points which had split the participants in the Conference in several camps in both formal and informal meetings. Only the representative of the Holy See reserved his delegation's position on the draft Plan as a whole in the Working Group, though the representative of China reserved his delegation's position on certain parts of the draft Plan.

Why was agreement reached? An unofficial checklist prepared by the United States' delegation at the beginning of the conference indicated that 15 countries were opposed to the draft Plan (Cuba, North Korea, Tanzania, Congo, Albania, Syria, China, Argentina, Senegal, Guinea, Mauritania, Algeria, Peru, Rwanda, Nigeria); 15 wanted major changes (Mexico, Czechoslovakia, Hungary, Bolivia, Byelo-Russia, Uruguay, Spain, Sudan, Mongolia, East Germany, Bulgaria, USSR, Romania, Ukraine and Yugoslavia); at least eight countries had certain reservations and wanted changes (Ecuador, Pakistan, India, Jamaica, Egypt, Sri Lanka, Mali, Colombia)[6].

By the end of the Working Group's deliberations, all these countries without exception were ready to approve the Plan as it was put to the Plenary. Mega-Conferences are no longer as fashionable as they were in the 1970s, but there is a certain alchemy in these massive events which makes it increasingly difficult for states, individually or severally, to hold out against an emerging consensus. In Mexico City ten years later it would ironically be the United States, the nation which at Bucharest pushed hardest for agreement, which would rock the boat most vigorously but, as we shall see, in Mexico City as at Bucharest the mysterious, magical all-important 'consensus' was finally attained.

At its 17th meeting on 30 August 1974, the Conference took note of the report of the Working Group on the World Population Plan of Action. At the same meeting the Conference adopted by consensus the draft World Population Plan of Action as presented by the Working Group.

Some of the statements made after the vote were of interest in that they shed further light on political attitudes. The representative of Japan, for example, said that the Plan was of immense significance for the future of mankind, but expressed regret that changes in the Plan had obscured the acute awareness in the earlier version that rapid population growth was one of the major obstacles to social and economic development. China, on the other hand, said that, although the document affirmed the principle of national sovereignty, the attempt to impose targets for reducing population growth was tantamount to interference in the internal affairs of a state. The delegate of the United States, predictably, regretted the references to the New International Economic Order but said that his country would do its part in providing financial assistance, especially to the lowest income countries, and would seek their progress through international trade, investment and technological transfer.

The representative of the Holy See said that the World Population Plan of Action, as finally approved by the Conference, constituted a clear improvement over the initial draft as submitted. Above all, the Plan placed population problems squarely within the broader context of development policies. It was unfortunate, however, that despite this perspective the Plan of Action remained in the domain merely of demographic policy instead of serving as a guide to a genuine population policy. The Holy See continued to be concerned about other points, notably the family, respect for life and indiscriminate recourse to means for birth prevention. These were matters on which the Holy See, by its very nature, was unable to compromise. Without denying the value of certain amendments of the draft Plan, the Holy See could not participate in the consensus that favoured the full text as it now stood.

The representative of Czechoslovakia spoke on behalf of ten other socialist states (including the USSR) to inform the Conference, lest there still be any doubt about their viewpoint, that the present economic difficulties of developing countries were the result of exploitation by imperialist Powers, a process in which socialist countries had no part.

The representative of Pakistan said that the Working Group which had prepared the Plan of Action had been dominated by countries where the problem of population did not exist with the intensity it existed in Asia. The amendments to the Plan had been the result of compromise and most of them had been adopted under the stress of physical fatigue and pressure of time. He hoped that the amended Plan would stand the close scrutiny to which it would be subjected.

Thus, even though consensus had finally been achieved, it was clear that the divergences of view which had been expressed throughout the course of the two-week Conference were real and persisted to the end. The representative of the United Kingdom, speaking last after the vote, said that the Plan provided a useful and potentially effective basis for action by Governments, by the United Nations and by all others concerned with population. Many went away from Bucharest wondering whether these words would turn out to be pious hopes or whether, on the contrary, the World Population Plan of Action would indeed prove to be a solid foundation for further action in the population field.

World Population Year

If Bucharest was a success (in the sense that it was not a failure), at least part of the reason is that the Conference was not a single isolated event, but one that took place within a wider constellation of events and activities.

As noted earlier, in its Resolution 1672 (LII) on population and development adopted on 2 June 1972 at its 52nd session, ECOSOC, *inter alia* designated the Executive Director of UNFPA as having responsibility for World Population Year (WPY)[7].

To launch the WPY campaign Salas expanded and transformed the UNFPA's public information section into the WPY Secretariat[8]. Tarzie Vittachi, an Asian journalist and recipient of a Ramon Magsaysay Award for Journalism and Literature, was appointed Executive Secretary of the unit. His task was to achieve the involvement of Governmental ministries, national groups, non-governmental organizations, business, social and youth clubs, churches of all creeds, universities, and schools. Mr Vittachi was to stay with UNFPA for almost a decade, before leaving to become Deputy Executive Director of UNICEF.

Vittachi was assisted by Jyoti Singh, former Secretary-General of the World Assembly of Youth, who took charge of non-governmental participation. Singh also was to stay with UNFPA to become its Director of Public Information. As Salas commented, 'virtually no outlet that would bring the Fund in touch with decision-makers, or the people who would be affected by the decisions, was barred. In the end the WPY programme was certainly a strange mixture of information and substantive projects, but there were few sectors in both the developed and the developing world which did not know about the population effort'[9].

In many respects, these were pioneering activities. Vittachi and Singh established a network of news-gathering and news dissemination centres in different parts of the world. In its report on its 17th session, which was held between 29 October and 9 November 1973, the Population Commission noted that:

> Newspaper and radio coverage of information on the Year had already increased substantially and the trend was very encouraging. As the Year approached, preparations for its launching were being developed rapidly. Supplements and special issues of newspapers and periodicals were also being developed. A popular book to be issued in paperback in eight, possibly 12, languages was now ready and was being edited to ensure accuracy of demographic data and to make it widely acceptable[10].

The knowledge and experience gained by UNFPA during World Population Year was to stand it in good stead. More than many other United Nations agencies, the Fund has realized that 'out-reach' is all-important. Preaching to the converted is easy and always has been. What the Fund recognized in the build-up to 1974 was that the *non-committed* were the primary targets and that both sides of the fence – developed and developing, donors and recipients, rich and poor – had to be worked with equal energy.

This double-process inevitably involved reaching out to all sorts and conditions of men – from senior politician to lowly villager. And it was a process which had to be carried out continuously and without respite.

Even senior politicians after all have a tendency to be replaced, while there are so many villagers in the world that it can never be time to stop. Building a constituency is one thing; maintaining a constituency is something else again.

As far as World Population was concerned, in addition to the press, a major programme of film and radio information was set in train. It was clear from the start that, if people could be reached by one means or another by news and information about World Population Year, then they could be reached in the course of on-going programmes of economic and social development, including family planning. In this sense, as Salas put it, every year was a World Population Year.

In the event, some 64 nations set up Commissions to prepare for World Population Year and the Conference. Many of these Commissions had an enduring existence and, in one form or another, served not merely for WPY/WPC activities but as a continuing umbrella for work at national level in the field of population.

8

Falling birth-rates:
Asia, Latin America,
Middle East and Africa

Introduction

A 'spectacular' decline

If any one recent historical trend is to be singled out as being of supreme importance for the future well-being of mankind, it is in the author's view not the progress made towards disarmament or towards the ending of racial discrimination, nor the steps taken to achieve international protection of the environment (though in all these areas some important achievements have been recorded); it is, rather, the widespread declines in fertility which have been registered in many parts of the world during this last third of the 20th century.

In its Concise Report on the World Population Situation in 1983, the United Nations summarizes this trend in the following terms:[1]

During the period between 1950–1955 and 1975–1980, the developed countries were nearing the end of a long transition towards lower fertility which began more than a century ago, while many less developed countries had just begun to experience a marked downward trend. The result was that there has been a *spectacular decline* [author's italics] in the birth rate for the world and its more developed and less developed components according to estimates prepared by the United Nations. In 1950–1955, the birth rate for the world as a whole was 38.0 per 1000 persons. The corresponding figures for the more developed and less developed regions were 22.7 and 45.4. By 1975–1980, the birth rate for the world had fallen to 28.9 and, for the more developed and less developed regions, to 15.8 and 33.5 per 1000, respectively. Over a 25-year period, the birth rate had fallen by 7 points in the developed countries and by 12 points in the developing countries.

131

Because birth rate trends are influenced by changes in the age structure, they are often studied in terms of the total fertility rate (which is expressed in terms of the number of children for women). During the period between 1950–1955 and 1975–1980, the total fertility rate for the world as a whole declined from 5.0 to 3.9; the rate declined from 2.8 to 2.05 in the developed countries and from 6.2 to 4.6 in the developing countries.

To speak, as the UN does, of a 'spectacular decline' in the birth-rate for the world is not of course to imply that attempts to 'defuse the population explosion' (to use U Thant's words quoted in the Introduction) have been successful in the sense that the 'fuse' has been removed from the Population Bomb or that those efforts may now safely be relaxed. On the contrary, the fact that there has been progress and that further progress can be realised is the best possible argument for a doubling and redoubling of efforts at both national and international level. The formula, whatever it is, seems to be working; but even in those areas of the developing world where birth-rates are falling, there is on the whole a long way to go before replacement levels of fertility are reached. And in some areas of the world most notably in Sub-Saharan Africa but also in Western South Asia and in some parts of Latin America, we have not yet witnessed the full or sometimes even the first onset of fertility decline.

To have a fuller sense of the achievements which had been registered by, say, 1984 – the year of the International Conference on Population held in Mexico City – it is worth considering what, demographically speaking, the world looked like at the beginning of the 1970s? Table 8.1 shows the total world population in 1970 in the principal regions, as well as birth-rate, death-rate and rate of natural increase.

Projections

The World Leaders' statement, first issued in 1967,[2] included the statement that there would be nearly seven billion people on this earth in the year 2000 at the then current rate of increase: in fact, since 1967 the rate of increase had itself accelerated and the United Nations had in 1970 revised its projections upwards. In making these projections, the UN then – as now – used four different variants: the 'constant fertility' variant assumed that the population of the less developed regions would maintain 1965 levels of fertility; the 'high', 'medium' and 'low' variants all assumed that the gross reproduction rate in the less developed countries would decrease by 5 per cent during the first five-year period, by 10 per cent within each of the next two five-year periods and by 15 per cent during

8 Falling birth-rates

Table 8.1. *World population, 1970 (mid-year estimates)*

	Population (in millions)	Rate of increase (%)	Birth rate	Death rate
			(per 1000)	
World	3633	2.0	34	14
Africa	344	2.6	46	20
Western Africa	101	2.5	49	24
Eastern Africa	98	2.5	43	18
Northern Africa	87	3.1	48	17
Middle Africa	36	2.1	45	24
Southern Africa	23	2.4	41	17
America	511	2.1	30	10
North America	228	1.2	18	9
Latin America	283	2.9	39	10
Tropical S. America	151	3.0	41	11
Middle America	67	3.4	44	10
Temperate S. America	39	1.8	26	8
Caribbean	26	2.3	36	13
Asia	2056	2.3	38	15
Eastern Asia	930	1.8	31	13
Mainland	765	1.8	33	15
Japan	103	1.1	18	7
Other Eastern Asia	61	2.5	34	9
South Asia	1126	2.8	44	16
Middle S. Asia	762	2.8	45	17
S.E. Asia	287	2.8	43	15
S.W. Asia	77	2.9	43	14
Europe	462	0.8	18	10
Western Europe	149	0.8	17	11
Southern Europe	128	0.9	19	9
Eastern Europe	104	0.8	17	10
N. Eastern Europe	81	0.6	18	11
Oceania	19.4	2.0	24	10
Australia and New Zealand	15.4	1.9	20	9
Melanesia	2.8	2.4	42	18
Polynesia and Micronesia	1.2	3.1	40	9
USSR	242	1.0	18	8

Source: UN Demographic Yearbook 1970

each of the next five-year periods, so that within 30 years the gross reproduction rate would be about half its initial value. What distinguished the 'high', 'medium' and 'low' variants from each other was the assumption made with regard to the date this pattern of fertility decline would begin. The 'low' variant made the assumption that the onset of fertility decline began in 1970. The 'medium' variant assumed a starting date of 1975 and the 'high' variant a starting date of 1980.

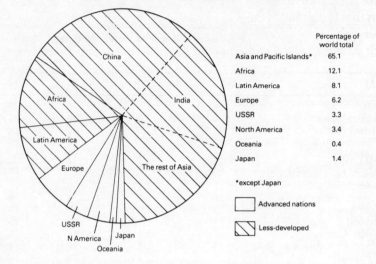

	Percentage of world total
Asia and Pacific Islands*	65.1
Africa	12.1
Latin America	8.1
Europe	6.2
USSR	3.3
North America	3.4
Oceania	0.4
Japan	1.4

*except Japan

☐ Advanced nations

▨ Less-developed

Figure 8.1. *Births throughout the world in 1970 divided by percentage among regions.*

Source: Estimates of International Demographic Statistical Center, Census Bureau, supplied by USAID

Tables 8.3–8.6 present the results of total population estimates and annual rates of growth by regions during the period 1965–2000, according to the above mentioned four variants. The world population of 3289 million in 1965 was expected, according to the 'medium' variant, to increase to 6494 million in 2000. The implied rates of growth indicated that the world population might be growing at almost a constant rate of about 2.0 per cent annually until the middle of the 1980s and then the rate would gradually decrease until it reached 1.7 per cent by the end of the century. During the period under consideration, the population of the less developed regions was anticipated to increase from 2252 million to 5040 million, with a rate of growth which would remain virtually constant and equal to about 2.4 per cent until 1985 and then gradually decrease to 2.0 per cent per annum. On the other hand, the population of the more developed regions might sustain an almost constant annual rate of about 1.0 per cent throughout the remainder of this century, thus increasing from 1037 million in 1965 to 1454 million at the turn of the century. As a result of these differing rates of growth, the projected population of the less-developed regions was expected to be about three-and-a-half times the projected figure for the developed regions at the end of the century, while the ratio in 1965 was only a little over two to one.

134

Table 8.2 shows the world population between 1960 and 1970. It can be seen that by the end of the period the world total was increasing at almost 2 per cent a year, which meant a net addition of almost 70 million persons each year, 58 million of them in the less-developed regions.

Table 8.2. *World population increase, 1960–70*

	Annual per cent increase		Annual absolute increase (millions)	
	1960–5	1965–70	1960–5	1965–70
World total	1.94	1.98	61.1	68.2
More-developed regions	1.15	0.95	11.5	10.0
Less-developed regions	2.32	2.45	49.6	58.2
East Asia	1.75	1.75	. 14.4	15.5
South Asia	2.48	2.75	23.1	28.6
Europe	0.84	0.78	3.7	3.4
Soviet Union	1.52	1.02	3.4	2.4
Africa	2.41	2.55	7.0	8.3
Northern America	1.34	0.98	2.7	2.2
Latin America	2.82	2.84	6.6	7.6
Oceania	1.69	1.45	0.2	0.2

Source: UN Demographic Yearbook 1970

In presenting high, medium and low projections based on anticipated declines in fertility (though, as we have seen, with different dates for the onset of the decline), the United Nations assumed:

> that the general level of development in less-developed countries would exert an effect on fertility, and that the existence of population and family-planning policies and their implementation would also affect fertility.

Thus the difference between the total of 6369 million inhabitants in the developing countries under the 'constant fertility' assumption and 4523 million under the 'low' assumption – a difference of almost 2000 million could be seen as a kind of maximum possible target figure. At the beginning of the 1970s it appeared that, if we went on the way we were going, we would have a world of almost 8 billion inhabitants in the year 2000, because to the 6400 million inhabitants of the LDCs must be added 1500 million inhabitants of developed countries (where a single 'medium' variant was assumed). Figure 8.2 demonstrates this graphically. If, on the other hand, development and population policies were successful, we might conceivably be able to 'lop off' 2000 million from this figure and achieve a population of 'only' 6000 million in the year 2000, with all the benefits this would bring for current and future generations.

Table 8.3. *Total population estimates (1970) and annual rates of growth by regions, 1965–2000: medium variant*

Regions	Total population (in thousands)					Annual rates of growth (per cent)				
	1965	1970	1980	1990	2000	1965 -70	1970 -5	1980 -5	1990 -5	1995 -2000
World total	3,289,002	3,631,797	4,456,688	5,438,169	6,493,642	2.0	2.0	2.0	1.8	1.7
More-developed regions	1,037,492	1,090,297	1,210,051	1,336,499	1,453,528	1.0	1.0	1.0	0.9	0.8
Less-developed regions	2,251,510	2,541,501	3,246,637	4,101,670	5,040,114	2.4	2.5	2.4	2.1	2.0
East Asia	851,877	929,932	1,095,354	1,265,343	1,424,377	1.8	1.7	1.5	1.2	1.1
Mainland region	700,076	765,386	901,351	1,042,864	1,176,176	1.8	1.7	1.5	1.3	1.1
Japan	97,950	103,499	116,347	125,330	132,760	1.1	1.2	0.8	0.6	0.6
Other East Asia	53,851	61,046	77,656	97,148	115,442	2.5	2.4	2.4	1.8	1.6
South Asia	981,046	1,125,843	1,485,714	1,911,819	2,353,841	2.8	2.8	2.6	2.2	2.0
Middle South Asia	664,868	761,809	1,001,046	1,279,761	1,564,963	2.7	2.8	2.5	2.1	1.9
South East Asia	249,349	286,925	380,367	491,775	607,709	2.8	2.9	2.7	2.2	2.0
South West Asia	66,829	77,109	104,302	140,283	181,169	2.9	3.0	3.0	2.7	2.4
Europe	444,642	462,120	497,061	532,636	568,358	0.8	0.7	0.7	0.7	0.6
Western Europe	143,143	148,619	158,214	168,679	179,266	0.8	0.6	0.6	0.6	0.6
Southern Europe	122,750	128,466	140,059	151,605	162,674	0.9	0.9	0.8	0.7	0.7
Eastern Europe	100,060	104,082	112,392	119,607	127,277	0.8	0.8	0.7	0.7	0.6
Northern Europe	78,689	80,953	86,396	92,745	99,141	0.6	0.6	0.7	0.7	0.7

Table 8.3 (continued)

USSR	230,556	242,612	270,634	302,011	329,508	1.0	1.0	1.2	0.9	0.8
Africa	303,150	344,484	456,721	615,826	817,751	2.6	2.8	3.0	2.9	2.8
Western Africa	89,546	101,272	133,406	180,059	240,158	2.5	2.7	3.0	3.0	2.8
Eastern Africa	86,448	97,882	128,757	173,639	233,245	2.5	2.7	2.9	3.0	2.9
Middle Africa	32,318	35,893	45,785	60,449	80,214	2.1	2.4	2.7	2.9	2.8
Northern Africa	74,520	86,606	119,385	163,230	214,404	3.0	3.2	3.2	2.9	2.6
Southern Africa	20,318	22,832	29,387	38,450	49,730	2.3	2.5	2.7	2.6	2.5
Northern America	214,329	227,572	260,651	299,133	333,435	1.2	1.3	1.5	1.1	1.0
Latin America	245,884	283,253	377,172	499,771	652,337	2.8	2.9	2.8	2.7	2.6
Tropical South America	129,854	150,660	203,591	272,495	358,447	3.0	3.0	2.9	2.8	2.7
Middle America (Mainland)	56,961	67,430	94,706	132,387	180,476	3.4	3.4	3.4	3.2	3.0
Temperate South America	36,000	39,378	46,731	54,783	63,266	1.8	1.7	1.6	1.5	1.4
Caribbean	23,068	25,785	32,145	40,107	50,148	2.2	2.2	2.2	2.2	2.2
Oceania	17,520	19,370	24,025	29,639	35,173	2.0	2.1	2.2	1.8	1.6
Australia and New Zealand	14,015	15,374	18,785	22,659	26,214	1.9	2.0	2.0	1.5	1.4
Melanesia	2,452	2,767	3,585	4,743	6,107	2.4	2.6	2.8	2.6	2.4
Polynesia and Micronesia	1,053	1,229	1,657	2,237	2,853	3.1	3.1	3.1	2.6	2.3

Source: UN Population Division: interim revision (1970) of 'World Population Prospects as Assessed in 1963' (*Population Studies*, No. 41, United Nations publication, Sales No.: 66.XIII.2).

Table 8.4. *Total population estimates (1970) and annual rates of growth by regions, 1965–2000: high variant, less-developed regions only*

	Total population (in thousands)					Annual rates of growth (per cent)				
	1965	1970	1980	1990	2000	1965 –70	1970 –5	1980 –5	1990 –5	1995 –2000
Less-developed regions	2,251,510	2,563,561	3,378,768	4,424,950	5,650,426	2.6	2.7	2.7	2.5	2.4
Mainland region	700,076	785,095	983,009	1,183,317	1,369,757	2.3	2.3	2.0	1.5	1.4
Other East Asia	53,851	61,046	78,845	102,115	123,424	2.5	2.5	2.7	2.1	1.7
South Asia	981,046	1,126,115	1,518,153	2,032,456	2,617,382	2.8	2.9	3.0	2.7	2.4
Middle South Asia	664,868	761,993	1,024,890	1,363,525	1,742,573	2.7	2.9	2.9	2.6	2.3
South East Asia	249,349	286,925	387,315	522,096	677,570	2.8	3.0	3.0	2.7	2.5
South West Asia	66,829	77,197	105,947	146,835	197,239	2.9	3.1	3.3	3.1	2.8
Africa	303,150	345,818	466,366	648,854	905,702	2.6	2.9	3.3	3.4	3.3
Western Africa	89,546	101,705	136,590	190,624	269,314	2.5	2.8	3.3	3.5	3.4
Eastern Africa	86,448	98,203	131,361	182,218	256,970	2.5	2.8	3.2	3.4	3.5
Middle Africa	32,318	36,013	46,754	63,457	88,626	2.2	2.5	3.0	3.3	3.4
Northern Africa	74,520	87,027	121,883	172,708	236,900	3.1	3.3	3.5	3.3	3.0
Southern Africa	20,318	22,871	29,778	39,847	53,892	2.4	2.6	2.8	3.0	3.0
Tropical South America	129,854	151,266	208,241	288,203	394,822	3.1	3.2	3.3	3.2	3.1
Middle America (Mainland)	56,961	67,498	96,505	138,609	196,659	3.4	3.5	3.7	3.5	3.5
Caribbean	23,068	25,851	32,754	41,915	53,842	2.3	2.3	2.5	2.5	2.5
Melanesia	2,452	2,771	3,645	4,963	6,625	2.4	2.6	3.0	3.0	2.8
Polynesia and Micronesia	1,053	1,230	1,737	2,472	3,337	3.1	3.4	3.6	3.1	2.9

Source: UN Population Division: interim revision (1970) of 'World Population Prospects as Assessed in 1963' (*Population Studies*, No. 41. United Nations publication. Sales No.: 66.XIII.2).

Table 8.5. *Total population estimates (1970) and annual rates of growth by regions, 1965–2000; low variant, less-developed regions only*

	Total population (in thousands)					Annual rates of growth (per cent)				
	1965	1970	1980	1990	2000	1965–70	1970–5	1980–5	1990–5	1995–2000
Less-developed regions	2,251,510	2,522,681	3,136,625	3,819,836	4,523,382	2.3	2.2	2.0	1.8	1.6
Mainland region	700,076	752,802	855,508	945,776	1,034,638	1.5	1.4	1.0	0.9	0.9
Other East Asia	53,851	61,046	76,468	92,659	107,712	2.5	2.3	2.0	1.6	1.4
South Asia	981,046	1,121,456	1,438,771	1,785,862	2,119,009	2.7	2.6	2.3	1.8	1.6
Middle South Asia	664,868	758,481	967,173	1,191,467	1,403,391	2.6	2.5	2.2	1.7	1.6
South East Asia	249,349	286,062	369,499	461,531	550,240	2.7	2.6	2.4	1.9	1.7
South West Asia	66,829	76,914	102,100	132,864	165,378	2.8	2.8	2.7	2.3	2.1
Africa	303,150	343,596	448,006	582,872	734,159	2.5	2.6	2.7	2.4	2.2
Western Africa	89,546	100,928	130,536	168,751	210,587	2.4	2.5	2.6	2.3	2.1
Eastern Africa	86,448	97,637	126,633	165,633	211,152	2.4	2.6	2.7	2.5	2.3
Middle Africa	32,318	35,766	44,757	57,033	71,306	2.0	2.2	2.4	2.3	2.2
Northern Africa	74,520	86,470	116,964	154,130	194,285	3.0	3.1	2.8	2.4	2.2
Southern Africa	20,318	22,795	29,117	37,325	46,829	2.3	2.4	2.5	2.3	2.2
Tropical South America	129,854	150,035	198,648	257,832	325,152	2.9	2.8	2.7	2.4	2.2
Middle America (Mainland)	56,961	67,136	92,831	127,219	167,641	3.3	3.2	3.2	2.9	2.6
Caribbean	23,068	25,762	31,713	38,814	47,677	2.2	2.1	2.0	2.1	2.0
Melanesia	2,452	2,765	3,533	4,579	5,786	2.4	2.5	2.6	2.5	2.2
Polynesia and Micronesia	1,053	1,213	1,632	2,179	2,733	2.8	3.1	3.0	2.4	2.1

Source: UN Population Division: interim revision (1970) of 'World Population Prospects as Assessed in 1963' (*Population Studies*, No. 41, United Nations publication. Sales No.: 66.XIII.2).

Table 8.6. *Total population estimates (1970) and annual rates of growth by regions, 1965–2000: constant fertility variant, less-developed regions only*

	Total population (in thousands)					Annual rates of growth (per cent)				
	1965	1970	1980	1990	2000	1965–70	1970–5	1980–5	1990–5	1995–2000
Less-developed regions	2,251,510	2,559,001	3,381,131	4,583,220	6,368,737	2.6	2.7	3.0	3.2	3.4
Mainland region	700,076	780,941	991,228	1,275,390	1,673,559	2.2	2.3	2.5	2.7	2.8
Other East Asia	53,851	61,573	82,445	113,879	156,700	2.7	2.8	3.2	3.2	3.2
South Asia	981,046	1,126,074	1,515,875	2,100,924	2,988,562	2.8	2.9	3.2	3.5	3.6
Middle South Asia	664,868	761,904	1,023,084	1,414,629	2,012,112	2.7	2.9	3.2	3.5	3.6
South East Asia	249,349	287,050	387,272	537,323	762,368	2.8	2.9	3.2	3.5	3.5
South West Asia	66,829	77,121	105,509	148,972	214,081	2.9	3.0	3.4	3.6	3.7
Africa	303,150	344,496	456,620	622,901	872,798	2.6	2.7	3.0	3.3	3.4
Western Africa	89,546	101,272	133,360	180,901	252,231	2.5	2.7	3.0	3.3	3.4
Eastern Africa	86,448	97,882	128,711	174,009	241,750	2.5	2.7	2.9	3.2	3.4
Middle Africa	32,318	35,958	45,603	59,449	79,683	2.1	2.3	2.6	2.9	3.0
Northern Africa	74,520	86,606	119,719	170,143	247,424	3.0	3.2	3.4	3.7	3.8
Southern Africa	20,318	22,779	29,227	38,399	51,710	2.3	2.4	2.7	2.9	3.0
Tropical South America	129,854	151,523	209,966	295,754	420,972	3.1	3.2	3.4	3.5	3.6
Middle America (Mainland)	56,961	67,485	96,413	140,425	206,814	3.4	3.5	3.7	3.8	3.9
Caribbean	23,068	26,041	33,725	44,540	60,115	2.4	2.5	2.7	2.9	3.1
Melanesia	2,452	2,767	3,612	4,886	6,798	2.4	2.6	2.9	3.2	3.4
Polynesia and Micronesia	1,053	1,229	1,733	2,478	3,544	3.1	3.3	3.6	3.6	3.6

Source: UN Population Division: interim revision (1970) of 'World Population Prospects as Assessed in 1963' (*Population Studies*, No. 41, United Nations publication, Sales No.: 66.XIII.2).

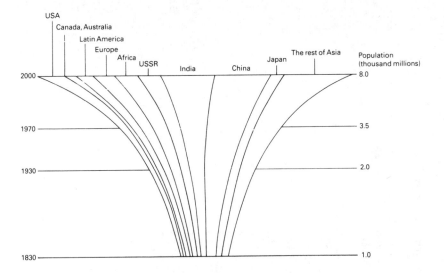

Figure 8.2. *Growth and distribution (1830–2000) under the 'constant fertility' assumption (1970 estimates).*

Source: United Nations Association of the United States of America: *World Population – a report of a National Policy Panel.* The projections shown are based on the United Nations interim revisions (1970) of 'World Population Prospects as Assessed in 1963' (*Population Studies*, No. 41, United Nations publication, Sales No: 66.XIII.2).

Progress made by 1984

By 1984, it was clear that already considerable progress had been made. At a global level declines in fertility had been recorded which were at least consistent with the assumptions made in the United Nations medium projections. In fact, the rate of world population growth which it was assumed (under the medium projections) would remain constant at around 2.0 per cent until the middle of the 1980s had already fallen by the time of the Mexico Conference to 1.67 per cent per year. Table 8.7 shows the total world population in 1984 by country or area in the world, according to the major areas or regions. It also shows birth-rates, death-rates, gross reproduction rate, expectation of life, percentage of urban population, 1980, and annual growth rates. A comparison with Table 8.1 shows that the main declines in the birthrate, contributing substantially to the decline in the world population growth rate, have occurred in Asia, although there have also been significant declines in some other regions. It also shows that the world population growth rate would have declined still further between 1970 and 1984 but for the fall in mortality recorded, especially in Africa and Latin America.

141

Table 8.7. Demographic indicators (1984) by country or area in the world, major areas and regions[a]

Country or area	Population (thousands)		Annual growth			Age distribution of population, 1980			Crude vital rates 1980–5 (per 1000 population)		Gross reproduction rate 1980–5	Expectation of life, 1980–5 (years)	Percentage of urban population, 1980
	1984	2000	1950–5	1980–5	1995–2000	0–14	15–64	65+	Births	Deaths			
World total	4,763,085	6,123,278	1.8	1.7	1.5	35.6	58.6	5.7	27.3	10.6	1.73	58.9	40.9
More-developed regions[b]	1,165,789	1,272,194	1.3	0.6	0.5	23.0	65.6	11.4	15.5	9.5	0.96	73.1	71.0
Less-developed regions[c]	3,597,297	4,851,083	2.1	2.0	1.8	40.0	56.2	3.8	31.2	11.0	2.00	56.6	30.6
A. Africa	536,589	877,061	2.1	3.0	3.1	45.2	51.7	3.1	46.4	16.5	3.16	49.7	28.5
1. Eastern Africa[d]	155,447	266,238	2.2	3.2	3.4	46.8	50.6	2.6	49.1	17.0	3.35	48.8	16.0
Burundi	4,503	6,951	1.7	2.7	2.7	43.4	53.4	3.3	47.6	20.9	3.17	44.0	2.4
Comoros	443	715	2.3	3.0	2.8	45.8	51.3	2.8	46.3	15.9	3.10	50.0	10.5
Ethiopia	35,420	58,407	2.0	2.6	3.1	45.5	51.9	2.6	49.2	21.5	3.30	42.9	14.2
Kenya	19,761	38,534	2.9	4.1	4.1	52.2	45.9	1.9	55.1	16.5	4.00	52.9	13.9
Madagascar	9,731	15,552	1.8	2.8	3.0	43.4	53.2	3.4	44.4	16.5	3.00	49.6	18.5
Malawi	6,788	11,669	1.9	3.2	3.4	47.7	50.1	2.2	52.1	19.9	3.45	45.0	34.7
Mauritius[e]	1,031	1,298	2.9	1.9	1.2	34.1	62.9	3.0	25.5	6.0	1.35	66.7	52.5
Mozambique	13,693	21,779	1.2	3.0	2.9	44.3	52.4	3.3	44.1	16.5	3.00	49.4	7.5
Réunion	555	685	3.1	1.4	1.2	35.0	61.3	3.7	20.5	6.5	1.10	66.4	54.9
Rwanda	5,903	10,565	2.3	3.5	3.7	48.2	49.2	2.6	51.1	16.6	3.60	49.5	4.0
Somalia	5,423	7,079	1.6	3.7	2.5	43.2	53.3	3.5	46.5	21.3	3.00	42.9	30.3
Uganda	15,150	26,774	3.1	3.5	3.5	48.0	49.4	2.5	49.9	14.7	3.40	52.0	11.9
United Republic of Tanzania	21,710	39,129	2.2	3.5	3.7	48.4	49.3	2.3	50.4	15.3	3.50	51.0	11.2
Zambia	6,445	11,237	2.4	3.3	3.5	46.9	50.4	2.6	48.1	15.1	3.33	51.3	38.8
Zimbabwe	8,461	15,132	4.0	3.5	3.6	47.2	50.0	2.7	47.2	12.3	3.25	55.7	23.1
2. Middle Africa[f]	60,723	95,693	1.8	2.7	2.9	43.6	53.2	3.2	44.9	18.1	2.97	47.2	33.6
Angola	8,540	13,234	1.4	2.5	2.8	44.2	52.9	3.0	47.3	22.2	3.15	42.0	19.2
Central African Republic	2,508	3,736	1.2	2.3	2.6	41.5	54.6	3.9	44.7	21.8	2.90	43.0	40.9
Chad	4,901	7,304	1.3	2.3	2.6	41.9	54.5	3.6	44.2	21.4	2.90	43.0	17.7

	1	2	3	4	5	6	7	8	9	10	11	12	13
Congo	37.5	46.5	2.95	18.6	44.5	3.3	53.5	43.2	2.9	2.6	1.7	1,695	2,646
Equatorial Guinea	55.4	44.0	2.79	21.0	42.5	4.2	55.1	40.7	2.4	2.2	1.1	383	559
Gabon	18.3	49.0	2.30	18.1	34.6	6.1	59.9	34.0	2.4	1.6	0.6	1,146	1,611
United Republic of Cameroon	34.3	46.0	2.85	19.2	43.6	3.8	54.3	41.9	2.6	2.4	1.9	9,371	14,045
Zaire	39.2	50.0	3.00	15.8	45.2	2.9	52.3	44.8	3.1	2.9	2.2	32,084	52,410
3. Northern Africa [g]	44.6	55.9	2.93	12.9	41.9	3.8	53.0	43.2	2.4	2.9	2.2	121,386	185,671
Algeria	61.7	57.8	3.40	12.3	45.1	3.9	49.4	46.6	2.9	3.3	2.1	21,272	35,194
Egypt	46.1	57.3	2.55	12.5	38.4	4.5	55.9	39.5	2.0	2.5	2.4	45,657	65,200
Libyan Arab Jamahiriya	52.5	57.9	3.50	10.9	45.6	2.2	51.1	46.7	3.3	3.8	1.8	3,471	6,072
Morocco	41.0	57.9	3.14	11.5	44.0	3.1	50.9	46.0	2.6	3.3	2.5	22,848	36,325
Sudan	24.4	47.7	3.22	17.4	45.9	2.7	52.4	44.9	2.7	2.9	2.0	20,945	32,926
Tunisia	51.4	60.6	2.40	10.1	34.1	4.3	53.7	42.0	1.7	2.4	1.8	7,042	9,725
4. Southern Africa	46.8	53.0	2.57	14.2	39.6	4.0	54.3	41.7	2.5	2.5	1.7	36,246	54,456
Botswana	26.2	54.5	3.20	12.7	50.0	2.0	48.4	49.7	3.7	3.5	2.1	1,042	1,865
Lesotho	4.6	49.3	2.85	16.4	41.7	3.6	54.5	42.0	2.6	2.5	1.6	1,481	2,251
Namibia	34.0	48.2	3.00	17.3	45.1	3.2	52.8	44.0	2.9	2.8	2.0	1,507	2,382
South Africa	50.8	53.5	2.50	13.9	38.7	4.1	54.7	41.3	2.4	2.5	1.7	31,586	46,918
Swaziland	8.8	48.6	3.20	17.2	47.5	3.0	51.6	45.4	3.2	3.0	1.9	630	1,041
5. Western Africa [h]	22.2	46.8	3.38	18.5	49.3	2.7	50.7	46.6	3.3	3.1	2.1	162,787	275,002
Benin	31.3	42.5	3.45	22.5	51.0	3.0	51.2	45.8	3.2	2.9	0.7	3,890	6,381
Cape Verde	6.3	57.0	1.30	10.3	23.9	3.5	61.1	35.4	1.0	1.4	2.7	317	382
Gambia	19.2	35.0	3.15	29.0	48.4	3.1	54.9	42.1	2.3	1.9	1.1	630	898
Ghana	36.6	52.0	3.20	14.6	47.0	2.8	50.9	46.3	3.2	3.2	4.8	13,044	21,923
Guinea	19.8	40.2	3.05	23.5	46.8	2.9	54.2	42.9	2.6	2.3	1.0	5,301	7,935
Guinea-Bissau	16.8	43.0	2.65	21.7	40.7	4.3	55.6	40.1	2.3	1.9	0.6	875	1,241
Ivory Coast	36.7	47.0	3.30	18.0	46.0	2.9	52.4	44.6	3.0	3.4	1.2	9,474	15,581
Liberia	34.6	49.0	3.40	17.2	48.7	3.1	51.3	45.6	3.3	3.2	1.9	2,123	3,564
Mali	19.7	42.0	3.30	22.4	50.2	2.8	51.4	45.9	2.8	2.8	1.7	7,825	12,363
Mauritania	35.7	44.0	3.40	20.9	50.1	2.8	51.5	45.7	3.1	2.9	2.0	1,832	2,999
Niger	12.5	42.5	3.50	22.9	51.0	3.8	50.3	45.9	3.2	2.8	1.0	5,940	9,750
Nigeria	19.5	48.5	3.50	17.1	50.4	2.4	49.5	48.1	3.6	3.3	2.4	92,037	161,930
Senegal	25.1	43.3	3.20	21.2	47.7	2.9	52.6	44.5	2.9	2.7	1.9	6,352	10,036
Sierra Leone	25.9	34.0	3.02	29.7	47.4	3.0	56.1	40.9	2.1	1.8	1.1	3,536	4,868
Togo	18.0	48.7	3.00	16.9	45.4	3.2	52.7	44.2	3.1	2.9	1.2	2,838	4,599
Upper Volta	9.5	42.0	3.20	22.2	47.8	2.8	53.1	44.1	2.8	2.3	1.4	6,768	10,542

Table 8.7 (continued)

Country or area	Population (thousands) 1984	Population (thousands) 2000	Annual growth 1950–5	Annual growth 1980–5	Annual growth 1995–2000	Age distribution of population, 1980 0–14	Age distribution of population, 1980 15–64	Age distribution of population, 1980 65+	Crude vital rates 1980–5 (per 1000 population) Births	Crude vital rates 1980–5 (per 1000 population) Deaths	Gross reproduction rate 1980–5	Expectation of life 1980–5 (years)	Percentage of urban population, 1980
B. Latin America	397,138	549,971	2.7	2.3	1.9	39.4	56.3	4.3	31.8	8.2	2.01	64.1	65.5
6. Caribbean	31,364	40,833	1.8	1.5	1.6	37.2	57.3	5.5	27.1	8.4	1.64	64.0	52.5
Barbados	262	307	1.5	0.8	1.0	29.5	61.2	9.3	19.9	8.6	1.10	71.6	40.6
Cuba	9,966	11,718	1.9	0.6	1.0	31.3	61.4	7.3	16.9	6.4	0.96	73.4	65.4
Dominican Republic	6,101	8,407	2.7	2.3	1.7	43.9	53.2	2.9	33.1	8.0	2.04	62.6	54.5
Guadaloupe	319	338	2.3	0.1	0.5	35.8	57.5	6.7	19.5	7.3	1.25	70.4	45.0
Haiti	6,419	9,860	1.7	2.5	2.7	43.6	52.9	3.6	41.3	14.2	2.80	52.7	24.9
Jamaica	2,290	2,849	1.9	1.4	1.3	40.6	53.6	5.8	28.3	6.7	1.65	70.3	41.6
Martinique	312	338	2.1	0.0	0.7	33.6	59.1	7.3	18.8	7.6	1.15	70.9	69.2
Puerto Rico	3,404	4,212	0.3	1.5	1.2	31.6	60.5	7.9	22.4	6.9	1.28	73.9	81.0
Trinidad and Tobago	1,105	1,321	2.5	0.9	1.0	34.2	60.8	4.9	24.6	6.2	1.40	70.1	23.5
Windward Islands[i]	418	525	2.0	1.2	1.4	41.2	54.3	4.5	30.4	6.2	1.75	69.1	0.0
Other Caribbean[j]	769	958	1.8	1.3	1.3	34.8	60.0	5.2	24.8	6.1	1.40	70.6	61.9
7. Middle America[k]	102,811	149,557	2.9	2.7	2.1	44.6	51.9	3.4	35.1	7.4	2.32	65.0	60.9
Costa Rica	2,534	3,596	3.5	2.6	1.9	38.5	58.0	3.6	30.5	4.2	1.71	73.0	42.1
El Salvador	5,388	8,708	2.7	2.9	2.9	45.2	51.4	3.4	40.2	8.1	2.71	64.8	41.1
Guatemala	8,165	12,739	2.9	2.9	2.7	44.1	53.1	2.9	38.4	9.3	2.52	60.7	38.9
Honduras	4,232	6,978	3.2	3.4	3.2	47.8	49.4	2.7	43.9	10.1	3.17	59.9	36.0
Mexico	77,040	109,180	2.9	2.6	1.9	44.7	51.8	3.6	33.9	7.1	2.25	65.7	67.0
Nicaragua	3,162	5,261	3.0	3.3	3.0	47.4	50.1	2.4	44.2	9.7	2.90	59.8	52.6
Panama	2,134	2,893	2.5	2.2	1.7	40.5	55.4	4.1	28.0	5.4	1.69	71.0	52.7
8. Temperate South America[l]	44,964	55,496	1.9	1.5	1.2	30.5	61.9	7.6	24.3	8.6	1.57	69.0	79.9
Argentina	30,094	37,197	2.0	1.6	1.2	30.0	61.8	8.2	24.6	8.7	1.66	69.7	78.9
Chile	11,878	14,934	2.0	1.7	1.3	32.5	62.0	5.5	24.8	7.7	1.42	67.0	81.1
Uruguay	2,990	3,364	1.2	0.7	0.7	27.1	62.5	10.4	19.5	10.2	1.35	70.3	84.5

9. Tropical South America	217,999	3.0	2.4	1.9	39.2	57.0	3.8	32.4	8.5	2.01	62.9	66.6
Bolivia	6,200	2.1	2.7	2.9	43.5	53.3	3.3	44.0	15.9	3.05	50.7	32.9
Brazil	132,648	3.2	2.2	1.7	37.7	58.2	4.0	30.6	8.4	1.86	63.4	67.5
Colombia	28,110	2.9	2.1	1.7	39.4	57.1	3.5	31.0	7.7	1.92	62.6	70.2
Ecuador	9,090	2.8	3.1	2.8	44.4	52.0	3.5	40.6	8.9	2.93	68.2	44.6
Guyana	936	2.8	2.0	1.3	39.4	56.8	3.7	28.5	5.9	1.59	65.1	22.3
Paraguay	3,576	2.7	3.0	2.3	42.7	53.9	3.4	36.0	7.2	2.37	58.6	39.4
Peru	19,197	2.6	2.6	2.1	41.8	54.6	3.6	36.7	10.7	2.44	69.4	68.7
Suriname	352	3.0	0.1	1.6	46.4	49.1	4.5	29.5	6.1	2.00	67.8	49.4
Venezuela	17,819	3.8	3.3	2.3	42.2	55.1	2.8	35.2	5.6	2.11		83.3
C. 10. Northern America	261,190	1.8	0.9	0.7	22.6	66.3	11.1	16.0	9.0	0.90	74.3	75.6
Canada	25,289	2.7	1.2	0.8	23.2	67.9	8.9	16.2	7.3	0.88	74.5	76.8
United States of America	235,764	1.7	0.9	0.7	22.5	66.2	11.3	16.0	9.2	0.90	74.2	75.5
D. East Asia	1,238,640	2.0	1.1	1.1	35.5	59.5	5.1	18.2	6.8	1.12	68.0	32.5
11. China	1,051,551	2.2	1.2	1.2	36.9	58.4	4.7	18.5	6.8	1.14	67.4	25.5
12. Japan	119,492	1.4	0.6	0.4	23.6	67.4	9.0	12.4	6.7	0.83	76.6	78.2
13. Other East Asia	86,697	0.6	1.8	1.4	34.9	61.1	4.0	23.8	6.6	1.42	66.7	59.5
Hong Kong	5,498	4.6	2.1	1.0	25.5	68.0	6.5	17.9	5.9	1.00	73.9	91.5
Korea	59,939	0.3	1.7	1.4	35.5	60.6	3.8	24.1	6.7	1.43	66.3	56.7
Korea, Democratic People's Republic of	19,630	−1.4	2.3	1.8	40.0	56.3	3.7	30.5	7.4	1.95	64.6	59.7
Korea, Republic of	40,309	1.0	1.4	1.1	33.4	62.7	3.9	21.0	6.3	1.20	67.5	55.3
Mongolia	1,851	1.9	2.7	2.0	43.0	53.8	3.2	33.8	7.2	2.35	64.6	50.6
E. South Asia	1,538,745	2.0	2.2	1.7	40.8	55.9	3.3	34.9	12.9	2.27	53.6	24.7
14. Eastern South Asia	393,082	2.0	2.1	1.6	40.7	56.0	3.3	31.7	10.9	2.01	56.8	22.8
Burma	38,513	1.7	2.5	2.0	41.3	55.0	3.7	37.9	12.7	2.60	55.0	27.5
Democratic Kampuchea	7,149	2.2	2.9	1.4	32.9	64.6	2.5	45.5	19.6	2.50	43.4	14.7
East Timor	638	1.3	2.5	1.5	34.2	63.4	2.4	48.0	23.0	2.85	39.9	14.1
Indonesia	162,167	1.7	1.8	1.3	41.0	55.6	3.3	30.7	13.0	1.90	52.5	19.8
Lao People's Democratic Republic	4,315	2.1	2.5	2.1	43.4	53.7	2.9	40.6	15.5	2.85	49.7	12.8
Malaysia	15,204	2.5	2.3	1.6	39.1	57.2	3.7	29.2	6.4	1.80	66.9	29.8

Table 8.7 (*continued*)

Country or area	Population (thousands)		Annual growth			Age distribution of population, 1980			Crude vital rates 1980–5 (per 1000 population)		Gross reproduction rate 1980–5	Expectation of life, 1980–5 (years)	Percentage of urban population, 1980
	1984	2000	1950–5	1980–5	1995–2000	0–14	15–64	65 +	Births	Deaths			
Philippines	53,395	74,810	3.0	2.5	1.8	40.6	56.6	2.9	32.3	6.9	2.05	64.5	36.9
Singapore	2,540	2,976	4.9	1.3	0.7	27.1	68.2	4.7	18.0	5.3	0.84	72.2	73.3
Thailand	50,584	66,115	2.7	2.1	1.6	40.2	56.6	3.1	28.6	7.7	1.75	62.7	14.6
Viet Nam	58,307	78,129	1.7	2.0	1.7	41.7	54.6	3.6	31.2	10.1	2.10	58.8	19.8
15. Middle South Asia [a]	1,036,011	1,385,652	1.9	2.2	1.6	40.7	56.1	3.2	35.8	13.9	2.33	51.8	22.4
Afghanistan	14,292	24,180	1.6	0.0	2.2	44.2	53.3	2.4	49.6	27.3	3.35	37.0	16.8
Bangladesh	98,464	145,800	1.6	2.7	2.2	46.2	50.4	3.4	44.8	17.5	3.00	47.8	11.2
Bhutan	1,388	1,893	1.6	2.0	1.8	40.4	56.4	3.2	38.4	18.1	2.70	45.9	4.0
India	746,742	961,531	1.9	2.0	1.3	39.2	57.6	3.2	33.2	13.3	2.15	52.5	22.1
Iran, Islamic Republic of	43,799	65,549	3.7	3.0	2.2	44.2	52.4	3.4	40.5	10.4	2.75	60.2	49.1
Nepal	16,107	23,048	1.2	2.3	2.2	43.5	53.5	3.0	41.7	18.4	3.05	45.9	4.8
Pakistan	98,971	142,554	2.1	3.1	2.2	45.0	52.1	2.8	42.6	15.2	2.85	50.0	28.1
Sri Lanka	16,076	20,843	2.6	2.0	1.4	36.9	59.0	4.2	27.0	6.7	1.65	67.5	26.6
16. Western South Asia	109,651	168,298	2.7	2.9	2.5	41.6	54.4	4.0	37.8	10.1	2.67	60.6	54.0
Arab Countries [r]	55,964	93,695	2.4	3.4	3.0	45.2	51.8	3.0	43.8	11.3	3.27	58.4	56.5
Bahrain	414	688	2.9	4.3	2.6	34.7	63.3	2.1	32.3	5.3	2.26	68.2	70.3
Democratic Yemen	2,066	3,309	1.8	2.7	2.9	46.1	51.3	2.7	47.6	18.8	3.35	46.5	36.9
Iraq	15,158	24,926	2.7	3.4	2.9	46.8	50.7	2.6	44.9	10.7	3.25	59.0	70.9
Jordan	3,375	6,400	3.1	3.7	4.0	49.4	47.5	3.1	44.9	8.4	3.60	64.2	62.5
Kuwait	1,703	2,969	5.4	5.3	2.8	42.6	55.9	1.4	36.8	3.5	3.00	71.2	87.1
Lebanon	2,644	3,617	2.2	–0.0	1.9	40.1	54.5	5.4	29.3	8.8	1.85	65.0	75.5
Oman	1,181	1,909	1.9	4.5	2.8	44.0	53.4	2.6	47.3	15.9	3.45	49.7	6.6
Qatar	291	469	6.7	4.0	2.7	32.6	65.1	2.2	30.1	4.6	3.30	70.6	82.9
Saudi Arabia	10,824	18,864	2.3	3.9	3.2	43.3	53.9	2.8	43.0	12.1	3.45	56.0	64.9
Syrian Arab Republic	10,189	18,102	2.5	3.7	3.3	47.5	49.3	3.2	46.5	7.2	3.50	67.0	51.3
United Arab Emirates	1,255	1,916	2.5	5.8	1.9	29.0	69.0	2.0	27.0	4.0	2.90	70.6	53.3
Yemen	6,386	9,859	1.8	2.4	2.8	45.8	51.0	3.3	48.5	21.6	3.30	44.0	10.2

Non-Arab Countries	51.5	63.8	2.10	8.8	31.7	5.0	57.0	38.0	1.8	2.3	2.9	74.602	53,686
Cyprus	45.6	74.3	1.12	8.2	19.7	10.3	65.4	24.3	0.8	1.1	1.4	759	659
Israel	90.5	74.0	1.50	6.8	23.6	8.4	58.4	33.2	1.3	2.1	6.6	5.376	4,216
Turkey	48.2	63.0	2.17	9.0	32.5	4.6	56.7	38.6	1.9	2.3	2.7	68.466	48,811
F. Europe	70.4	72.9	0.93	10.9	14.0	13.0	64.7	22.3	0.2	0.3	0.8	510.197	490,259
17. Eastern Europe	59.3	71.5	1.05	10.9	16.4	11.9	64.6	23.5	0.4	0.6	1.0	120.393	112,285
Bulgaria	4.0	72.4	1.09	10.7	15.4	12.0	65.8	22.2	0.3	0.5	0.7	9.685	9,184
Czechoslovakia	63.0	71.3	1.07	12.0	16.1	12.7	63.3	24.0	0.5	0.4	1.1	16.679	15,575
German Democratic Republic[s]	77.3	72.4	0.80	13.9	12.5	16.3	64.2	19.5	-0.0	-0.1	-0.5	16.459	16,647
Hungary	54.6	70.6	1.00	13.1	14.4	13.5	65.0	21.5	0.1	0.1	1.0	10.816	10,772
Poland	56.6	71.8	1.09	9.1	18.5	10.0	65.9	24.1	0.6	0.9	1.9	41.222	37,216
Romania	48.1	70.8	1.19	9.8	17.4	10.4	63.1	26.5	0.7	0.8	1.4	25.531	22,891
18. Northern Europe[t]	85.1	73.7	0.87	12.0	12.8	14.6	64.1	21.4	0.0	0.1	0.4	82.929	82,054
Denmark	84.2	74.6	0.74	11.1	11.1	14.2	64.9	20.9	-0.1	0.1	0.8	5.091	5,138
Finland	63.1	73.4	0.78	10.2	12.7	12.0	67.9	20.1	0.0	0.4	1.1	4.947	4,861
Iceland	88.7	76.5	0.99	6.9	17.0	9.6	63.5	27.0	0.6	1.0	2.0	269	240
Ireland	56.2	72.7	1.55	10.0	20.9	11.1	57.9	31.0	1.1	1.1	-0.3	4.228	3,553
Norway	52.4	75.5	0.82	10.7	12.3	14.6	63.2	22.2	0.0	0.3	1.0	4.204	4,137
Sweden	87.2	75.9	0.75	11.5	10.5	16.2	64.3	19.6	-0.2	0.0	0.7	8.071	8,286
United Kingdom	91.2	73.4	0.87	12.6	12.8	14.8	64.1	21.1	0.0	-0.0	0.2	55.849	55,592
19. Southern Europe[u]	62.7	73.0	1.03	9.7	15.4	11.7	64.3	24.0	0.4	0.6	0.8	152.262	141,722
Albania	36.8	70.7	1.75	5.9	27.8	4.8	57.9	37.3	1.7	2.2	2.4	4.089	2,984
Greece	59.9	75.0	1.12	9.5	15.8	13.3	63.9	22.9	0.5	0.6	1.0	10.752	9,900
Italy	70.3	73.6	0.88	10.8	12.8	13.5	64.7	21.8	0.0	0.2	0.6	57.635	56,644
Malta	77.5	71.9	0.95	10.4	17.3	9.9	67.1	23.0	0.5	0.7	0.1	418	380
Portugal	30.9	70.5	1.11	10.0	17.8	10.4	63.5	26.1	0.5	0.7	0.5	10.949	10,005
Spain	74.1	74.0	1.17	8.9	17.0	10.9	63.2	25.9	0.6	0.8	0.8	43.217	38,700
Yugoslavia	42.3	71.0	1.00	8.9	16.4	9.2	66.4	24.4	0.5	0.8	1.4	25.103	23,022
20. Western Europe[v]	77.5	7.39	0.77	11.3	11.7	14.2	65.4	20.4	-0.0	0.1	0.8	154.613	154,198
Austria	54.0	72.7	0.79	12.8	12.1	15.5	64.1	20.4	-0.0	-0.1	0.0	7.454	7,484
Belgium	72.2	73.1	0.78	12.3	12.1	14.3	65.6	20.1	0.0	0.0	0.5	9.867	9,872
France	77.5	74.1	0.89	10.7	13.8	13.7	64.0	22.2	0.2	0.3	0.8	56.588	54,453
Germany, Republic of[s]	83.7	73.3	0.69	12.0	10.2	15.0	66.3	18.6	-0.2	-0.2	0.9	59.456	61,212

Table 8.7 (*continued*)

Country or area	Population (thousands)		Annual growth			Age distribution of population, 1980			Crude vital rates 1980–5 (per 1000 population)		Gross reproduction rate 1980–5	Expectation of life 1980–5 (years)	Percentage of urban population, 1980
	1984	2000	1950–5	1980–5	1995–2000	0–14	15–64	65 +	Births	Deaths			
Luxembourg	363	356	0.6	−0.1	−0.1	19.7	66.3	14.0	10.1	12.0	0.67	72.6	76.7
Netherlands	14,452	14,957	1.2	0.4	0.1	22.1	66.4	11.5	11.6	8.7	0.70	75.7	75.5
Switzerland	6,309	5,871	1.2	−0.3	−0.5	18.1	67.1	14.8	8.1	10.7	0.65	75.8	58.9
G. Oceania	24,458	30,410	2.2	1.5	1.3	29.5	62.6	7.9	21.1	8.4	1.32	67.6	74.9
21. Australia-New Zealand	18,781	22,368	2.3	1.2	1.0	25.9	64.8	9.3	16.1	7.8	0.96	74.1	87.4
Australia	15,518	18,675	2.3	1.3	1.1	25.6	65.1	9.3	16.2	7.7	0.97	74.3	87.4
New Zealand	3,263	3,693	2.3	0.8	0.7	27.1	63.6	9.3	15.6	8.1	0.90	73.4	87.4
22. Melanesia	4,158	6,165	1.6	2.8	2.2	42.8	54.1	3.2	40.4	12.7	2.92	55.0	27.5
Papua New Guinea	3,601	5,292	1.6	2.7	2.2	42.4	54.3	3.2	40.4	13.6	2.92	53.3	27.3
Other Melanesia w	557	873	2.0	3.2	2.5	45.0	52.2	2.8	39.9	6.6	2.90	66.8	28.7
23. Micronesia-Polynesia	1,519	1,877	2.8	1.7	1.1	40.7	56.1	3.1	32.1	5.4	2.08	69.3	40.9
Micronesia x	348	437	2.7	1.7	1.3	41.1	55.6	3.3	34.9	8.5	2.43	62.7	39.1
Polynesia	1,171	1,440	2.8	1.7	1.0	40.6	56.3	3.1	31.3	4.4	1.98	71.6	41.5
Fiji	674	821	3.0	1.7	1.0	36.9	60.0	3.1	27.2	4.1	1.55	72.5	42.2
Other Polynesia y	498	619	2.5	1.7	1.1	45.6	51.3	3.1	36.8	4.9	2.70	70.6	40.6
H. 24. USSR	276,066	313,940	1.7	1.0	0.7	24.3	65.6	10.0	18.8	9.0	1.15	71.3	63.2

Source: Data compiled by the population division of the Department of International Economic and Social Affairs of the United Nations Secretariat. This table is published as an Annex to the 'United Nations Concise Report on The World Population Situation in 1983': ST/ESA/SER.A/85. Department of International Economic and Social Affairs. No. 85, United Nations. New York, 1984.

Notes: Crude vital rates are average annual births and deaths per 1,000 population at the middle of the period. Gross reproduction rates are sums of average rates of female births to women by age during the period indicated. Expectation of life is average of expectations for males and females at birth, based on average death rates by age during the period indicated. Population totals may not agree with sums of figures for component areas because of rounding or omission of small populations.

^{a} Data for small countries or areas, generally those with a population of 300,000 or less in 1975, are not given separately in this table but have been included in the regional population figures.

[b] More developed regions include Northern America, Japan, all regions of Europe, Australia-New Zealand and the Union of Soviet Socialist Republics.

[c] Less-developed regions include all regions of Africa, all regions of Latin America, China, other East Asia, all regions of South Asia, Melanesia and Micronesia-Polynesia.

[d] Including British Indian Ocean Territory, Djibouti and Seychelles.

[e] Including Agalesa, Rodrigues and St. Brandon.

[f] Including Sao Tome and Principe.

[g] Including Western Sahara.

[h] Including St. Helena.

[i] Including Dominica, Grenada, Saint Lucia and Saint Vincent and the Grenadines.

[j] Including Antigua, Bahamas, British Virgin Islands, Cayman Islands, Montserrat, Netherlands Antilles, St. Kitts-Nevis-Anguilla, Turks and Caicos Islands and United States Virgin Islands.

[k] Including Belize and Panama Canal Zone.

[l] Including Falkland Islands (Malvinas).

[m] Including French Guiana.

[n] Including Bermuda, Greenland and St. Pierre and Miquelon.

[o] Including Macau.

[p] Including Brunei.

[q] Including Maldives.

[r] Including Gaza Strip (Palestine).

[s] The data which relate to the Federal Republic of Germany and the German Democratic Republic include the relevant data relating to Berlin for which separate data have not been supplied. This is without prejudice to any question of status which may be involved.

[t] Including Channel Islands, Faeroe Islands and Isle of Man.

[u] Including Andorra, Gibraltar, Holy See and San Marino.

[v] Including Liechtenstein and Monaco.

[w] Including New Caledonia, Norfolk Island, Solomon Islands and Vanuatu.

[x] Including Canton and Enderbury Islands, Christmas Island, Cocos (Keeling) Islands, Johnston Island, Midway Islands, Pitcairn Island, Tokelau and Wake Islands, Kiribati, Guam, Nauru, Niue, Pacific Islands and Tuvalu.

[y] Including American Samoa, Cook Islands, French Polynesia, Samba, Tonga and Wallis and Futuna Islands.

Presented in this summary and aggregate form, these tables are perhaps less than wholly illuminating. They do not, for example, say anything about the extent to which national population policies and family-planning programmes have contributed to recorded declines in birth-rates (see Table 8.8). Nor *a fortiori* do they indicate the part that may have been played in such declines by international assistance in general and by the United Nations in particular. It seems sensible therefore to consider some of the key countries around the world where the birth-rate has been falling with a view to indicating, as far as this is possible, what part population and family-planning programmes have played in this process and what, if any, contribution has been made by external assistance, including that of the United Nations.

Caveats

Any such attempt has, of course, to be preceded by a large number of caveats. Professional demographers are in no doubt about the difficulties involved in distinguishing between declines in fertility which as it were 'happen anyway' as a result of the process of economic and social development (the classic theory of 'demographic transition') and those that are brought about as a result of the deliberate adoption of population policies and family-planning programmes. Even the most sophisticated regression analyses leave room for residual uncertainties. And it is perhaps even more difficult to estimate the importance of the role played by external assistance. If resources had not been found from outside, would they nevertheless have been provided somehow from within a country's own budgetary possibilities? In that case it could hardly be argued that fertility declines (or some proportion of them) occurred purely as a result of external assistance. If, on the other hand, the external assistance was *genuinely additional* (not substituting for national spending), then such a case could be made.

Quite apart from the question of external funding of population projects, there are other extraneous contributions to be considered. All the international symposia, seminars and conferences held on the subject of population over the years; all the broadcasts made, speeches given, articles written must surely have had their effect – directly, indirectly, homeopathically or even subliminally – on the formulation of policy at a national level. How is that effect to be assessed except by the crudest of yardsticks? Yet in the long-run the promulgation of ideas and influence through the medium of the United Nations and its agencies may have had just as important an impact in lowering birth-rates around the world as, say, the provision of direct assistance to a national family-planning programme.

Table 8.8. *Number and population of developing countries by governmental policy position and date* [a] *of initial governmental support of family planning, by region (1980)*

Region	Support: demographic rationale [b]	Support: health and human rights rationale [c]	Nonsupport [d]
South Asia	5	2	0
Population (millions)	882.1	1.4	0
% Regional population	99.8%	0.2%	0

Demographic support: Bangladesh 1960, India 1951, Nepal 1965, Pakistan 1960, Sri Lanka 1953

Health and human rights support: Bhutan 1979, Maldives 1978

East Asia	4	0	3
Population (millions)	1035.8		19.9
% Regional population	98.1%		1.9%

Demographic support: China 1956, Hong Kong 1955, South Korea 1961, Taiwan 1959

Nonsupport: North Korea, Macao, Mongolia

Southeast Asia and Oceania	14	4	7
Population (millions)	311.1	3.3	44.4
% Regional population	86.7%	0.9%	12.4%

Demographic support: Indonesia 1967, Malaysia 1964, Philippines 1969, Singapore 1959, Thailand 1967, Vietnam 1962 (South Vietnam 1968), Cook Islands 1974, Fiji 1962, Kiribati 1970, New Hebrides 1972, Samoa 1970, Solomon Islands 1970, Tonga 1958, Tuvalu 1970

Health and human rights support: Papua New Guinea 1968, American Samoa 1973, Guam 1967, St Helena 1975

Nonsupport: Brunei, Burma, Kampuchea (support 1971–7), Laos (support 1971–6), Nauru, Tahiti, Tokelau Island

Latin America and the Caribbean	15	22	6
Population (millions)	120.4	203.9	6.1
% Regional population	36.4%	61.7%	1.8%

Demographic support: Colombia 1967, Dominican Republic 1968, El Salvador 1968, Guatemala 1969, Mexico 1972, Puerto Rico 1967, Barbados 1955, Grenada 1974, Guadeloupe 1968, Jamaica 1966, Martinique c. 1976, St Kitts-Nevis 1971, St Lucia 1975, St Vincent 1972, Trinidad & Tobago 1967

Health and human rights support: Brazil 1974, Chile 1962, Costa Rica 1967, Cuba early 1960s, Ecuador 1968, Haiti 1971, Honduras 1966, Nicaragua 1967, Panama 1969, Paraguay 1972, Peru 1976, Venezuela 1965, Anguilla 1979, Antigua 1973, Bermuda 1937, Cayman Islands 1977, Dominica 1970, Guyana 1977, Montserrat 1976, Netherlands Antilles 1965, Br. Virgin Islands 1979, US Virgin Islands 1970

Nonsupport: Bolivia (support 1968–76), Bahamas, Belize, French Guiana, Suriname, Turks and Caicos

Table 8.8 (*continued*)

	5	11	10
Middle East			
Population (millions)	153.6	93.3	19.5
% Regional population	57.7%	35.0%	7.3%

Demographic support: Iran 1967, Turkey 1965, Egypt 1965, Morocco 1965, Tunisia 1964

Health and human rights support: Afghanistan 1970, Bahrain 1974, Iraq 1971, Jordan 1976, Lebanon 1970, Syria 1974, North Yemen 1975, South Yemen 1973, Algeria 1971, Somalia 1977, Sudan 1970

Nonsupport: Kuwait, Oman, Palestine (Gaza), Qatar, Saudi Arabia, United Arab Emirates, Djibouti, Libya, Mauritania, Albania

	8	10	1
English-speaking Sub-Saharan Africa			
Population (millions)	45.0	176.9	6.1
% Regional population	19.7%	77.6%	2.7%

Demographic support: Botswana 1970, Ghana 1968, Kenya 1966, Lesotho 1974, Mauritius 1964, Seychelles 1975, Swaziland 1971, Uganda 1971

Health and human rights support: Ethiopia 1972, Gambia 1968, Liberia 1973, Namibia 1972, Nigeria 1970, Sierra Leone 1976, South Africa 1966, Tanzania 1970, Zambia 1974, Zimbabwe 1968

Nonsupport: Malawi

	1	16	8
French and Portuguese-speaking Sub-Saharan Africa			
Population (millions)	5.7	90.1	32.2
% Regional population	4.5%	70.4%	25.2%

Demographic support: Senegal 1976

Health and human rights support: Benin 1969, Burundi 1979, Cameroon 1975, Cape Verde 1978, Central African Republic 1978, Comoros 1979, Congo 1976, Guinea-Bissau 1976, Madagascar 1976, Mali 1971, Mozambique 1977, Niger 1977, Réunion 1966, Rwanda 1977, Togo 1974, Zaire 1972

Nonsupport: Angola, Chad, Equatorial Guinea (Spanish-speaking), Gabon, Guinea, Ivory Coast, São Tomé & Principe, Upper Volta

Developing world total			
Countries	52	65	35
Population (millions)	2553.7	569.0	128.2
% Regional population	78.6%	17.5%	3.9%

Source: International Encyclopedia of Population, 1982.

Notes: ᵃ Earliest date with reasonable evidence of *governmental* commitment to family planning (e.g. by formal programmatic effort, by initial *governmental* budgetary or facilities support of family-planning association, or by *governmental* agreement with or submission of request to UNFPA for family planning support.)
ᵇ Countries supporting family planning to reduce threat of rapid population growth to development or for related demographic reasons usually also support it for health and human rights.
ᶜ Some countries supporting family planning for health and human rights reasons recognize that a programme may have demographic consequences and thus affect development.
ᵈ Position of some countries unclear; several seem to be moving toward support.

There is only one way, it seems, of reaching any kind of judgement and that is to proceed on a country-by-country basis. Since China looms so large – because of her sheer size and because of the particular population policy which she had adopted – we begin this review there. The discussion of China's programme is followed by a section on India, whose official family-planning programme is the oldest in the world and which has known its successes as well as its vicissitudes. Other Asian countries where declines in fertility have been recorded and where the United Nations has been involved include Indonesia, Thailand and Sri Lanka, and some account is given of developments in each of those countries.

What happens in Asia is, from the global point of view, crucial. As a whole, Asia accounts for 56 per cent of the world's population and 75 per cent of the developing world's population. If the battle to bring down birth-rates cannot be won in Asia, it will not be won at all.

But there has been some important progress also in Latin America where some tropical South American countries – Brazil, Colombia and Venezuela – as well as Costa Rica and Panama have entered into an nearly stage of the transition, that is the beginning of a significant decline in fertility and sharp declines in mortality rates. Mexico has also experienced a marked decline in fertility and improved life expectancy[3]. This Chapter summarizes the recent demographic history in three of those countries: Brazil, Colombia and Mexico.

As far as the Middle East is concerned, the Governments of Egypt and Tunisia have launched national programmes for population activities designed to accomplish explicit demographic objectives of reductions in fertility and population growth; some account is given of these though progress can at best be described as patchy.

Many challenges still lie ahead, most notably in Sub-Saharan Africa, but also in those areas of Latin America and Asia where birth-rates have not yet begun to fall significantly and where, therefore, intensified efforts are required at the national and international level. An attempt is made in this chapter to indicate what some of those challenges are.

ASIA

Half of mankind

In 1975, two out of every four persons in the world lived in Asia. Excluding those in Soviet Asia and Western South Asia (or the Middle East) there were more than two billion Asians in the total world population of

3.9 billion. The region had the world's two most populated countries – India and China – which together accounted for 36 per cent of the world total. According to the United Nations' figures, China's population at the end of 1975 stood at 838.8 million and India's at 613.2 million. Each was considerably bigger than Europe's 473 million, Latin America's 324 million, the Soviet Union's 255 million, North America's 236 million, and Oceania's 21.3 million. Indonesia and Japan had over 100 million each, and outside Asia, their populations were exceeded only by those of the Soviet Union and the United States. Despite their separation in 1971, Pakistan with 70.5 million people and Bangladesh, with 73.7 million, still counted among the world's ten most populated countries. Three Asian countries – Re-unified Viet Nam, Thailand and the Philippines – had each gone past the 40-million mark and were experiencing an annual population increase of 1 million or more.

A prominent feature of the region's population was its rapid growth. In the first half of the decade (1970–5) that growth averaged 2.3 per cent growth annually, higher than the world average of 1.8 per cent for the same period and exceeded only by Africa's 2.6 per cent and Latin America's 2.7 per cent. Other regions had far lower growth rates. Europe averaged only 0.6 per cent, the Soviet Union 0.9 per cent and the United States of America 0.8 per cent. A notable exception in Asia was Japan which, after a long, almost imperceptible process spanning a century, completed its demographic transition in the 1950s. In 1975, Japan had low birth-rates and low death-rates, a fairly stable age structure, and a low net reproduction rate – factors which pointed to eventual cessation of growth. A few other countries, like China and other areas in East Asia, seemed to be moving in the same direction, but paucity of data (as in China's case) and the presence of many variables, made it difficult to predict how soon their transition would be completed.

The most rapid population growth was being experienced in Middle South, Eastern South, and Western South Asia, where growth rates had gone up to 2.4–2.8 per cent annually, compared to just 2 per cent for all Asia in the 1950s and less than 1 per cent in the first half of this century.

In numerical terms, the dimensions of such growth seem even starker. In 1800 Asia's population was only about 600 million. It took a century to grow to 925 million – a gain of slightly over 50 per cent. By 1920, the figure had exceeded 1 billion. Net additions have grown progressively larger ever since. The population doubled only 50 years after reaching the billion mark. The third billion was expected by 1990 and, if growth rates remained at their current high levels, Asia in the year 2000 would have had 3.6 billion people – exceeding the earth's total population in 1970.

China

Census results

At midnight on June 30, 1953, a few days after man's first ascent of Everest, the Government of China undertook the first systematic census for the whole country. The results, announced on November 1, 1954, revealed that the population of the mainland as of June 30, 1953 (or the 20th day of the fifth moon of the kuei-szu year) stood at 582.6 million persons. Since the highest working estimate had not exceeded 500 millions, and many had settled for something nearer the Kuomintang's 1945 estimate of 450 millions, the census results came as a surprise and a shock to much of the world.

Subsequently a total of over 646 million at the end of the year 1957 was obtained from the National Population Registration System. In 1964 a second census counted a total of 691 million and a registration total of 982 million was announced for the end of 1980.

According to official estimates, the birth-rate was 37 per 1000 population in 1952 and the death-rate was 17, the rate of natural increase being therefore 2 per cent per annum. During the food-crisis years, 1960–1, mortality rose sharply as fertility declined, but official data show a rebound in the birth-rate to 43.6 per 1000 and a peak in natural increase at 33.5 per 1000 in 1963. Fertility and natural increase remained high during the rest of the 1960s reaching a secondary peak towards the end of the decade. Fertility began to decline sharply after 1971, according to official sources, and by 1979 the birth-rate was reported as 17.9 per 1000. The death-rate was said to be around 7 per 1000 in the middle 1970s and had declined further to 6.2 per 1000 by 1979. The rate of natural increase had thus fallen by the end of the decade to around the 1 per cent level[4].

Population planning in China

When the People's Republic of China was established in 1949, the new leaders explicitly rejected any notion that the country might be faced with problems because of the size or rate of growth of its population. However, under the aegis of the Hundred Flowers movement in the spring of 1957, leading Chinese scholars began to speak out on the need to control population growth and on the problems that population growth posed for national economic development. The Big Leap Forward launched in the spring was a big step backward as far as population planning was concerned. Mao stated that a large and impoverished population was an asset in building socialism. China's peasants were said to have overthrown the law of diminishing returns in agriculture and 'put the final nail in the coffin of Malthus'. Birth-control efforts languished and the production of contraceptives all but ceased.

Early in 1962, a new birth control campaign was started, and a major effort was made to popularize late marriage. Intrauterine devices, which had been tried out experimentally during the first campaign, were publicly promoted for the first time. The second birth-control campaign was interrupted by the Cultural Revolution in the summer of 1966.

The third birth-control campaign began in 1968 as the United Nations was gearing itself up for more vigorous action in the population field, but the initial stages were tentative and not very forceful. By about 1972, the efforts had been greatly intensified, and from that time onward a considerable decline in the national birth-rate was reported. Controlling population growth was seen as being of critical importance to China's programme of modernization and to the prospects for improving living standards in rural and urban areas alike. The objectives for the future included popularizing the one-child family as an ideal for all of China and limiting the size of the population to less than 1.2 billion by the year 2000[5].

Probably, no other country in the world has embraced the concept of population planning as wholeheartedly as China. Liu Zheng, Director of the Population Research Institute at the Chinese People's University of Beijing has described China's position as follows[6]:

In view of what had been learned from past experience China has decided to bring the population growth under control by planning. Hence, it has planned the development not only of the production of material goods but also of the population growth, in both the 5-year plan and the yearly plans to surmount the blind increase of population and enhance its planned development. Past experience indicates that setting definite target for the population growth and having a correspondingly feasible target plan to control that growth are indispensable conditions for realising the plan to control the population.... It is essential to take appropriate economic measures to coordinate the interrelationship of the Government, the collective and the family.

Liu Zheng goes on to discuss in unambiguous terms what is perhaps the most remarkable feature of China's population policy; the system of incentives and disincentives.

Married couples are encouraged to have only 1 child throughout their life time. They are awarded an allowance for the child's health care.... The 1-child family could occupy a living space as large as that for a 2-children family in urban areas. In rural areas a 1-child family may have the same amount of land for housing-building and a private plot as a 2-children family.

In order to dispel the worries of parents having no children or only one, it is necessary to ensure the social security of the elderly. In urban areas staff and workers, being insured by retirement pensions, have fewer worries. For the encouragement of 1-child bearing (for those couples who have either no children or only 1) a certain percentage of ordinary pensions are added. In rural areas the social security for the elderly varies from place to place. China stands firm against not only the use of 'economic constraint' instead of ideological education but also 'coercion and commandism' in disguise, which ignore the interests and the consciousness of the masses. It consistently favours the use of propaganda and education to bring the broad masses out of their state of ignorance to awareness, and from unconsciousness to consciousness in family planning, so that it could be practised as a normal social custom....

Strengthening technical guidance in birth-control and providing contraceptives promptly are the main practical guarantees of realising the goal of birth control. In order to control the fertility rate in a planned way, it is necessary to let the vast number of fertile couples know of the various contraceptive methods and to obtain the necessary contraceptives. As regards to contraceptive methods, China advocates the adoption of comprehensive measures in consonance with an individual's conditions, i.e. each couple, in accordance with its own wishes and physical conditions, decides to adopt the kind of contraceptive method which would give the best contraceptive effect. All contraceptives supplies are free of charge, and induced abortion and sterilisation are free of charge as well. Moreover, the Government has introduced a uniform system of giving certain leave with full pay wages or work points to the people undergoing induced abortion or sterilisation. So for the purpose of strengthening technical guidance in contraception and birth control, the health care departments are staffed by the medical personnel who are well trained in planned birth services. They endeavour to perfect their skill and to improve their technique and have made contributions to the control of the fertility rate. Among medical personnel some have performed 10,000 operations without accidents....

The people's highest organ of state power, the National People's Congress and its standing committee paid great attention and concern to the worker family planning and population control. In March of 1978, at the Second Plenary Session of the Fifth National People's Congress, 'the Government promotes and pursues family planning' was written into the Constitution of the People's Republic of China. This is the first time since the founding of the Republic that family planning was made one of the fundamental organs of the country.... In 1980, the National People's Congress passed a new marriage law, in which 'carry out family planning' was indefinitely stipulated in the second clause of the General Principles....

This lengthy quotation is important since, given the source, it can be regarded as official statement of policy. Indeed, such is the level of political commitment to population planning in China, that she must inevitably be categorized as a major 'donor' as far as United Nations population activities are concerned – not so much, of course, from the point of her financial contribution (though by 1985 her annual payments to the Fund had risen to US $500,000) but rather from the point of view of the approach taken to demographic questions and the experience acquired in bringing down birth rates.

Salas' own comment is instructive[7]:

> At the invitation of the Government I visited the country in late 1972 and had an opportunity to discuss population problems with the officials directing the various Birth Planning Programs in Shanghai and Peking.... Before the trip I knew about the policies of China on late marriage, birth spacing, and the teaching of small-family norms. But observing at first hand the manner in which these policies were worked out in the smallest political and administrative units of the country was the most instructive part of the visit.
>
> China views its birth planning programmes as an integral part of its development efforts. Specifically, these programmes are part of the health services available to all citizens who need them. All forms of contraception from pills to sterilisation are utilized. But what was interesting to me in the management of these programmes was not the wide variety of techniques employed but the emphasis given to motivating couples to make a decision on the size of their families.
>
> This motivational work is done through formal education, neighbourhood group discussions, and even by home visits from both medical personnel and the 'barefoot doctors'. The message is for parents who have smaller families. Whether in factories or in communes, the couples are encouraged and assisted to make the decision for themselves on how to achieve their own birth-planning objectives. This type of participatory decision making and the skilful use of small groups strongly reminded me of the methods we used in my country to increase food production.
>
> I left China with a feeling that I had found a really good example of how to integrate family planning programs into development and even more significant to do all these without any external assistance at all but as a sheer act of will of both people and government. This was to influence my thinking and the Fund's.

The Chinese experience is perhaps of special interest as an example of the so-called 'revised theory' of demographic transition. As the World Bank put it in its World Development Report 1984[8]:

> It was once assumed that reducing fertility in developing countries would require a typical sequence of economic advance: urbanisation, industrialisation, a shift from production in the household to factory production, and incomes rising to the level enjoyed by today's developed countries. This view seemed to be confirmed by the fertility declines of the 1960s, which were largely confined to the industrialising economies of Korea, Singapore, and Hong Kong. But fertility declines beginning in other developing countries in the late 1960s, and spreading to more in the 1970s, have been related to a different kind of development: education, health, and the alleviation of poverty. Birth-rate

declines have been much more closely associated with adult literacy and life expectancy than with GNP per capita.

Professor Norman Uphoff of the Centre for International Studies at Cornell University points out

A number of Third World countries have already begun to reverse their rate of population growth at per capita income levels of $150, $200 or $300 in conjunction with strategies of development that stressed not so much the expansion of a modern industrial sector starting out with advanced technology, but rather the development of agriculture in the rural areas, using throughout most of the economy production techniques that are appropriate to the existing factor endowments, particularly their abundant labour[9].

Citing particularly the case of China and Sri Lanka, he suggests that

The equivalent of the demographic transition can be achieved at per capita income levels well below those observed historically in Europe and North America.... The development strategy followed by these early developers, with its unequal distribution of benefits concentrated in the urban-industrial sector, meant that average per capita incomes had to reach, say US $600 to US $1000 before the rural majority began to receive some improvement in income, welfare and security that would be conducive to reducing fertility... even small reductions in the fertility rate of the rural majority will contribute more to bringing down national population growth rates than will achieving much larger drops for the urban middle and upper classes, who constitute a definite minority.

And Freedman and Berelson observe that the delivery system for family planning in China, including services and supplies in the traditional sense as well as motivational activity, is integrated not only into the health structure from locality to central hospital but into the entire administrative, economic, social and political structure of the country as well. This last is a key and distinctive feature of the system, enabling the Government to launch mass campaigns, and therefore reach down to the household in a systematic and potentially powerful way, like national Chinese campaigns in other fields rather than family-planning programmes in other countries. Up to 70 per cent of Chinese couples of child-bearing age are estimated to be using modern contraceptives[10].

It is of course quite unrealistic to suppose that other countries in the developing world will wish or be able to follow the Chinese experience in all aspects. And, indeed, it would have been quite ironic if an organisation like UNFPA, with its historic reliance on the United States as a major source of funds and with important support from other Western donors, had come to the conclusion that the Chinese approach was the only viable one. But the Chinese case seemed to illustrate that the 'uncoupling' of fertility and income was possible at least in certain circumstances and to a certain extent. The lesson to be learned was, not that it was unnecessary to pursue development at the same time as population planning; rather it was that certain kinds of development would have a bigger impact on fertility control than other kinds.

A two-way street

Though Mr Salas in the comment noted above spoke of China's ability to carry on its affairs 'without any external assistance at all', China has in fact received substantial assistance from the United Nations. In June 1980, the Governing Council of UNFPA approved assistance to China in the amount of $50 million for five years. The programme emphasized the introduction of new technologies and equipment not available in China, and the improvement of technical training, research and institutional development. For example, the National Training Centre for Family Planning Personnel in Nanjing, established with UNFPA assistance, was providing training for 70,000 full-time family planning workers. China was being helped to expand the supply of intrauterine devices (IUDs) which accounted for approximately 50 per cent of contraceptive use. UNFPA and WHO were together supporting applied and basic research on contraceptives and human reproduction. $15.6 million was provided in support of the 1982 census which included assistance for preparation and publicity, census-taking, data processing, printing, analysis and dissemination of findings.

A second comprehensive programme of assistance to China in the amount of US $50 million was approved by the UNDP Governing Council at its 1984 session. Among the projects to be supported over the five-year period, 1985–9, were several relating to the production of contraceptives. ($8 million to be provided over five years). The new programme would also include projects relating to: population policies and planning; basic data collection and analysis; support of MCH/FP services; population education; demographic research and training; programmes for the aged; and research into contraception and human reproduction[11].

The United Nations' relationship with China over population matters must therefore be seen as a two-way street. The UN gained much from the Chinese experience. At the same time it is clear that, even though in this field as in so many others it is China's own determined efforts which have finally made the difference between success and failure, the contribution of the United Nations to China's population policies and programmes has been both real and important. Whether, in retrospect, it was sensible for the United Nations to become quite so heavily involved with a programme which anyway already had a successful momentum of its own given the price which later had to be paid in terms of the US reaction to the 'abortion issue' is an intriguing but perhaps academic point. The reality is that, at the time the United Nations's commitments in China were being expanded, it would have been difficult to foresee the 'volte-face' which the United States would spring on an unsuspecting world at Mexico City in August 1984[12]. And, in any case, even if future troubles could have been anticipated, would it have been right for the United Nations to have withdrawn its support for a Member State merely because in the legitimate exercise of national sovereignty it determined to implement certain population policies which another Member State found to be distasteful? The Chinese way of birth control might not be to everyone's liking, but that was neither here nor there. The management of UNFPA was satisfied that no coercion was involved and that no UNFPA monies were being used to finance any such activities including abortion. That being the case, the United Nations might have lost far more than it gained by bowing, and being seen to bow, before US pressure.

India

The family-planning programme

If China must be awarded the palm for actual achievements in the population field, there is no doubt that India deserves the prize for perseverance. In 1951, India became the first government in the world to adopt a comprehensive national family-planning policy as an integral part of its development plans. The beginning was modest enough. Over the period 1951-6 1.45 million Rupees were spent; 147 clinics were established. The method promoted was, principally, rhythm, and the impact – so far as could be judged – was negligible.

Not much more progress was achieved in the second five-year plan, from 1956 to 1961. Expenditure increased to 22 million rupees and the number of clinics rose to 4165. But still Anglo-Saxon attitudes prevailed with their emphasis on specialized birth control clinics. There was no thought of a mass educational campaign nor would the clinic staff, committed to the time-honoured and time-consuming procedures of doctor–patient consultations and overburdened by record keeping, have been able to conduct one in any case. Perhaps the most significant event of the Second Plan period was that in 1958 the Government of India officially endorsed sterilization as a main method of contraception. In 1960, it began to reimburse the states for the cost of sterilization operations.

161

When the census revealed that population had grown from 360 millions to 439 millions, an increase of 78 millions or 21.5 per cent over the period 1951–61, the government realized how badly it had underestimated the rate of population growth in the previous decade; it looked at the future and saw what a gloomy prospect lay ahead unless something could be done to close the 'widening gap'. Clearly what had been achieved in the first two Plan periods was nowhere near enough. New approaches were required.

Thus the 'extension' approach was born. The old Anglo-Saxon pattern of specialized birth control clinics was discarded. Family planning was to be incorporated into general health work, becoming a regular part of the activities of health centres, child and maternity clinics and so forth. According to the new philosophy, the services would seek out the people. Systems of mass communication and mass education would be devised to supplement the 'informational' and 'motivational' efforts of medical, paramedical and other personnel engaged in the work. Community participation was to be of paramount importance; there was to be a total mobilization of resources, whereby the energies of the 'panchayats' – village councils, 'gram Sewaks' – village level workers, 'dais', village midwives, Ayurvedic physicians and other 'practitioners of indigenous systems of medicine', women's organizations, social workers, business and industrial leaders, civil servants, religious bodies, Gandhian 'sarvodaya' workers, etc would all be harnessed to the task. It was an immense and exciting vision, founded on the belief that the tools now existed to change basic human behaviour on a vast scale and in a most radical way.

The Indian family-planning programme was, to use the words of the Minister of Health and Family Planning, Dr S. Chandrasekhar, the most imaginative attempt at 'engineered social change' that had ever been launched.

The vision did not spring fully grown from the head of the Government of India as soon as the results of the decennial census of 1961 were published. It grew piece by piece. The Chinese invasion in the autumn of 1962 forced government departments to reexamine their priorities; the 1962–3 Report on the Family-Planning Programme, for example, emphasized the 'need for family planning programmes in the emergency; especially the need to extend the community education extension aspect of the programme and to increase the use of non-clinical approaches to the promotion of family planning'. In early 1965, a World Bank team headed by Bernard Bell visited India and made, *inter alia*, a report on the family-planning programme. Shortly afterwards the United Nations sent an expert mission, headed by Sir Colville Deverell – then Secretary-General of IPPF – to undertake a general review of the progress and effectiveness of

162

the family-planning programme to date and to make recommendations for future action. The reports of both missions served to confirm and strengthen the Government of India (GOI) in its pioneering endeavours.

The most significant development of all, however – and one on which GOI placed the highest hopes for an expanded and effective programme – was technological. To say that the intra-uterine device was the answer to the maiden's prayer would be to exaggerate, since its use was recommended only for women who had already borne a child. That limitation aside, the IUD appeared to represent the real breakthrough the whole world was waiting for. This, indeed, was the term the UN mission used. It wrote:

A major breakthrough in the family planning programme is now in sight with the recent acceptance of the Government of India of the intrauterine device, the loop, as a contraceptive method to be offered after various successful trials in India and some other countries. This method has the advantage of being cheap, reversible, safe and highly effective and as it involves only one decision it does not need constant follow-up to ensure the continuance of motivation. The Mission expects that the intrauterine device will be readily accepted by the majority of Indian women as it has been by women in other countries where it has been introduced. It is hoped that the method will be accepted not only by women who do not wish to have any more children but also by younger women as a method of spacing child births[13].

The Government of India seized on the IUD with alacrity. With a successful IUD campaign, there was a faint hope that the 'target' declines in the birth-rate – down to 25 births per 1000 population by 1973, down to 22 per thousand by 1978–9 – could be achieved. And the GOI's commitment to the family-planning programme, at the end of 1968, was certainly impressive. Expenditure under the Third Plan (1961–2 to 1965–6) amounted to 250 million Rupees. But in 1966–7 alone 139 million Rupees were spent and in 1967–8 265 million Rupees, while 370 million Rupees was budgeted for 1968–9. Until the brief but bitter Indo–Pakistan war in the autumn of 1965 and some disastrous harvests upset the even succession of five-year plans, 2290 million Rupees had been allocated in the Fourth Plan, which was about eight times the allocation of the previous plan. The Government of India had accorded 'top priority' to the programme which had been launched on a 'war footing'.

When, after an interregnum of one-year plans, the five-year cycle was resumed, this 'top priority' was maintained. The Planning Commission stated in its 'Approach to the Fourth Five-Year Plan 1969–74' that 'This programme has already been accepted as a centrally-sponsored scheme for a period of ten years. Whatever can usefully be spent on the programme may be provided ...'. The programme had been given what, in theory, amounted to a blank cheque. The budget for family planning amounted to 2.1 per cent of total public sector outlays. By comparison, health had 3.0 per cent of public sector outlays, agriculture 15 per cent, power 14 per cent, industry and minerals 21.5 per cent, transport and communications 22 per cent and education 5.6 per cent. (Other categories of expenditure accounted for the rest.)

In 1969, India had asked the United Nations to evaluate the programme and the immediate result was a substantial increase in government expenditures and in bilateral support. UNFPA, for its part, had agreed to contribute $1 million for an innovative vasectomy campaign – a decision which demonstrated rather clearly that the Fund did not intend to be squeamish about the use to which its money was put[14]. As Salas put it in his first speech to the UNDP Governing Council: 'The Fund never seeks to urge any particular population policy or programmes on any country. It is neutral with respect to policy'[15] – a statement which implied that, if the Fund did not seek to persuade, it would not seek to dissuade either. If the Government of a country, in the full exercise of sovereignty, chose to go down one particular road, then – as long as it was clear that the voluntary and non-coercive nature of the programme was not in question – the Fund was prepared to follow with whatever support it could muster.

At the time, the $1 million UNFPA aid for the mass vasectomy camps was the largest direct assistance agreement which the Fund had so far concluded. India took the view that in the population field they had sufficient experts of their own and had no need of foreign consultants. Salas agreed with this assessment. Thus a precedent for large-scale direct assistance was set, which would as time went on become increasingly important.

In spite of the commitment of human and material resources, progress in the Indian family-planning programme was slow. Impatience with poor performance led to an unprecedented increase in the extent of political support from the top echelons of the central government during the period of 'Emergency' declared in June 1975. In April 1976, the central government issued a 'national population policy statement' which promised measures to raise the age at marriage, improve literacy and education among women, and enhance the nutritional status of all children. Monetary compensation was increased to individuals undergoing sterilisation, and group incentives were to be introduced. The intensity of the family-planning programme, particularly the sterilization drive, became the focus of attack by opposition parties during the elections in March 1977; and with the defeat of Mrs Indira Ghandi and the ruling party, the widely feared backlash occurred, leading to a sharp decline in programme performance in June 1977–8. The programme slowly recovered during the succeeding two years; and the performance in June 1979–80 exceeded that during the pre-Emergency Year (1974–5).

India enacted a quite lenient law permitting abortion in 1971. Between April 1972 and March 1980, some 1.6 million registered abortions were performed; and non-registered abortions done by both medical and non-medical personnel were thought to number from 2 to 4 million per year. The minimum legal age of marriage for girls, difficult to enforce because of poor age reporting and absence of a tradition of birth registrations, was raised from 15 to 18 in 1978.

Role of the United Nations

With a family-planning programme of such considerable dimensions, involving the expenditure of billions of Rupees, it would plainly be implausible to argue that assistance provided through the UN system has been the determining factor in bringing the services to the people. The input of the UN has, nevertheless, not been insignificant. Mention has been made of the reports of the World Bank and United Nations missions to India in 1965, and of UNFPA's early support of the vasectomy campaign. UNFPA's major association with India began in 1974, when a small mission from the Fund visited the country to have discussions with the Government and to prepare a five-year programme of assistance. The programme was formulated on the basis of the Government's perception of the population problem and of measures required to cope with this problem. The strategy was based on providing family-planning services through the health care system. Because of the health network's limited infrastructure, terminal methods were seen as the most practical. As an interim plan, the infrastructure itself was to be extended by the creation of a national cadre of multi-purpose health workers at the field level.

In addition, the Fund was also responsible for developing two innovative programmes. The first was the establishment of a documentation centre, which was to provide a sound data base and statistical base for the planning and implementation of the programme. The other involved enlisting the support of organized labour institutions in promoting the small-family norm. The total package of assistance covered by these proposals was $40 million. Implementation of the programme began in 1975. It soon became evident, however, that this strategy would not achieve the reduction in population growth rates projected in the Government's development plan. Other activities, such as increasing the supply of pills, increasing the availability of IUDs and designing communication programmes aimed specifically at community leaders in rural areas, were added to the original components of the First Country Programme.

Several important lessons were learned during this first phase. First, it became clear that the allocation to India was insufficient for effective apportionment over the entire national programme. Second, it was obvious that the population problem was not uniform throughout all India. Population growth rates varied widely among the states, and a single uniform national policy was unlikely to produce the required results. Third, it was realized that in certain northern states, growth rates were so high that special measures were required.

To examine this complex situation, a needs assessment mission visited India in 1979 and carried out an in-depth analysis of the principal problem areas[16]. After the mission presented its report and after consultation with Government, UNFPA designed a second programme of assistance that was both selective and comprehensive. Two states in India with very high growth rates were chosen by the Government of India as the principal focusses for assistance. Six districts in the State of Bihar with population of 15 million and three districts in the State of Rajasthan with a population of six million were to be the principal programme areas. The programme was comprehensive in that, in these nine districts, the Fund agreed to support all the new activities required by a multisectoral programme. The plan was to prepare a programme based on an overall development strategy instead of limiting it to a narrow approach through health care. Special attention was given to programme management, problem solving, interpersonal communication and popular participation, by enlisting voluntary and non-government agencies. Most important, the district administration was given overall responsibility for the programme.

The new comprehensive programmes in Bihar and Rajasthan were expected to provide important information and experience to assist planners in resolving the difficult problems of the northern states. The main task of these programmes would be to introduce a wider framework of administrative responsibilities and improved management and communication systems, designed to make the family-planning programme an effort not merely of the Government but of the entire community. These efforts, of course, had to contend with the formidable obstacle of low rural literacy and widespread rural poverty. In addition to these new comprehensive programmes in the states of Bihar and Rajasthan, the Fund continued to support the large national sterilization and paramedical training programmes.

Other activities were also supported, including several supply projects (IUDs, condoms, laparoscopes and oral pill raw materials); several projects – executed by ILO – aimed at creating information for the introduction of family-planning activities and the provision of contraceptive services in the organized sector, and a major national population education programme which was being carried out in co-operation with UNESCO[17].

Achievements

Today there are undoubtedly parts of India with clear indications of a significant fertility decline. In Kerala, the rural birth-rate declined from more than 37 in 1966 to 25 in 1978. Independent evidence of a decline in fertility is available in the reduced growth rate of enrolments in the first year of primary school – from 4.0 per cent during 1961–2 – 1965–6 to 1.6 per cent during 1965–6 – 1971–2. In Punjab the estimated birth-rate increased from about 33.6 in 1968 to 35.8 in 1972. But this was followed by a decline in the birth-rate to 32 in 1976 and 28 in 1978. The estimate of the rate of natural increase in Punjab was confirmed by the rate of intercensal population growth between 1971 and 1981.

The most recent evidence of fertility rates in India is that these declines have continued and have begun to spread to other states. In its World Development Report 1984, the World Bank notes that the total fertility rate in India fell from 6.5 in the 1950s to 4.8 in 1982, and comments: 'No other country at India's level of socio–economic development – measured by low literacy and per capita income and high infant mortality – has a lower level of fertility.'

The Bank asks what accounts for this impressive record. It notes that continued progress in raising female literacy and lowering infant mortality, as well as a concerted effort to expand access to family planning, have both been important. Within India there is wide variation which closely corresponds to patterns of social development. For example, in the state of Kerala which has the lowest total fertility (2.7 in 1978), 75 per cent of rural women are literate, infant mortality is 47 per 1000 live births, and 32 per cent of couples are protected by modern contraception. By contrast, in the state of Uttar Pradesh, total fertility was 5.6 in 1978, infant mortality was almost four times higher (171 per 1000), and female literacy and contraceptive use were, respectively, one-seventh and one-third the levels found in Kerala.

New departures

In the course of 1986 a new family-planning strategy was prepared by the Government of India to be launched on 1 September of that year. The new strategy laid down some revised targets both for population growth and for family planning. Whereas population growth for the period 1979–84 had continued at 2.2 per cent, the new strategy envisaged a reduction to 1 per cent by the end of 1989. And whereas during 1985–6 some 35 per cent of couples accepted family planning, by the end of 1989 that proportion would hopefully rise to 60 per cent. The new policy would also mean an increase in the funds sanctioned for family planning from RS 3256 crore to RS 3787 crore.

Among the means envisaged to enable India to reach these new goals were:

Shifting the accent from sterilizations to spacing children. No target had been set but the number of couples practising preventive methods at the end of the campaign was expected to be far in excess of the 14.5 million couples target for the seventh plan.

Preparing an eligible couples register, rather like an electoral roll, which would be displayed at all 83,000 health sub-centres and also given to the million workers in the family-planning programme as their 'medicentre catchment area'.

Setting up popular FP committees in every one of the thousands of blocks and panchayats in the country, with the participation of officials, non-officials and opinion-makers.

Creating a women's corps of 2 million volunteers with each volunteer being assigned 60 couples to work with, modelled on the neighbourhood health worker scheme in China. The volunteers, all of them acceptors, would have the incentive that the best among them would be given regular government jobs in the programme.

Establishing the two-child norm by providing more incentives for couples limiting families to two children. These would include an 'honoured citizen' status entitling them to extra benefits, an old-age pension for the needy, low premium insurance policies and a national lottery. To counter the preference for sons, long-term bonds maturing at the time of marriage would be given free to those with two daughters.

Using the skills of 400,000 practitioners of Indian systems of medicine for the programme.

Involving the organized industrial sector (which has 25 million employees) by making it obligatory for all industrial units to provide incentives and family-planning services to employees.

Involving the corporate sector by giving tax incentives not only for activities directly related to the programme (like running a medicentre) but also for linked activities, like employing adolescent girls in areas where child marriages are common.

Involving the country's 35,000 co-operatives (with a membership of 120 million) by creating FP cells in all apex co-operatives.

Making FP motivation part of the curriculum for the country's 50,000 medical students[18].

It remains to be seen how successful these new initiatives will be. But there can be no doubting the seriousness of the undertaking. Rajiv Gandhi has picked up where his mother left off. The task before him now – and before India – is to convert the important declines in fertility which have been realized in certain states, as noted above, into nationwide achievements. If this can be done, then India's 35-year-old family planning will have more than justified the resources which have been devoted to it. And, because India, like China, exerts a dominant influence on global population totals, the demographic panorama as a whole will look considerably brighter.

If India does indeed reach the 1% population growth rate target by the end of 1989 as now scheduled, this will be applauded as a stupendous achievement by all those who are concerned with development, environment and the quality of human life. The lion's share in that achievement will of course belong to India herself. Yet some part has been played by external assistance, including that of the United Nations, a fact which India with her characteristic generosity of spirit will certainly be the first to recognize.

Indonesia

Demography and family planning

The third most populous country in the developing world, after China and India, is Indonesia. An official Dutch estimate in 1940 said Java had a population of 48.4 million, and all of Indonesia had 70.4 million. The new Republic's first official estimate, made in 1950 and based on reports from village heads, placed Java's population at 50.5 million and Indonesia's at 77.2 million. A 1961 census put the country's population at 97 million, 63 million of whom lived in Java. By 1971 the figure stood at 119 million for Indonesia and 76 million for Java. (This meant that around two-thirds of the population lived on one island, the size of Nepal.) The population was growing at well over 2 per cent annually and was headed towards at least 250 million people by the year 2000. The crude birth-rate was about 44 per 1000 and the total fertility rate (the number of children an average woman would give birth to) was around 5.8.

For the first two decades after independence, Indonesia had followed a pro-natalist policy. But President Sukarno and other nationalist policy planners soon became concerned about the dense population on the island of Java and thought that encouraging the Javanese to migrate to other thinly populated islands would solve the problem. However, between 1952 and 1965, a total of only 383,475 people were moved from Java and Bali to the Outer islands. During that period, the population of Java and Bali rose by more than 15 million.

In 1967, President Sukarto joined 29 other heads of state in signing the Declaration on Population by World Leaders; in 1968 a National Family Planning Institute was established; and in 1969 the first Five-Year Development Plan introduced the target of three million family planning 'acceptors' by 1973–7, while stating 'Family Planning is not only important in reducing the rate of population growth to below the increase in national income, so as to raise per capita income, but is also beneficial for the health of the mother in particular and the family in general.'

Three presidential decrees in 1970 changed the National Family-Planning Institute (LBKM) into the National Family-Planning Co-ordinating Board (with the Indonesian acronym BKKBN) directly responsible and reporting to the President on family-planning activities.

In 1974, the family-planning programme, promoted at first only in Java and Bali, was expanded to 10 outer-island provinces and subsequently to all provinces. The new strategy was to place the family-planning programme in villages not clinics and de-centralize it to give responsibility to village officials and volunteers.

One key element in the new strategy was the use of trained field workers who would promote family planning in their home communities. This was considered a more effective way than relying on unknown, untrusted outsiders. By the end of the decade of the 1970s, more than 7000 field workers had been trained.

Another key element in the strategy – the heart of the new programmes – was the idea of making use of traditional village institutions to promote the new concepts of family planning and a 'small family norm'. For example, Bali has more than 3500 *banjars*, which are the traditional centres for mutual aid and cooperative work plus the gathering point for recreation and ceremony. Each of Bali's *banjars* displayed a map of all houses in the district, based on information collected from household heads. Apparently, houses of IUD users were outlined in blue, pill-users in red, and condom-users in green while houses of non-users were left blank.

The achievements of the family-planning programme within a few years exceeded most expectations. BKKBN officials believed that by late 1978 the national crude birth-rate (which had been around 45 at the end of the 60s) had already been reduced to between 34 and 36. They further contended that nationwide 30 per cent of the eligible couples were currently practising family planning and there had already been a reduction of 30 per cent in fertility compared with the beginning of the programme. If the momentum could be maintained, they believed the goal of reducing total fertility by 50 per cent (in comparison with 1971 levels) could be achieved by 1990 instead of by 2000. They hoped to achieve a reduction in the birth-rate of 35 per cent nationwide by the end of the Third Plan Period (1983–4) as compared with 1971 levels. This meant that around 40–50 per cent of eligible couples should be protected from pregnancies.

Deliberate steps were taken to extend the family-planning programme beyond Java and Bali to the outer islands where total fertility rates (and rates of population growth) were higher than in Java and Bali. The hope was that it would be possible to reduce the birth-rate in the outer islands by between 15 and 25 per cent as compared with 1971. (At the same time the highly ambitious targets set for the 'transmigration' programme in the third Five-Year Plan period (1979–84) called for the movement of half a million households, or more than two million people altogether, from the Java–Bali–Lombok areas.)

External assistance

In Indonesia, as in the other countries of densely populated Southern and Eastern Asia, external assistance for population and family planning has played its part. As a co-ordinating body, the BKKBN has its own budget. In 1970, the first year of full operation, this stood at US $4.6 million of which 70 per cent was supplied by foreign donors. In 1978, the budget had increased nearly 10 times to US $45.8 million but the amount supplied by foreign aid had fallen to 28 per cent. During the Third Plan period, the BKKBN expected to need a total operating budget of around 90 Rupiahs (about US $225 million before the Rupiah was devalued by one-third in November 1978) and a budget for contraceptives of about 40 billion Rupiahs (about US $100 million) making a total family planning budget of 1.3 billion Rupiahs (about US $325 million). Of this about 31 per cent was expected to come from foreign sources.

Seen in the light of these fairly considerable sums of money, the debate population versus development seems by no means academic. Though there are, of course, ancillary effects of a developmental nature from the family-planning programme (e.g. increase in trained workers, rural health centres, etc), it must also be recognized that the failure of the family-planning programme to deliver 'success' in the sense of lasting declines in fertility would be serious and would certainly strengthen the hand of those who argue that monies spent on family planning could be better used.

Bilateral assistance to Indonesia in the population field has come from the United States Agency for International Development (USAID) and the

Australian Development Assistance Bureau. Non-Governmental assistance to Indonesia has been provided by, amongst others, the Ford Foundation, the International Planned Parenthood Federation (with which the Indonesian Planned Parenthood Association is affiliated), the Japanese Organization for International Co-operation in Family Planning (JOICFP), Oxfam, the Pathfinder Fund, the Population Council and the Rockefeller Foundation.

UNFPA assistance to Indonesia began in 1969 with approval of a 'study tour on Family Planning for Indonesian Ministers and officers'. In 1971, UNFPA funded health education projects, including US $300,000 for the UNICEF-executed project: 'Development of a Transport Fleet in support of the Health and Family Planning Programme'.

On April 18, 1972, UNFPA signed an agreement with the Government of Indonesia on UNFPA participation in a joint project with the World Bank (International Development Association). The project, with an estimated total cost of US $33 million, was assisted by an IDA credit of US $13.2 million and a UNFPA grant of $13.2 million. Included in this programme were: the construction and equipment of about 320 maternal child health/family-planning centres in East Java, Bali and Jakarta; the construction and equipment of six provincial training centres and 10 sub-provincial centres; salary support for 7000 non-medical field workers; construction and equipment of one central and six provincial family-planning administrative centres; the provision of 115 mobile information units, technical assistance, fellowship and studies for information and communication activities; and support for a population education programme.

This project formed part of the Fund's First Country Programme agreement with Indonesia, lasting from 1969 to 1979, which included a wide range of projects: health and family planning, information, education and communication; population education; population dynamics; population policy formulation; and a 'women's participation in development' programme.

Since then, substantial progress has been made on a number of fronts. As Dr Nafis Sadik reports, nearly all the 11 outer-island provinces joining the national family-planning/population programme in 1979 have received the vehicles and medical equipment necessary for bringing services to remote areas. The hospital-based family-planning effort has been greatly strengthened by a strong commitment from hospital administrators both for increasing the range of services and for expanding the participation of other hospital divisions in the family-planning effort. This commitment is largely the result of study tours throughout the Asian region for administrators, the provision of equipment to upgrade the hospitals and the training of staff. The integrated family planning and nutrition project on Sumatra has demonstrated its viability; this and similar projects on the outer islands are increasingly being absorbed into the routine budget of the Government[19].

The urban project, which has aimed at expanding contraceptive prevalence in five cities by increasing supplies and encouraging demand for such services, 'is one of the most exciting undertakings in the Second Country Programme, 1980–4, and has been an ideal experimental project'. The project has demonstrated that it is possible for the Government and the private sector to join forces for social service projects and that the resourcefulness of the commercial advertising world can be effectively used on behalf of family-planning issues. On the service delivery side, the project has demonstrated the value of the private clinic, with private doctors supplementing the Government's efforts in the cities. The project has also shown that, as Government family-planning clinics have improved the quality of their services, utilization has increased[20].

Several seminars and workshops have resulted in strengthening the role of the communications branch within the total programme. The Fund's assistance to the Central Bureau's capability in the collection of demographic data, research and training activities, under way at three demographic research institutes, promises to substantially increase Indonesia's pool of fully qualified demographic analysts. The creation of a Population and Development Research Committee will promote the integration of population and development concerns. The project on women in development is a major innovation; it has greatly boosted the earning power of women participating in the scheme, making them less dependent on traditional money-lenders. Considered a model project, it is being replicated by several other donors.

A long way to go

This enthusiastic account of the involvement of the United Nations with Indonesia's population and family-planning programme must of course be seen in the context of the colossal tasks which still confront the Indonesian authorities in their attempt to reduce birth-rates. Even the most optimistic observers concede that the conditions for attaining population stability will not be reached for all of Indonesia by the year 2000, though it is possible that Java will attain a Net Reproduction Rate of 1 by that time which in itself would represent substantial progress. If, on the other hand, an NRR of 1 was not to be achieved for the whole country until, say, 2010 the total population would still rise to 370 million as compared with a 1985 figure of 165 million.

Nevertheless, a start has been made. Of particular interest as far as the subject of this book is concerned is the early collaboration of the UNFPA and the World Bank on a large-scale country project, a clear indication that population policy and projects were moving to the very centre of the development process.

Sri Lanka

Fertility decline

Sri Lanka's first census in the modern sense was taken in 1871. The era of British rule, which had begun in 1796 when the British took over the maritime provinces from the Dutch, had witnessed far-reaching changes in the political, social and economic life of the people which included the development of tea and rubber plantations, the opening of roads and railways, the introduction of English and the development of the administrative system. These changes had undoubtedly a demographic impact. The 1871 census enumerated a population of 2.4 million. It took 58 years – until 1929 – for the population to double. The next doubling, however, took only 30 years. The population had reached 10.6 million by 1963 and the census of 1971 gave a population of 12.7 million.

At that time the strength of the various ethnic groups was: Sinhalese 72.0 per cent; Sri Lanka Tamils 11.2 per cent; and Indian Tamils 9.3 per cent. The remaining 7.5 per cent was made up of Moors (Sri Lanka and Indian), Burgers (a group of Dutch descendants), Malays and others. The majority of the Sinhalese were Buddhists, while most Tamils were Hindus. The Moors and the Malays were Muslim. In total, around 67 per cent of the people were Buddhist, about 18 per cent were Hindus, the remainder being Christians and Muslims.

Sri Lanka had a population density of 508 persons per square mile at the census of 1971, which had increased to around 550 by 1978. This made the island one of the most densely populated agricultural countries of the world. Moreover, nearly 75 per cent of the population was concentrated in around 35 per cent of the land area, almost exclusively in the wet zone, while the remaining 25 per cent occupied 65 per cent – mostly in the dry zone[21].

From the turn of the century to around 1960 the crude birth-rates in Sri Lanka remained consistently high, ranging from 35 to 42 births per 1000 population. During the decade of the 70s, however, a steady decline of the crude birth-rate had been observed. In 1971 it was approximately 30 per 1000 falling to 27.3 in 1974. The first major finding of the 1975 World

Fertility Survey in Sri Lanka showed a continued rise in the average age of marriage – urbanization and education being cited as the main causes. (According to the 1971 census, the mean age of first marriage was 23.5 for women and 28.0 for men[22].)

The second major finding of the 1975 World Fertility Survey was that fertility continued to decline at a rapid rate, decreasing approximately 6 per cent annually 'sufficient to halve the rate of population growth in ten years'. The survey further stated that if women achieved their stated intentions the mean completed family size would be 2–4 children.

Economic background

The economic setting at the time Sri Lanka attained independence in 1948 was relatively favourable. The prices for the principal export crops – tea, rubber, coconut – were good, and accumulated foreign exchange reserves were substantial. The Central Bank in its First Annual Report in 1950 observed that Sri Lanka was in a very sound financial position on account of the favourable balance of trade and the large amount of external assets that it held. The first Parliament of independent Sri Lanka of 1948 reflected some concern for the population problem, but this was largely understood as a problem of the overcrowded wetter zone of the island and of immigrant Indian labour living and working on the plantations. It was hoped that the large-scale colonization of the dry zone would, on the whole, look after the population problems of the wet zone. The economic situation deteriorated in the late 1950s and 1960s, particularly as a result of Sri Lanka's dependence on a few exportable primary commodities. An upward turn of the economy in the late 1960s could not be maintained in the 1970s even though the government made a vigorous attempt between 1970–7 to restructure the economy, improve productivity and reduce the level of unemployment. Though the Sinhalese Buddhists who formed the majority of the population had been averse to any limitations on the size of their families, tending to view any restrictions on the growth of the Sinhala Buddhist population as a threat to the future of Sri Lanka itself, in 1968 a Family-Planning Bureau was established within the Ministry of Health, with the responsibility of implementing family-planning activities. The programme aimed at a reduction in the birth-rate from 33 per thousand in 1965 to 25 per thousand in 1976.

The Five-Year Plan 1972–6 stated that 'the continued growth of population at the present high rates will pose problems which would defy every attempt at solution'. It noted that family planning for the whole population was a routine activity of the Ministry of Health and that it was fully integrated in the maternal and child welfare programme. A reduction in the rate of population growth through fertility control was accepted as an important component of social and economic development, although such a reduction was not considered to be a substitute for vigorous economic development efforts. The official 1978 policy aimed at lowering the rate of growth by decreasing fertility (a targeted crude birth-rate of 23 per thousand in 1980, compared with the then current 26 per thousand) and maintaining immigration at its current level (i.e. guarding against any further increases in immigration). The Government hoped to reduce Sri Lanka's population growth rate from 1.6 per cent to 1.2 per cent by 1981.

The demographic achievements of Sri Lanka between 1965 and 1980 can be summarized as follows: Sri Lanka's crude birth-rate (per 1000 population) fell from 32 over the period 1965 to 1970 to 28 over the period 1975 to 1980, a fall of 12 per cent and the general fertility rate (per 1000 women aged 15–49) fell from 141 to 115, a decline of 18 per cent.

United Nations involvement

United Nations' involvement with Sri Lanka's population and family planning programme goes back to 1971 when a United Nations inter-agency mission to Sri Lanka (then Ceylon) was organized by the United Nations in co-operation with UNESCO and WHO, at Sri Lanka's request, and with the financial assistance of the UNFPA. The mission was led by Sir Colville Deverell, former Director-General of the International Planned Parenthood Federation; its rapporteur was Mr B. Aromin, a demographer with the population division of ECAFE (now ESCAP) and two members each appointed by UNESCO and WHO. The mission was requested by the Government of Ceylon: 'to make a comprehensive review of the national family planning programme'.

The mission's report, completed at the end of February 1971, noted that there appeared to have been some decline in fertility in Ceylon in the previous decade, and that social and economic conditions considered vital to such a decrease were currently present, so that 'a steady decline in the birth-rate' might be expected, provided that 'the public demand is matched by the provision of adequate information and services'. The report revealed that at the time the family-planning programme had barely reached 50 per cent of its target[23].

In 1973 UNFPA signed a country agreement with Sri Lanka covering assistance of the US $6 million over four years until the end of 1976. The 12 projects include a health manpower survey; strengthening of nursing/

midwifery education; family health; a law and population study; support for a demographic research and training unit; two projects dealing with workers' population education and information on family planning in the urban and plantation sectors; teaching of human reproduction, family planning and population dynamics to medical students; a project on communication strategy; support for health education; and population education in the formal school system. The twelfth project was a mid-term review of the UNFPA-funded programme scheduled to take place in November 1975.

By the end of 1977, orientation courses in family planning had been given to 14,000 health personnel and service delivery capacity had been built up. In nursing and midwifery education, a revised curriculum had been introduced, and further training needs in demography and child health had been met. Under the urban section of the workers' population education and family planning project, around 1400 meetings of workshops were organized, in which 45,000 people participated. In the plantation sector, 1200 estates participated. In all, around 800 meetings were held and over 55,000 workers attended.

Two new UNFPA-funded projects, started in 1979, involved the preparation of the 1981 census and the creation of a new family welfare workers' group to serve as a liaison between the health staff and the employees of the state. The 1973 agreement ended in 1979. The second programme of UNFPA assistance to Sri Lanka, approved by the Governing Council in June 1981, covered family planning, population education and communication, population and development and the advancement of women, and brought to 27 the total number of UNFPA-funded operational projects in the country at the end of 1982.

While some of the projects under the second country programme were a continuation or expansion of old projects, there were a number of new projects which stressed integration of population with development activities, strengthening family health services and improving the co-ordination and management of population programmes.

UNFPA supported the Mahaweli Resettlement Scheme in 1982 with provision of some equipment and preparation of training programmes for 225 worker-settlers in basic health care, 150 women settlers in education, 50 volunteers in health service, and 30 Mahaweli Scheme Staff in management, all aimed at close links between public health and family planning, and between population and development.

In August 1979 the International Conference of Parliamentarians on Population and Development was held in Colombo, and in September 1982, Sri Lanka was host to the Third Asia and Pacific Population Conference.

Thailand

Past population growth and future targets

In 1900 Thailand's population numbered about 6 million. It had grown to 14.5 million in 1937, about 27 million in 1960, with the figure for 1968 at 33.5–35 million. Since 1947 the rate of growth at 3.2 per cent or greater – had been one of the highest in the world. A continuation of such rapid growth meant that 1960's population would have doubled by 1980. As in most developing countries, Thailand's high population growth rate stemmed from two factors: high fertility and a sharp decline in mortality.

Though, during the first half of this century, the government's policy was to encourage large families, by the mid-1960s there was increasing concern that high population growth rates were creating pressure on food supplies and that increasing domestic demand was threatening to affect Thailand's agricultural surplus, its major foreign exchange earner.

On March 17, 1970, the Thai Cabinet declared: 'The Thai Government has the policy to support voluntary family planning in order to resolve various problems concerned with the very high rate of population growth which constitutes an important obstacle to the economic and social development of the nation.'

With this statement was born the National Family Planning Programme (NFPP). Its specific objectives, as incorporated in the Third Five-Year Plan (1972–6) were:

> to reduce the annual population growth rate from over 3% to about 2.5 per cent by the end of 1976. (The total population at the time was around 36 million.)
>
> to inform eligible women, particularly those living in the rural and remote areas, about the concepts of family planning; to motivate them to use contraception; and to make family-planning services readily available throughout the country.
>
> to integrate family-planning activities with overall maternal and child health services and thus mutually strengthen the activities in these closely related fields.

In 1978, a new official target was set which aimed at a reduction in the rate of population growth from 2.5 per cent in 1977 to 2.1 per cent in 1981.

Achievements

Thailand is currently in the midst of a major decline in fertility. Between 1969 and 1979, marital fertility appears to have declined by close to 40

178

per cent. Contraceptive knowledge has increased rapidly and is now almost universal among women. The practice of contraception has increased dramatically as well. As of 1981, more than 58 per cent of women in the reproductive ages were practising some method, compared with less than 15 per cent ten years ago.

Although an increase in age at marriage may have reduced the birth rate in the years before 1960, since then changes in patterns of nuptiality have not been important in reducing the birth-rate. The mean age at marriage for women is now about 22 years. Changes in the age structure also have not contributed significantly to declining birth-rates. The recent decline in fertility is thus largely a product of changing reproductive behaviour within marriage. The reduction of fertility has occurred despite a trend towards shorter duration of breast-feeding in both rural and urban areas.

The decline in fertility and the increase in contraceptive use are pronounced in the rural sector. The urban–rural gap in fertility decline has almost disappeared. Women of all educational backgrounds, including the least educated women, have participated in the changes taking place.

The growth rates in the early 1960s ranged from 3.2 to 3.4 per cent, falling to between 2.6 and 2.9 per cent by 1970, and continuing to fall to between 2.3 and 2.6 per cent by 1975. The Government estimated that the growth rate was 1.95 per cent in 1981; thus, the goal of reaching a 2.1 per cent growth rate by the end of 1981 was achieved. The Government expected to reduce the growth rate to 1.5 per cent by the end of 1986.

The explanation for Thailand's 'reproductive revolution', most observers conclude, lies in a combination of socio–cultural factors and the relative accessibility of contraceptive information and services.

The Thai people have been receptive to the idea and practice of fertility regulation, including sterilization. One important supporting factor is the nature of Thai Buddhism, which encourages personal responsibility for behaviour and individual autonomy; these principles carry over into social and family relationships, shielding couples from pro-natalist family influences and providing higher status for women. Thai women tend to act independently of their husbands with regard to contraception. The high literacy rate for both sexes further contributes to informed decision-making and the advanced status of women.

The Thai people have relatively good access to contraceptives. The credit for providing services to most Thais can be attributed to the activities of the National Family-Planning Programme of the Ministry of Public Health. It is estimated that, overall, at least 80 per cent of all contraceptive users receive their supply of contraceptives from programme sources.

The number of family-planning acceptors attributed to the programme grew steadily from an average of about 60,000 new acceptors annually during 1965–8 to 1,000,000 by 1980. The success of the programme in reaching a large number of acceptors is the result of a variety of factors. Of particular importance is the involvement of health personnel at all levels in family-planning activities and especially the delegation of family-planning tasks to non-physicians. The 1971 decision to allow auxiliary midwives and nurses to provide contraceptive pills, and the 1976 decision to provide pills free of charge, increased dramatically the acceptance of the pill, the main contraceptive used. Women obtain the pill mostly from Government sources (73 per cent) although pharmacies provide pills to another 21 per cent of users. Another factor in the success of the National Family-Planning Programme is the wide variety of methods available, including injectables.

Contribution of United Nations

UNFPA has been assisting population activities in Thailand since 1971. During this period, more than $20 million has been provided through three country programmes. More than 90 per cent of this amount has gone to support the National Family-Planning Programme in its service delivery activities; training; and information, education and communication activities.

Although Thailand's National Family-Planning Programme still has important and difficult tasks ahead, it is now a mature undertaking. As the programme has evolved, UNFPA assistance has also changed in order to remain of maximum use and relevance. Thai–UNFPA co-operation now emphasizes assistance only for specific inputs that well-advanced programmes need. This collaboration is also aimed at making the Thailand programme self-reliant in human resources, supplies and financing as soon as possible.

Amongst other things, UNFPA support has permitted the purchase of 5000 motorcycles and 450 bicycles to provide greater mobility for personnel engaged on family-planning activities. Whether the founding fathers of the United Nations, as they set up the Population Commission at those early post-war meetings, foresaw the extension of the United Nations population activities to cover the supply of two-wheeled transport for Thai field-workers is not easy to establish with certainty, but the odds are against it. Yet 30 years later fertility reductions were being achieved in Thailand which were at least in part due to the comprehensive nature of the assistance provided from all sources, including the United Nations system.

Asia: a summary view

In its World Development Report 1984, the World Bank observes that the 930 million people of Bangladesh, India, Nepal, Pakistan and Sri Lanka comprise between one-fifth and one-quarter of the population of developing countries. Although incomes in South Asia are among the lowest in the world, the region's fertility has already fallen substantially (see Table 8.9). In Sri Lanka, for example, the total fertility rate fell from 5.5 in 1960 to 3.5 in 1974; in India, as noted, it dropped from 6.5 in the 1950s to 4.8 in 1982. The Bank notes that progress in South Asia has not been uniform and rapid population growth is a source of continuing concern. The experience in Sri Lanka and in some Indian states suggests that much more could be done to bring about fertility decline. In every country there is considerable scope for reducing infant mortality, raising the legal marriage age and increasing female education – all of which would have a profound effect on fertility. To satisfy unmet needs, family-planning programmes must resolve important issues of access and quality.

Turning to East Asia, the Bank notes that countries there have experienced marked declines in fertility in the last decade. Total fertility (less than 3) and rates of natural increase (about 1.5 per cent a year, 2.2 per cent excluding China) are the lowest of any developing region. For the most part, the Bank observes, recent declines in fertility have occurred in countries where fertility was already lower than would be expected, given the region's income. The most dramatic reductions have been in China: total fertility drop from 7.5 to 2.3 over the past two decades, despite a per capita income of only \$310 in 1982. Indonesia, the Philippines and Thailand have also experienced remarkably rapid falls in fertility with only modest increases in income. However, the Bank notes that replacement-level fertility is still a long way off for Burma, Indonesia, Malaysia, the Philippines, Thailand and Viet Nam with total fertility rates of at least 3.6; total fertility in Korea, at 2.7, is also still above replacement level.

Though contraceptive use is higher in East Asia than in most other developing regions, the Bank notes there is still considerable unmet need for contraception. Low and high estimates of unmet need are 19 to 49 per cent of married women of child-bearing age in the Philippines (1978); 20 to 31 per cent in Indonesia (1976), 15 to 26 per cent in Thailand (1981), and as much as 30 per cent in Korea (1979).

Some countries have overlooked potentially important methods of family planning (for example, the Indonesian programme does not offer sterilization.) The Bank observes also that, given the relatively advanced state of population policies, more use could be made of incentives and disincentives.

Table 8.9. *Birth-rates and change, 1965–70 and 1975–80, ESCAP region (Asia and the Pacific)*

Country or area	Crude birth rate (per 1000 population)		Percentage change 1965–70 to 1975–80	General fertility rate (per 1000 women aged 15–49)		Percentage change 1965–70 to 1975–80
	1965–70	1975–80		1965–70	1975–80	
ESCAP region	37	29	−20	164	124	−24
East Asia	31	21	−32	137	87	−36
China	32	21	−34	149	90	−40
Hong Kong	24	19	−21	104	74	−29
Japan	18	15	−15	63	56	−11
Mongolia	42	37	−11	182	162	−11
Republic of Korea	32	25	−21	138	100	−28
South East Asia	42	35	−16	180	147	−18
Burma	40	39	−4	166	164	−1
Democratic Kampuchea	44	31	−30	189	123	−35
Indonesia	43	34	−22	183	139	−24
Lao People's Democratic Republic	45	44	−2	190	190	0
Malaysia	39	33	−15	181	140	−23
Philippines	41	36	−11	183	153	−16
Singapore	25	17	−31	109	63	−42
Thailand	42	32	−23	187	137	−27
Vietnam	41	40	−3	173	168	−3
Middle South Asia	43	38	−13	194	164	−15
Afghanistan	50	48	−3	219	219	0
Bangladesh	50	47	−6	233	217	−7
Bhutan	45	43	−4	192	187	−3
India	42	35	−16	186	151	−19
Iran	45	44	−2	213	202	−5
Nepal	46	44	−4	191	194	2

Pakistan	47	43	−8	224	199	−11
Sri Lanka	32	28	−12	141	115	−18
Oceania	24	22	−11	106	91	−14
Australia	20	17	−16	84	68	−19
Fiji	32	29	−11	140	111	−21
New Zealand	23	18	−21	100	74	−26
Papua New Guinea	42	42	0	191	193	1

Source: Selected papers: Third Asian and Pacific Population Conference (Colombo, September 1982), *Asian Population Studies Series* No. 58, Economic and Social Commission for Asia and the Pacific, Bangkok, Thailand. Published by the United Nations, New York, 1984.

Among the countries of East Asia, China, Singapore, and, to a lesser extent Korea, have made greatest use of measures to promote small families. The Bank notes that most governments have not chosen to promote such drastic measures as those in China with its complex structure of incentives, disincentives, and birth quotas to promote a one-child family. And few have the administrative control necessary to implement national schemes of deferred payments or social security to promote smaller families.

In China the one-child policy has been challenged by an apparent preference for sons. The same bias in favour of sons exists in Korea, and has been partly responsible for keeping total fertility, now at 2.7, from declining to replacement level. 'To counteract this bias' the Bank suggests 'governments need public information campaigns and legal reforms of inheritance, property rights and employment. Incentives might also be offered to one- or two-child families with girls such as lower educational and medical costs or preferred access to schooling.'

These comments by the World Bank are instructive. They make it clear that though much has been achieved in Asia, much more remains to be done if fertility rates are to be brought down towards replacement levels for the continent as a whole.

As Table 8.10 indicates, over the period 1969–83, 36 per cent of all UNFPA expenditures were made in Asia and the Pacific. Table 8.11 shows UNFPA expenditures over the same period in the Asia and the Pacific region by work plan category. It can be seen that 60 per cent of the funds were spent on, or allocated to, family planning programmes, and that more than three-quarters of the funds were spent on, or allocated to, 'priority countries'. Given the dimensions of the job still to be done in the region, it is clear that Asia – and particularly the family-planning programmes of priority countries – will continue to have a large call on the Fund's resources.

At the same time, it is plain that Asia has much to offer the rest of the world.

Asia has had longer experience than any other developing region with interventions to modify reproductive behaviour. As already noted, the region has witnessed the adoption of family planning as a national policy by India in the 1950s and in a few other countries such as Pakistan, which then included Bangladesh, and Malaysia in the 1960s. By the time of the World Population Conference in Bucharest in 1974, 17 Asian countries had population policies and almost all countries had family-planning programmes. As Sadik comments[25]: 'In general, Asian countries have had the least problems in legitimising family planning as a means of achieving smaller family size and, consequently, lower fertility rates. The first United

Table 8.10. *Percentage distribution of UNFPA expenditures by regions, 1969–83*

Regions	Years												Total 1969–83
	1969–72	1973	1974	1975	1976	1977	1978	1979	1980	1981	1982	1983	
Sub-Saharan Africa	9.0	9.6	9.9	12.4	13.0	13.2	11.5	14.4	13.9	15.7	16.1	20.4	14.3
Asia and the Pacific	27.5	30.5	29.0	30.7	30.0	33.4	37.0	38.1	37.3	39.2	41.4	38.3	36.1
Latin America and the Caribbean	7.7	11.1	20.3	21.1	25.2	19.8	19.2	16.4	17.2	14.3	13.8	13.2	16.8
Middle East and Mediterranean	9.7	7.0	10.4	10.1	13.2	12.8	11.3	9.9	9.2	9.8	10.1	10.9	10.4
Europe	0.5	0.7	0.3	0.3	0.5	0.6	0.7	1.1	1.1	1.2	1.0	0.9	0.9
Interregional and global	45.6	41.1	30.1	25.3	18.1	20.2	20.3	20.1	21.3	19.8	17.6	16.3	21.5
Total	100.0	100.0	100.0	100.0	100.0	100.0	100.0	100.0	100.0	100.0	100.0	100.0	100.0
(Thousands of US dollars)	(26,501)	(30,067)	(54,103)	(66,673)	(69,368)	(66,551)	(89,230)	(123,624)	(136,357)	(122,543)	(106,244)	(127,165)	(1,018,426)

Source: UNFPA Fact Sheet No. 1.10 (September 1983); UNFPA Fact Sheet No. 1.11 (November 1983). Table given in *Population, the UNFPA Experience*, edited by Nafis Sadik and published for the United Nations Fund for Population Activities by New York University Press, 1984.

Note: Figures for 1969 to 1982 are project expenditures; figures for 1983 are project allocations as of 30 November 1983.

Table 8.11. *Percentage distribution of UNFPA expenditures by work plan categories, Asia and the Pacific 1969–83*

Work plan categories	Years												Total
	1969–72	1973	1974	1975	1976	1977	1978	1979	1980	1981	1982	1983	1969–83
Basic data collection	3.8	5.5	7.7	5.1	4.4	4.1	4.1	9.2	13.7	26.0	12.3	4.9	10.3
Population dynamics	6.4	1.8	2.1	2.3	2.8	2.9	1.4	2.3	2.7	5.0	6.7	8.3	4.1
Formulation and evaluation of population policies and programmes	2.7	0.9	2.1	1.2	2.9	2.4	1.9	1.5	1.9	4.7	4.2	4.1	2.8
Implementation of policies	0.0	0.0	0.0	0.0	0.0	0.2	0.0	7.2	0.6	1.2	0.7	1.8	1.5
Family planning	71.4	68.0	64.9	70.9	73.5	71.2	71.2	61.8	62.7	40.5	56.0	51.7	60.2
Communication and education	11.0	19.1	17.9	15.2	10.8	11.0	8.6	8.6	11.4	13.1	10.4	17.8	12.3
Special programmes	0.7	0.5	0.1	0.2	0.6	0.6	1.3	1.3	0.5	1.3	0.6	0.9	0.8
Multisectoral activities	4.0	4.2	5.2	5.1	5.0	7.6	11.5	8.1	6.5	8.2	9.1	10.5	8.0
Total	100.0	100.0	100.0	100.0	100.0	100.0	100.0	100.0	100.0	100.0	100.0	100.0	100.0
(Thousands of US dollars)	(7.283)	(9.165)	(15.663)	(20.447)	(20.805)	(22.258)	(32.981)	(47.150)	(50.845)	(48.040)	(43.981)	(48.628)	(367.246)

Source: UNFPA Fact Sheet No. 1.08 (September 1983); UNFPA Fact Sheet No. 1.09 (November 1983). Table given in *Population, the UNFPA Experience*, edited by Nafis Sadik and published for the United Nations Fund for Population Activities by New York University Press, 1984.

Note: Figures for 1969 to 1982 are project expenditures; figures for 1983 are project allocations as of 30 November 1983.

Nations meeting on family planning in the region, sponsored by ESCAP (then ECAFE) in 1966, was on the management of family planning rather than on the justification for family planning.'

It will be easier perhaps for the United Nations, than for other organizations, to draw on this Asian experience in the formulation and implementation of population policy so as to deploy Asian expertise both within and outside the region.

LATIN AMERICA

Demographic background

From a demographic point of view, Latin America is commonly divided into three sub-regions: Temperate (Argentina, Chile, and Uruguay); Central or Middle America (Mexico, Panama, Nicaragua, Costa Rica, Guatemala, Honduras, and El Salvador); and Tropical which includes the other nations of South America, along with the Caribbean Islands of Cuba, the Dominican Republic, and Haiti[26].

The three temperate-zone countries are fairly homogeneous. These populations are characterized by large proportions of European migrants, high educational levels, low rates of population growth, small proportions engaged in agriculture, and low fertility and mortality. With a total population of approximately 45 million (1984) and an average density of 16 persons per square kilometre, their annual growth rate, on average, is 1.6 per cent and life expectancy at birth is 68 years[27].

In contrast, the regions of Middle America and tropical South America show markedly higher growth rates, 2.7 per cent and 2.4 per cent respectively. With fertility levels of 4.8 per woman and 4.1 per woman as well as a lower expectation of life – about 65 and 63 years, respectively – those regions have much in common with other developing areas of the world.

According to CELADE estimates for the latter half of the 1950s, birth-rates were 45 or more in 14 of the 20 Latin American countries. In a number of them, birth-rates seemed to be rising; and, with few exceptions, the high and possibly rising rates were sustained in the face of low death rates, high urbanization, moderately high literacy, and rising per capita product. According to J. Mayone Stycos 'Impressive post-World War II economic gains and moderate social progress in the ten largest countries appeared to have no impact on overall fertility levels, leading to speculation that Roman Catholic resistance to birth control and a Luso-Espanic culture favouring large families make Latin America an exception to the theory that economic modernisation eventually leads to low fertility[28]'.

Stycos notes that there have been other ideological streams as important as Catholicism in inhibiting family-planning programmes. Nationalism coupled with the belief that a nation's economic and military power is enhanced by a large and rapidly growing population has been characteristic of the political right, while the Marxists' traditional opposition to Malthusian doctrines has been salted with the notion that population pressures are a useful precipitant of revolution.

'Both left and right have been vociferous in identifying family planning with North American Imperialism. US President Lyndon Johnson's dictum that five dollars invested in population control is worth a hundred dollars in economic growth was widely interpreted as proof that pills at worst were being substituted for Imperialist bullets, or at the very best were to be a cheap substitute for economic assistance.'

In such an atmosphere, Stycos suggests, the pioneering efforts of private family-planning organizations were critical. Spearheaded by organisers from the International Planned Parenthood's Western Hemisphere Branch, local footholds were established before 1960 only in the English-speaking Caribbean and Puerto Rico, but by the mid-1960s they were in nearly all the Latin American nations. The later private programmes met much less opposition from governments than the earlier ones, for the international climate had become favourable to family planning. Also, policy-makers had available, in many instances for the first time, two consecutive decennial censuses that conclusively demonstrated extraordinary rates of population growth.

By the early 1970s, most governments had added family planning to Social Security and Health Ministries' services, usually rationalised as anti-abortion or maternal and child health programmes. By the mid-1970s some countries were evidencing case loads of a magnitude sufficient to effect substantial reductions in birth-rates.

Towards the mid-1970s, most governments had come to accept the view that demographic factors played a significant role in the process of socio–economic planning. Today, seven Latin American countries – Costa Rica, Dominican Republic, El Salvador, Guatemala, Mexico, Nicaragua and Peru – perceive their rates of growth as being too high, and pursue policies to alter spatial distribution and international migration patterns, and directly or indirectly to lower fertility. Brazil, Colombia, Cuba, Ecuador, Haiti, Honduras, Panama and Venezuela perceive their rates of growth and fertility rates as satisfactory. Nonetheless, they all provide some form of government support for family planning, sometimes directly through the public health structure; less frequently, by tacit endorsement of a non-governmental group[29].

According to their official statements, Argentina, Bolivia and Chile desire high rates of growth. Argentina and Bolivia do not limit access to family-planning services but do not provide government-subsidized services, whereas Chile provides some direct support for family planning.

Most Caribbean governments have at least an implicit policy to slow down the rate of population growth and many have enacted measures to achieve this objective. Barbados, Dominica, Grenada, Jamaica and Trinidad and Tobago have implemented a family-planning programme. Although the Bahamas, St Lucia and St Vincent do not have government support and interventions for this purpose, access to contraceptives is not restricted. Guyana and Suriname regard their growth rate and fertility rates as acceptable.

Because three countries, Brazil, Colombia and Mexico, account for 60 per cent of the region's 370 million people (1984 figure) and because each of the three has experienced fertility declines though of varying orders and because, again, there have been different degrees of United Nations involvement, it is instructive to look at their record a little more closely. We begin with Mexico; first, because it would serve as host to the International Conference on Population held in August 1984; second, because that country has in some senses had a pivotal role as far as the evolution of population policies in Latin America is concerned.

Mexico

Part of the constitution

Mexico's population increased from 14.3 million in 1921 to around 20 million in 1940 and 50 million in 1970. The average annual growth rate rose from 1.1 per cent in the 1920s to 1.7 per cent in the 1930s and to 3.4 per cent in the period 1970–6. At the time of the International Conference on Population, held in 1984, Mexico's population was around 77 millions.

Lester Brown comments:

> In Mexico, one of the earliest manifestations of population stress was rising unemployment. Political leaders became alarmed when they realised that even the rather impressive 7% annual economic growth simply could not provide enough jobs for the new entrants into the labour force. coupled with the return to food-deficit status in the '70s following the dramatic Green Revolution gains in food production during the '60s, the unemployment rate induced an abrupt turnabout in Mexican population policy. In April 1972, the Government abandoned its pro-natalist stance and announced that it was launching a nationwide family planning programme[30].

189

Mexico's 1973 General Population law, which was introduced under President Echeverria, provided for the establishment of an institution which would be concerned with the demographic aspects of development. The National Population Council (CONAPO), an inter-ministerial body which began functioning in 1974, was headed by the Secretary of the Government and included representatives from the Ministries of Health and Welfare, Public Education, Finance, Foreign Affairs, and Labour and Social Security; it also had representatives from the Ministries of Programming and the Budget, Agrarian Reform, Human Settlements and from other decentralized agencies of the health sector.

As well as the new Law on Population, Article 4 of the Constitution which came into effect in 1974 stated that 'every person has the right to decide in a free, responsible and informed manner on the number and spacing of their children'. The Constitution provides for 'carrying out family-planning programmes ... with absolute respect for human rights ... inorder to rationally regulate and stabilise the country's population growth'.

In 1978 a Regional Demographic Policy was submitted to the President by CONAPO, marking a new stage in Mexico's demographic planning. Emphasizing the need to consider all aspects of demographic behaviour and not merely fertility, the Policy sought to modify demographic variables at the regional level by means of direct and indirect intervention. As a means of achieving its objectives, it defined quantitative targets for fertility, natural increase and spatial distribution at the national level and for each of the states.

The states were divided into four groups according to their current levels of fertility. Those states with the highest levels of fertility – as well as those with high levels of illiteracy and with a large proportion of rural inhabitants and indigenous groups – were designated as priority areas, and efforts would be made to intensify family planning. In contrast, in the more-developed areas, such as the State of Mexico and the Federal District, greater emphasis would be placed on such measures as education and communication programmes. The Government's objectives for some states, for example Baja California (*norte* and *sur*), were to lower the birth-rate per 1000 from 44.1 to 37.4 over the four-year period 1978–9, and the rate of natural increase from 3.4 to 2.9 per cent per annum, whereas in other parts of the country, for example, Oaxaca and Tlaxcala where the rate of population growth was already relatively low, the objective was to reduce birth rates from 33.7 per 1000 to 28.0 and the rate of natural increase from 2.5 to 2 per cent per annum. Overall, the Government's target was to reduce the rate of population growth to 2.5 per cent per annum by 1982 and to 1.0 per cent after the year 2000.

By 1985, the net population growth rate had fallen to 2.1 per cent from the rate of 3.5 per cent a decade earlier. Fertility rates over the decade dropped from 43.1 to 32.5 per 1000 births.

A unique position

In many ways, Mexico occupies a somewhat unique position as far as population policy is concerned. In 1975, it acknowledged that it was the only country in the world with a population of more than 60 million inhabitants and a rate of growth as high as 3.5 per cent. It is also the only country (apart from Ecuador) to have included family planning in its Constitution. The explicit nature of its population policy, and the disaggregation of fertility-reduction targets to the state level, is probably without parallel in other countries of Latin America. Mexico provided the Secretary-General for the World Population Conference in Bucharest in 1974 in the person of Dr Antonio Carrillo-Flores and, as noted, it provided also the venue for the International Conference on Population which took place in August 1984.

Mexico is also unique among Latin American countries in that it has entered into a comprehensive and trusting relationship with the United Nations in the field of population. Whereas other Latin American countries have, as noted above, had their doubts and hesitations about external assistance in this most sensitive of areas (assuming of course that they were ready to take action in the first place), and whereas those doubts and hesitations have often extended – though perhaps to a lesser degree – to assistance proffered through the United Nations system, Mexico appears to have decided early on that UN aid for population was more than acceptable; it was essential.

UNFPA assistance to Mexico began with a 1972 grant to the Foundation for Population Studies and, in 1973, to the Government's maternal and child health and family-planning programme. Assistance continued throughout the 1970s and, in 1980, following a needs assessment mission, the Fund and the Government undertook a comprehensive programme that included attention to population and development planning, migration and employment policy, projects in population dynamics, maternal and child health and family planning, education and communication, and the integration of women into development. Linked to a sex education project supported by a Swedish Trust Fund, the programme – Sadik comments – constituted a complete population programme[31].

Within this framework, one project of special interest was designed to assist CONAPO in establishing the methodological and institutional bases and co-ordinating mechanisms for the integration of population policy into socio–economic development plans carried out by the governmental institutions at the national and state levels. Among project activities were the preparation of a demographic diagnosis and population policy for 15 states and the sponsoring of a Latin American Regional Seminar on the integration of population policies into development strategy, held in Mexico City in November 1982. One result of the project was the signing of agreements with 21 states interested in the integration of population policies into their development and the preparation of 21 monographs on demography for these states.

Overall, UNFPA assistance to Mexico totalled $22 million between 1973 and 1983. In the course of this period the Government of Mexico, recognizing the role the MCH/FP programme has played in improving health services and extending services to rural communities, has shown an increasing readiness to expand the programme and to assume expenditures for local staff. In summary, the United Nations role in Mexico has not only been to contribute to a successful programme; it has also helped move the programme towards the goal of self-reliance. In matters of population, as in all other spheres of development, successful self-reliant programmes must indeed be the ultimate objective.

Colombia

Adoption of population policy

Colombia's initial demographic patterns were typical of a number of other countries in the Latin American region. There was a substantial decline in mortality between the periods 1938–51 and 1951–64, with life expectancy at birth rising from 41.0 to 45.5 years for males and from 43.8 to 50.7 years for females. High levels of fertility – with crude birth-rates of the order of 45 per 1000 – prevailed until the mid-1960s, when the country entered a fertility transition that has been one of the most rapid on record.

In the drafting of its first comprehensive development plans in the early 1960s, the Government was concerned by the impact of high rates of population growth on the employment situation. Colombia's first national population policy, which was presented to Congress in 1970, had as its principal aim the achievement of 'a significant reduction in the rate of population growth through decreasing the level of fertility'. Since the promulgation of its law on responsible parenthood in 1968, Colombia has had one of the most far-reaching family-planning programmes of any country in Latin America, and it was the first to have a large-scale *rural* family-planning programme. During the decade of the 1960s, Colombia's rate of natural increase was an estimated 32 per 1000 population. By 1979, it had declined to 21 per 1000 and, given significant emigration, the annual rate of population growth was estimated to be 1.9 per cent.

Overall socio–economic development, which was rapid during the period 1963–73, appears to have contributed to the emerging demand for fertility limitation. Among other things, there was a significant decline in the labour force employed in agriculture, appreciable economic growth (that was not, however, accompanied by major changes in income distribution), rising levels of education, growing participation of women in the labour force, and improvements in the status of women. Thus, when the Government declared in 1979 that it had no explicit policy with regard to population growth and fertility, it was in effect acknowledging that fertility levels had changed in a fashion considered by the Government to be desirable without the need for direct intervention.

However, the Government continued to support family-planning programmes. In 1981, about half of Colombia's family-planning services were provided by Pro-familia, the private family-planning association that was established in 1965 (and affiliated to IPPF). About 40 per cent of the services were provided the Ministry of Health, and the rest by private physicians.

Sterilization, which is legal without conditions, is widely practised throughout Colombia, with operations performed in Pro-familia's urban clinics and in its mobile programmes in rural areas, and in the regional hospitals in the Ministry of Health. Abortion remains strictly restricted under Colombian law, although an estimated 200,000 to 250,000 such operations are performed each year (1981 estimate).

UN support

Next to Mexico, Colombia was the largest recipient of UNFPA funds in the Latin American and Caribbean region over the period 1969–81 with some US $10 million being spent there. The main project was support of the Government's maternal and child health programme with WHO/ PAHO serving as the executing agency. First approved by the UNDP Governing Council in 1974, the scope of the project was expanded in 1977 and again in 1980. In 1983 and 1984 the Italian Government joined with UNFPA in funding the project. UNFPA also agreed a pilot project in natural family planning with the Church in Colombia and a project on family-planning information with the private organization, Pro-familia.

In February 1980, a UNFPA Evaluation Mission visited Colombia for three weeks in order to evaluate the past performance of the Colombia Maternal and Child Health and Population Dynamics (MCH/PD) Programme. The mission concluded that the programme had been particularly effective in extending services through the national health system to previously unserved rural areas, and in contributing to fertility decline. Its impact on maternal and child morbidity and mortality could not be measured because of lack of data. The strengths of the programme were found to be in its general strategy, services, training and community education. Weaker areas were programming, administration, supervision and evaluation.

The mission found the funding and monitoring mechanism inefficient and concluded that it constrained programming and programme operations. As a result, the recommendation was made that UNFPA should establish more direct links with the programme by making the Government the executing agency. UNFPA considered this recommendation when appraising the project proposal submitted by the Government for assistance over the period 1980 to 1983, but the Executive Director decided to keep WHO/PAHO as executing agency, in view of the time constraints which made the necessary negotiations with both PAHO and the Government impossible[32].

Role of the World Bank

Within the United Nations system, the role of the World Bank in Colombia has been of particular interest as far as population policy is concerned. In the 1960s when Colombia was a major borrower, the Bank's country economic reports stressed the macro-economic impact of continued high population growth rates on Colombia's development prospects. The impact of these reports was one of the factors which contributed to the adoption, in 1970, of Colombia's national population policy.

Brazil

Population policy

Brazil's population grew from 17 million inhabitants in 1900 to about 119 million in 1980, making it the sixth most populous country in the world and one of the relatively few countries to have sustained rates of population growth of more than 2 per cent for over a century. Immigration was a significant factor at the end of the last century and in the early years of the 20th century. However, natural increase is now the overwhelmingly dominant force in total population increase.

Brazil's rate of population growth averaged 2.3 per cent between 1930 and 1940, increased to 3.0 per cent between 1940 and 1950, and remained virtually unchanged at about 2.9 per cent between 1950 and 1960. The rate of population growth slowed after about 1955, having averaged 2.5 per cent per annum between 1960 and 1970. The rate of population growth (1982–3) stood at 2.23 per cent per annum.

The total fertility rate in Brazil declined nearly 8 per cent from 1930–40 to 1961–70. This is attributed to the drop in fertility levels in the more developed regions of Brazil, particularly São Paolo and the South, and, to a lesser extent, to declines in Minas and Rio de Janeiro. This downward trend stands in contrast to the marked increase in fertility recorded in the less developed regions, including Amazonia, the northern regions, Bahia and Parana. Moreira comments[33]:

> Concerned both about the national security aspects of population size and distribution and about the need to integrate vast empty regions of the country into the national economy, Brazil's leaders have been reluctant to embrace in their policy anything that seemed to threaten future population growth. 'Birth control' and even 'family planning' were for many years phrases that produced strong reactions... traditional pronatalist thought in Brazil has also drawn from the teaching of the Roman Catholic church, whose union with the state was made official in the first constitution of 1824. Church and state were separated in 1889, with the proclamation of the Republic, but it is fair to say that many of Brazil's leaders have been strongly influenced by the church's doctrines about family life and procreation.

Prior to its participation in the World Population Conference of 1974, the Government conducted a number of lengthy discussions on population issues, which culminated in the inclusion of a statement on population policy in its Second National Development Plan (1975–9). The Government noted:

> It is hoped that by allowing each family to make its own decisions, taking into consideration their moral conscience and socio–economic conditions, Brazil will achieve a population growth rate that will reconcile the various needs and demands. It is hoped that during this decade the population growth rate will decline, with the average between 1970 and 1980 being 2.7 – 2.8 per cent. In the following decades, the decline should be more rapid.

Since then the Government has given this population policy little publicity although there appears to have been a recent evolution in perceptions as shown by a Presidential statement expressing the view that the country's 'demographic explosion' is among the basic factors affecting the welfare of the society and calling for the establishment of guidelines to deal with the problem.

At the World Population Conference, the Brazilian delegate expressed support for the right of individual couples to determine their family size[34] and in July 1977 the Minister of Health announced that federal health agencies would offer family-planning services as part of the new programme for the Prevention of High-Risk Pregnancy. In practice, official policy towards family planning has remained ambiguous. A *de facto* policy of 'states' rights' apparently exists. Five states of Brazil's underdeveloped north-east have implemented agreements with BEMFAM (Sociedade Civil Bem-estar Familiar do Brasil) which since 1965 has been the chief source of organized family-planning services (BEMFAM is IPPF's largest affiliate). In addition to the agreements with the five state governments which have led to the development of the world's largest private programme of community-based services, BEMFAM also provides services through a network of more than 220 clinics and conducts highly creative and wide-ranging information and education programmes for the general public and specialized groups such as parliamentary groups and professional groups.

External assistance

Given the state of policy development in Brazil, it is not surprising that the non-governmental donors remain an important source of international assistance to Brazil in the population field. For example, IPPF's support has been running at around $3 million a year. But the United Nations has also been involved. By the end of 1982 the Fund had provided US $1.3 million for a maternal and child care demonstration project in Rio de Janeiro with the Government being the executing agency. Another project, with the United Nations as the executing agency, aimed at strengthening the technical and institutional capability of the State of Maralhao's planning system, so as to ensure the explicit incorporation of population variables in planning for socio–economic development. UNFPA expenditures for this purpose totalled around $900,000 by the end of 1982.

This relatively modest level of engagement by the United Nations was not a reflection of a lack of interest on the part of the World Organization. On the contrary, since Brazil accounted for the population of almost half of South America, it was clear that demographic developments on that continent would be powerfully influenced by evolutions in policy and practice in Brazil. It was rather a reflection of the lack of real political commitment by the Brazilian government to the goals of population policy.

The activities of the private sector and in particular BEMFAM, IPPF's affiliate in Brazil, however laudable these might be, could never be a wholly adequate substitute for an official government-sponsored commitment to fertility control. In the last resort, IPPF's affiliates around the world – including BEMFAM – are concerned primarily with the health and welfare of individuals, particularly women and children. In the 1960s and early 1970s the organization underwent considerable soul-searching as it tried to decide to what extent it might, in parallel with considerations of individual welfare, pursue or be associated with the pursuit of broader demographic objectives. That dilemma was never finally resolved, in the sense that there were still member organizations within IPPF, particularly in the European region, who were reluctant to see the Federation diverted from what they believed its primary mandate should be.

Towards the end of the period covered by this book, there were indications that changes were in the wind. In 1985, the UNDP Governing Council approved a five-year (1985–9) project in maternal and child health care for a total of $15 million, the aim being to improve management and technical capacity in the public health system and train medical and paramedical personnel, the Government of Brazil, WHO/PAHO and UNFPA being jointly responsible for the execution of the project. Since the new 'integrated approach' to maternal-child health care was firmly understood to include the principle of free decision on the number and spacing of children as accepted by the Brazilian government at the Mexico Conference, there seemed to be no doubt that an important step had been taken by both Brazil and the United Nations. The time for trumpeting the news abroad had not yet arrived, and indeed may not arrive for quite some while. That in the end may not matter very much. As the poet put it, heard melodies are sweet, but those unheard may be sweeter still.

Latin American perspective

Country differentials

In its World Development Report 1984, the World Bank points out that almost all of the countries in Latin America and in the Caribbean are middle-income, but with great demographic diversity. In four countries with per capita incomes exceeding US $2,500 – Argentina, Chile, Trinidad and Tobago, and Uruguay – population growth has slowed to below 2 per cent a year and total fertility is nearing replacement level. The highest fertility in the region is in six lower-middle-income countries: Bolivia, Ecuador, El Salvador, Guatemala, Honduras, and Nicaragua. Total fertility in these countries exceeds five and population growth ranges from 2.5 to 3.4 per cent. Fertility is high in the Caribbean, with the exception of Cuba, but emigration moderates population growth[35].

The Bank comments that in three countries, Brazil, Colombia, and Mexico (which as noted account for almost two-thirds of Latin America's population), fertility is consistently and inversely related to household income and to education. Surveys in Brazil indicate that poor rural women bear twice as many children as do women from the upper 40 per cent of urban households. Brazilian women who neither have paid jobs nor have completed primary school have more than twice as many children as working women who completed secondary school. Similar differentials occur in Mexico and Colombia. The well-to-do are able to spend more per child than are the poor and they have fewer children. But the Bank goes on to say

> Population policies have helped to reduce fertility in Latin America. In 1966 Colombia's Ministry of Health signed an agreement with a private medical association to provide a programme of training and research that included family planning. By combining low-key public support with private family-planning programmes, the Colombian Government has helped facilitate a rapid fertility decline.
>
> The Mexican Government adopted a population policy to reduce fertility in 1973 and began providing family-planning services in 1974. By 1976 contraceptive use had doubled, almost entirely because of public programmes. Between 1970 and 1980 fertility fell in both Mexico and Colombia by about one-third; in contrast, it declined by less than 20% in Brazil, a country in which the national Government had not committed itself to a population policy or programme.
>
> This contrast becomes even sharper when it is noted that per capita real incomes nearly doubled in Brazil but were up only 50% in Colombia and Mexico. Whereas Colombia and Mexico managed a sharp decline in fertility in relation to income growth, Brazil's fertility decline was more modest. If Brazil had followed the pattern of Colombia and Mexico, its total fertility rate would have fallen to 3.0 by 1982 given its income growth; in fact it was 3.9. With a population policy no more vigorous than that of Colombia and Mexico during the 1970s, Brazilian fertility might now be one-quarter lower than it is. Most of the difference would come from lower fertility among the poor, since it is they who would be assisted most by a public policy.

Lessons for the future

The lesson for government planners in Latin America and for concerned aid-givers seems to be clear. First, make sure there is a firm government commitment to population policy. Second make sure that other policies in the social field stress female education and other aspects of female emancipation. Such a recipe, of course, may be easier to advocate in countries and among cultures where the notion of female independence (including independence in decisions about whether or not to become pregnant) is more highly developed than it is, say, on a continent where 'machismo' has not yet become an obsolete word.

Nevertheless, there has been progress at least as far as the first requirement is concerned – as can be seen from the pattern of UNFPA allocations over the period. In the early years of UNFPA operations, assistance to the Latin American and Caribbean region consisted mainly of support for demographic research, compilation and analysis of data, and evaluation missions in the field of family planning.

Up to 1972, the annual allocations to the Latin American region were under $1 million. In 1978 they amounted to over $20 million, and the total spent by UNFPA between 1969 and 1978 was $82 million[36].

Before 1969, only a few governments had a policy of supporting population activities (although a number of countries had conducted censuses regularly). (See Table 8.10.) From its earliest years, UNFPA assisted the Latin American Demographic Centre (CELADE) at the Economic Commission for Latin America, as well as census-taking in El Salvador, Guatemala, Haiti, Honduras, Nicaragua and Uruquay. The first support to maternal and child health and family-planning programmes went to Chile, Colombia, Costa Rica, Haiti and to some Caribbean countries in 1970–2.

After 1972, the programmes were greatly expanded and the emphasis shifted gradually from demographic and census-oriented assistance to maternal and child health and family-planning programmes with supporting activities in information and communications and sex education. Prior to the 1974 World Population Conference, 71.2 per cent of the Fund's resources in the region went to areas other than family planning; resources devoted to family planning amounted to 28.8 per cent only. During the period 1974–8, UNFPA assistance to Latin America in areas of basic population data and population dynamics continued to increase but the fastest increase was registered in the area of family planning. In 1978, close to 56 per cent of the approved budgets were for this purpose and that proportion has been broadly maintained over the subsequent years (Table 8.12).

Looking to the future, apart from family planning (either as part of broader maternal and child health programmes, or as independent elements), United Nations assistance is likely to stress education and communication programmes in support of MCH/FP programmes as well as – for the reasons noted above – projects aimed at increasing the participation of women in the development process. One such exercise took place in 1983

Table 8.12. *Percentage distribution of UNFPA expenditures by work plan categories, Latin America and the Caribbean, 1969–83*

Work plan categories	Years												Total
	1969–72	1973	1974	1975	1976	1977	1978	1979	1980	1981	1982	1983	1969–83
Basic data collection	28.7	17.7	18.2	13.6	15.8	8.1	4.6	11.3	18.5	19.9	12.3	6.8	13.3
Population dynamics	8.7	7.4	3.4	1.9	9.5	11.1	10.6	11.7	15.0	13.5	11.9	9.6	10.3
Formulation and evaluation of population policies and programmes	32.7	27.4	18.5	16.9	4.7	7.3	7.6	8.5	7.3	12.3	15.7	14.0	11.3
Implementation of policies	0.0	0.0	0.0	0.0	0.0	0.0	0.0	0.0	0.0	0.0	0.0	0.0	0.0
Family planning	14.3	27.8	47.3	56.4	57.9	62.0	66.3	54.0	45.0	37.3	42.5	50.4	50.8
Communication and education	13.9	14.4	9.1	8.3	8.5	7.4	7.7	8.8	9.4	9.0	8.6	10.1	8.9
Special programmes	1.6	0.0	0.0	0.3	0.0	0.1	0.1	1.2	0.4	0.6	1.0	2.2	0.6
Multisectoral activities	0.1	5.3	3.5	2.6	3.6	4.0	3.1	4.5	4.4	7.4	8.0	6.9	4.8
Total	100.0	100.0	100.0	100.0	100.0	100.0	100.0	100.0	100.0	100.0	100.0	100.0	100.0
(Thousands of US dollars)	(2,054)	(3,339)	(10,983)	(14,147)	(17,443)	(13,163)	(17,171)	(20,318)	(23,465)	(17,570)	(14,608)	(16,808)	(171,069)

Source: UNFPA Fact Sheet No. 1.08 (September 1983); UNFPA Fact Sheet No. 1.09 (November 1983). Table given in *Population, the UNFPA Experience,* edited by Nafis Sadik and published for the United Nations Fund for Population Activities by New York University Press, 1984.

Note: Figures for 1969 to 1982 are project expenditures; figures for 1983 are project allocations as of 30 November 1983.

when the Fund organized a travelling seminar on population and family planning for women leaders – the First Ladies – from the Caribbean. Among all possible methods to influence attitudes in the male-dominated world of Latin American politics, an approach 'via the pillowcase' stands as good a chance as any.

NORTH AFRICA AND MIDDLE EAST

Demographic background

Karol J. Krotki, in his regional survey of North Africa and the Middle East, writes that the area has an ideological unity, having become Muslim within a few decades of the Hegira (AD 622) and having remained so ever since.

> The religious, cultural, political, and economic explosion of the seventh century is the last of the three mono-theistic movements of this area, after Judaism and Christianity. The population of the area, more than 200 million by 1980, is a minor although central part of the Islamic populations of the world. Religious uniformity is paralleled by an ethnic and linguistic unity, for 19 of the 23 units are predominantly Arabic (the exceptions are Cyprus, Israel, Sudan, and Turkey[38].)

Population size in the Arab countries differs substantially from one country to another. At one extreme is Egypt with a population of about 46 million in 1984, and on the other Qatar with around 290,000.

Population size and growth rates in the Arab countries are shown in the following Table 8.13.

During the period 1970 to 1975, the rate of population growth in the Arab countries was generally high with some variation between countries. The highest rate was registered for Kuwait (7.13 per cent per year), due to high fertility, decline in mortality, and substantial immigration. Among other countries, Saudi Arabia had high fertility but its mortality rate was high enough to offset the population growth rate somewhat, keeping it at a level of 2.9 per cent per year. High population growth rates were shared by Algeria, Jordan, Morocco, Oman, Sudan, Syria and the Yemens. Mauritania had the lowest growth rate, probably due to the high mortality rate of 25 per 1000. In Lebanon, the high growth rate was attributed to declining mortality[39].

The demography of each country is almost the same throughout the region: early marriage of females, high proportions of the population marrying, no illegitimacy, high marital fertility, high remarriage rates of

Table 8.13. *Population and growth rates – Arab countries (in thousands)*

Country	Official population based on census		Population 1975		Growth rate 1970-5 % per year	Years for population to double	Population 1980*
	Year	Population	UNESCO	UN			
Morocco	1971	15,380	17,540	17,504	2.92	24	20,255
Mauritania	1972	1,180	—	1,283	1.99	35	1,417
Algeria	1966	12,000	16,908	16,792	3.35	21	19,854
Tunisia	1975	5,810	5,810	5,810	2.25	33	6,502
Libya	1973	2,291	2,255	2,255	3.50	20	2,686
Egypt	1976	38,000	37,140	37,543	2.38	29	42,278
Sudan	1973	14,900	18,268	18,268	3.04	23	18,312
Somalia	1972	2,941	—	3,170	2.56	27	3,603
Syria	1970	6,303	7,606	7,259	3.30	21	8,561
Lebanon	1970	2,126	2,720	2,869	2.50	27	3,251
Jordan	1970	2,320	—	2,688	3.29	21	3,169
Iraq	1965	8,262	11,124	11,067	3.36	21	13,092
Kuwait	1975	995	1,188	1,085	7.13	10	1,550
Bahrain	1971	216	262	251	7.10	10	358
Qatar	1976	180	163	92	7.10	10	232
Emirates	1971	217	345	222	7.10	10	492
Oman	no census		700	766	3.50	20	912
Saudi Arabia	1974	7,013	—	8,966†	2.94	24	8,124
Yemen, A.	1975	5,300	5,300	6,668	2.90	24	6,127
Yemen, D.	1973	1,590	1,695	1,660	2.90	24	1,959

Source: Cairo Demographic Center, 1970; UNESCO 1977; UN Secretariat, 1975; UN Statistical Office, 1974. Table given in *Population in the Arab World: Problems and Prospects* by Abdel-Rahim Omran, published by Croom Helm, London 1980.

Notes: * Based on 1970-5 annual growth rate.
† Overestimate.

males, with simultaneous or consecutive polygamy taking up the remaining females[40].

High fertility

With the exceptions of Cyprus and Israel, and to a lesser extent Egypt, Lebanon, Tunisia, Turkey, the countries of North Africa and the Middle East experience high fertility. Krotki comments: 'It is seldom that such high rates are reliably reported for large human populations.' And Omran remarks that there is no doubt that the fertility level of the Arab populations is probably the highest in the world.

Over the five-year period 1970–1975, the average birth rate for the Arab World was 45 per 1000 population, with several countries reaching 50 births per 1000 population. These figures can be compared with 32 in the world as a whole and 17 in the more developed countries ... in general, fertility is higher in the Asian than in the African regions of the Arab World. It is also relatively high in the oil-rich countries, both Asian and African, than in other countries. Fertility is moderate only in Tunisia, Egypt, and possibly certain areas of Lebanon[41].

Omran goes on to say

Reproductive behaviour among Arab women in different countries has some common features. In most countries, fertility is high with child-bearing starting early and continuing throughout the reproductive span. The age at marriage is generally low with marriage being universal. There is a traditional preference for sons and large families. Fertility in the Arab World is still viewed as a major basis for determining the wife's status in the family and community and a sign of virility for men.

Signs of hope

Omran does not, however, conclude that the situation is without hope. He believes there is convincing evidence from at least three Arab countries – Tunisia, Lebanon, and Egypt – that fertility can decline in response to family-planning efforts without drastic changes in societal values and beliefs and without substantial socio–economic development comparable to the Western model[42].

Because this book is concerned specially with falling birth-rates and the part the United Nations may play in bringing these about, we now look at two of the three countries cited by Omran: Egypt and Tunisia.

203

Egypt

Population growth

Apart from those early efforts by King Herod, the first census of the population was taken in 1822 and it showed that Egypt had 7.8 million inhabitants. Subsequent efforts at census-taking proved sporadic, and it was not until 1900 that any regular system for determining population growth was set up. Between 1900 and 1960, a census was taken every ten years, and, according to the Egyptian Central Agency for Public Mobilization and Statistics (CAPMAS), these censuses show an average rate of population increase of about 1.7 per cent per annum. By 1960-6, the rate of population growth had risen to 2.5 per cent[43].

In 1952, according to CAPMAS, the population of the country was 21.4 million; by 1960, it had risen to 25.8 million; in 1965, it was 29.3 million.

Government concern

Egypt's concern with its growing population dates back 40 years. The Ministry of Social Affairs, formed in 1929, was charged amongst other things with the study of Egypt's population problems. A National Population Commission was established by President Nasser in 1953 to examine population issues. The first formal population policy statement was included in the new National Charter in 1962; and a Supreme Council for Family Planning was established in 1965. During the 1970s, the Government considered population issues to be of great importance; President Sadat stressed the critical nature of Egypt's population problems in a speech to the Arab Socialist Union in 1971, and a National Population Policy for the decade 1972–82 was announced in 1973. The target was to reduce the annual rate of population growth to 1.0 per cent by 1982 and to achieve a population size of not more than 41 million by 1982. (In 1972, population stood at 34.8 million.) The Government also reaffirmed its fairly ambitious target – which was first announced in 1969 – of lowering the crude birth-rate by 1 per 1000 population per year over the next ten years, or from 33.7 per 1000 population in 1973 to 23.6 by 1982.

In February 1982, President Mubarak stated that 'the current population growth rate impedes development efforts and frustrates our hopes for improving the quality of life for every Egyptian. It confines our ambitions to preventing further deterioration in living standards, and that is unacceptable'. Emphasizing the massive size of projected near-term population growth, the President further reported:

The total number of those employed in 1976 was 11.6 million; this number is expected to double to 24.1 million in the year 2000 and to jump to 53.3 million in the year 2025. The number of children of primary school age would be 12 million in the year 2000 as compared to not more than 6 million in 1976. In housing, eight million new units will need to be provided by the year 2000 and another 7 million units during the following ten years.

These figures are indicative of the serious constraints population growth places on our efforts to achieve development and a higher standard of living.

Official family-planning policy

Egypt was the first Arab country to adopt a national family-planning policy. There were various official and private efforts to encourage family planning beginning in the 1950s; the National Population Commission (1953), for example, set up its first family-planning clinics in 1955. It was not until 1965, however, that the Government formally announced a national family-planning programme and established the Supreme Council for Family Planning (later renamed the Supreme Council for Population and Family Planning). Subsequently, the voluntary organizations that had been operating during the preceding decade were officially recognized, and the Egyptian Family-Planning Association, an affiliate of the International Planned Parenthood Federation (IPPF) since 1963, was formally established in 1967 to co-ordinate their activities.

A Director-General for Family Planning, a High Committee for Family Planning, and a Technical Advisory Board was established by the Government in 1977. By the late 1970s services were being provided in some 3750 health units located throughout the country. Contraceptives were also being distributed through street vendors and other commercial outlets.

The Government also placed increasing emphasis on direct client motivation activities such as information, education, and communications programmes. Egypt was in fact the first Muslim country in which the religious authorities supported the view that family planning was not incompatible with Muslim religious teachings.

Setbacks

In the event, the crude birth-rate increased to 37.6 per 1000 by 1975. The somewhat unexpected rise in fertility prompted a reevaluation of approaches to family planning. The 'traditional' clinic-oriented approach, with its emphasis on the distribution of contraceptive supplies and information, was complemented by a broader approach, the 'development' approach, which stressed not only direct intervention to modify fertility (increasing the coverage of services; and improving communications programmes), but also wider programmes involving improving and extending educational facilities; providing more employment opportunities for women; increasing the mechanization of agriculture; promoting industrialization; improving social security measures; reducing infant mortality; and improving the socio–economic level of the family.

External assistance

Aid for population policies and family planning in Egypt has been significant. On 29 April 1971, the Egyptian Government and UNFPA signed a comprehensive agreement under which UNFPA undertook to assist the National Family Planning Programme in the amount of US $5.8 million over the four years 1971–4. A second phase of support was agreed for the five-year period beginning 1976. This Second Country Programme Agreement reflected the shift in policy towards the 'development approach' and included projects for the creation of employment opportunities for women, literacy classes and other community-based activities to motivate the population for accepting family planning[44].

In 1976, as part of the Egyptian Government's decentralization, governors were given the responsiblity for preparing development plans most appropriate for their respective governorates. On the basis of the 1976 population census carried out with United Nations support, each governor was advised of the number of women in the reproductive age group in the governorate so that a target could be set for increasing the number of family-planning acceptors. One activity financed by UNFPA under the Second Agreement was the Population and Development Project (PDP), initiated in 1977. This, Sadik states, was: 'a significant step in amplifying the new, broader approach to population issues'. With assistance from UNFPA and subsequently from other donors, this project has financed, through a fund that awards interest-free loans, projects of importance to communities as a reward for achieving specified numbers of family-planning acceptors. A trained population co-ordinator advised on the priority to be given projects bearing on fertility behaviour, such as women's employment projects or literacy classes for women.

By 1983, the project was operational in 12 of 26 governorates serving 14.5 million people. The Federal Republic of Germany, The Netherlands and the United States Agency for International Development (USAID) all substantially contributed to expanding this programme nationwide. The grand total of UNFPA's expenditure in Egypt as of 30 June 1983 was nearly $21 million.

Another important source of multilateral assistance has been the World Bank which in 1974 contributed US $5 million to enable the Government to put its Integrated Health Services System into operation in four governorates; and, in 1979, a further US $25 million for a second project designed to help reduce fertility, infant mortality and morbidity, and maternal mortality and morbidity, in seven of the country's 25 governorates, containing 26 per cent of the population. The British Overseas Development Administration (ODA) also contributed £8.0 million for this project, while the Egyptian Government put in the equivalent of US $27.3 million.

Achievements

It has to be said that in spite of these considerable efforts both by the Government of Egypt and by external aid-donors, the achievements so far have not been spectacular. In 1982–3, Egypt's population stood at 41.2 million, around 45 per cent being urban dwellers. Crude birth-rates had risen to 38.4 and the population growth rate was 2.52 per cent per annum. The programme was clearly not on target.

In its issue of 2–8 August 1986, in an article entitled 'The Baby Machine', the *Economist* commented:

The most striking thing about Egypt's population is not just that it is ballooning (at the present annual growth rate of 2.7 per cent, it should rise from 50m now to 70m by the end of the century). The really odd thing is that Egyptians, grand or lowly, have made practically no attempt to do anything about the problem. As with the economy in general, 'Allah will provide'.

To be fair to Mr Mubarak, he has told Egyptians plainly that they should breed less. But a whole array of obstacles, ranging from the torpor of bureaucracy to the strength of tradition, makes mock of the president's appeals. The national family planning council set up a year and a half ago has met only once. The health minister sounds, at best, lukewarm about taking vigorous action. The Government has been spending less than £3m a year on family planning, while American agencies alone have spent £61m on it in Egypt in the past eight years. Egypt has used less than a third of the £25m soft loan for population control it got in 1978; it may have to give back the unused portion.

Tradition and religion obstruct family planning. Abortion is illegal, and sterilisation is discouraged as 'contrary to religious values'. The health minister, Dr Helmy Hadidi, has banned Depoprovera, the contraceptive injection women need only once a quarter, although it is now medically acceptable. Religious fundamentalism, Christian as well as Muslim, resists all forms of birth control.

So women still average nearly seven births each. Nearly half marry before they are 17. Nearly half the population is under 16. Almost all mothers want sons, and tend to breed on until they have several. Overcrowding torments the town-dwellers: some 7% of Cairenes, according to one recent survey, actually live in tombs. In the countryside, the average family holding has been squeezed down from seven acres to one.

Not a glimpse of hope anywhere? The number of people using contraception has risen – from 24 per cent in 1980 to perhaps a third today. But $10m worth of food is imported every day[45].

Leaving aside one statistical inaccuracy (the number of births per woman is nearer five than seven), the moral of this story seems to be that it is not always sufficient to have political will at the highest levels of government. It must also be present at the other echelons as well. Furthermore, even though it may prove possible in Egypt, as it has elsewhere, to achieve fertility reductions without necessarily achieving rises in per capita income according to the classic theories of demographic transition, the 'drastic changes in societal values and beliefs' (which Omran suggests might also be dispensed with) may – at least in some parts of the Arab world – be a necessary precursor of fertility decline. In such circumstances, it will behove national planners – and international aid-givers – to take the widest possible view of the development process. Information, education and communication may be as important as the contraceptives themselves.

In 1985, a new thrust was given to the Egyptian population programme with the establishment of a National Population Council chaired by the President. The intention was to intensify family planning, especially in rural areas, ensuring the availability of a mix of contraceptive methods, improving and extending family-planning services, and establishing effective outreach and information, education and communication (IEC) programmes to reach women. A new programme for 1986–90 was being prepared to achieve these goals.

Tunisia

Targets and fertility declines

According to the early censuses, the Tunisian population increased gradually from a total population of 2 million in 1921 to over 2.4 million by 1936, at an estimated average annual rate of growth of between 1.2 and 1.5 per cent during this period. After the Second World War the population underwent a much more rapid growth, rising from 2.9 million in 1946 to over 6 million in 1980. The period of the highest rate of growth was between 1956 and 1966 (2.9 per cent).

An official family-planning programme was launched as early as 1963, and in the subsequent development plans the importance of population issues was stressed repeatedly. In 1973, the Government provided centralized leadership by establishing the National Office of Family Planning and Population as a semi-autonomous agency of the Ministry of Health.

Official targets have been set regularly by the Government. In 1975 the National Office of Family Planning and Population aimed at reducing the general fertility rate to 137.8 per 1000 by 1981 and at achieving a rate of natural increase of 1.2 per cent by the year 2001. The Fifth Plan (1977–81) projected, assuming a continuous fertility decline, a crude birth-rate of 32.3 per 1000 by the end of the planned period, which was expected to decrease to 29.9 by 1986. The general fertility rate as projected in the plan was expected to reach 135.3 per 1000 in 1981 and 120 per 1000 in 1986. These targets were obtainable, according to Tunisian planners, provided 40,000 births could be prevented in 1981 increasing to 90,000 in 1986. The Government considered this to be possible if the rate of protection through the family-planning programme could be increased, particularly for women in rural areas and for the increasing number of women in the reproductive age group. The plan also aimed at the promotion of family health, which included family-planning activities at all levels of the health infrastructure.

Fertility levels in Tunisia have gradually declined over the past two decades. According to Government registration data, the rate fell from 44.5 per 1000 in 1966 to 37.0 per 1000 in 1971. (Prior to 1966 the crude birth-rate was estimated to have fluctuated between 43 and 46 per 1000.) After 1971, the rate continued to decline with minor fluctuations and for the period 1975–80 it was estimated by the United Nations Population Division to have reached a level of 36.7 per 1000. The gross reproduction rate at this time was estimated to be 2.8.

Assistance to family-planning programme

On 10 April 1975, the Government of Tunisia and UNFPA signed an agreement under which the UNFPA, over a three-and-a-half-year period beginning in 1974, committed $4 million in assistance to the Tunisian Family Planning Programme. The projects under the agreement covered the whole range of family-planning activities including support for clinical delivery services and population education in schools and in the rural and labour sectors as well as equipment and training. A second programme of assistance was approved by the UNDP Governing Council at its 25th session in June 1978 in order to ensure continuation of the earlier programme. The estimated UNFPA contribution was $4 million, with the Government's contribution some $13.7 million for the five-year period 1978–82. Consulting agencies were the ILO, UNESCO and UNICEF. In June 1981, a further comprehensive programme of assistance to the Government of Tunisia was approved by UNDP Governing Council, in the amount of US $5 million. UNFPA support was to cover such areas as data collection and analysis, population dynamics, maternal and child health and family planning, and population information, education, and communication (IEC). The estimated value of the Government's contribution was US $57 million. Assisting agencies were the United Nations, UNESCO and WHO.

In September–October 1982 a UNFPA Evaluation Mission visited Tunisia with the aim of analysing and assessing the achievements of the Family-Planning and Population Education Programme in Tunisia, in the areas assisted by UNFPA, over the period 1974–82[46]. The mission concluded that in a general sense much progress had been made over the period under review. It was, for example, favourably impressed with the comprehensiveness of the family-planning programme, with the expansion of service units and personnel resulting in much increased availability of family-planning services, with a large number of IEC activities undertaken and with the existing network of population education co-ordinators in the school sector.

However, the mission concluded that progress had been somewhat slow in certain areas (for example, in terms of increasing contraceptive prevalence and in terms of actually integrating population education into all schools at all levels) and that some objectives had not been fully achieved (for example, the targets of new FP acceptors had not been met in the last three years). Moreover, the mission noted that in some cases objectives and targets had been too ambitious because they were set without proper analysis of needs in comparison with available resources. However, although progress in increasing contraceptive prevalence and in decreasing fertility and birth-rates had been somewhat slow over the 1974–82 period, it was still noteworthy given the cultural context of the programme.

The World Bank has also provided support to the Tunisian Government. A first Population Project, implemented from December 1971 to 1980, was designed to improve programme performance and relieve a shortage of accommodation in maternity hospitals. The total project cost was US $33 million, with the Bank providing a US $4.8 million IDA credit, the

Norwegian Agency for International Development providing a US $4.8 million grant and the Government of Tunisia the equivalent of US $23.4 million.

A second World Bank Health and Population Project became effective on 15 October 1981. Total project cost was $41 million, of which $12.5 million was provided by a World Bank loan and $28.5 by the Government of Tunisia. The project was designed to help the Government develop its integrated health delivery system including family planning by strengthening the planning and management capabilities of the Ministry of Public Health and extending the decentralization process begun in 1977. It also included the construction or remodelling of health facilities, health education, training of health workers and paramedicals, and a programme of studies and applied research.

Status

It is not clear that Tunisia's early progress in reducing birth-rates has been maintained. UNFPA comments in its Annual Report for 1984:

> While family planning activities continued apace in Tunisia in 1984, the realization that the population growth rate (2.5 per cent) was virtually unchanged since the national programme began in 1966 gave pause to those concerned with its effectiveness. Most fertility decline has resulted from the rising age of marriage over the last two decades. The proportion of women still unmarried at ages 15–24 rose from 43 to 75 per cent between 1956 and 1980. Some observers have long thought that the lack of reliable service in rural areas, which account for only about one-third of acceptors, may be a major factor in the failure to reduce the birthrate.

In fact, in 1984 the Tunisian birth-rate still stood at around 34.1 per 1000 while the total fertility rate was 4.92, i.e. a national average of almost five births per woman.

The regional perspective

Population policies

In a review of population policies in the region, Sadik notes that there is a wide variation in countries' perception of their population problems and their readiness to adopt population policies[47]. The Governments of Egypt and Tunisia have launched national programmes for population activities designed to accomplish explicit demographic growth objectives of reduction in fertility and population growth, even though as we have seen these efforts have not yet been crowned with a substantial degree of success. The Governments of Algeria and Morocco have, to a lesser extent, defined the magnitude of their population problems and have initiated programmes to provide their populations with information and services about family planning as part of basic health services. In Western Asia, Democratic Yemen, Jordan, the Syrian Arab Republic and Yemen, have proceeded to integrate family planning with maternal and child health services as part of the basic health services. Somalia and the Sudan have similar activities. Other countries, such as the Gulf States and Iraq, have no stated population policy and no direct national population programmes except for policies regulating immigration of the exogenous labour force.

Sadik notes that, by and large, almost all the countries of the region lack adequate infrastructure for population data collection and analysis; generally, they have weak, or no, civil registration systems. Their development plans generally do not take demographic variables sufficiently into account.

Priorities for UN

What of the future? It is clear that the efforts of the United Nations and its agencies must be directed towards assisting countries in the region with the formulation of appropriate population policies where this has not yet been done. This will require, as Sadik puts it, 'policy-relevant research identifying the socio–economic determinants and consequences of (population) trends and shedding light on the policy options available for their modification[48]'.

As far as family-planning progammes are concerned (where these have been introduced), Sadik comments that 'means of reaching non-urban communities must be found if reductions in crude birth rates are to be achieved'. This is likely to involve training of non-medical or paramedical personnel – village motivators, rural health workers, mobile teams, traditional birth attendants – who must be counted on to participate not merely in the family-planning programme but in the broad-based efforts to reduce infant and child nutrition and mortality. 'In rural areas' Sadik writes, 'the death toll on infants and children still remains unacceptably high. Without a reduction in this burden, the possibility of wide acceptance of family planning methods in these areas remains slim.' (See Table 8.14.)

Table 8.14. *Percentage distribution of UNFPA expenditures by work plan categories, Middle East and Mediterranean, 1969–83*

Work plan categories	Years												Total
	1969–72	1973	1974	1975	1976	1977	1978	1979	1980	1981	1982	1983	1969–83
Basic data collection	8.4	42.0	26.1	35.2	24.4	33.2	14.6	23.7	26.7	29.5	29.7	13.3	24.8
Population dynamics	3.1	2.8	2.5	1.8	3.0	4.2	15.0	12.7	16.6	12.0	13.2	19.0	11.0
Formulation and evaluation of population policies and programmes	2.6	4.8	3.7	2.4	0.8	0.6	3.2	1.4	3.0	4.1	3.5	4.3	2.8
Implementation of policies	0.0	0.0	0.0	0.0	0.0	0.0	0.6	0.5	0.4	0.4	0.1	0.4	0.3
Family planning	78.8	32.2	54.1	47.0	55.4	46.6	46.9	41.7	29.7	26.4	26.6	31.4	39.4
Communication and education	6.1	5.4	0.7	5.0	7.5	6.0	9.7	8.2	10.2	13.9	13.8	20.0	10.4
Special programmes	0.0	0.0	0.0	0.0	0.1	0.6	0.9	0.7	1.2	0.8	0.2	1.2	0.6
Multisectoral activities	1.0	12.8	12.9	8.6	8.8	8.8	9.1	11.1	12.2	12.9	12.9	10.4	10.7
Total	100.0	100.0	100.0	100.0	100.0	100.0	100.0	100.0	100.0	100.0	100.0	100.0	100.0
(Thousands of US dollars)	(2,561)	(2,112)	(5,605)	(6,736)	(9,187)	(8,487)	(10,075)	(12,180)	(12,513)	(11,947)	(10,739)	(13,888)	(106,030)

Source: UNFPA Fact Sheet No. 1.08 (September 1983); UNFPA Fact Sheet No. 1.09 (November 1983). Table given in *Population, the UNFPA Experience*, edited by Nafis Sadik and published for the United Nations Fund for Population Activities by New York University Press, 1984.

Note: Figures for 1969 to 1982 are project expenditures; figures for 1983 are project allocations as of 30 November 1983.

Country-programming

Once again, it seems clear that effective family planning requires, often if not always, associated efforts in the field of health, nutrition and education. Thus, country-programming in the widest sense and continuing collaboration over a broad field between the World Bank, UNFPA/ UNDP, the Specialized Agencies of the UN system and, more widely, the other actors in the field of development co-operation, e.g. the major bilateral aid programmes (USAID, ODA, SIDA, etc), or the EEC Development Fund, will become of increasing importance.

SUB-SAHARAN AFRICA

Current perspective

In its recent survey of population growth and policies in Sub-Saharan Africa, the World Bank notes that Sub-Saharan Africa has about 9 per cent of the world's population and about one-fifth of its land, divided into some 48 countries with over 800 ethnic groups. By world standards, nearly all African countries have small populations. Only six (Nigeria, Ethiopia, Sudan, Tanzania, Kenya and Zaire) exceeded 20 million in 1984; except for Nigeria and Ethiopia with about 94 and 44 million respectively, none exceeded 35 million. Three-quarters of Sub-Saharan countries had fewer than 10 million people and nearly half had fewer than 5 million[49].

The rate of population growth in Sub-Saharan Africa is extraordinarily rapid. Africa is the only region that has not had a fall in population growth rates. Apart from a brief baby boom after World War II, growth rates in the industrial countries have been declining for decades and in some countries are at or below zero. The population growth rate for Latin America peaked at 2.9 per cent a year in the early 1960s and has now fallen to 2.4 per cent in the late 1960s falling to 2.1 per cent. Only in Sub-Saharan Africa are growth rates continuing to rise, from 2.5 per cent a year in 1960 to 3 per cent a year in 1983. If these rates were to continue, Sub-Saharan Africa's population of 459 million (1985) would double in just 22 years.

The World Bank notes that Africa's rapid population growth results from a steady fall in death-rates and no fall – indeed, in some countries an increase – in birth-rates. In the last 20 years the average crude death-rate for all of Sub-Saharan Africa fell by one-third to 15.9 per thousand – in itself a success. Yet the average crude birth-rate changed hardly at all. (See Table 8.15.) By contrast, birth-rates as well as death-rates were declining in all other continents. Table 8.15 shows current levels for African and other selected countries: in Africa, birth-rates are almost all very high; death-rates vary more but, compared to non-African countries, are not

Table 8.15. *Birth-rates, death-rates, and rates of natural increase: Sub-Saharan Africa and selected other developing countries*

Region and country	Crude birth-rate per thousand population 1983	Crude death-rate per thousand population 1983	Growth rates 1983 (per cent)
Sub-Saharan Africa			
Cameroon	46	15	3.2
Ethiopia	41	20	2.1[a]
Ghana	49	10	3.9
Ivory Coast	46	14	4.2
Kenya	55	12	4.3
Mali	48	21	2.3
Nigeria	50	17	3.3
Senegal	46	19	2.8
Sudan	46	17	2.8
Tanzania	50	16	3.4
Uganda	50	19	3.3
Zaire	46	16	3.1
Zambia	50	16	3.4
Zimbabwe	53	13	4.0
Other regions			
Bangladesh	42	16	2.6
China	19	7	1.2
Colombia	28	7	1.9
India	34	13	2.2
Indonesia	34	13	2.1
Mexico	34	7	2.5
Philippines	31	7	2.3
Peru	34	11	2.3
Thailand	27	8	1.9

Source: World Bank: *World Development Report 1985*, p. 212.

Note: [a] This unusually low rate for Ethiopia reflects the famine in 1983.

particularly low. Indeed, they can be expected to fall further in the decade ahead.

Over the past 40 years life expectancy has risen substantially in Africa, to average about 50 years at birth. In the 1950s life expectancy of under 40 years, with corresponding infant mortality rates of 200 or more, was common; life expectancy over 50 was rare. By the 1980s, however, few countries had life expectancies below 45. Some had climbed above 55, with corresponding infant mortality rates of less than 100. Although the average level of mortality in Africa is still the highest in the world, some countries in eastern and southern Africa have achieved life expectancies comparable to countries in other developing regions.

By contrast, fertility in Africa is extremely high by world standards. In most African countries, total fertility rates are over 6. Several are over 7, with rates in Eastern Africa generally higher than in Western Africa. Most rates below 6 reflect involuntary pathological sterility. Meanwhile total fertility rates in China, Thailand and Indonesia have fallen from the peak of 5–6 to 2–4 today. In other areas such as Central America, the Middle East and North Africa, and the Muslim parts of the Indian sub-continent, total fertility rates of up to 7 can be found. But the rates of 7–8 in Eastern and Southern Africa and occasionally in West Africa are almost unparalleled elsewhere. The Bank summarizes the situation as follows:

> Other developing regions have achieved a demographic transition; both death rates and birth rates have declined from high levels. Africa has begun its demographic transition with death rate declines but has yet to achieve the second stage of falling birth rates. With the exception of Zimbabwe, no documented cases of national fertility decline has occurred in Africa.

McNamara's Crawford lecture

In November 1985, Mr Robert McNamara, former president of the World Bank, delivered the Sir John Crawford Memorial lecture in Washington DC, on 'the Challenges for Sub-Saharan Africa'[50].

> The most important long-term issue is the rampant growth of population. For most countries in Africa that issue constitutes a ticking time-bomb.

The following Table (Table 8.16) was used by McNamara to illustrate the possible course of African demographic development. The assumptions concerning the future tempo of fertility decline in the African countries, incorporated in the projections, reflect the judgement – or the hope – that the high fertility rates, which are still increasing in some countries, will start to decline well before the century's end, and that then the downward trend will be precipitous and sustained until replacement-level fertility is achieved. These are, McNamara says, 'heroic assumptions. They require that the move from high fertility to replacement-level fertility – which took about a century and a half in the United States – be completed within a drastically shorter time span in Africa. They envisage no possibility of temporary reversals or pauses on the downward course of fertility. They allow for no 'baby booms' such as the West experienced once replacement fertility had been attained'. He continues:

> And yet the populations that must conform to these demanding assumptions are largely poor and rural. They are populations in which security and old age is still derived primarily from the support of one's children. Many are populations with religious and cultural values that place a high premium on fertility.

And even if such heroic assumptions prove to be borne out by events, by the year 2025 Kenya would be four times the size it was in 1980; Nigeria

216

Table 8.16. *African population projections, 1980–2100 (population in millions)*

Selected Countries	1950	1980	2000	2025	2050	2100	Total fertility rate, 1983	Year in which NRR = 1 [a]
Cameroon	4.6	8.7	17	30	42	50	6.5	2030
Ethiopia	18.0	37.7	64	106	142	173	5.5	2035
Ghana	4.4	11.5	23	40	53	62	7.0	2025
Kenya	5.8	16.6	37	69	97	116	8.0	2030
Malawi	2.9	6.0	11	21	29	36	7.6	2040
Mozambique	6.5	12.1	22	39	54	67	6.5	2035
Niger	2.9	5.5	11	20	29	38	7.0	2040
Nigeria	40.6	84.7	163	295	412	509	6.9	2035
Tanzania	7.9	18.8	37	69	96	120	7.0	2035
Uganda	4.8	12.6	25	46	64	80	7.0	2035
Zaire	14.2	27.1	50	86	116	139	6.3	2030
Other Sub-Sahara	59.8	121.7	218	381	524	651	6.5	2040
Total Sub-Sahara	172.4	363.0	678	1,202	1,658	2,041	6.7	2040
Other Africa	42.6	89.6	148	225	282	319	5.5	2025
Total Africa	215.0	452.6	826	1,427	1,940	2,360	6.5	2040

Source: Sir John Crawford memorial lecture. *The Challenges for Sub-Saharan Africa* by Robert S. McNamara, November 1, 1985, published by the World Bank.

Note: [a] NRR refers to net reproduction rate. When NRR = 1, fertility is at replacement level.

and Ghana would have grown more than three-fold; all of the other countries would have at least tripled; and the population of Sub-Saharan Africa as a whole would have risen from 363 million to 1201 million.

Looking at the implications of rapid population growth for Sub-Saharan Africa, McNamara notes that countries 'will find it increasingly difficult to reverse the 20-year decline in per capita food production'. Sub-Saharan Africa will almost certainly find it impossible to achieve and maintain a rate of growth in food production that exceeds its current population growth rate of 3.2 per cent. Agricultural growth rates that high have been achieved by very few countries, and only then under the most favourable conditions. 'The reality is that agriculture in Sub-Saharan Africa is unlikely to grow at more than 2.5 per cent per year for at least the next two decades. Thus, the already high levels of malnutrition will grow even worse, and punishing years of famine will become even more frequent.'

Another serious consequence of the runaway population growth rate will be mounting unemployment. Between now and the end of the century, industry and agriculture combined will be able to absorb only about half of the projected increase in the labour force.

217

The present population explosion will also aggravate the ecological vulnerabilities of the continent. Already the pressures have led to a significant decline in the wood resources. The demand for firewood has increased so intensely that it has resulted in widespread deforestation. This in turn has brought on severe fuel shortages.

> In many countries of West Africa families that traditionally cooked two meals a day now have fuel for only one hot meal a day, or one every other day. Thus deforestation is beginning to lead to an accelerated degradation of the basic life-support system.... The population problem in Africa is clearly related to its growing ecological difficulties.

High population growth rates will also put heavy strains on already overburdened educational and health care systems. Countries such as Kenya face a doubling or tripling of their school-age population within the next 15 years. Growth rates such as these will immensely exacerbate the problems of expanding these services to anything approaching required levels.

The high fertility rate – an average of 6.7 children per woman in 1983 – is the result of a broad mix of economic, social and cultural forces. These include such factors as the early age of marriage for African girls; the diminishing practice of prolonged breast feeding, and of sexual abstinence after childbirth; and the very limited use of modern contraception. Fewer than 5 per cent of couples use contraceptives in Sub-Saharan Africa, as compared with some 30 per cent in India and some 70 per cent in China.

The high fertility rates, McNamara suggests, are due in part also to the low relative status that women have in African societies. Though both males and females derive benefits from children, it is generally the women who bear most of the costs. In addition to the health risks of bearing children women often have the major financial responsibility for raising them. This is particularly true in polygamous households where each wife has primary responsibility for her own children.

> Men, on the other hand, enjoy the benefits of children at a much lower cost. They are less involved in their day-to-day care, less concerned with their health, educational and emotional needs, and hence less conscious of the costs to the children of having many siblings. Thus, to the extent that males continually dominate the decision to have another child, fertility is likely to remain high.

McNamara points out, however, that recent surveys of a number of African countries have indicated that women too express a very high demand for children. The surveys show that even though most married women already have six children, more than 80 per cent want still more. In six of the countries surveyed, women said they wanted between six and nine offspring.

McNamara notes that until quite recently many African leaders regarded population growth as a distinct asset, rather than a potential hazard. They had not fully realized the inevitable consequences of runaway growth rates. Population control, furthermore, is often a sensitive political issue in Africa, particularly when different groups in a society compete for power and resources.

The perception, moreover, that much of the pressure for small families comes from western aid donors leads to resentment and inaction on the part of the officials. Government commitment is further constrained by the lack of recent and reliable demographic data. Many countries do not have a history of census-taking, and even when censuses have been taken, political controversy has often prevented them from being public. The result is that the size of the population and its rate of growth in countries such as Guinea, Nigeria and Zaire are not known with any degree of certainty.

McNamara notes that as recently as 1974 – the year of the United Nations Conference on Population at Bucharest – only two countries, Kenya and Ghana, had adopted policies to moderate their population growth. However, there are signs that 'at least on the surface, the attitudes of Sub-Saharan African Governments are beginning to change'. He cites the Kilimanjaro Programme of Action on Population, a document adopted in January, 1984, when representatives from most African Governments met at the Second African Population Conference sponsored by the United Nations in Arusha, Tanzania. The Conference recommended, among other things, that 'population should be seen as a central component in formulating and implementing policies and programmes for accelerated socio–economic development plans', and that 'Governments should ensure the availability and accessibility of family planning services to all couples or individuals seeking such services freely or at subsidised prices.'

If McNamara's memorial lecture has been quoted at some length, it is because he summarizes in stark terms the demographic situation in Africa today and the dimensions of the task which confronts most countries in Africa if they are to bring their birth rates down. That task involves:

First, improving understanding in African countries as to the nature of the problems posed by population growth and promoting greater support and political commitment to the solution of those problems;

Second, implementing development strategies and information and education programmes that build demand for smaller families;

Third, supplying safe, effective and affordable family planning and other basic health services targetted particularly at the reduction of high infant and childhood mortality and focussed on the poor in rural and urban settings.

Priority countries

Up until the time of the Bucharest Conference, and in the years immediately following it, the allocation of UNFPA resources to countries had been based largely on the size of Government requests, the types of programme for which assistance was sought, and the availability of other internal and external resources. In 1976, for example, countries in Asia and the Pacific received the largest share of the Fund's programme resources, just over 30 per cent; Africa received around 13 per cent, Latin America around 25 per cent and Europe, the Mediterranean and the Middle East 13 per cent, while the remainder supported inter-regional and global activities (See Table 8.10).

The large amounts alloted to countries in Asia and the Pacific could be explained by the fact that particularly in the earlier years of the Fund's existence they were, and in general terms remained, more 'population conscious' and had more comprehensive action programmes than elsewhere. But now that the Fund had, as it were, come of age, it became clear that a special system of selection of high priority countries for population assistance would have to be designed in order to take fully into account the general principle that the Fund was to assist particularly countries with urgent population problems. By applying the criteria of a per capita national income below $400 per annum or two or more of the following demographic criteria:

1. Annual rate of population growth of 2.75 per cent or higher;

2. Fertility in terms of gross reproduction rate of 2.75 per cent or higher;

3. Infant mortality of 176 infant deaths or more per 1000 live births; and

4. Agricultural population density on arable land of 2.2 persons or more per hectacre,

the UNFPA in 1976 designated a group of 40 developing countries as priority countries for population assistance (PCPAs) out of a total of 128 developing countries. Of the group, 17 were in Africa, 14 in Asia and the Pacific, 5 in Europe, the Mediterranean and the Middle East and 4 in Latin America.

In 1982, after reviewing its experience, the Fund revised the selection criteria to include the following:

1. An annual gross national product per capita of $500 or less:

2. Annual population increase of 100,000 persons or more;

3. A gross reproduction rate of 2.5 or more;

4. An infant mortality rate of 160 per 1000 live births or above;

5. A density of two or more persons per hectare of arable land.

Table 8.17. *Regional distribution of UNFPA priority countries for population assistance*

Africa, Sub-Saharan	
Angola	Malawi
Benin	Mali
Burundi	Mauritania
Central African Republic	Mozambique
Chad	Niger
Comoros	Rwanda
Equatorial Guinea	Sao Tome and Principe
Ethiopia	Senegal
Gambia	Sierra Leone
Ghana	Uganda
Guinea	United Republic of Tanzania
Kenya	Upper Volta
Lesotho	Zambia
Liberia	Zaire
Madagascar	Zimbabwe
Asia and the Pacific	
Afghanistan	Lao People's Democratic Republic
Bangladesh	Maldives
Bhutan	Nepal
Burma	Pakistan
China	Samoa
Democratic Kampuchea	Solomon Islands
India	Sri Lanka
Indonesia	Vietnam
Latin America and the Caribbean	
Dominica	Haiti
Middle East and Mediterranean	
Democratic Yemen	Sudan
Egypt	Yemen
Somalia	

A country had to be at or below the income threshold and to meet two of the demographic variables mentioned above. On this basis 53 countries qualified as priority countries, of which 30 were in Sub-Saharan Africa as can be seen from the following Table 8.17.

By 1985, almost 20 per cent of UNFPA assistance was being spent in Africa. As the data in Table 8.18 illustrate, the highest proportion of UNFPA expenditures in Africa during the period 1969–83 was for data collection – an average of 37 per cent, and more than 50 per cent in 1974, 1975, 1976. The most interesting pattern, however, has been the pronounced increase in the proportion of expenditures for family planning, from 14 per cent in 1969–72 to 33 per cent in 1983, as a growing awareness of the deleterious effects of population trends prompted Governments to seek external support for remedial actions.

Of course, the distance already covered is as nothing when compared to the length of the journey that still lies ahead. For UNFPA, and for all the

Table 8.18. *Percentage distribution of UNFPA expenditures by work plan categories, Sub-Saharan Africa, 1969–83*

| Work plan categories | Years | | | | | | | | | | | | Total |
	1969–72	1973	1974	1975	1976	1977	1978	1979	1980	1981	1982	1983	1969–83
Basic data collection	31.1	42.0	52.1	51.3	50.6	34.1	40.3	38.1	35.1	38.0	33.9	28.4	37.4
Population dynamics	22.2	19.3	11.0	13.2	13.8	14.8	14.0	14.4	18.8	16.7	18.3	15.2	15.9
Formulation and evaluation of population policies and programmes	3.3	4.4	3.7	2.1	1.4	0.4	0.8	1.6	4.0	4.1	3.5	5.8	3.2
Implementation of policies	0.0	0.0	0.0	0.0	0.0	0.0	0.0	0.1	0.0	0.0	0.0	0.0	0.0
Family planning	13.7	10.8	7.2	15.7	16.6	27.4	20.3	22.0	18.1	19.0	23.3	32.8	21.8
Communication and education	22.0	20.0	13.5	12.0	9.4	12.2	13.6	13.1	12.7	9.9	7.6	6.9	10.9
Special programmes	1.0	0.9	1.1	1.0	1.8	3.4	0.4	1.5	1.3	2.0	1.4	0.5	1.3
Multisectoral activities	6.7	2.6	11.4	4.7	6.4	7.7	10.6	9.2	10.0	10.3	12.0	10.4	9.5
Total	100.0	100.0	100.0	100.0	100.0	100.0	100.0	100.0	100.0	100.0	100.0	100.0	100.0
(Thousands of US dollars)	(2.374)	(2.893)	(5.366)	(8.253)	(9.029)	(8.769)	(10.229)	(17.732)	(18.908)	(19.217)	(17.153)	(25.962)	(145.885)

Source: UNFPA Fact Sheet No. 1.08 (September 1983); UNFPA Fact Sheet No. 1.09 (November 1983). Table given in *Population, the UNFPA Experience*, edited by Nafis Sadik and published for the United Nations Fund for Population Activities by New York University Press, 1984.

Note: Figures for 1969 to 1982 are project expenditures: figures for 1983 are project allocations as of 30 November 1983.

bodies which work with UNFPA support, Africa must inevitably remain a priority region. This is one area of the world where expressions such as 'onset of the demographic transition' or 'take-off into self-sustaining fertility decline' (to paraphrase Walt Rostow's famous dictum) do not yet apply.

Key role for World Bank

It is also clear that Africa will become increasingly important in the context of the World Bank's work in the field of population.

Two groups of high-level leaders from 40 African countries were brought together to discuss population policy issues and next steps with Bank staff in Berlin in the summer of 1985; 'sector' studies of the population situation in 26 countries of Sub-Saharan Africa were carried out by the Bank between 1981 and 1985; a major policy paper on population in Sub-Saharan Africa was published in 1986.

Most important of all is the Bank's intention to increase dramatically its lending (IBRD loans and IDA credits) for population, health and nutrition projects in Sub-Saharan Africa. As the bank notes,

> fertility reduction is PHN's dominant objective. But reducing child mortality may indirectly affect fertility by persuading parents that the children they want will survive. Family planning is itself a major means of reducing infant and maternal mortality, along with basic maternal and child health care, immunization, improved food supplies, better sanitation and control of key diseases .... This approach is most effective not only because of the behavioural links between health status and population change, but also because in many settings, particularly in Africa, targeting fertility objectives without giving consideration to other aspects of family health is politically insensitive, administratively impractical and, in the long run, ineffective[52].

The World Bank's PHN lending programme has grown steadily since its first loan was signed in 1970. At the beginning of 1986, there were approximately 30 current World Bank financed population and health projects in 28 countries in each of the six regions of the developing world (of these, 12 were classified as population projects, 15 as health projects while three projects worked towards both population and health objectives – though precise distinctions were, for the reasons noted, difficult to draw).

Figure 8.3 shows that the Bank's PHN lending programme was projected to expand substantially from current levels. The bulk of this growth was expected to occur in Sub-Saharan Africa, with total lending projected to grow by 181 per cent and 466 per cent. The resources involved, as can be seen, are substantial. Taken together with other resources available for population planning through the United Nations

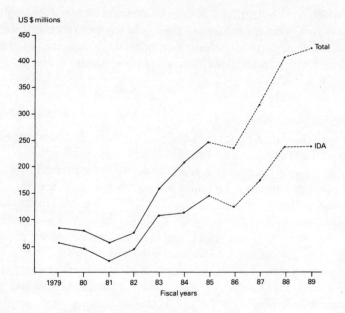

Figure 8.3. *Current and projected World Bank lending programmes for population, health and nutrition, FY78–FY90 total and IDA loan commitments in millions of $US[1].*

Source: *Current and Planned Activities in the Population Field: a brief review,* World Bank, 1986.

[1]Figure shows three-year moving average of total loan and credit amounts committed (FY79–FY85) and projected (FY85–FY90). Projections are based on future lending programme as estimated September 19, 1985 and are subject to change.

system and through bilateral donors, they could spell the difference between, on the one hand, a progressive continent-wide deterioration in basic economic and social systems, leading to a succession of acute human and environmental crises or, on the other hand, the slow recovery of hope. The chances of resources of this magnitude being available for population and family-planning programmes in Africa *without* external assistance are under present circumstances extremely thin. In spite of hopeful developments like the Kilimanjaro meeting, most of Africa has not reached the point on the 'continuum of population concern' where Asia stood well over a quarter of a century ago.

Review and appraisal of the World Population plan of action

Looked at in the round, what were the achievements of the decade of the 1970s?

With the approach of the tenth anniversary of the World Population Conference, the United Nations undertook a substantive Review and Appraisal of progress made in implementing the World Population Plan of Action (WPPA) adopted at Bucharest[53]. The Review and Appraisal noted that in the decade since Bucharest, world population had grown from 4 billion to 4.8 billion, or roughly by one-fifth. Of the increase, 90 per cent occurred in the less-developed regions of the world. During the ten-year period, it was estimated that the annual rate of growth of the world population had declined from 2.0 per cent to 1.7 per cent. Declines had occurred in the developed as well as in the developing countries. Among the latter group, the decline observed in China was of the most significance. Birth-rates had dropped to around 20 per thousand with the rate of natural increase around 1.3 per cent per annum. Since 1971, birth planning in China had been considered as an integral part of other social and economic planning. If China was excluded from the group of developing countries, the decline in the rate of growth of this group, although still noticeable, was far less significant (from 2.5 to 2.1 per cent per year). This was due to the fact that the fertility decline in developing countries, a decline of about 15 per cent in terms of the total fertility rate, was almost offset by a corresponding decline in mortality.

The deceleration did not occur evenly among the various regions. For the developing countries as a whole, the decline in the rate of growth was from 2.5 per cent in 1970–5 to 2 per cent in 1980–5; the corresponding decline for the developed countries was from 0.9 to 0.6 per cent. The declines were most marked in Asia, which reduced its rate of growth by 50 per cent (from 2.4 to 1.2 per cent) and least in Africa, where the rate probably rose (from 2.7 to 3.0 per cent).

There was evidence that an increasing number of countries had formulated policies concerned with population growth as such. As of mid-1983, about two-thirds of all countries indicated that they had formulated an explicit policy with respect to population growth. The most important change that was observed over the decade was a decline in the number of countries that viewed their rate of population growth as too low. It was estimated that one country in five held that position in 1974, whereas a survey among governments showed that it had declined to one in ten by 1983.

The latest population projections (Tables 8.19, 8.20, 8.21) indicated that the growth rate of the world population would decline much slower than during the past ten years or it might even turn to increase between 1984 and the end of this century. During this period, the growth rate was projected to reach 1.5 or 1.8 per cent (from the present 1.7 per cent) according to the medium and high variant of the United Nations

Table 8.19. *Projected (1983) population and percentage increase according to three variants:
world more-developed and less-developed regions, 1975–2100*

Year	Population (millions)			Period	Percentage increase		
	Medium variant	High variant	Low variant		Medium variant	High variant	Low variant
World							
1975	4,076	4,076	4,076	1975–2000	50.2	56.1	44.6
2000	6,123	6,363	5,895	2000–25	33.3	44.1	23.2
2025	8,162	9,171	7,263	2025–50	16.6	26.8	5.8
2050 *ᵃ*	9,513	11,629	7,687	2050–75	6.1	14.8	−0.3
2075 *ᵃ*	10,097	13,355	7,662	2075–2100	0.9	6.3	−1.8
2100 *ᵃ*	10,185	14,199	7,524				
More-developed regions							
1975	1,095	1,095	1,095	1975–2000	16.2	19.9	12.8
2000	1,272	1,313	1,235	2000–25	8.6	15.8	2.1
2025	1,382	1,521	1,261	2025–50	1.4	5.8	−5.3
2050 *ᵃ*	1,402	1,610	1,194	2050–75	1.2	5.6	−3.6
2075 *ᵃ*	1,419	1,701	1,151	2075–2100	0.1	1.9	−1.2
2100 *ᵃ*	1,421	1,733	1,137				
Less-developed regions							
1975	2,981	2,981	2,981	1975–2000	62.7	69.4	56.3
2000	4,851	5,050	4,660	2000–25	39.7	51.5	28.8
2025	6,779	7,649	6,002	2025–50	19.6	31.0	8.2
2050 *ᵃ*	8,111	10,018	6,493	2050–75	7.0	16.3	0.3
2075 *ᵃ*	8,677	11,654	6,511	2075–2100	1.0	7.0	−1.9
2100 *ᵃ*	8,764	12,466	6,387				

Source: Results of United Nations demographic estimates and projections as assessed in 1982.
Table printed in 'United Nations Concise Report on the World Population Situation in
1983': ST/ESA/SER.A/85, Department of International Economic and Social Affairs,
No. 85, United Nations, New York, 1984.

Note: ᵃ The long-range projections, 2050–2100, are taken from: United Nations Secretariat.
'Long-range global population projections, as assessed in 1980'. *Population Bulletin of
the United Nations.* No. 14–1982 (United Nations publication. Sales No. E.82.XIII.6).

projections, respectively. The major reasons why the growth rate was
expected to decrease more slowly or even turn to increase in the future
were:

(a) because of the already low level of fertility in East Asia and the effects of a
less favourable age composition, a further reduction of the growth rate in this
region would become more and more difficult in the near future;
(b) the very low fertility rates in the developed countries were expected to
remain near the current levels;
(c) a moderate rise of growth rate could continue in Africa for the rest of this
century owing to the persistently high level of fertility levels and the slow but
continuing improvement in life expectancy for the region.

Table 8.20. *Population and annual rate of increase: world and major areas, 1980–2025*

Area	Population (millions)								Annual rate of increase (percentage)							
	1980	1985	1990	1995	2000	2010	2020	2025	1975–80	1980–5	1985–90	1990–5	1995–2000	2000–5	2010–15	2020–5
World	4,453	4,842	5,248	5,677	6,123	6,987	7,793	8,162	1.77	1.68	1.61	1.57	1.51	1.38	1.15	0.93
Africa	476	553	645	753	877	1,170	1,488	1,642	2.99	3.00	3.08	3.09	3.05	2.96	2.56	1.96
Latin America	362	406	453	501	550	647	742	787	2.37	2.30	2.19	2.02	1.85	1.69	1.43	1.17
North America	252	263	275	287	298	319	339	348	1.07	0.90	0.88	0.83	0.75	0.68	0.66	0.49
East Asia	1,182	1,252	1,317	1,390	1,470	1,589	1,662	1,696	1.42	1.14	1.02	1.08	1.11	0.91	0.48	0.40
South Asia	1,408	1,572	1,740	1,909	2,074	2,379	2,654	2,771	2.30	2.20	2.03	1.85	1.65	1.44	1.17	0.86
Europe	484	492	499	505	510	515	518	518	0.40	0.32	0.28	0.24	0.22	0.13	0.05	0.02
Oceania	23	25	27	29	30	34	38	40	1.65	1.50	1.43	1.37	1.28	1.20	1.08	0.90
USSR	265	279	291	303	314	334	352	361	0.93	0.97	0.90	0.76	0.72	0.64	0.55	0.52

Source: Results of United Nations demographic estimates and projections as assessed in 1982. Table printed in 'United Nations Concise Report on the World Population Situation in 1983': ST/ESA/SER.A/85. Department of International Economic and Social Affairs, No. 85, United Nations, New York, 1984.

Table 8.21. Population of the 12 most populous countries, 1980, and annual rate of increase, 1980–2025

Country	Population (millions)								Annual rate of increase (percentage)							
	1980	1985	1990	1995	2000	2010	2020	2025	1975–80	1980–5	1985–90	1990–5	1995–2000	2000–5	2010–15	2020–5
China	1,003	1,063	1,120	1,184	1,256	1,362	1,429	1,460	1.44	1.17	1.04	1.12	1.17	0.95	0.51	0.43
India	689	761	832	899	962	1,113	1,154	1,189	2.15	1.99	1.78	1.55	1.34	1.09	0.87	0.58
USSR	265	279	292	303	314	334	352	361	0.93	0.97	0.90	0.76	0.72	0.64	0.55	0.52
United States of America	228	238	248	259	268	287	306	313	1.05	0.87	0.86	0.82	0.75	0.68	0.65	0.49
Indonesia	151	165	178	192	204	228	248	255	2.14	1.77	1.57	1.46	1.27	1.15	0.89	0.62
Brazil	121	136	150	165	179	207	234	246	2.31	2.23	2.07	1.87	1.67	1.51	1.26	1.00
Japan	117	120	123	125	127	130	129	128	0.91	0.57	0.43	0.40	0.40	0.29	-0.09	-0.15
Bangladesh	88	101	115	130	146	177	206	219	2.83	2.73	2.61	2.46	2.24	2.04	1.61	1.26
Pakistan	87	102	113	128	143	173	201	213	2.96	3.08	2.16	2.44	2.16	2.02	1.63	1.17
Nigeria	81	95	113	135	162	228	302	338	3.49	3.34	3.49	3.56	3.57	3.49	3.01	2.27
Mexico	69	79	89	99	109	128	146	154	2.86	2.59	2.39	2.16	1.92	1.70	1.36	1.08
Germany, Federal Republic of	62	61	61	60	59	57	54	53	-0.06	-0.18	-0.15	-0.17	-0.22	-0.39	-0.49	-0.50

Source: Results of United Nations demographic estimates and projections as assessed in 1982. Table printed in 'United Nations Concise Report on the World Population Situation in 1983': ST/ESA/SER.A/85. Department of International Economic and Social Affairs, No. 85, United Nations, New York, 1984.

These projections suggested that world population growth would continue to be sustained during the rest of this century unless further actions significantly altered the projected trends. For the world as a whole, the present annual increment of 78 million was projected to increase to 89 million by 1995–2000, which was more than the current population of Mexico. In the 16 years from 1984 to 2000, the world population was expected to increase by 1.3 billion, from 4.8 billion in 1984 to 6.1 billion in 2000, an increment greater than the combined present populations of Africa and Latin America. Of this increase, 56 per cent would occur in Asia, 25 per cent in Africa and 11 per cent in Latin America.

Uncertainty about the future course of demographic changes, which depended in part on the future paths of social and economic development and on the intensity of Governments' actions in the field of population, was reflected in the high and low variants of projections. It was noted that such a range of possible outcomes was by no means trivial. For example, the difference between the high and low variants for the world population in the year 2000 was 500 million (6.4 and 5.9 billion, respectively), which was approximately the current size of the population of Africa.

Since the present unprecedented rapid growth of world population was likely to continue for quite a while, it was only natural to ask what would eventually happen to the size and structure of the world population. In the United Nations, experimental calculations had been attempted, assuming that life expectancy at birth in all parts of the world would eventually reach the level currently considered as maximum (78.7 years for both sexes), and that fertility levels would eventually converge to, or fluctuate around, the replacement level (net reproduction rate of one).

According to these long-range projections (medium variant), the world population would reach 8.2 billion by 2025, exceed 9.5 billion by 2050, and ultimately stabilize at 10.2 billion near the end of the twenty-first century. The expected maximum size of the world population would be slightly more than twice the current one. By then, the proportion of the world population living in the currently developing countries would have risen from the present 74 per cent to 86 per cent. The average annual increment to the world total during the first quarter of the next century would be over 80 million. In the second and third quarters, there would be significant reductions in the annual increment, down to 53 and 23 million per year, respectively. The average annual increment was expected to become minimal only in the last quarter of the 21st century.

In the low variant, it was calculated that the total population of the world would peak at 7.7 billion in 2060, but in the high variant it would exceed 14 billion in the 22nd century (it would be even higher under the 'constant fertility' assumption). The difference between the high and low

Table 8.22. *Percentage distribution of UNFPA expenditures by work plan categories, 1969–83*

Work plan categories	Years												Total 1969–83
	1969–72	1973	1974	1975	1976	1977	1978	1979	1980	1981	1982	1983	
Family planning	51.7	41.0	39.8	49.3	50.0	50.4	51.1	44.5	41.3	31.8	39.8	40.5	43.0
Communication and education	7.5	11.5	10.8	10.5	9.7	10.7	10.5	10.7	11.7	12.3	10.8	14.2	11.3
Basic data collection	7.4	12.6	15.9	16.5	17.3	14.5	12.1	15.8	18.6	24.3	17.1	11.5	16.2
Population dynamics	8.4	7.8	7.4	6.8	9.0	9.1	8.8	9.6	11.3	10.7	12.4	13.0	10.2
Formulation and evaluation of population policies and programmes	4.9	4.7	6.0	5.6	3.4	3.7	4.2	4.4	5.6	6.0	6.4	6.0	5.2
Implementation of policies	0.0	0.0	0.0	0.0	0.0	0.1	0.1	2.9	0.7	1.1	0.8	1.2	0.8
Special programmes	1.4	2.8	2.5	2.0	1.3	1.3	1.7	2.0	1.5	1.9	1.2	1.4	1.7
Multisectoral activities	18.7	19.6	17.6	9.3	9.3	10.2	11.5	10.1	9.3	11.9	11.5	12.2	11.6
Total	100.0	100.0	100.0	100.0	100.0	100.0	100.0	100.0	100.0	100.0	100.0	100.0	100.0
(Thousands of US dollars)	(26,501)	(30,067)	(54,103)	(66,673)	(69,368)	(66,551)	(89,230)	(123,624)	(136,357)	(122,543)	(106,244)	(127,165)	(1,018,426)

Source: UNFPA Fact Sheet No. 1.06 (September 1983); UNFPA Fact Sheet No. 1.07 (November 1983). Table given in *Population, the UNFPA Experience*, edited by Nafis Sadik and published for the United Nations Fund for Population Activities by New York University Press, 1984.

Note: Figures for 1969 to 1982 are project expenditures; figures for 1983 are project allocations as of 30 November 1983.

variant estimates, which was more than 6 billion, was mainly caused by the differing fertility assumptions. The year in which the replacement level is reached in all the regions of the world (Africa happens to be the last region to do so) is assumed to be 2065 in the high variant, 2010 in the low variant, and 2035 in the medium variant.

Not withstanding the progress made over the last decade or so, these projections illustrated dramatically the magnitude of the tasks which still lay ahead.

9

Evolving perceptions

Perspectives

How do people look at the 'population problem'? Have perceptions changed over the last 20 years? Has there, for example, been an evolution in the perception of United Nations bodies both of the population question and of their own potential contribution? The delivery of programmes of assistance in the field, of whatever nature, depends ultimately not merely on the willingness of countries to receive aid but also on the readiness of the external organizations to provide it. Both are influenced, directly or indirectly, by the prevailing climate of intellectual and political opinion. At any moment, one or more of several themes may appear to dominate the population debate. Sometimes Malthusianism, having flown out by the window, seems to be creeping back through the door and books with titles like *Standing Room Only* or *Our Crowded Planet* reappear on the shelves. At other times, the economic arguments predominate. It is not population growth *per se* which matters, we are told, it is the *rate* at which populations are growing in any particular country and the ability of the national economy to absorb the annual increase[1]. This latter viewpoint certainly predominated in the 1960s and early 1970s when weighty volumes like the National Academy of Sciences' massive study: *The Consequences of Rapid Population Growth* were to be found on the desks of officials in the World Bank, UNDP, USAID and the Ford Foundation[2].

In the 1970s other themes began to emerge. The impact of population on the environment, and the contribution of population pressures to ecological degradation, began to be examined more closely and this in turn necessitated some rethinking. If there were after all 'limits to growth'[3] in the long-term, and real environmental problems in the shorter terms (like desertification) associated with population pressures, perhaps the classic economic theories needed to be looked at again. Perhaps population *per se* was indeed a problem, seen in terms of its impact on non-renewable

9   Evolving perceptions

Table 9.1. *Proportion of the population living in urban areas: world, more-developed and less-developed regions, and major areas, 1950–2000.*

Area	1950	1960	1970	1975	1980	1985	1990	1995	2000
World	29.4	33.6	37.0	38.3	39.9	41.6	43.6	45.8	48.2
More-developed regions	53.6	60.3	66.4	68.7	70.6	73.4	74.2	76.0	77.7
Less-developed regions	17.4	21.4	25.3	27.1	29.4	31.8	34.4	37.3	40.4
Africa	14.8	18.4	22.9	25.6	28.7	32.1	35.5	38.9	42.2
Latin America	41.1	49.3	57.4	61.5	65.4	69.0	72.1	74.7	76.9
Northern America	63.9	69.9	73.8	73.9	73.8	74.3	75.2	76.4	78.0
East Asia	17.8	23.1	26.3	27.0	28.0	28.9	30.2	32.0	34.2
South Asia	16.1	18.3	21.2	23.2	25.4	27.7	30.4	33.5	36.8
Europe	55.9	60.5	66.2	68.6	71.1	73.7	75.4	77.2	78.9
Oceania	61.2	66.3	70.8	71.7	71.6	71.7	71.9	72.3	73.1
USSR	39.3	48.8	56.7	60.0	63.2	66.3	69.2	71.9	74.3

Source: Results of United Nations demographic estimates and projections as assessed in 1982. Table printed in *Population, the UNFPA Experience,* edited by Nafis Sadik and published for the United Nations Fund for Population Activities by New York University Press, 1984.

ecological resources. In which case, of course, it could no longer be presented as a problem purely of the developing world since it was clear that the rich industrialized world – in particular, the United States, Western Europe and Japan – consumed far more resources on a per capita basis than did most of the inhabitants of Asia, Africa and Latin America. Thus even though the industrial world might have much lower rates of population growth, and in some cases be well on the way to attaining replacement levels of fertility, the impact of the average American man (or even the average American dog for that matter) on limited world resources might far outweigh that of, say, 100 villagers in Bihar or Rajasthan.

The process of urbanization has forced another rethink of the classic approaches to population. Urban problems are not purely economic problems, capable of being 'solved' through the application of economic measures. In the developing world, many urban problems are linked to the phenomenon of urbanization, itself a function both of population growth and internal migration (the latter itself often a result of rural population pressures). (See Table 9.1.)

The new emphasis on women's rights and female emancipation has also led to an evolution in thinking about population. Though historically the issue of human rights – and the impact of high fertility on the well-being of individuals and families – has long been to the fore in the population argument, the last decade or so has given a much sharper focus to this issue. A woman's right to bear a child, one of the most fundamental human rights of all, has increasingly become linked to a woman's right *not*

233

to bear a child. She is, in other words, to be master (or rather mistress) of her own body. Population policy, in so far as it encompasses information about and programmes for contraception and family planning, is clearly of the greatest relevance here, even though abortion – an area where different human rights appear to come into conflict with each other like ignorant armies clashing by night – is likely to remain a matter of considerable controversy.

And if family planning is an integral part of female emancipation, a solid blow struck against the Dark Ages which still prevail in large parts of the world, for example, the Middle East and much of Africa, so female emancipation (as expressed, for example, in the goals and objectives of the United Nations Women's Decade) is a necessary concomitant of successful family-planning programmes. The link between fertility and social patterns extends in both directions. Nothing could be more fundamental. As T. S. Eliot put it, 'birth, copulation and death are all the facts, when you come down to brass tacks'.

Population and human rights; population and development; population, resources and the environment; population and urbanization; population and women – all these are themes which have played their part in the process of building the consensus for action.

Ultimately questions of population growth can be linked to the maintenance of world peace itself. The validity of such a linkage was, at the time this book was being written, being increasingly explored in academic and official circles. It was, for example, as we shall see, specifically mentioned by UN Secretary-General Perez de Cuellar in his own speech to the International Conference on Population in 1984.

Without in any way seeking to be exhaustive, this Chapter outlines some of the different threads in the population debate as it developed in the years which followed the Bucharest Conference of August 1974. Though the vast bulk of activity at national and international level has been rightly concerned with activities in the field, there is nevertheless an intellectual counterpoint which inevitably influences to a greater or lesser extent the practical agenda.

Post-Bucharest

In its own way, Bucharest 1974 was a major landmark on the path towards the acceptance by the nations of the world that the population problem was of real and vital concern and that it was a legitimate subject for concerted action at all appropriate levels ranging from the humblest village hut with barefoot doctor at the door to the loftiest podium of the

United Nations. Though, as noted, the debate at Bucharest was long and at times anguished, what finally precipitated the general consensus was the sense that something had to be done and a way found of reconciling the views of opposing camps.

In the quinquennium which followed Bucharest, more and more countries began to realize that no development effort could afford to ignore the question of population. Its interrelationship with policies on education, food and agriculture, industrialization, urbanization, employment, health facilities, the improvement of the status of women and other disadvantaged sectors and with numerous other areas of development was increasingly acknowledged as a pivotal consideration for all societies irrespective of their differences in political creed or economic standing. By 1978, 18 countries in Asia, 18 in Africa, 16 in Latin America and 2 in the Middle East – comprising 82 per cent of the population in the developing world – indicated in response to an enquiry by the United Nations that they considered their fertility levels 'too high'. Not all these countries, of course, had developed effective population policies and programmes. Deeds had not always followed words. But already, five years or so after Bucharest, it could be said that a deeper and more lasting consensus than had been possible to attain at that time was rapidly being built. That new consensus was based on the premise, increasingly validated by real experiences in real countries, that population policy was not a substitute for social and economic development, nor was development an alternative to population policy but that both were inextricably linked sides of a single coin and, taken together, the vital ingredients of change.

The Colombo Conference of parliamentarians

Nor was this new consensus confined to official circles, or restricted to the rarefied domain of planners or economists. One meeting which the author attended when he was a newly elected member of the European Parliament took place in Colombo, Sri Lanka, in August 1979 was of special interest. Co-sponsored by UNFPA and the Inter-Parliamentary Union, it brought together parliamentarians from 58 countries to proclaim their commitment to the goal of linking Population and Development.

> Today most countries have recognised that population and development are inextricably bound together and that no population programme should be considered in isolation from policies and plans on health, housing, education, employment, the environment and the use of resources. Equally, there is increasing recognition that development programmes should reflect population policies.

The Colombo Declaration referred to the first United Nations review and appraisal of the effectiveness of the World Population Plan of Action (WPPA), which had just been carried out and stressed that such progress as had been achieved did not go far enough:

In the 25 years up to 1975 the total world population increased from just under 2,500 million to over 4,000 million; by the year 2000 it is expected to reach 6,200 million, of which four-fifths will be in the developing countries, with a substantial majority living in desperate poverty.

The implications of such increases are staggering. In the developing countries, between now and the end of the century, 800 million additional jobs will need to be created. This is more than the entire actively employed population of the developed world at the present time. Problems of similar magnitude will be posed as far as the provision of food, water and shelter is concerned.

Though its primary focus was on the link between population and development, the Conference did not ignore other themes.

In the developed countries, per capita consumption of resources – so much higher than in the developing world – has been a cause of much pollution, waste and environmental degradation. It has also contributed to world-wide shortages in key resources. Other questions such as the ageing of the population and internal and international migration are becoming important.

At the global level, continuously expanding human demands have created intolerable pressures on resources, particularly energy. The pressures on biological resources – fisheries, forests, grasslands and croplands – are mounting steadily and will continue to do so. Human needs have already begun to outstrip the productive capacity of many local biological systems as currently managed.

The Conference then addressed itself explicitly to the link between population and development. 'Peace itself, which is the precondition of development, will be put in jeopardy. For one of the principal threats to peace is the social unrest caused by the accumulation of human fear and hopelessness.'

The fact that parliamentarians from almost 60 countries responded to the invitation to come to Colombo to discuss population and development is an example of what we have called earlier the growing 'outreach' of United Nations' influence in this field and of the awareness, particularly on the part of UNFPA's management, that no efforts should be spared in the process of building wide political support. Bureaucrats administer funds, but politicians vote them. This obvious fact, sometimes seemingly forgotten or ignored by those who run UN programmes, was very much in the forefront of Salas' mind as he sought to nurse UNFPA from infancy to maturity with scant regard for the normal biological rhythms that apply to most new institutions.

To give one small but concrete example, the author recalls that the British delegation at the Colombo Conference of Parliamentarians included Mr Edward Heath, a former British Prime Minister; Mr Kenneth Baker who would, in Mrs Thatcher's second term of office serve successively as Minister for Information Technology, Secretary of State for the Environment and Secretary of State for Education; and Mr Alastair Goodlad, who after a spell in the Government's Whip's office would become Minister for Energy. The delegations of other countries were similarly endowed with political talent.

1979, the year of the Colombo Conference, was also the tenth anniversary of UNFPA. In the previous decade the Fund grew from a $2.5 million Trust Fund of the Secretary-General into a major funding body with cumulative resources of almost $600 million in 1979. During the period, 125 countries and territories requested and received assistance from UNFPA and 94 governments made one or more voluntary contributions to the Fund. As requested by ECOSOC, the Fund had played 'a leading role in the United Nations system in promoting population programmes'; it was also playing a co-ordinating role outside the United Nations system by working closely with donor and recipient governments and non-governmental organizations in extending population assistance. More than a quarter of the total global population aid to developing countries was now channelled through the UNFPA.

Population and the urban future

Another important step in the evolution of perceptions about the nature of the population problem was marked by the International Conference held in Rome in September 1980 on Population and the Urban Future[4]. Imaginatively, the Conference, organized by UNFPA with the co-operation of the Italian Government and the City of Rome, brought together mayors, administrators and planners from 41 cities whose populations were projected to be five million or more by the year 2000, as well as national planners from the 31 countries in which these cities were located. The author who was present in an 'expert' capacity recalls that the Conference was not only opened by the Mayor of Rome amid the splendours of the ancient Capitoline Palace; it was also addressed – if in somewhat guarded tones – by His Holiness Pope John Paul II.

The Rome Declaration on Population and the Urban Future began by noting that in 1950 there were only six cities with populations of 5 million or more, and their combined population was only 44 million. By 1980, this had risen to 26 such cities with a combined population of 252 million.

By the year 2000, the indications were that this number would rise to approximately 60 cities, with an estimated population of nearly 650 million. Whereas in 1950 there was only one city, Shanghai, with a population of 5 million or more in the less-developed countries, by the year 2000 there would be 45 such cities in the Third World, and most of these would be in Asia (Table 9.2).

The Declaration recognized that, historically, the city has been 'the engine of development and the forge of human creative energies. In fact the city has often been the place in which civilization has blossomed'. The process of urbanization could be harnessed to achieve mankind's goal of just, peaceful and lasting progress. But if this were to happen, urbanization must take place under 'planned and orderly conditions'.

The eminent delegates to the Rome Conference took a look at the world around them and concluded that:

> planned and orderly conditions for urbanization for the most part do not exist. We find that the problems confronting urban settlements are in fact already acute in many parts of the world. They include shortages in virtually every service, amenity and support required for tolerable urban living. Housing and shelter, basic health services, sanitation, clean air and potable water, education, transport, energy supplies, open spaces and recreational facilities – all these are lacking in many parts of the world. Moreover, under conditions of unplanned urbanization, the situation is becoming worse rather than better.

Economic problems – such as unemployment and underemployment – loomed large. It was estimated that, during the next two decades, over 600 million people would be added to the labour force in the less-developed countries alone, and many of these would be flocking to the cities in search of jobs. Social problems – crime, delinquency, social segregation and the exploitation of certain groups, e.g. migrants and urban squatters – were becoming increasingly acute, as were environmental problems such as congestion and pollution.

> Unplanned urbanization may generate tension between groups and classes within the city itself; it may also generate tension between urban and rural areas within national boundaries.

The Conference recalled the language of the Colombo Declaration on Population and Development when it concluded that 'peace itself, which is the precondition for development, may be put in jeopardy'. It re-affirmed that:

> one of the principal threats to peace is the social unrest caused by the accumulation of human fear and hopelessness. Fear and hopelessness can accumulate both quickly and enduringly in the hearts of the urban poor when their aspirations are not realized.

Table 9.2. *Twenty largest agglomerations in the world, ranked by size, 1950–2000 (population in millions)*

Rank	1950	Population	1970	Population	1980	Population	1990	Population	2000	Population
1	New York/north-eastern New Jersey	12.4	New York/north-eastern New Jersey	16.3	Tokyo/Yokohama	17.0	**Mexico City**	21.3	**Mexico City**	26.3
2	**London**	10.4	Tokyo/Yokohama	14.9	New York/north-eastern New Jersey	15.6	São Paulo	18.8	São Paulo	24.0
3	Shanghai	10.3	Shanghai	11.4	**Mexico City**	15.0	Tokyo/Yokohama	17.2	Tokyo/Yokohama	17.1
4	Rhein-Ruhr	6.9	**London**	10.6	São Paulo	12.8	New York/north-eastern New Jersey	15.3	Calcutta	16.6
5	Tokyo/Yokohama	6.7	Rhein-Ruhr	9.3	Shanghai	11.8	Calcutta	12.6	Bombay	16.0
6	Beijing	6.7	**Mexico City**	9.2	Greater Buenos Aires	10.1	Shanghai	12.0	New York/north-eastern New Jersey	15.5
7	Paris	5.5	Greater Buenos Aires	8.5	**London**	10.0	Bombay	11.9	Seoul	13.5
8	Tianjin	5.4	Los Angeles/Long Beach	8.3	Calcutta	9.5	Greater Buenos Aires	11.7	Shanghai	13.5
9	Greater Buenos Aires	5.3	Paris	8.3	Los Angeles/Long Beach	9.5	Seoul	11.5	Rio de Janeiro	13.3
10	Chicago/north-western Indiana	5.0	Beijing	8.2	Rhein-Ruhr	9.3	Rio de Janeiro	11.4	Delhi	13.3
11	Moscow	4.8	São Paulo	7.6	Rio de Janeiro	9.2	Los Angeles/Long Beach	10.5	Greater Buenos Aires	13.2
12	Calcutta	4.4	Osaka/Kobe	7.2	Beijing	9.1	Cairo/Giza/Imbaba	10.0	Cairo/Giza/Imbaba	13.2
13	Los Angeles/Long Beach	4.1	Rio de Janeiro	7.1	Paris	8.8	**London**	9.5	**Jakarta**	12.8
14	**Osaka/Kobe**	3.8	Moscow	7.1	Bombay	8.5	Beijing	9.5	Baghdad	12.8
15	Milan	3.6	Calcutta	6.9	Seoul	8.5	**Jakarta**	9.3	Teheran	12.7
16	Rio de Janeiro	3.5	Tianjin	6.8	Moscow	8.2	Moscow	9.2	Karachi	12.2
17	**Mexico City**	3.1	Chicago/north-western Indiana	6.7	Osaka/Kobe	8.0	Delhi	9.2	Istanbul	11.9
18	Philadelphia/New Jersey	3.0	Bombay	5.9	Tianjin	7.7	Rhein-Ruhr	9.1	Los Angeles/Long Beach	11.3
19	Bombay	2.9	Milan	5.6	Cairo/Giza/Imbaba	7.3	Teheran	9.0	Dhaka	11.2
20	Detroit	2.8	Seoul	5.4	Chicago/north-western Indiana	6.8	Paris	9.0	Manila	11.1

Source: Results of United Nations demographic estimates and projections as assessed in 1982. Table printed in *Population, the UNFPA Experience*, edited by Nafis Sadik and published for the United Nations Fund for Population Activities by New York University Press, 1984.

The pace and pattern of urbanization, and the nature of the economic and social development that took place, was crucially influenced by demographic trends. In the less-developed countries, migration from rural areas formerly contributed the major part of urban growth. By the time of the Rome Conference, natural increase – the excess of births over deaths – generally contributed 60 per cent of urban growth.

The Conference believed that

> the process of urbanization can only be managed where the demographic factors contributing to this process are themselves managed through economic, social, political and cultural measures. We must seek to match population with resources in cities, in regions, in countries and – ultimately – in the world itself.

The Conference called on countries to develop a strategy for national planning for the urban future. Such strategies, supported by appropriate legislation and funding, should include the formulation of comprehensive national population policies, policies for balanced development between urban and rural areas and between small, intermediate and large cities; and policies for the improvement of urban areas.

The Brandt report

The Rome Declaration on Population and the Urban Future stands as a precursor to the equally powerful conclusions of the Brandt report published in early 1980 under the title 'North–south: A Programme for survival'[5]. The Commission's 18 regular members included several former prime ministers, and ten persons from the developing countries, though none from the Communist world. The report noted that

> the present staggering growth of world population will continue for some considerable time. It will be one of the strongest forces shaping the future of human society.... Depending on whether the decline in fertility accelerates or slows down, world population could, as projections show, stabilize – or possibly turn down – at levels anywhere between 8 and 15 billion in the course of the next century. Even on the assumption of continued fertility decline, the populations of most countries in the developing world are likely to reach at least twice their present size. Nigeria and Bangladesh are projected to have as many people as the United States and the USSR today, and India will have at least 1.2 billion inhabitants. The cities of the Third World are growing even faster than the total populations, and the biggest of them are likely to exceed 30 million by the end of this century.

The Brandt Commission observed, in a passage which is as striking as any in the report, that:

It is easy to feel a sense of helplessness at these prospects. The growth of population at rates between 2 and 3 per cent per annum will produce a doubling of population in 25 to 35 years. This compounds the task of providing food, jobs, shelter, education and health services, of mitigating absolute poverty and of meeting the colossal financial and administrative needs of rapid urbanization.

Like the Parliamentarians who met in Colombo in 1979, the Brandt Commission saw the vital link between population, development, environment and peace. Would the ecological system itself suffice to meet the needs of a greatly increased world population at the economic standard that was hoped for? Could sustainable development take place where biological systems were taxed beyond the limit?

> Population growth in some parts of the Third World is already a source of alarming ecological changes, and its industrialization is bound to lead to greater pressure on resources and environment.

In effect, the Brandt Commission expanded the population–development relationship to incorporate explicitly the dimension of environmental management. The Brandt Commission did not argue that population growth is the only, or even (necessarily) the major, factor in environmental overload. But it is seen as an important contributing factor, leading – via ecological degradation – to important constraints on growth. Thus the impact of population on development can be seen in the classic terms of demand (numbers to be fed, housed, clothed and watered) and also in terms of its impact on supply in terms of resource availabilities – forests and fisheries, croplands and water catchment areas, etc. These environmental and resource constraints will sometimes have a local or regional impact, to be felt primarily in those developing countries where the resource pressures are most acute. But sometimes, as in the case for example of climatic change induced through deforestation, the consequences may be wider and even global, adding new north–south tensions to those that already exist.

Looking ahead, the Brandt Commission found it

> difficult to avoid the conclusion that a world of 15 billion people would be marked by a host of potentially devastating economic, social and political conflicts. Whether the nightmarish vision of a hopelessly overcrowded planet in the next century can be averted depends gravely on what is done now to hasten the stabilization of population.

Global 2000

The decade of the 1980s, which had begun with the publication of the Brandt Report, saw other landmarks in the process of building an integrated view of the interrelationships between population, development and environment. The Global 2000 Report to the President, which was prepared by the Council on Environmental Quality and the United States Department of State, and published in 1980[6], came to the conclusion that

> already the populations in Sub-Saharan Africa and in the Himalayan hills of Asia have exceeded the carrying capacity of the immediate area, triggering an erosion of the land's capacity to support life ... yet there is reason for hope. It must be emphasized that the Global 2000 Study's projections are based on the assumption that national policies regarding population stabilization, resource conservation and environmental protection will remain essentially unchanged through the end of the century. But, in fact, policies are beginning to change. In some areas, forests are being replanted after cutting. Some nations are taking steps to reduce soil losses and desertification. Interest in energy conservation is growing and large sums are being invested in exploring alternatives to petroleum dependence. *The need for family planning is slowly becoming better understood.* [author's italics] Water supplies are being improved and waste treatment systems built. High-yield seeds are widely available and seed banks are being expanded. Some wild-lands with their genetic resources are being protected. Natural predators and selective pesticides are being substituted for persistent and destructive pesticides.

The Report concluded that, though these developments were encouraging, they were far from adequate to meet the global challenges projected in the Study.

> Vigorous, determined new initiatives are needed if worsening poverty and human suffering, environmental degradation and international tension and conflicts are to be prevented. There are no quick fixes. The only solutions to the problems of population, resources and environment are complex and long-term. These problems are inextricably linked to some of the most perplexing and persistent problems in the world – poverty, injustice and social conflict.

The World Conservation Strategy

Another landmark study, the World Conservation Strategy (WCS) launched in June 1981, was prepared by the International Union for the Conservation of Nature and Natural Resources (IUCN) with the advice, co-operation and financial assistance of the United Nations Environment Programme (UNEP) and the World Wildlife Fund (WWF) with the collaboration of FAO and UNESCO[7]. The Strategy had three main objectives:

to maintain essential ecological processes and life-support systems;
to preserve genetic diversity;
to ensure the sustainable utilization of species and ecosystems.

These objectives, according to WCS, had to be achieved as a matter of urgency because the planet's capacity to support people was being irreversibly reduced in both developing and developed countries. Thousands of millions of tonnes of soil were lost each year as a result of deforestation and poor land management; at least 3000 km² of prime farmland disappeared annually under buildings and roads in developed countries alone. Hundreds of millions of rural people in developing countries, including 500 million malnourished and 800 million destitute, were compelled to destroy the resources necessary to free them from starvation and poverty. The rural poor were stripping the land of trees and shrubs for fuel in widening swathes around their villages, so that many communities did not have enough food to cook or to keep warm. The rural poor were also obliged to burn every year 400 million tonnes of dung and crop residues badly needed to regenerate soils.

The energy, financial and other costs of providing goods and services were growing. Throughout the world, but especially in developing countries, siltation was cutting the life-time of reservoirs supplying water and hydro-electricity, often by as much as half. Floods were devastating settlements and crops (in India the annual cost of floods ranges from $140 to $150 million). At the same time, the resource base of major industries was shrinking. Tropical forests were contracting so rapidly that by the end of the century the remaining area of unlogged productive forest would have been halved. The coastal support system of many fisheries were being destroyed or polluted (in the USA the annual cost of the resulting losses was estimated at $86 million).

WCS addressed itself explicitly to the links between population, development and conservation, arguing that much habitat destruction and over-exploitation of living resources by individuals, communities and nations in the developing world was a response to relative poverty, caused or exacerbated by a combination of population growth and inequities within and among nations.

Peasant communities, for example, may be forced to cultivate steep, unstable slopes because their growing numbers exceed the capacity of the land and because the fertile, easily managed valley bottoms have been taken over by large landowners. Similarly, many developing countries have so few natural resources and operate under such unfavourable conditions of international trade that they often have very little choice but to exploit forests, fisheries and other living resources unsustainably. In many parts of the world population pressures are making demands on resources beyond the capacity of those resources to sustain.

The WCS concluded that:

> every country should have a conscious population policy to avoid as far as possible the spread of such situations, and eventually to achieve a balance between numbers and the environment.

At the same time it was essential that the affluent constrain their demands on resources, and preferably reduce them, shifting some of their wealth to assisting the deprived. 'To a significant extent the survival and future of the poor depends on conservation and sharing by the rich.'

Population and peace

Over the last 15 years, there has been a growing realization that the population issue is not only central to development and environment but also that it is linked, both directly and indirectly, to the maintenance of peace itself.

On the occasion of the International Conference on Population, which took place in Mexico City in August 1984 (see following chapter), 92 Heads of State or Heads of Government presented brief statements of their views on population[8]. A review of these statements indicates a growing concern with the relationship between demographic factors and situations which can or do give rise to tensions, instabilities and conflicts whether within nations or between nations. To cite just one example: Turgut Ozal, Prime Minister of Turkey, wrote:

> Population issues cannot be confined within national boundaries. They are closely related to the attainment of our ideals for peace, security and stability in the world.

The relationship can be presented positively or negatively. Where it is evident, for example, that population planning contributes to economic and social development and where – as presumably it should – economic and social development contributes to national and individual well-being, and therefore to stability (both internal and external), we have a virtuous cycle – a case of positive feedback. On the other hand, it can be argued that an absence of population planning and other appropriate demographic policies can make orderly development more difficult to achieve. Where the prospects for improvement are low or non-existent, fear and hopelessness accumulate (to use the language of the Rome and Colombo Declarations) and, under such conditions, tensions and instabilities may be caused which themselves may impact negatively on the development process, either by causing a diversion of scarce resources towards military or security expenditures or through other forms of disruption. Here we have a vicious cycle – a case of negative feedback.

Among its Recommendations for the Further Implementation of the World Population Plan of Action, the International Conference on Population included a section on Peace, Security and Population. It stressed that it was

> of great importance for the world community to work ceaselessly to promote, among nations, peace, security, disarmament and co-operation, which are indispensable for the achievement of the goals of humane population policies and for economic and social development[9].

Without peace there could be no orderly development, and therefore no orderly approach to population planning now recognized to be an integral part of development.

But the reverse might apply as well. As Mr Salas, Executive Director of UNFPA and Secretary-General of the 1984 Conference, pointed out in his speech on the opening day:

> Population policies and programmes by looking towards a moderation of population growth and a rational spatial distribution of population thus represent humane efforts to reduce imbalances and disparities that lead to crises.

In saying this, Mr Salas reiterated, in explicit terms, a theme which had been developed over the years in different fora, such as the Colombo meeting of Parliamentarians on Population and Development, the Rome Conference on Population Growth and the Urban Future and the UNA–USA Panel Report, previously quoted, on World Population[10].

This latter report stated with considerable cogency:

> In the widest sense the population issue is the world's concern. It is as important as peace itself because it may indeed be the precondition of peace. We live in an age when the internal stability of countries is constantly threatened by the massive disaffection or disappointment of those whose expectations have not been met; it is an age when the growing polarization between rich and poor nations makes the conduct of orderly external relations increasingly difficult. If it is true that internal stability and external order are influenced, however indirectly, by the rate of population growth, then the commitment of the international community to the cause of peace should be matched by a parallel commitment to population planning.

As we look towards the future, it is becoming increasingly apparent that – in addition to the destabilizing effects caused by the 'accumulation of human fear and hopelessness' as development objectives are vitiated by demographic pressures – environmental degradation and the wastage of renewable natural resources caused, in part at least, by population pressures, are playing important and growing roles in causing wars, regional and national insecurity, internal strife and bloodshed.

For example, in its final report in 1981, the UN Group of Governmental Experts on the Relationship between Disarmament and Development stated:

> There can no longer be the slightest doubt that resource scarcities and ecological stresses constitute real and imminent threats to the future well-being of all people and nations. These challenges are fundamentally non-military and it is imperative that they be addressed accordingly. If this is not recognised, if the international community fails to accept and persevere in the view that these challenges can only be addressed through voluntary and cooperative measures, there is a grave risk that the situation will deteriorate to the point of crisis where, even with low probability of success, the use of force could be seen as a way to produce results quickly enough. This is far from being a remote possibility. In recent years there has been a marked tendency in international relations to use or to threaten to use military force in response to non-military challenges to security.

And the UN Environment Programme's 'State of the Environment, 1984' report noted that 'the processes of environmental despoliation constitute a threat to the future of humankind' no less insidious than nuclear war. But 'at present this threat lies hidden – obscured by a pre-occupation with an economic, social and political analysis that pays little or no heed to the environmental destabiliser'.

According to an Earthscan document published in November 1984[11], it is possible to distinguish at least three types of environmental factors, often linked to demographic pressures and associated with recent and current strife:

> The accelerating trends in forest and soil degradation, combined with growing populations and a stagnant world economy, are rapidly marginalizing hundreds of millions of Third World people – especially in ecological zones already troubled by deep social and political unrest: the Andes, the Himalayas, the Sahel region of Africa.
>
> As water needs increase (for irrigation, electricity and simply to supply growing populations), the year-round yield of many shared rivers decreases, because deforestation and soil erosion have reduced the 'sponge effect' of the land to rapidly absorb and slowly release water. Rivers now tend to flood after the rains and run low in the dry season, making it impossible for governments to realise their needs from these rivers.
>
> Many shared marine fisheries are declining in yield due to overfishing, at the same time as demand and exploitation are increasing.

In states where governments give little priority to ordering their rural sectors, but where large proportions of the people (in many cases the vast majority) live on the land, the result is often profound disorder. People seeking livelihoods leave the land in uncontrolled waves to:

> move across national boundaries as refugees or migrant workers, creating tension between states;
>
> move into regions of better agricultural land, creating conflicts with people already settled there;
>
> convert forests to fields, disrupting the societies of and often fighting with forest peoples;
>
> move into swollen cities, which can offer few opportunities and which are often already stretched far beyond what their infrastructures can support. Large numbers of new arrivals can have a deep effect on urban political stability of cities.

The Earthscan survey restricts itself to cases where significant bloodshed has been caused – riots, guerrilla movements, revolutions and wars – or where significant interstate conflict has occurred short of war (the Soviet–Japan fisheries dispute and the tension between Brazil and Argentina over shared rivers). It does not argue that all the security problems it examines have led, or are likely to lead, to wars between states. The violence between indigenous peoples and settlers in forest lands, though it results in thousands of deaths a year, is almost always a purely internal affair.

The survey does, however, examine cases in which a government's neglect of its resources base has led to 'internal' strife which has resulted in the fall of that government. Often the new government is of a radically different political persuasion than the previous regime – and this can affect governments of almost any political colour. Regional security may be seen to be threatened, and the attention of larger powers drawn to the scene of instability. Examples include Nicaragua, Ethiopia, Iran, Afghanistan and Poland.

The possibility of escalation cannot be ruled out in any of these conflicts. Thus, what may begin, in Harold Macmillan's immortal words, as a 'little local difficulty', fundamentally caused by the imbalance between population and resources in one particular country or region, may grow and spread like a forest fire until the flames of that fire may one day truly engulf the world[12].

Looking at matters from this perspective we could argue that Professor Richard Gardner even understated the case when he wrote in the essay already quoted that 'a really effective response by the UN to the challenge of population growth... might prove to be the Organization's most vital contribution to human welfare second only to keeping the peace[13]'. The United Nations population activities could in fact be seen as an essential part of its *primary* mandate: the maintenance of peace itself.

10

The International Conference

on Population, 1984

Background

In 1981, in a report addressed to the Economic and Social Council, the
Population Commission recommended 'the convening of a new population
conference'. In the light of that report and of other considerations, the
Council adopted Resolution 1981/87 of 20 November 1981 by which it
decided, *inter alia*

> to convene in 1984, under the auspices of the United Nations, an International
> Conference on Population open to all States as full members and to the
> specialised agencies, bearing in mind that it should be conducted with the
> utmost economy in size, duration and other cost factors and the need to utilise
> extrabudgetary resources for its financing to the maximum extent possible.

The Council further decided the Conference should 'be devoted to the
discussion of selected issues of the highest priority', and made certain
recommendations concerning preparations for the Conference. By the
same resolution the Council designated the Population Commission as the
Preparatory Committee for the Conference and requested the Secretary-
General to appoint the Executive Director of the United Nations Fund for
Population Activities to serve as Secretary-General of the Conference and
the Director of the Population Division of the Department of International
Economic and Social Affairs as Deputy Secretary-General.

The decision to appoint the Executive-Director of UNFPA as the
Secretary-General of the International Conference on Population was a
recognition that the Fund, *de jure* as well as *de facto*, was now central to the
United Nations' population activities. Whereas in 1974, as we have seen,
the Fund's task was mainly concerned with organizing the activities of
World Population Year, with the Population Division of the United Nations

being responsible for the management of the Conference, ten years later it was another story.

It is interesting to note that in the discussions in the Population Commission on the question of holding a conference, the strongest support for the idea came from the members of developing countries, anxious to maintain the momentum of the last decade at a time when other issues – energy, inflation, unemployment, the arms race – were competing for international attention. And when the Population Commission's draft resolution was considered by the Economic and Social Council during its three succeeding sessions over the course of 1981, it was again developing countries who were mainly in favour, while the developed countries showed far less enthusiasm. One exception to this pattern was the delegate of Brazil, whose sceptical queries challenged the need for the conference.

The reticence of developed countries was, no doubt, partly inspired by their reluctance to see the north-south confrontation brought back into the population issue and by their concern for the budgetary implications of the decision. In the event, as far as the latter was concerned, the budget for the Conference was set at the comparatively very modest level of $2.3 million ($1.5 million from extra-budgetary sources and $0.8 million from the regular budget of the United Nations). By early 1984, Mr Salas – as Secretary-General of the Conference — was able to announce that $1.3 million in extra-budgetary support had been pledged by 22 governments.

The Government of Mexico offered to act as host to the Conference, an offer which was accepted by the Economic and Social Council with gratitude in its resolution of 27 July 1982[1].

The Opening of the Conference

World population stabilization

In his speech to the World Population Conference at Bucharest, on 20 August 1974, Mr Rafael Salas – speaking as Executive Director of UNFPA – had said that the World Population Plan of Action was 'an affirmation of certain fundamental principles of action in the field of population. It emphasizes the different needs and priorities in the various parts of the world. In order to give the Plan substance' he added, 'it will be necessary for countries and communities to design and put into effect their own national plans of action in accordance with their own special conditions, and with their own resources. ...To solve the population problems of countries will require more from us in a shorter time than ever before in the history of mankind.'

Ten years later, Mr Salas addressed the International Conference on Population not only as Executive Director of UNFPA, but also as Secretary-General of the Conference. He spoke at the inaugural ceremony, held at the Palacio de Bellas Artes, Mexico City on 6 August 1984. He set out on that occasion, in clear and unambiguous language, his own views of what, as T. S. Eliot put it, might be called 'the goal of all our striving'. Listening to that statement, the author could not help reflecting what a long way the United Nations had come as far as population was concerned from those uncertain beginnings forty years earlier. For Salas left none of his listeners in any doubt that the ultimate objective of policy was indeed the stabilization of world population. Tiny acorns; mighty oak trees.

The passage is worth quoting in full because it is possibly the most explicit statement on the subject made by a high official over the United Nations, speaking in an official capacity and in the most public way. Salas said:

> Our goal is the stabilization of global population within the shortest period possible before the end of the next century. The combination of rapid population growth, slowly growing incomes and inadequate level of technology continue to widen the disparities in international levels of living and frustrate the efforts of developing countries to improve the quality of life of their people. Even a high growth rate of 5 to 6% in national income of the developing countries between 1985 and 2000 would still leave over 600 million persons below the poverty line. Population stabilization will make it less difficult for the developing countries to improve their levels of living. Voluntary family planning is a vital means of reaching this global goal provided it is in accord with individual human rights, religious beliefs and cultural values. It is essential that population programmes be maintained until the promise of stabilization is within sight.
>
> Only the determined, rational and humane national population policies of countries can bring about a more satisfying future for the forthcoming generations. Governments must plan and work to bring about a global society that is secure and viable, one in which individuals can develop their full potential free from the capricious inequalities of development and threats of environmental degradation. This should be done without violating the dignity and freedom of the human person and by giving all people the knowledge and the means to bring forth only the children for whom they can provide the fullest opportunities for growth ...

The President of Mexico

We shall see later the manner in which the Conference approached the concept of world population stabilization. The opening session, a formal occasion, was the time for tone-setting speeches rather than textual

250

proposals. Another such contribution was made by the President of Mexico, Miguel de la Madrid Hurtado, who described, amongst other things, Mexico's own population policies. Before Bucharest, Mexico had foreseen the consequences of its excessive population growth rate, then 3.5 per cent per year. The interest of the authorities had been complemented by a social demand for family-planning services which the State had been unable to ignore. At the end of 1973, the country's constitution had been amended to establish the right of all individuals to decide freely, responsibly and in an informed manner the number and spacing of their children. A general population law had been approved by Congress.

The legal basis had thus been established for a population policy, which had been in force since 1974 and included action in the areas of family planning, women's participation, social communication, health and education. National goals had been set in 1978 for lowering the population growth rate from 2.5 per cent by 1982 and to 1.9 per cent by 1988. The growth rate in 1983 was estimated at 2.3 per cent.

Despite the progress made, the President said 'We are not satisfied with the prevailing situation'[2].

President de la Madrid thus confirmed Mexico's special place on the world stage as far as population matters were concerned. Mexico had provided the Secretary-General, in the person of Dr Carillo Flores, for the Bucharest World Population Conference; it had been one of the first Latin American countries to adopt a population policy with specific demographic targets; it had offered its capital city as the venue of the 1984 conference. Now the Mexican President himself had publicly confirmed his country's commitment to population goals. In international conferences such gestures can have more than symbolic significance.

It was also significant that the man who was instrumental in Mexico's 'revolution' in population policy in 1974 was elected President of the International Conference on Population. Lic. Manuel Bartlett Diaz, Minister of the Interior, had – in an earlier capacity – been intimately involved in the formulation of Mexico's population policy and his work had been incorporated in the New General Population Act of 1974, which formed the basis of the present National Population Policy.

At the same time Dr Frederick Sai of Ghana was elected President of the Main Committee, another key appointment which augured well for the eventual outcome of the conference. Dr Sai, an ebullient, witty yet compassionate man, had previously served as director of Ghana's Health Services and, subsequently, as IPPF's Medical Director. He would later, after Mexico, join the World Bank as a Senior Advisor in its Population, Health and Nutrition Department. To paraphrase the remark made by the Chinese Delegate to the Bucharest Conference: of all population experts,

Sai was the most precious. With Sai chairing the Main Committee, the future of the Conference, if not of mankind itself, might indeed be made infinitely bright.

Another speech made on the first day which was of more than symbolic significance was that given by Queen Noor al Hussein of Jordan.

Queen Noor of Jordan

The woman of the family, she said, is 'the single most effective agent for improving the socio–economic welfare of a community'. Improving women's status may be 'the most cost-effective and efficient investment possible in the long run'. Queen Noor pointed out that of the 700 million illiterate people in the world, two-thirds are female; that women are generally in poorer health than men and that wage-earning women in industrialized countries work longer hours, earn less money, have less free time and enjoy fewer hours of sleep than men. If women's lot was improved, women would pass on their knowledge to their families, dramatically improve their welfare with an awareness of family planning and nutrition, and increase the family's standards of living with their extra income from work.

As important as Queen Noor's actual words was the fact that she had been accorded, as a high Arab dignitary, a privileged position in the Conference proceedings, speaking as she did at the start of the General debate. Much time would later be taken up by discussion of Recommendation 36 relating to 'illegal settlements' submitted by a number of Arab states. As the Conference began, the organisers must clearly have hoped that Recommendation 36 would not disrupt the smooth ordering of the proceedings. Giving the spotlight to Queen Noor of Jordan was a tactically astute move. In the event, the Conference managed to avoid an all-out clash over Recommendation 36 though certain quite nasty skirmishes took place as it was adopted with only Israel and the United States of America voting against[3].

UN Secretary-General

On August 13, 1984, the Secretary-General of the United Nations, Mr Perez de Cuellar, who had been unable to attend the opening session, addressed the Conference Plenary. He began by taking stock of progress since Bucharest:

Ten years ago in Bucharest the World Population Plan of Action was adopted by the World Community. It was an ambitious plan, commensurate with the seriousness and breadth of the population problem itself. The present Conference has provided first of all a much needed opportunity to take stock of where we stand in terms of the Bucharest Plan. There has been general agreement, I believe, that in these ten years, significant progress has been made. A wide consensus on population issues has developed in the international community which has facilitated the mobilization and allocation of resources to priority programmes and countries. National and international research and training programmes have enabled countries formulate population programme policies on the basis of greatly broadened knowledge and understanding. This has in many cases included increased attention to the close relationship between population, resources, environment and development. In a good many countries, there has been notable improvement in the integration of development and population policies. And more resources are being devoted to population programmes. Developing countries, on the average, are spending from their own resources 3 to 4 times the amount they receive for this purpose in foreign assistance.

Demographic phenomena, he continued, varied greatly in terms of geography. It was especially fortunate that delegations had stressed the importance of regional circumstances in defining priorities for action with regard to population. Some of these circumstances gave reason for alarm. High population growth rates, and rapid, unregulated urban expansion would continue to cause concern in the Latin American and Asian regions. Conversely, the drastic decline in the birth rate of developed countries had resulted in extremely low or even negative population growth. One of the consequences was the considerable ageing of the populations with attendant economic and social problems.

The Secretary-General of the United Nations singled out Africa for special mention.

I would particularly like to mention the problems generated by rapid population growth combined with slow economic growth in the African region. While growth of food output has kept pace with the growth of population in many developing countries, this has not been so in Sub-Saharan Africa. In this region, per capita food availability has been declining and the technology, human skills, infrastructure and the resources needed to reverse this trend do not appear presently within the means of the countries of this region. These long-term tendencies have been reinforced by the drought of the past 2 or 3 years thus aggravating the already adverse balance between food output and the size of population. I have sought to mobilise the resources of the United Nations and the entire international community to alleviate this situation. It is clear that a lasting solution to this imbalance also must include a reduction in the rate of population growth, which is close to or exceeds 3 per cent per annum in many countries of the region.

Not unnaturally, towards the end of his remarks, the Secretary-General turned his attention to the role of the United Nations itself.

> Ever since the establishment of the Population Commission in 1946 as a subsidiary body of the Economic Social Council, the United Nations has highlighted the importance of population questions. Since the Bucharest Conference, the organizations of the United Nations system have redoubled their efforts to assist Member States in finding solutions to crucial population problems and in emphasizing the importance of demographic factors in international plans and strategies, including the International Development Strategy for the Third United Nations Development Decade.

And he went on to stress, in unambiguous terms, the link between population and peace.

> ... I consider these activities are directly related to the first objective of the United Nations, the preservation of peace, since future political stability, like economic development, will depend heavily on the way in which population policies are handled.

Major controversies

The United States drops a bombshell

The big surprise of Mexico, 1984 was the position of the United States. Looking back at the Conference, Leon Tabah, the former director of the Population Division of the United Nations Department of Economic and Social Affairs, and a member of the French Delegation to the International Conference on Population in Mexico, wrote:

> For the few participants of the International Population Conference held in Mexico City last August who had the good fortune to attend the Bucharest Conference ten years ago, the contrasts between the two conferences were both striking and fascinating. Participants had the feeling they were witnessing a topsy-turvy world as each Conference protagonist used the very arguments at Mexico used by his antagonists at Bucharest 10 years earlier ... the most conspicuous change came from the American delegation which was more open than the other delegations in reversing a previously strongly-held position ...[4].

This reversal was even more surprising in that at the two sessions of the Preparatory Committee held in January and March 1984 in New York, the United States gave no indication of the stunning *volte-face* which it was about to spring. On the contrary, the United States Ambassador, Richard Benedick, who represented his country at those two sessions, complained that the documents prepared by the secretariat did not dramatise enough the fact that, apart from China, the growth rate of the Third World was still at the same level that it was at the time of the Bucharest Conference. It was not until the United States, shortly before the Mexico Conference, distributed a position paper on its policy towards family planning in the Third World, that the world had a warning of the surprises in store. The US policy statement asserted that the 1960s and 1970s saw a 'demographic overreaction' in which 'too many governments pursued population control measures without sound economic policies that create the rise in living standards historically associated with decline in fertility rates'. The policy appeared to challenge one of the basic assumptions of the Conference: namely, that the current world programme, emphasising efforts to cut back population growth through government-initiated family planning, was on the right course and it would simply be built upon to reflect advances in technology and changes in demographic patterns such as the growth in rural–urban migration. On the contrary it attributed to the free market economy, rather than to directive intervention, the only effective way to modify population trends.

On 8 August, James L. Buckley, a former Conservative Senator and head of the United States delegation to the Conference, elaborated on the themes already advanced in the policy paper. Blithely ignoring the fact that it had been largely US influence and US pressure which had contributed to the dramatic expansion of population activities at the international level over the last two decades, Buckley assured the conference that:

> First, and foremost, population growth is, of itself, neither good nor bad. It becomes an asset or a problem in conjunction with other factors, such as economic policy, social constraints, and the ability to put additional men and women to useful work. People, after all, are producers as well as consumers.

He went on to refer to the experience of Hong Kong and South Korea.

> They have few natural resources, and over the past 20 years they have experienced major increases in population, yet few nations have experienced such rapid economic growth. We believe it is no coincidence that each of these societies placed its reliance on the creativity of private individuals working within a free economy.

The second main theme of Buckley's speech was its clear statement of US policy on abortion. He said that over the past decade, the United States had not allowed its population assistance contribution to be used to finance or promote abortion. The present policy tightened this existing restraint in three ways.

> First, where US funds are attributed to nations which support abortion with other funds, the US contribution will be placed into the segregated accounts which cannot be used for abortion; second, the US will no longer contribute to separate non-governmental organisations which perform or actively promote

abortion as a method of family planning in other nations; and third, before the US will contribute funds to the United Nations Fund for Population Activities, it will first require concrete assurances that the UNFPA is not engaged in, and does not provide funding for, abortion or coercive family planning programmes. Should such assurances not be possible, and in order to maintain the level of its overall contribution to the international effort, the United States will redirect the amount of its intended contribution to other, non-UNFPA family planning programmes.

When efforts to lower population growth are deemed advisable, US policy considers it imperative that such efforts respect the right of couples to determine the size of their own families. Accordingly, the United States will not provide family planning funds to any nation which engages in forcible coercion to achieve population goals.

To what extent the US position at Mexico, as set out in the position paper and Buckley's speech, was simply a reflection of domestic politics was a matter of speculation. Writing in the London *Sunday Times*, Rosemary Righter clearly took the view that internal political considerations were a determining factor.

The Reagan administration's team, headed by the Conservative ex-Senator James Buckley, a Roman Catholic, will arrive with speeches and policies which pander to the phobias of the anti-abortion Moral Majority and the arch-conservative lobbies in the US, and which also plainly have an eye on the Republican Party convention the following week[5].

The same newspaper commented in its lead editorial[6]:

Two immensely powerful leaders, the Pope and President Reagan, are combining to do mankind a profound disservice.

Even though human fertility has diminished in the past ten years, the prospect is still that today's 4.8 billion people will grow to something between 10 billion and 12 billion before the numbers finally stabilise. Even attaining the lower figure will require an unprecedently determined mobilisation of the world's social resources. Yet the Vatican with its grim opposition to any 'artificial' form of birth control, and the White House, with its decision to withhold funding from anybody that even countenances abortion, are sabotaging much of the necessary effort before it can even begin.

If the US statements amazed journalists and leader-writers around the world, it disturbed the delegates at Mexico even more. Tabah comments wryly:

the developing countries gave the impression they were living in a baffling world and attending a no less baffling Conference. After being to some extent upset by the impatience and the excessive eagerness of rich countries to obtain prompt results on the family-planning front, they heard at Mexico, voiced by the most activist, that population was a mere 'neutral factor' at a moment when they, the developing countries, were finally ready to accept the idea of curbing their population growth. At a working group dealing with redrafting a proposed American amendment on population and development trends over the last decade which took a generally 'rosy' view of things, I was struck by the attitude of African delegates. They were insisting that development in Africa had proceeded at a slower rate than stated by the American draft. They said that poverty was growing in Africa while population growth was continuing at a high pace, mortality levels were falling short of the objectives set by the Bucharest Conference, and food availability was declining[7].

Reaction was not confined to members of official delegations to the Conference. Pradman Weerakon, Secretary-General of the International Planned Parenthood Federation, said in a statement that IPPF 'does not promote abortion; it promotes contraception as the first line of defence against unwanted pregnancy'. He said that it would be people in the poorest countries that would be affected if American aid was cut off to IPPF 'since it is in developing countries that alternative facilities are absent and the dependence on the non-government sector is greatest. The incidence of abortion would certainly rise if access to contraception services is denied'.

Sharon Kamp of the Population Crisis Committee, the US-based lobbying organization which was the creation and legacy of General Draper, described the US statement as 'Voodoo demographics'. 'The idea that there is a correlation between rising income and falling birthrates may be valid over a 200-year period, but that has not been the experience over the past 10 years.' She cited Mexico as a country that a decade earlier had a very high rate of per capita income but also high population growth rates. It was only after Mexico initiated its family-planning programmes that there was a 'precipitous' decline in the birth-rate. Camp said that a 'rigid' interpretation of the new US language on abortion 'potentially dismantled' $US 75 million in currently funded US population programmes. 'The abortion policy attempts to impose on the world a minority view which is contrary to US law and to majority public opinion in the US'[8].

China's response

The US bombshell rocked the Bucharest consensus, but it did not destroy it. Counter-attacking in measured tones, China's delegate, Mr Wang Wei, stressed that China 'as a developing socialist country' had been making unremitting efforts to develop her economy while controlling rapid population growth. The natural population growth rate had dropped to 1.154 per cent in 1983 from 2.089 per cent in 1973. 'All this has proved that the policy decision of promoting family planning to control population growth along with planned economic development is a correct one.'

And he defended not only the decision itself but also the programme methods.

Since 1979, the Chinese Government has advocated the practice of '1 couple, 1 child'. This, however, does not mean that one couple should have one child only in every case. The Government gives guidance for the implementation of family planning programmes in the light of specific conditions such as economic developments, cultural background, population structure and the masses' wishes in different localities. The requirements are more flexible in rural areas than in urban areas and more so among the people of national minorities than among the people of the Han nationality. In rural areas, those couples who have actual difficulty and wish to have two children may have a second birth with planned spacing. At present, the women with single-children account for only 21.2 per cent of all the married women of reproductive age who have children. The advocacy of the practice of '1 couple, 1 child' is a policy of a specific historical period in China. Our family planning policy is based upon actual conditions and is reasonable, and thus has gained the masses' support.

Mr Wang Wei did not, in this Plenary speech, speak directly about abortion. He affirmed that in carrying out its family planning programme, China has consistently adhered to the principle of 'integrating state guidance with the masses' voluntariness'.

The Government has always emphasised the importance of encouraging the people's own initiatives, through publicity and education, which is the key link in implementing the family planning programme. We rely upon hundreds of thousands of full-time and part-time family planning workers, masses' organizations and other social potentials in disseminating constantly and extensively family planning policies and the knowledge about contraception and prevention of genetic and birth defects. We have maintained the principle of taking contraception as the main method, providing multiple services, free of charge, for the users to choose from.

And as though he intended deliberately to indicate China's view of the threats and warnings contained in the stated US position, the Chinese delegate addressed himself deliberately to the area of international collaboration.

In the past decade, the relevant organizations of the United Nations, especially the UNFPA headed by Dr Salas, have exerted fruitful efforts and made important contributions to the implementation to the World Population Plan of Action and so did some international non-governmental population and family planning organizations. In seeking the solution to its population problem, China mainly relies upon its own efforts. At the same time, it also attaches great importance to the development of friendly international co-operation with the

United Nations population agencies and some non-governmental organizations in the population and family planning field; it has also established bi-lateral relations of co-operation with some countries. We wish to make further efforts to strength such friendly co-operation'.

Abortion

If the Chinese defence of abortion was implicit rather than explicit in the speech of that country's delegate to the International Conference on Population, Sweden's Minister of Health and Social Affairs, Mrs Sigurdsen was more forthright.

Effective contraception liberates women from unwanted pregnancies and induced abortion, and improves considerably the health of both mothers and children. Prevention of unwanted pregnancies must always be our aim. I note, however, that illegal abortion, performed under unsafe medical conditions, is a very serious health problem in many countries today. Therefore I would like that all women in the world have access to legal and safe abortions.

In draft recommendation number 13, governments were urged, *inter alia*:

to take appropriate steps to help women avoid abortions and, whenever possible, to provide for the humane treatment and counselling of women who have had recourse to illegal abortion.

Sweden fought hard, but unsuccessfully, to have that paragraph maintained in the final recommendations. In the event, the final text adopted by the conference read:

Governments are urged... to take appropriate steps to help women avoid abortion, which in no case should be promoted as a method of family planning, and whenever possible, provide for the humane treatment and counselling of women who have had recourse to abortion. (Paragraph 18e)

Sweden, in the explanation of their vote on the whole report, regretted that the paragraph which dealt with 'steps to help women avoid abortion' did not refer to illegal abortion, thereby implying that all abortions are illegal and should be avoided without mentioning the use of legal abortion.

The addition of the words to paragraph 18e 'which in no case should be promoted as a method of family planning' was accepted by a consensus. However, the fact that the amendment was proposed by the French delegation was another revealing example of the way in which even as late as 1984 the Old Guard – namely the Catholic countries of Western Europe – were still ready to be mischievous, fighting and sometimes, as on this occasion, winning small rearguard victories even though they had essentially lost the main battle almost 20 years before, when the United Nations adopted those historic resolutions of the 1960s.

The Holy See

None of this, however, went far enough for the delegate of the Holy See. Bishop Jan Schotte speaking on the morning of August 8th expressed the Vatican's 'concern about the setting of quantitative population growth targets. There is always' he said, 'the danger that the achievement of such targets, especially in terms of declines in population growth and/or fertility rates, will be used as a condition for economic assistance'. And he also expressed the Church's opposition, on moral grounds, to abortion, sterilization and contraception.

> Despite affirmations to the contrary, and often contrary to the explicit formulations of national legislation, abortion is more and more used as an integral part of family planning programmes, financed even by governments and international organizations.

As far as sterilization was concerned, Bishop Schotte told the Conference that, in the ten years since Bucharest, sterilization had 'become more and more widely used in family-planning programmes in many nations'.

> The Holy See has constantly opposed the practice of sterilization because of the finality with which it destroys one of the person's prerogatives, the ability to procreate, and because as a demographic measure it can be too easily used in violation of human rights, especially among the poor and the uninformed.

If there was any comfort to be had in the Bishop's remarks it was in that he gave the Holy See's support to the proposal in the draft recommendations (recommendation 20, retained in the final text as Recommendation 25) which urged governments to make available access to natural family planning and which therefore suggested

> *'that Governments should in this matter provide concrete assistance for couples, which respects their religious and cultural values in making responsible decisions regarding the spacing of births'.*

Bishop Schotte stated that:

recent specific studies underscore the validity and reliability of the newer natural methods, and pedagogical techniques have been developed that can be properly implemented and evaluated in various cultures.

He went on to assert confidently that:

women achieve a better understanding and appreciation of their sexuality from instruction in the natural methods, and couples who commit themselves to natural family planning strengthen their communication, mutual respect and shared responsibility in regard to parenthood.[9]

Not surprisingly, the Holy See disassociated itself, as it had done at Bucharest, from the adoption by the Conference of the recommendations of the Main Committee 'by consensus and by acclamation' being, as at Bucharest, the only delegation to do so. Though it recognized that the recommendations contained some valuable proposals with regard to development, the important role of the family, migration and ageing, the Holy See could not agree with or give approval to those sections that 'asserted for individuals, including unmarried adolescents, the prerogatives that belonged to married couples in regard to sexual intimacy and parenthood'. Furthermore, the recommendations endorsed and encouraged methods of family planning that the Catholic Church considered morally unacceptable.

The Holy See's problems with the reference to 'individuals' as well as 'couples' were not new, but they had been compounded since Bucharest. Whereas the World Population Plan of Action referred to the basic right of 'all couples and individuals to decide freely and responsibly the number and spacing of their children and to have the information, education and means to do so' the recommendations for the further implementation of the World Population Plan of Action, adopted in Mexico City went further. Recommendation 25 read:

Governments should, as a matter of urgency, make universally available information, education and the means to assist couples and individuals to achieve their desired number of children.

While under Recommendation 30:

Governments are urged to ensure that all couples and individuals have a basic right to decide freely and responsibly the number and spacing of their children and to have the information, education and the means to do so.

In other words, while Bucharest had stated a 'basic right', Mexico not only restated that right but also urged governments to ensure that it was respected. A nuance, perhaps, but an important nuance, nevertheless.

Targets for population growth

In his speech of 6 August 1984, delivered to the opening session of the international Conference on Population, Mr Rafael Salas, Executive Director of UNFPA and the Secretary-General of the Conference, had stated: 'our goal is the stabilization of global population within the shortest period possible before the end of the next century'. To what extent did the Mexico Conference represent an advance on Bucharest as far as the adoption of population growth targets was concerned? Was there in any sense an international commitment to the concept of 'population stabilization'.

In purely formal terms, the answer is: no or not much. Recommendation 8 of the draft Recommendations for the further implementation of the World Population Plan of Action[10] attempted to reintroduce the notion of quantitative targets which, as we have seen, was lost at Bucharest. It read:

> Countries which consider their population growth rate detrimental to their national purposes are invited to consider setting quantitative population growth targets, within the framework of socio–economic developments.

The attempt failed in the final recommendations as adopted by the Mexico Conference. Recommendation 8 became Recommendation 13 and read:

> *Countries which consider their population growth rates hinder the attainment of national goals are invited to consider pursuing relevant demographic policies, within the framework of socio–economic development. Such policies should respect human rights, the religious beliefs, philosophical convictions, cultural values and fundamental rights of each individual and couple, to determine the size of its own family.*

By dropping the reference to 'quantitative population growth targets' in favour of the more neutral expression 'relevant demographic policies' the Conference could hardly be said to have improved upon the language agreed at Bucharest[11].

A fortiori, there was no mention in the final Mexico recommendation of a global target for reducing population growth or attaining population stabilization.

The United Nations' own official account of this aspect records in typically neutral tones:

> Many delegations stressed that, while it would be useful for the Conference to approve broad general guidelines, it was in the final analysis the responsibility of Governments in the exercise of their sovereign authority, to formulate the population policies which they considered most appropriate and consistent with national social, economic and cultural conditions and factors. Several delegations considered that it was utopian to aspire to the formulation of global policies, in view of the diversity of national situations. It was generally recognised, however, that conscious efforts had to be made by Governments to frame coherent population policies adapted to the conditions in their countries

and consistent with plans or programmes relating to social and economic development as a whole. It was also stressed that population policies were integral parts of the long-range socio-economic development policies of each country[12].

In spite of the fact that there was no explicit commitment to the goal of world population stabilization, there was nonetheless an underlying current of interest in such an idea. R. P. Kapoor, who was a member of the Indian delegation to the Conference, wrote:

Even though it has not been specifically stated, it was clear in Mexico that in the long term, global population policies should aim at a stabilised population size in a limited time-frame and at a level of around 8 billion people. Bucharest made the world conscious of the need to *slow down* population growth; Mexico has brought about an awareness regarding the urgency of *halting* the population growth. [author's italics][13].

Though, as noted above, it is doubtful whether the actual text adopted at Mexico would allow of such a bullish interpretation, it is certainly true to say that other speakers besides Mr Salas specifically advocated the goal of World Population Stabilization in the statements they made to the Plenary. Thus His Excellency the Honourable Mwai Kibaki, M.P. vice-president of the Government of Kenya after describing Kenya's own objectives ('the projections indicate that if we do not curb the population increase now an incredible total of 160 million people will be reached by the year 2050'), went on to exhort the Conference: 'let us commit ourselves to the goal of stabilization of World Population within the next 50 years'.

Coming from an African such a statement was especially significant. Nor was Mr Kibaki alone in using such explicit language. The delegate from Mauritius spoke of a 'race against time' and said that 'the challenge is ours – not for the past nor for the future generations'. The delegate from Pakistan told the Conference that 'the good news is that population planners have not failed the world; globally there is an overall decline in fertility'. But he added that 'ours is an expanding world, and population growth rates continue to deny a quality of life and macro socio–economic development which mankind is worthy of'.

The delegate from the Philippines indicated that the Commission on Population in his country had 'established a strategy that should make it possible to reach replacement levels of fertility by the year 2000'. And the delegate from the Republic of Korea indicated that: 'Korea hopes to achieve its population replacement level by 1988.'

The delegate from Turkey spoke of 'hopes that the world population may eventually be stabilized' if the trend towards lower population growth in the developing countries continued. And the delegate from Nepal told the Conference that: 'It has become all too clear that the World at large must accelerate efforts to control population growth if the citizens of the Third World are to enjoy a reasonable level of living.'

Among the developed countries, Sweden, Norway and New Zealand spoke in the most emphatic terms about the need for global population planning.

The Swedish Delegate told the Conference that the review and appraisal of the World Population Plan of Action showed that, in absolute terms, the population growth figures were still 'staggering'. 'The global population could increase by 1.3 billion to reach 6.1 billion by the year 2000 – only 16 years from now.'

Most of this tremendous increase will take place in countries which already have difficulties providing their people with a decent quality of life. Population growth will result in major strains on the already limited availability of food, clean water, shelter, energy, education, health services and job opportunities. It will also increase the strains on fragile environments and speed up desertification, deforestation and soil erosion. This will negatively affect food and agricultural production on which the survival of millions of human beings depends. It will also affect our climate. Furthermore, population growth may cause tensions which can lead to war and unrest. All this underscores the importance of the links between population, resources, environment and development and of unfair consumption patterns which were recognised already in Bucharest, and the need for action now.

What is urgently needed are effective measures to promote economic and social development and to increase the productive resources available to the developing countries to combat poverty, starvation and disease. But this is not enough. Measures to slow down rapid population growth are also imperative. If such measures are not taken the future will look bleak. Mortality rates will increase and Governments may feel forced to take drastic measures to halt the population growth, measures that will infringe on human rights. Do we want this to happen?

Norway took a similar position. Norway's delegate told the Conference that:

The World Population Conference in Bucharest agreed on a World Population Plan of Action, which became a landmark in our joint task of coming to grips with a threat of over-population of our planet. Despite the achievements reached in Bucharest, my Government feels that the population problems we face today are as serious as they were ten years ago, even though their nature is different. Whereas some countries have demonstrated that it is indeed possible to bring population growth under control through determined policies, other countries, accounting for about one-fourth of the world population, have not yet experienced any significant decline in their fertility rate. At the current growth rate the population in these areas will double in twenty-five years. Unless a reduction of fertility is brought about, the growth of the population may be checked by a tragic increase in mortality, especially among the poor, infants and children. It will seriously affect political and social stability, human rights, economic development and the possibilities of orderly change.

The delegate from Norway told the Conference that it was:

imperative that this Conference generate a new powerful momentum at the national and international levels in the struggle to curb the growth of the world population.

Finally, from the other side of the world, the New Zealand delegate told the meeting:

ultimately, in a finite world with finite resources only a dramatic decline in population growth can assure the majority of the world's people of adequate food and shelter and access to other basic human requirements.

The general debate

The Mexico City consensus, itself building upon the Bucharest consensus so hardly won ten years earlier, was reflected not only in the Recommendations and Declaration of the Conference but also, broadly speaking, in the statements made by delegates on the central questions of population and development. There were, of course, echoes of the debate about the relative merits of family planning versus development as a means of attaining lower fertility, but – apart from the surprising contribution of the United States discussed above – the old interest and sparkle, political as well as intellectual, seemed no longer to be present.

In achieving the Mexico consensus, the position of China was crucial. Actions spoke louder than words. China's demographic achievements were plain for all to see. Privately there were several even among the United States delegation (which included veteran 'populationists' like Philander P. Claxton) who were ready to admit that those achievements were not all brought about by the unfettered operation of the 'free-market economy'.

But quite apart from China's conversion, since Bucharest, into a whole-hearted protagonist of population policies, it was clear to anybody who heard the speeches in the Plenary or read the texts that the basis of the consensus was a good deal stronger at Mexico than it had been at Bucharest[14]. Some countries, whose enthusiasm for population policy and family planning had in 1974 been at best lukewarm, were far more positive ten years later. Other countries who at Bucharest had been actively hostile had, by the time the Mexico Conference came round, modified their views even to the point of adopting a position of guarded neutrality. Brazil was a case in point.

It was symbolic perhaps of the new atmosphere that the leader of the Brazilian delegation, Dr Walyr Mendes Arcoverde, Minister of State for Health, was the first to speak in the Plenary debate after the formalities of the opening session were over.

Dr Arcoverde reminded delegates that Brazil was firmly convinced that the deliberations of the 1984 International Conference on Population must be based, as in 1974, on two premises: (a) strict respect of states' sovereignty with regard to the definition and implementation of their national population policies; and (b) the recognition that social and economic development is the central factor in the solution of demographic problems.

Brazil rejected the 'apocalytpic perspective which preceded both the convening of the Bucharest Conference and the 1972 Stockholm Conference on the Human Environment'.

> We cannot accept the simplistic diagnosis which blames demographic growth as the source of the developing countries' ills. Moreover, we cannot admit that the population control prescription be one more magic solution for the problems of poverty, hunger and disease which affect the greater part of humanity. The seriousness of our subject does not allow the uncritical acceptance of imported demographic models, nor does it lend itself to pious exhortations of the 'put-your-own-house-in-order' type, a kind of advice that can certainly be applied both ways. In short, my delegation understands that population policies must not be considered as a replacement for development policies, nor can they constitute a form of escapism from the responsibilities of international co-operation.

Dr Arcoverde referred in particular to the debt crisis among developing nations, and especially in Latin America. 'The world goes today through an economic crisis of unprecedented proportions. Nevertheless, contrary to the conservationists' diagnosis, this did not come about as a result of an exhaustion of resources or of a demographic explosion.'

Having thus established his credentials as it were, the Brazilian delegate went on to deal with the population situation in his own country. Brazil had the world's sixth largest population: 120 million inhabitants according to the 1980 census. For more than a century, the Brazilian population had been doubling practically every 30 years. Approximately 3.1 million individuals were being added each year to the country's population. Though, since 1960, the rate of total growth of the population, which was at 2.48 per cent between 1970 and 1980, had been declining, the relatively young age of the Brazilian people would lead to an absolute increase in the population for many years, with a probable duplication of the present stock in little more than four decades.

> . The Brazilian Government is wholly conscious of the challenge presented by the growth of its population. The acuteness of this challenge is particularly noticeable in a time of economic crisis induced by factors which are largely beyond national control and in a situation where the levels of consumption and employment are being compressed.

Dr Arcoverde went on to explain in very clear terms the present position of the Brazilian Government as far as population policy and family planning were concerned:

> The Government is aware of the fact that today the Brazilian people increasingly demands knowledge and adequate means for planning its reproduction. As I have already stressed, my Government's answer to this demand is ethically grounded: it is based on the recognition that the planning of the number of offspring is one of the fundamental rights of the human being. As the Brazilian Government sees it, this matter must not be subject to goals which are established beforehand; on the contrary, it should be the result of a social consensus. According to this view, the legitimate growth-rate for Brazil is that which corresponds to the sum total of the free and well-informed decisions of these couples and individuals who aim at planning their reproductive life.

For these reasons Dr Arcoverde explained, Governmental interference in birth control was not to be found in Brazil. However, the state played a decisive role, namely that of assuring everyone's right to health care, whether or not the population was on the increase.

> As the Minister of Health for my country, I wish to lay particular stress on this point. In fact, since the 1970s, the Brazilian Government has been willing to incorporate into the field of health-care those activities related to family planning. The President of the Republic has just approved a set of guidelines, according to which family planning will be considered as an integral part of public health activities.

Nigeria

If Brazil was an example of one major country which was moving, however cautiously, in the right direction along the spectrum of demographic policies, Nigeria was another. The Nigerian delegate told the meeting that, at the Bucharest Conference, his country's position was that the capacity of the Nigerian economy, which was then growing at the rate of 12 per cent per annum (during a period of economic boom) to cope with a population growth rate of 2.5 per cent per annum was not in doubt. However, two national development plans had been launched since the

1974 conference in Bucharest and there had been a certain evolution in thinking. The crude birth-rate was about 50 per 1000 while the crude death-rate was about 17 per 1000, resulting in an annual growth rate of 3.6 per cent. Average family size was about six children. The estimated population for 1984 was slightly over 90 million and by the year 2000, the population was expected to increase to well over 150 million.

The Government now recognises, more than ever before, the fact that the overall rate of growth has to be brought down to the level which will not impose excessive burdens on the economy in the long run. The Government plans to achieve this through an integrated approach to population planning. The Government is not only concerned about the rate of growth of the population but also the spatial distribution and the effects of early and frequent child-bearing on mothers and their children. The primary concern is with the well-being of the family as a social unit and of the nation in general.

The issue of fertility regulation and child-spacing is being viewed within the context of national goals and objectives, as well as the aspirations of the people. These goals and objectives include the provision of basic health care for the entire population by the year 2000 through the Nigerian Primary Health Care System and active support for family planning activities during the current Plan period as part of the basic health care system, so such families willing to take advantage of such services may have easy access to them.

Given the importance of Nigeria in the context of African demography, this shift of position was highly significant, even if any practical effect in terms of fertility reductions had yet to be realised.

Kenya

Kenya, on the other side of the African Continent, was another example of a country where there had been an evolution since Bucharest, though – in Kenya's case – the significant developments were more at the level of practical implementation of a long-agreed programme than of basic policy formulation. (The Kenyan Government adopted an official population policy and family planning programme as early as 1965 – the first Sub-Saharan country to do so.)

Mr Mwai Kibaki in his speech outlined the basic demographic facts. Population growth in Kenya had been rapid. The population grew from 5.4 million in 1948 to 8.6 million in 1962, a 59 per cent increase in 14 years. It increased from 10.9 million in 1969 to 15.3 million in 1979, an increase of 78 per cent in only ten years. In the period before 1962 the population grew by less than 3.0 per cent, between 1962 and 1969 by about 3.3 per cent, and between 1969 and 1979 by just over 3.5 per cent.

Data from the 1977–1978 Kenya Fertility Survey recorded a rate of 4.1 per cent and it was evident from these data that the rate of population growth had been increasing since around 1962.

The Government had established the National Council for Population and Development in December 1982. This Council which brought together all the Governmental and non-Governmental agencies dealing with family-planning matters had the primary responsibility of developing national policies. The Council was also charged with the responsibility for introducing information and education programmes towards the establishment of a small family norm.

Mr Kibaki went on to outline the steps that Kenya was actually taking to put its population policy into practice.

Kenya has realised that rapid population growth frustrates her efforts to provide the population with the basic-needs services of education, health, housing, food and employment. For this reason we have given a lot of thought on how to mount an effective family planning programme while at the same time realising that family planning is not the panacea of all population issues. The strategies that are going to be enacted will basically involve recruiting a large force of family planning acceptors through:

(a) Making contraceptives accessible to all clients by increasing service delivery points from 400 now to 800 by 1986;

(b) Using medical practitioners to dispense contraceptives freely to suitable clients;

(c) Using rural and urban shops to sell certain types of contraceptives through an organised 'social marketing';

(d) Using community-based delivery systems.

Kenya has realised that satisfied clients are the best recruiters. For instance, in agriculture, introduction of hybrid maize or high grade dairy cattle has been very successful because neighbours have been able to observe the benefits enjoyed by the participating farmers in the form of higher yields. Kenya will be using local and satisfied family planners as educators, informants, recruiters and promoters.

Higher yields in terms of maize, lower yields in terms of babies – two facets of the same problem!

Turkey

Progress too was to be noted in the Middle East.

Mr Mehmet Aydin, Turkey's Minister of Health and Social Assistance, told the Conference that Turkey believed that by adopting effective population policies she would be able to maintain a rate of population growth which was in harmony with her economic and development goals. He drew attention to a pronouncement about family planning in the Muslim scriptures:

the Holy Koran in its Surah Enfal set out the family edict 14 centuries ago: 'Beware that you will be examined and put to test on account of your children and property'. This edict imposes on the parents the responsibility of proper upbringing of their children. Should they be unable to fulfil this duty because of their economic and social position they would suffer divine responsibility. For this reason parents should have no more children than they can appropriately care for. The rationale for all this is a self-imposed discipline which encompasses flexibility of choice.

He said that the fall in Turkey's rate of population increase had been sustained during the past decade. While the percentage increase was 2.50 in the 1970s, in the 1980s it had been brought down to 2.06. Measures were now being taken so that family planning services could be made available to those requesting them throughout the country, as affirmed by the Turkish Constitution. 'With the new measures' Mr Aydin said, 'we are hoping to bring the population growth rate down to 1.76 per cent by the year 2000'.

Indonesia

As at Bucharest, some of the most powerful advocates of population policies and programmes came from the Asian countries.

Emil Salim, Indonesia's Minister of State for Population and Environment, told the Conference that achievements since Bucharest were 'significant, but not sufficient'. The annual rate of world population growth had declined from 2.03 per cent in 1974 to 1.67 per cent in 1984. This reduction, however, had been influenced mainly by the achievements of China and the industrialized countries.

The world is already facing today the problem of poverty, heart-rending and spirit-killing poverty in most developing countries. Population growth in many developing countries already outstrips the rate of development. Population pressure already threatens to deplete resources beyond our capabilities for sustaining the environment. Employment opportunities are already inadequate and unevenly distributed between and within countries, leading towards higher unequal distribution of income between and within countries. Population growth has raised population density and increased population mobility.

If the total population of 4.8 billion persons today is already overburdened by these broad range of social problems which are undermining social solidarity among nations of the globe, then the impact of a rapidly increasing number of population under these circumstances may well lead towards a global social upheaval.

'Global social upheaval' – this was strong language but it was used deliberately. To avoid such upheaval, Salim told the Conference, it was 'imperative to launch a two-prong approach to development; first, a population centred development policy, i.e. a development policy aimed at solving population problems; second, a development-oriented population policy, i.e. a population policy which stimulates development.'

He spoke of Indonesia's own commitments and argued strongly for concerted global action.

> We have passed the journey from Bucharest to Mexico City. Let us now move forward for the next journey from Mexico City to the goal of life with quality for all by the year 2000.

India

Similarly, Mr B. Shankarananda, India's Minister of Health and Family Welfare, left the Conference in no doubt about India's determination to carry on with its family-planning programme.

> India is the first country in the world to have adopted an official family planning programme as early as 1952. Since then increasing emphasis is being laid on this programme in our successive Five-Year Plans. Family planning is an important component of our Prime Minister's new twenty-point Programme of socio–economic development. Recent trends in the Programme have raised hopes that we may be able to reach the goal we have set for ourselves of achieving a net reproduction rate of 1 by the year 2000. Our greatest hope is that a vast majority of people wish to limit the size of their families. We intend to cover 60 per cent of all eligible couples with effective contraception and achieve a crude birth rate of 21 per 1000, a crude death rate of 9 per 1000 and infant mortality rate of less than 60 per 1000 live births by the year 2000. This is a stupendous task. But we are confident that the goals are attainable. While we have spent over RS 14.5 billions in the Sixth Five Year Plan, we plan to spend RS 64 billion in the Seventh Five Year Plan. This is an indication of the growing resource needs of the population programme for developing countries in an atmosphere of resource constraints.

Mr Shankarananda warned the Conference that although the interplay between population and development was increasingly being recognized, the slogan 'development is the best contraception' had yet to move from the realm of rhetoric to something more serious. Poverty and rapid population growth reinforced each other in a vicious cycle. In breaking this cycle the donors and the developing countries had to co-operate with each other.

The developed world

What then was the position of the donors at Mexico City? Had there been any evolution in attitudes since Bucharest, any strengthening or weakening of commitment? Leaving aside the initial reservations that had been expressed by some of the industrialized countries at the idea of holding another World Population conference, as well as the particular circumstances of the United States discussed above, the answer on the whole is: yes.

The Scandinavian countries stood four-square behind the recommendations which emerged from the Mexico Conference, just as they had at Bucharest ten years earlier. The delegate from Sweden indicated that the Government would extend a 'substantial share' of Swedish official development assistance to population, family planning and related programmes. The delegate from Norway told the meeting that Norwegian development assistance was at present 1.15 per cent of the gross national product (GNP). Norway had decided in 1971 that 10 per cent of those allocations should be earmarked for population activities. In 1983, the Norwegian Parliament had stressed that '10 per cent should be considered as the lower limit for such allocations'. The delegate from Denmark spoke of his Government's 'high priority to continue to support developing countries in their efforts to implement population policies'.

Lord Glenarthur, leader of the United Kingdom delegation and parliamentary secretary of the Ministry of Health and Social Security, confirmed that the British Government was 'committed to continuing our development efforts and, within them, our support for population-related activities'. He announced that in 1985, subject to Parliamentary approval, the United Kingdom Government intended to increase its overall contribution to multilateral organizations working in the population field by £1.5 million, bringing total contributions from the United Kingdom to such organizations to £9.5 million, a 50 per cent increase over the level of support provided in 1982.

The delegate of France, though not committed to massive support of family-planning activities, nevertheless indicated that his Government was ready to extend considerable assistance in the field of demographic studies and spoke of the renowned and venerable institutions in France for whom the science of demography was meat and drink.

272

Most of the donors indicated that not only were they committed to increasing their support for population assistance, they also intended to increase the proportion of their aid given through multilateral channels. The United Nations Fund for Population Activities (UNFPA) and the International Planned Parenthood Federation (IPPF) were usually singled out for special mention in this connection. The delegate of the Federal Republic of Germany, for example, stated that his Government considered population policy to be an important component of its development aid strategy, believed that this was an area which, as much as any other, demanded the respect of national sovereignty, and concluded that 'an international organization is thus particularly suitable to act as impartial counsellor and helper in this delegate field'. The Federal Republic of Germany would therefore continue its support through such international organisations as UNFPA and IPPF.

In view of the trouble which loomed on the not-so-distant horizon regarding the United States' contribution to UNFPA and IPPF, this announced readiness on the part of other donors to maintain or even increase their assistance for population activities was specially significant. Indeed, it might spell the difference between life and death as far as the continuation of viable international programmes was concerned.

The role of the agencies

The general debate which took place in Mexico City in August 1984 also provided the platform for the main intergovernmental and non-governmental bodies with an interest in the subject matter of the Conference to reaffirm their participation in what could be seen as one of the most remarkable efforts of international co-operation so far attempted.

The World Bank

The World Bank, in its World Development Report 1984, not only provided an essential background document for the Conference. Its then President, Mr A. W. Clausen, made an extended visit to Mexico City in the course of which he addressed the Plenary in sombre terms. He warned delegates on the second day of the Conference that, unless there was renewed effort to check population growth, development for the Third World would be 'postponed indefinitely'. Clausen said that the evidence was overwhelming that rapid population growth impeded efforts to raise living standards in most of the developing world. 'There must therefore be a continuing effort to contain population growth if pervasive poverty is to ease and development accelerate.'

We believe that the international community has no alternative but to cooperate with a sense of urgency. Rapid reductions in population growth, and indeed rapid improvements in living standards, plainly require a combination of economic and social development with family planning.

Mr Clausen offered delegates the World Bank's approach to development, which included dialogue between all those involved in the development process so as to understand the causes of population growth and to forge appropriate policies. It also involved education for women, improving economic opportunities for the poor; and assistance for the extension and improvement for family planning and basic health services.

He said that over the past 14 years the World Bank had spent US $500 million for population projects and more than $100 million for health projects. He added that the Bank was 'both willing and able' to do more in the population field.

Requests for population assistance are rising; and where there are programmes that we can effectively support, we shall certainly respond. We plan to at least double our population and health-related lending over the next few years and our major focus will be on Africa and Asia, where population related health problems are still the most dramatic.

Clausen said that the Bank felt that population assistance could usefully triple, or even quadruple, between now and the end of the century, from its present US $500 million – less than 2 per cent of the official aid – per year to US $2 billion by the year 2000.

A quadrupling of population assistance in real terms could raise the level to some US $2 billion per annum by the year 2000. Even such a relatively small volume of donor assistance could, given effective policies in developing countries, make a vast difference to population growth, to maternal and child health, and thus to the future we share. Surely all donors can recognise that fact, and respond accordingly.
But a few donors should not be expected to carry the bulk of the burden. The whole donor community must help.

Mr Clausen added that good family-planning services existed at present and cost very little.

If donors and developing countries were each to make similar adjustments in their budget allocations, the resources would be there to make such services available to most people in the developing world as well.

World Health Organization

Of equal interest was the address given by Dr H. Mahler, the Director-General of the World Health Organization. For those in his audience who recalled the traumatic events of the 1950s and 1960s, when the World Health Organization was trying to come to terms with the implications of the population problem for its own work, Dr Mahler's speech must have seemed little short of a miracle. The central thrust of his remarks was his affirmation that the decisions taken at the Alma Ata Conference in 1977 by the World Health Assembly at which the policy 'Health for All by the Year 2000' was adopted was of direct relevance to the theme of the Mexico City Conference[15].

In 1977 WHO's Member States took a major policy decision when they declared that a main social goal in the coming decades should be the attainment by all the people of the world by the year 2000 of a level of health that will permit them to lead a socially and economically productive life. This is popularly known as Health for All by the Year 2000. And they decided that primary health care is the key to attaining health for all. Then, they adopted a Strategy for attaining their goal and are currently active in carrying out .... A very important feature of the Strategy is the care of families, and essential to that are respect for the status of women and maternal and child care including family planning. I should like to emphasise that family planning can lead to striking improvements in health and well-being of mothers and children and indeed of the whole family. For in all societies, the family in one form or another is the central nucleus for people, for the lives, their loves, their dreams, their health and their development. In keeping with this, the Strategy aims at ensuring that every child born is truly wanted and enjoys the best possible opportunity to grow into a healthy member of a decent and just society.

Dr Mahler said WHO's task was to obtain the consensus of its Member States on policies and strategies that acted as levers for people's development, not the least of which related to family health and family planning.

What it does do is to generate appropriate health technology that can be adapted to various circumstances, including technical, social and behavioural measures for family planning. What it does do is to cooperate with Member States and people in applying all that through sound health infrastructures.

At a press conference later, Dr Mahler referred particularly to the role men should play. 'Men must be "dragged screaming into family planning".' And he went on to add that:

in the spirit of primary health care, it is quite inconceivable that women be left alone when it comes to family planning. Primary health care tries to take the community and the whole family – first and foremost the man and woman together – in order to have a dialogue between them, to solve what is very often a problem for the woman if she faces strong male resistance or indifference.

275

In this context, WHO was involved in research to study the possibility of a male pill. 'It is absolutely within reason that a male pill will be developed in the not too distant future.' Another male contraceptive would be the possibility of a vaccine which 'would put a man out of action for one to three years, in the sense that he would not be able to fertilise the egg'[16].

A far cry indeed from those anguished debates of earlier years!

The International Planned Parenthood Federation

Mrs Avabai Wadia, President of the International Planned Parenthood Federation, and a woman who had been associated with IPPF since its foundation in 1952, made a similar point. She said:

> The development of a wide range of effective and acceptable methods of family planning must become universal, as well as advice on periodic abstinence and help for the infertile.

Mrs Wadia stressed that the promotion of family planning had so far met with only partial success on a global level. She reminded delegates of the findings of the World Fertility Survey that there were about 500 million women in different parts of the world who did not have knowledge of or access to family planning.

Mrs Wadia spoke of the important role the non-governmental organizations had to play. 'NGOs are part of the community and can evoke widespread voluntary participation at the grass roots level. They can instil confidence in new ideas.' IPPF, as a federation of autonomous member associations in 119 countries, 'represents a people's movement and derives its policies, purposes and strengths from its family planning associations'. She concluded her speech by saying that IPPF was 'much encouraged' by the strong support many conference delegations had demonstrated for NGOs in general, and for IPPF and its family-planning asssociations in particular. 'We have great satisfaction in acknowledging our gratitude in this form for such support.'

It is not often at United Nations conferences that a non-governmental body speaks with such authority. But, as Julia Henderson (a former senior United Nations official and former Secretary-General of IPPF) points out, the non-governmental movement has been especially important in the population field and IPPF, together with the IUSSP – the International Union for the Scientific Study of Population – and (among national, as opposed to international NGOs) the Population Council of New York, has occupied a privileged position within this movement[17]. In 1985 the International Planned Parenthood Federation received the United Nations

Population Award in recognition of its 'outstanding awareness of population questions and of its contribution to their solutions'.

Mexico City: an advance on Bucharest

In the article already cited, R. P. Kapoor concluded that the Mexico Conference was necessary to seek affirmation from the world community that whatever the other competing issues might be, population continued to be central to the development agenda of the Third World. 'Who knows that without Mexico, population matters may have lost their primacy for global action?' The history of the last few decades had shown that the world community gets bored with one subject and moves on to accord priority to new areas and subjects. In the 1950s, development planning predominately focussed on economic issues. In the 1960s, social planning was added and over the course of the 1970s, increasing attention was given to population. More recently, concern had broadened to encompass resources and the environment. The Mexico conference, Kapoor suggests, preempted a switching of priority from population. It was a 'notable success'.

An analysis of the texts adopted at Mexico, and a comparison of these texts with those agreed at Bucharest, bears out this assessment of the Conference.

Access to family planning

Of special interest were the 11 recommendations which the Conference adopted on *reproduction and the family*. Though the World Population Plan of Action had recognized the basic human right of all couples and individuals to decide freely and responsibly the number and spacing of their children, many couples and individuals had been unable to exercise that right effectively, either because they lacked access to information, education and/or services or because, although some services were available, an appropriate range of methods and follow-up services were not. Data from the World Fertility Survey for developing countries indicated that, on average, over one-fourth of births in the year prior to the survey had not been desired. The Conference therefore recommended *inter alia*:

Recommendation 25

Governments should, as a matter of urgency, make universally available information, education and the means to assist couples and individuals to achieve their desired number of children. Family planning information, education and means should include all medically approved and appropriate methods of family planning, including natural family planning, to ensure a voluntary and free choice in accordance with changing individual and cultural values. Particular attention should be given to those segments of the population which are most vulnerable and difficult to reach.

This emphasis was also reflected in the Declaration on Population and Development which was adopted by acclamation at the 12th (closing) plenary meeting on 14 August 1984. Paragraph 13 of that Declaration read:

Although considerable progress has been made since Bucharest, millions of people still lack access to safe and effective family planning methods. By the year 2000 some 1.6 billion women will be of child bearing age, 1.3 billion of them in developing countries. Major efforts must be made now to ensure that all couples and individuals can exercise the basic human right to decide freely, responsibly and without coercion, the number and spacing of their children and to have the information, education and means to do so. In exercising this right, the best interests of their living and future children as well as the responsibility towards the community should be taken into account.

Status of Women

Another area where Mexico represented a net advance on Bucharest was in the treatment it gave to the status and role of women. The Conference recalled that the World Population Plan of Action as well as other important international instruments – in particular the 1975 Mexico City Plan of Action, the 1980 Copenhagen programme of action for the United Nations Decade for Women and the Convention on the Elimination of all Forms of Discrimination Against Women – stressed the urgency of achieving the full integration of women in society on an equal basis with man and of abolishing any form of discrimination against women. Comprehensive strategies to address these concerns would be formulated at the 1985 Nairobi Conference which was being convened to review and appraise the achievements of the United Nations Decade for Women.

The Conference observed that the ability of women to control their own fertility formed an important basis for the enjoyment of other rights; likewise, the assurance of socio–economic opportunities on an equal basis with men and the provision of the necessary services and facilities enabled women to take greater responsibility for their reproductive lives. The

Conference therefore made several recommendations aimed at ensuring that women could effectively exercise rights equal to those of men and in all spheres of economic, social, cultural and political life, and in particular those rights which pertained most directly to population concerns.

These recommendations, too, were reflected in the Mexico City Declaration on Population and Development which stated:

> Improving the status of women and enhancing their role is an important goal in itself and will also influence family life and size in a positive way. Community support is essential to bring about the full integration and participation of women into all phases and functions of the development process. Institutional, economic and cultural barriers must be removed and broad and swift action taken to assist women in attaining full equality with men in the social, political and economic life of their communities. To achieve this goal, it is necessary for men and women to share jointly responsibilities in areas such as family life, child-caring and family planning. Governments should formulate and implement concrete policies which would enhance the status and role of women.

Strengthening international co-operation

It would have been ironic, to say the least, if the Mexico City Conference had produced a less ringing endorsement of the need for international co-operation in the population field than had been the case at Bucharest ten years earlier. Yet, as the Conference opened, there seemed a real risk that this might indeed prove to be the situation. The United States had after all for almost 20 years been the leading proponent of international population assistance. Now it was precisely the United States which appeared to have the gravest doubts about the wisdom of such activities. Had that country's delegation pressed its new-found philosophy to a logical conclusion, tabling dozens of amendments as Argentina had done at Bucharest, a worthwhile consensus – certainly a consensus that represented an advance on Bucharest – would probably have been impossible to achieve. So the last state would have been worse than the first.

In the event, wiser counsels prevailed. The Recommendations for the further implementation of the World Population Plan of Action contained a substantial section on the role of international co-operation (Recommendations 79 to 87). Governments, for example, were urged to '*increase their level of assistance for population activities*'; the '*international community should play an important role; organs, organizations and bodies of the United Nations system and donor countries... are urged to assist governments at their request*'; the importance of non-governmental organizations and activities was stressed. In all this, the co-ordinating and catalytic role of UNFPA in particular was firmly recognized. Whereas the recommendations of Bucharest were somewhat hesitant in recognizing the place of UNFPA in the population field, the delegates at Mexico knew no such inhibitions. Recommendation 83 stated unambiguously:

> *In view of the leading role of the United Nations Fund for Population Activities in population matters, the Conference urges that the Fund should be strengthened further, so as to ensure the more effective delivery of population assistance, taking into account the growing needs in this field. The Secretary-General of the United Nations is invited to examine this Recommendation, and submit a report to the General Assembly on its implementation as soon as possible but not later than 1986.*

When the United Nations General Assembly came to deal with the results of the Mexico Conference at its 39th session, the importance of international co-operation and of the role of UNFPA was confirmed. The General Assembly Resolution adopted on 10 December 1984:

> Emphasises that international cooperation in the field of population is essential for the implementation of recommendations adopted at the Conference, and in that context calls upon the international community to provide adequate and substantial international support and assistance for population activities, particularly through the United Nations Fund for Population Activities, in order to ensure more effective delivery of population assistance in the light of growing needs in the field and the increasing efforts being made by developing countries.

One practical consequence of Recommendation 73 of the Bucharest Conference and of the General Assembly Resolution of December 1984 was that in June 1986 the Governing Council of the UNDP passed a resolution which among other things:

> urged the Executive Director to increase the attention given to countries of the Sub-Saharan Africa region in the light of the General Assembly's Special Session on the Critical Economic Situation in Africa, held in early 1986;

> requested the Executive Director to strengthen the capacity of the Fund to deal with the issues of women in development;

> endorsed the Fund's efforts to achieve effective evaluations, both internal and independent of United Nations population activities.

The Governing Council of the UNDP also decided in the same resolution, to review at its 1987 organizational session the number of sessions to be allocated to UNFPA in the course of Governing Council meetings, the object being to provide adequate time for consideration of UNFPA items.

It could be argued therefore that by 1986 the process of institution-building which has been one of the underlying themes of this account (the strengthening of institutions being inseparable from an expansion of international population activities) was virtually complete. In 1969 the

UNA–USA Panel had called for the Fund to be governed by a Special Population Committee of the UNDP Governing Council. In a sense the solution finally arrived at was an improvement on the UNA Panel's recommendation. Today, when the UNDP Governing Council considers population matters, it meets in a plenipotentiary manner as a Governing Council, not as a committee of the Council. But it meets for that part of its agenda as the *Governing Council of the Fund*. One set of hats is taken off; another set of hats is put on. Thus it has, eventually, been possible to square the circle. UNFPA in practice now exists as a fully fledged independent intergovernmental agency with an annual budget far larger than many other agencies operating in the UN system. Yet at the same time, because the Fund's governing body is one and the same as UNDP's governing body, it remains totally integrated into the United Nations development system. To attempt to break this link with UNDP, now or in the future, would be to render both the Fund and the United Nations development efforts a grave disservice.

The Mexico City Declaration on Population and Development

At the 12th and last plenary meeting on 14 August 1984, the draft text of a 'Mexico City Declaration on Population and Development', which had been prepared by a 12-nation Friends of the President group, was adopted by acclamation. It was a short document, some 23 paragraphs in all, intended to serve both as inspiration and guidance to those who would have to put into effect the recommendations for the further implementation of the World Population Plan of Action. The last five paragraphs of the declaration were as follows:

19. As the years since 1974 have shown, the political commitment of Heads of State and other leaders and the willingness of Governments to take the lead in formulating population programmes and allocating the necessary resources are crucial for the further implementation of the World Population Plan of Action. Governments should attach high priority to the attainment of self-reliance in the management of such programmes, strengthen their administrative and managerial capabilities, and ensure co-ordination of international assistance at the national level.

20. The years since Bucharest have also known that international co-operation in the field of population is essential for the implementation of recommendations agreed upon by the international community and can be notably successful. The need for increased resources for population activities is emphasised. Adequate and substantial international support and assistance will greatly facilitate the efforts of governments. It should be provided whole-

heartedly and in the spirit of universal solidarity and enlightened self-interest. The United Nations family should continue to perform its vital responsibilities.

21. Non-governmental organizations have a continuing important role in the implementation of the World Population Plan of Action and deserve encouragement and support from Governments and international organizations. Members of Parliament, community leaders, scientists, the media and others in influential positions are called upon to assist in all aspects of population and development work.

22. At Bucharest, the world was made aware of the gravity and magnitude of the population problems and their close inter-relationship with economic and social development. The message of Mexico City is forge ahead with effective implementation of the World Population Plan of Action aimed at improving standards of living, and the quality of life for all peoples of this planet in promotion of their common destiny and peace and security.

23. IN ISSUING THIS DECLARATION, ALL PARTICIPANTS AT THE INTERNATIONAL CONFERENCE ON POPULATION REITERATE THEIR COMMITMENT AND REDEDICATE THEMSELVES TO THE FURTHER IMPLEMENTATION OF THE PLAN.

Looking back at the Mexico Conference

Looking back at the Mexico City Conference a few months later, Rafael Salas described it as 'one of the shortest, one of the most economical and one of the best attended, among recent United Nations Conferences'. The results of the Conference provided 'definitive guidelines for population policies and programmes to be undertaken by governments and the international community in the next decade'.

There were 147 delegates at the Conference (including Namibia), as compared with 136 countries represented at Bucharest. The number of official participants exceeded 1000, including more than 200 women. 22 delegations were headed by women. All UN agencies and organizations concerned with population were represented, as well as 154 non-governmental organizations with 367 representatives. Sixteen NGOs were given their opportunity to speak at the plenary sessions. Forty-one papers prepared by NGOs were distributed as background documents.

No separate secretariat was established for the Conference. The responsibility for substantive preparations was assigned to the Population Division of the Department of International Economic and Social Affairs, which worked in close co-operation with UNFPA and DTCD. The preparatory meetings as well as the Conference itself were serviced by existing units and organizations in the United Nations system. The total amount budgeted for the Conference was approximately US $2.3 million ($1.5 million from extra budgetary sources, with up to US $800,000 from the regular budget.) In fact, conference expenditures remained well within the budget established.

Mr Salas concluded his review of the Mexico City Conference by writing:

> The task before us now is to sustain the momentum generated by the Conference. This will require a concerted effort by national governments to implement the recommendations of the Conference, in the framework of their own national needs and requirements; and a redoubled effort by the international community to keep population developments and issues in focus and to provide increasing support for population activities.

Salas's article appeared towards the end of 1984. In September 1985, the Administrator of USAID announced that the United States Government would not pay US $10 million of its pledged contribution of US $46 million to the UNFPA because of the alleged participation of UNFPA in the 'management' of the China Population Programme which in its judgement included coercive abortions. The Administrator of the USAID laid down conditions for its 1986 contribution: a drastic change in China's population policies or the reduction of UNFPAs multi-sector assistance to China so as to limit it solely to the supply of contraceptives. In the judgement of the management of the Fund, both of these conditions were difficult for UNFPA to fulfil because of the principle of the national sovereignty which it observed strictly, and because of UNFPA's inability to alter unilaterally agreements which had been previously approved by its Governing Council.

Salas recognized that a total United States withdrawal of its 1986 contribution would mean a 25 per cent reduction of UNFPA assistance to the 134 developing countries. However, it would not stop UNFPA from operating. Including increases from pledges, the organization could still operate with a budget of about US $120 million in 1986. But such withdrawal was certain to disrupt current programmes, diminish the Fund's ability to support new and needed projects and stall the momentum generated by UNFPA in developing countries.

Thus, at the time this book was being written, a question mark still hung over the Mexico City Conference. Should it be seen as the consolidation of the Bucharest consensus, setting the stage for new commitments by developing countries and by the international community? Or should it in the end by registered as a setback, if only because in Mexico the major supporter of international population programmes, certainly the major supporter of United Nations efforts in this field, was seen to waver in its dedication to these goals?

Table 10.1. Population assistance by major donors (1971–81)

	1971	1972	1973	1974	1975	1976	1977	1978	1979	1980	1981	Avg. annual growth rate
Governments: Official Development Assistance for Population												
Australia	–	357	579	659	711	680	1,591	2,815	3,150	2,532	3,340	26.2
Belgium	147	18	75	667	772	965	1,773	2,252	1,868	923	761	33.5
Canada	3,140	3,846	5,817	7,879	9,169	12,198	13,951	15,958	15,076	13,298	14,023	15.6
Denmark	1,801	2,248	3,155	3,392	3,561	5,061	5,924	7,722	9,306	11,662	8,546	18.0
Finland	512	900	1,126	2,623	2,079	1,587	1,918	648	969	1,676	3,142	7.5
Germany, Fed. Republic of	1,657	2,435	4,392	5,770	9,906	8,789	14,421	14,653	36,284	21,366	22,537	27.6
Italy	–	–	–	100	–	–	–	–	–	126	1,006	n.a.
Japan[a]	2,090	2,196	2,812	5,293	7,289	9,908	11,843	15,744	21,883	26,419	33,449	29.7
Netherlands	1,000	2,736	4,001	6,041	7,205	8,119	8,919	12,083	13,774	15,343	13,186	22.8
New Zealand	22	24	270	578	831	591	591	627	611	589	501	27.9
Norway[a]	3,870	5,539	8,600	10,800	13,678	21,789	20,914	32,760	32,703	34,356	32,388	22.3
Sweden[a]	7,446	12,739	17,123	21,468	26,652	32,272	35,764	31,829	34,209	35,814	30,685	13.1
Switzerland	168	191	189	190	200	242	500	1,149	1,506	1,841	1,408	27.7
United Kingdom	2,311	3,257	3,861	3,032	6,756	7,270	10,866	14,104	19,490	17,653	13,127	21.7
United States[b]	109,567	121,133	115,106	110,146	106,036	119,027	145,367	165,618	173,255	168,519	193,457	5.9
Others	1,283	1,592	1,747	2,325	3,580	11,356	3,918	2,562	1,696	2,214	2,370	4.2
ODA Subtotal	135,014	159,211	168,853	180,963	198,485	239,854	278,260	320,524	365,778	354,326	373,926	11.0
World Bank[c]	1,600	5,700	10,990	14,840	20,340	25,940	27,730	31,380	59,100	80,340	77,260	33.5
Major private donors												
Ford Foundation	21,261	16,864	15,149	14,791	10,586	11,315	10,352	10,366	7,993	7,819	7,592	–9.9
Rockefeller Foundation	5,981	6,846	6,346	3,803	4,194	3,797	3,120	3,253	3,549	3,573	4,885	–4.4
Other	5,308	–	7,904	36,894	45,050	22,339	28,716	25,771	14,828	29,854	27,442	3.8

Total excluding double-counting:[d]

A. in current US dollars	169,164	186,851	209,242	251,291	278,655	303,245	348,178	391,294	451,246	475,912	491,105	11.3
B. in constant 1970 US dollars	162,190	173,492	182,904	197,867	201,050	206,852	222,905	232,913	241,308	224,275	209,784	3.2

Sources: UNFPA Report on Population Assistance, 1981, Table 1, New York, 1983, and Population Reports J-26, Johns Hopkins University, Baltimore, 1983.

Notes: All figures refer to the calendar year. Any changes in data of earlier years reflect revisions to the original data.

[a] Official estimates for Norway, for Sweden from 1975 and for Japan from 1980 include a one-fifth share of assistance to maternal and child health programmes provided through the UNICEF programme.

[b] Data are expenditures with some exceptions. While the data for USAID from 1978 are expenditures, annual estimates prior to 1978 are commitments.

[c] All World Bank data are UNFPA estimates based on commitments according to loan or to credit agreements and the planned duration of project execution.

[d] The totals, exclusive of double-counting, were arrived at by summing up the project expenditures recorded in Table 2 in the Source.

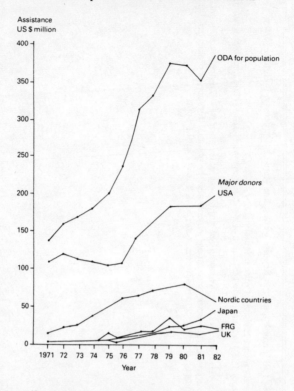

Figure 10.1. Official development assistance for population (DAC).

Source: Sources of Population and Family-Planning Assistance, Population Reports J-26, 1-2/83, Population Information Program, Johns Hopkins University, Baltimore, MD, 1983, published in World Bank staff working paper No. 688.

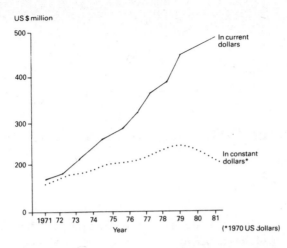

Figure 10.2. *Population assistance (1971–81) in current and constant dollars (expenditures).*

Source: UNFPA Report on Population Assistance, 1981, New York, 1983. Published in World Bank staff working paper No. 688.

11

China, the United States and the United Nations

In December 1986, when much of the work on this book had already been completed, I had the chance to visit China to discuss population issues with a number of interested parties and from various perspectives.

In the context of an account of the United Nations' involvement in population questions, this Chinese mission was important for at least three reasons.

There was, in the first place, and as an immediate and pressing problem, the continuing dispute between the United States and the United Nations Fund for Population Activities over UNFPA's involvement with China's family-planning programme. One effect of this dispute was to throw into question the continued support of the international community for multilateral population activities, particularly those conducted through the United Nations.

The second question had to do with the demographic situation in China itself. What precisely was happening to the birth-rate in that vast country? What were the projections for the future? Was the family-planning programme on target? Given the importance of China from the point of view of the world demographic perspective, a clear understanding of Chinese realities was essential if there was to be an informed judgement about the progress being made towards the ultimate stabilization of the world's population.

The third of these interrelated questions had to do with the extent to which the Chinese experience in reducing birth-rates could be repeated in other countries. Had the Chinese found, at least, the magic formula (like the ingredients of Coca Cola) for organizing successful family-planning activities on a vast scale – a formula born out of their 6000-year old history and their instinctive genius for social organization? If so, could that formula be transplanted elsewhere with equal effect?

In the course of my Chinese trip I visited several of the main population centres outside Beijing, including Xian, Chongking, Wuhan and Guangzhou (Canton). I also had the chance to undertake an extended journey through Sichuan and Hubei provinces, some of the most densely populated regions in the world (Sichuan itself has a population of over 100 million people). This journey in December 1986 complemented an earlier trip I had made to China in the summer of 1975. On that occasion I visited Beijing, Shenyang, Tsinan, Wuxi, Shanghai and Guangzhou. Though Mao Tse Dong was still alive at the time, the Gang of Four was in effective control. Amid the turmoil of the 'Cultural Revolution', most orderly economic and social planning had been thrown out of the window, including of course China's population policy and family-planning programmes. Eleven years later, it was quite another story.

The dispute between China, the United States and the United Nations over the Chinese family-planning programme

At the time of writing, the facts on the UNFPA dispute can be briefly stated. In 1985, the US Administration withheld US $10 million from its contribution to UNFPA, the sum being equivalent to UNFPA annual spending to China. At that time USAID cited 'evidence ... that UNFPA participates in the management of the China family planning programme and also that the implementation of China's one-child-per-family policy has resulted in abuses' such as forced abortion and sterilization.[1] Reacting to the United States' decision, China vigorously defended its policy and programme. For example, in the remarks before the Second Committee of the 40th Session of the United Nations General Assembly, the Chinese representative Li Luye criticized the United States, without mentioning that country by name, for distorting China's population policy and interfering with China's internal affairs.

> This policy is in the interest of the Chinese people and is also in conformity with the plan of action, declarations and recommendations adopted by the two World Population Conferences held in 1974 and 1984 respectively.[2]

An attempt by the Population Council and others to block USAID's 'reprogramming' of the funds withdrawn from UNFPA failed when a US Court of Appeals ruled in December 1985 that the Administrator of USAID, Mr Peter McPherson, could allocate the money that had been earmarked for UNFPA to voluntary family-planning programmes run by

Ecuador, Jamaica, Kenya, Nepal and Tunisia and to similar programmes run abroad by five private US groups.

On 27 August, 1986, USAID announced that the US Government would not contribute the $25 million it had budgeted for UNFPA in 1986, the reason given being the same as that used when the US withheld payment of the $10 million out of the $46 million pledged to UNFPA in 1985, namely that UNFPA was supporting or participating 'in the management of a programme of coercive abortion or involuntary sterilization in China'.

The *New York Times* commented on 29 August, 1986, that the USAID decision followed 'months of lobbying by anti-abortion activists who say the United Nations group supports a programme of coerced abortion in China'. The report recalled a measure passed by the United States Congress in 1985 which banned all Federal aid for groups that 'support or participate in the management of a programme or coercive abortion or involuntary sterilization'.

The *International Herald Tribune* on 10 September, 1986, reprinted an editorial from the *Washington Post* which began with the damning indictment

> The United States is no longer part of the great international effort to aid population planning ... without the American contribution, this important and effective international programme, whose mission is so critical in the world's poorest nations, will be crippled and perhaps permanently damaged. This is misguided policy at its worst.

In his own speech to the Second Committee, at the Forty-First Session of the United Nations General Assembly, delivered in New York on 18 November, 1986, Mr Rafael M. Salas, UNFPA's Executive Director, stated that there was absolutely no truth in the allegation that UNFPA was supporting or participating in the management of a programme of coercive abortion or involuntary sterilization in China and no evidence had to date been produced by USAID to prove its claim.

> As we have stated on many previous occasions, UNFPA does not support abortion or coercion in any country, including China – a statement which has been confirmed by USAID itself in the reviews of UNFPA's assistance to China in April 1984 and March 1985.

Salas recalled that the support UNFPA had provided to China was approved by the UNDP/UNFPA Governing Council (of which the United States was a Member) by consensus in June 1980 and once again in June 1984. Opportunities for reviewing this programme were available at the meeting of the Governing Council in June 1985 and again in June 1986.

'At neither of these meetings did the United States raise any questions concerning the China programme'.

If Salas' response to the action of the United States government was forthright and unequivocal, so too was China's. The Chinese delegate to the Forty-First Session of the United Nations General Assembly indicated (before the Second Committee) that China would not change its population policy despite US criticism of it.

China's population policy has achieved tremendous success and has been set down in our constitution. The Chinese delegation cannot but regrettably point out that a particular country, out of its needs in domestic politics, has four years running attacked our population policy, interfered in our domestic affairs and attempted to change the mandate and direction of UNFPA.

Mr Bai went on to say that China appreciated the role the UNFPA played in seeking solutions to the world's population problems.

China will work to contribute its share to the stabilization of the world's population. Population is not a sole problem for China but a problem of global dimension[3].

As far as further US contributions to United Nations population activities are concerned, Mr Peter McPherson, Administrator of USAID, indicated in a letter to Mr Salas dated 10 November, 1986, that the United States Government would

be able to consider funding UNFPA in 1987 and subsequent years only if there are significant changes in either UNFPA's 1987–1989 programme in the People's Republic of China or in the Chinese population programme, which would permit the US Government to conclude that UNFPA does not support or participate in the management of coercive abortion or involuntary sterilization.

What in concrete terms has been the impact of the United States' action on the funding available to UNFPA? UNFPA's income from governmental contributions in 1985 (including the partial United States contribution) was approximately $135.9 millions resulting in a total income for the year, including interest income, of $142.9 million. Pledged income for 1986 amounted to $129 million and total anticipated income for 1986, including interest, to $133.5 million. It is worth noting that, in the absence of the United States, Japan has stepped clearly into the lead among donor nations with a pledge of $33.9 million for 1986. The Netherlands which had contributed $9.6 million in 1985, pledged an extra $5 million for 1986 bringing its total to $14.7 million, the additional resources being voted with the explicit objective of helping to cover the shortfall left by the withdrawal of US support. Other major donors pledging for 1986 included the Federal Republic of Germany – $17.6

million, Norway – $14.0 million, Sweden – $9.3 million, Canada – $18.2 million, Denmark – $7.3 million, the United Kingdom – $6.6 million, Switzerland – $3.4 million, Finland – $2.8 million and Italy – $1.96 million. It can be seen, therefore, that, at least as far as 1986 is concerned, the Fund's operations have not been seriously disrupted.

Following the annual United Nations pledging conference held in New York in November 1986, pledges to UNFPA from 74 countries, both developed and developing, amounted to nearly $140 million[4]. The United States, traditionally the largest donor, made no pledge. China, somewhat ironically in view of the circumstances, pledged $500,000 to UNFPA, an increase of $50,000 on its 1985 contribution. Overall, it seems likely that for the immediate future, United Nations population activities could continue at their present levels or even experience some modest growth – in itself a fairly remarkable testimony on the part of the international community to the importance of this particular programme.

The longer-term effect, however, of the 'China problem' on United Nation's population activities could be severe. Though other nations, such as Japan, the Scandinavian bloc and certain western European countries may, for the time being, make increased contributions to make good the shortfall, it is not certain that their efforts will continue at this level without the assurance that the United States, that powerful erstwhile champion of multilateral population activities, will once again pick up the hand which it has now laid decisively on the table.

The World Bank may, of course, make good some of the deficit through increased lending. But there are constraints on World Bank activity (for example, the need to keep a balance between IBRD loans and IDA credits) which do not affect the United Nations. Nor is it to be expected that the World Bank will for ever be immune to the climate of political opinion in the United States on population, as on other issues.

The new President of the World Bank, former Congressmen Barber H. Conable, spoke in forthright terms on 30 September, 1986 at the joint annual meeting of the Bank and the International Monetary Fund held in Washington about the need to 'reflect new attention to the role of population'. Realistically, however, the United States remains the World Bank's largest shareholder, and provides the largest share of the regular 'replenishments' of the Bank's soft-loan affiliate, the International Development Association. It is not likely that the US Executive Director would readily agree to a situation in which the Bank simply picked up that part of the multilateral population load which UNFPA had been forced to shed, unless there was a radical change in the political situation in Washington (with the anti-abortion lobbies, and the right-to-life-groups being effectively sidelined). But if there were such a change, the need for a shift of emphasis as between the United Nations and the Bank, the two main sources of multilateral population lending, would be less obvious.

The present crisis is not of course limited to UNFPA. The US has also withdrawn its support completely from the International Planned Parenthood Federation and that pioneer organization, which in so many respects acted as a pathfinder in the field of population and family planning for the other international bodies, has had to undertake some severe retrenchment and regrouping. IPPF supporters – and they are to be found in considerable numbers on all five continents – fervently hope that it is a question of 'reculer pour mieux sauter'. But for the 'private sector' of international population assistance, as for the official or governmental sector, the outcome of the present dispute is by no means clear. A cutback in IPPF assistance to areas of the world such as Africa and Latin America will be all the more serious in that it is precisely there that the 'comparative advantage' of private sector activities, preparing the ground for programme activities of a public character, is most clearly to be seen.

The real facts in the US–China dispute

What are the real facts in the US–China dispute over population and family planning? Do the US charges have any basis in reality?

It seems sensible to split the indictment into its two component parts. First, does UNFPA 'support, or participate in, the management' of China's population and family planning programme? Secondly, is that programme itself coercive?

As far as the first question is concerned, the realistic answer must be that UNFPA does not participate in the 'management' of the Chinese programme in any accepted sense of the word. Total Chinese allocations for family planning are around US $1 billion annually. China has some 200,000 full-time family planning workers, and perhaps 20 times that number working in a volunteer capacity. UNFPA support to China was at $10 million a year and the Fund's staff within the country number no more than a handful.

Overall, the first cycle programme of UNFPA in China (1980–4) allocated $50 million, more than a quarter of the funds going to support China's first modern census. Another $50 million was approved for the second cycle (1985–9), with the emphasis being shifted to:

contraceptive production

China produces all the contraceptives needed in the country, but UNFPA has assisted in buying factory equipment to produce enough contraceptive pills for 12.5 million women per year and injectibles for 2.5 million women. Two IUD factories assisted by UNFPA can annually produce 5.5 million copper-Ts and three plants produce more than 550 million condoms. The UNFPA is also helping to improve quality control of Chinese contraceptives and improving the distribution of contraceptives.

communication and education

UNFPA has assisted in setting up one national family-planning information centre, two regional and eight provincial level centres. Audio-visual equipment as well as training has been included in the programme.

training in population management

UNFPA provides assistance to the training of family-planning administrators at a national school in Nanjing and another school for family-planning professionals in Chengdu. In addition, training programmes both locally and abroad are provided to family-planning personnel.

demographic training and research

The 1982 Census generated voluminous data on China's population. To help analyse the data, UNFPA is assisting 22 population research institutes in as many universities. In addition, eight institutes under the China Academy for Social Sciences are being assisted. At least 20 fellowships for long-term studies abroad are provided by UNFPA for faculty members from key universities each year. Short-term training and mid-career fellowships are also provided.

family planning research

China has taken a leading role in developing contraceptives and UNFPA is assisting research institutes in Beijing, Tianjin, Guangzhou and Chengdu with the technical guidance of the World Health Organization (WHO). Improvements of existing contraceptives and development of new ones is going on in all these centres. Promising family-planning techniques, chemical contraceptives, reversible sterilization and immunization are being pursued. UNFPA has provided advanced research equipment for these centres, offered training opportunities abroad, and facilitated the exchange of scientific information with other researchers in other parts of the world.

basic data collection and dissemination

Although the bulk of China's census work has been done, UNFPA continues to assist in the analysis of census results as well as the printing and dissemination of population reports.

material and child health/family planning

Under the technical guidance of WHO, UNFPA assistance is used to update provincial/municipal, country and district level maternal and perinatal health care systems in hospitals. In addition, three medical colleges receive assistance in maternal, perinatal and family-planning training.

policy research

UNFPA is assisting the State Planning Commission to strengthen integration of population into the development planning process.

UNFPA's financial allocations to China in 1985–6 are set out in Table 11.1.

This level of United Nations effort in China is important and it is welcomed by the Chinese, as they have made clear on many occasions. But it cannot by any stretch of the imagination be said to involve the Fund in a management role. To believe that, would be to believe that the tail of a very small Dachshund could wag a very large St Bernard!

But even if that were the case, what is the evidence that the Chinese programme is coercive?

Chapter 47 of the Seventh Five-year Plan (1986–90) which was presented to the Fourth Session of the Sixth National People's Congress by the Premier of the State Council, Zhao Ziyang, on 25 March, 1986, consists of two short sentences under the heading: Population.

At the end of 1990 China's total population should not exceed 1.113 billion. We shall continue to attach great importance to family planning and make every effort to ensure its success.

The longer term target is to keep the population within 1,200 million by the year 2000, thereby permitting per capita gross value of industrial and agricultural production to increase from 719.6 yuan* in 1980 to 2,333.3 yuan in 2000.[5]

*At the official exchange rate there were about 4 yuan to one US dollar (end 1986)

Table 11.1. *UNFPA financial allocations to China in 1985-6*

Programmable areas	1985	1986
Contraceptive production[a]	1,509,354	3,210,385
Communication and education	2,604,148	2,043,502
Training in population management	1,292,060	721,288
Demographic training and research	1,201,112	1,070,338
Family-planning research[a]	1,141,591	750,000
Basic data collection/dissemination	893,812	618,260
MCH/FP[a]	1,713,688	919,396
Policy research	168,528	186,283
	10,524,293	9,519,452

Note: [a] UNFPA funding directly related to family planning, including maternal and child health in China amounted to $4,364,633 in 1985 (41.4 per cent). In 1986, the proportion of funds for Family Planning and MCH went up to 51.2 per cent ($4,879,781).

Source: UNFPA.

The Twelfth National Congress of the Communist Party of China which convened in September 1982 took the implementation of family planning as a basic policy of the State. Article 25 of the Constitution of the People's Republic of China stipulates that 'The State promotes family planning so that population growth may fit the plan for economic and social development'.

Presumably, not even the most ardent opponents of China's policies would argue that the adoption of the population targets quoted above is of itself coercive (unless of course they question the very legitimacy of the institutions under which these measures were endorsed). The case that 'coercion' is being used in China seems therefore to relate to the instruments which have been put in place with a view to ensuring that the overall policy objectives are achieved. Here a close look at the realities of the situation is in order.

What are the instruments? They are essentially:

— late marriage and late childbirth;
— having fewer babies;
— having healthy babies.

Late marriage and late childbirth

In 1950, the Chinese Government issued the first section of the Marriage Law, abolishing the feudalistic arranged marriage and implementing free choice of partner, monogamy, equal rights for both sexes, and protection of the lawful rights and interests of women and children. A marriage could be contracted only after the man had reached 20 years of age and the woman 18 years of age. In 1981, the Chinese government issued a new Marriage Law which, amongst other things, stated that husband and wife are duty bound to practise family planning, while raising the legal marrying age from 20 to 22 for men and from 18 to 20 for women.[6] Today, the average age for women's first marriage has gone up from 19 years in the late 1950s to more than 22 years in the late 1970s.

In advocating reasonable late marriage and late childbirth, the government was certainly aware of the significant role these measures could play in cutting birth peaks and reducing population growth (by widening the gap between generations), but these provisions could hardly be labelled coercive for that reason. Indeed, the way in which women's rights and women's opportunities have been increased in China since 1949, the determination with which feudal practices have been stamped out (foot-binding is just the striking tip of this iceberg), represent one of the most significant expansions in the freedom of choice of a large section of the population (in this case no less than 'half of heaven' to use that ancient Chinese proverb) that any nation has ever achieved. Most societies have sumptuary laws of one kind or another. The object of such laws, like most other laws, is either to prevent people from doing what they want to do (e.g. having sexual intercourse with minors) or to encourage them to do things which they may not want to do (like practising family planning). If this is coercion, then coercion is inevitable wherever laws are made and enforced.

Having fewer babies

As described elsewhere in this book, China has advocated 'one couple, one child' since 1979 in order to keep within the target of 1.2 billion people by the end of the century. Though this policy has been adopted at

Table 11.2. *Population and family-planning statistics in China*

Year	Number of first-born births (M)		Number of second-born births (M)		Number of third-born births (at and above) (M)		Total
1980	7.47	41.8%	4.75	26.6%	5.65	31.6%	17.87
1981	9.67	46.5%	5.27	25.4%	5.84	28.1%	20.78
1982	10.97	51.6%	5.15	27.1%	5.14	24.2%	21.26
1983	10.71	56.4%	4.66	24.6%	3.63	19.1%	19.00
1984	10.00	55.6%	4.51	25.0%	3.51	19.5%	19.02

Source: State Family Planning Commission, People's Republic of China

this specific period in Chinese history, it is not something which will necessarily endure unchanged for a prolonged period. Second, though the concept 'one couple, one child' is central to the family-planning effort, there may be variations on the theme. In carrying out the family-planning programme, the government sets different requirements and offers specific guidance to people of various localities with different economic and cultural background and population structure. The requirements are more flexible in rural areas than in urban areas (and China is still 80 per cent rural, though much depends on the definitions used for the terms 'urban' and 'rural') and more so among the people of national minorities (for example, the Zhuang, Hui, Uygur, Yi, Miao, Manchu, Tibetan, Mongolian groups) than among people of the Han nationality who at the last census accounted for 93.3 per cent of the total population. According to official policy statements:

> Those couples with actual difficulties and wishing to have two children in the rural areas may give birth to a second child with planned spacing. Married couples who are both single children themselves in the urban and rural areas may have two children if they wish.[7]

This last provision is designed to deal with the problem where a single grandchild finds that he or she has to look after two sets of grandparents. Table 11.2 shows the distribution of births in recent years.

Throughout my time in China, I in no way gained the impression that the policy of one couple, one child has been imposed coercively on the Chinese people. Indeed, since the target population, i.e. those of child-bearing age, is some 520 million, it is hard to imagine how any policy based on coercion could be effective. (It is estimated that so far about 70 per cent of married couples of a reproductive age have adopted contraceptive measures). China's family-planning policy and programme is firmly based on the 'voluntariness of the masses' to use the phrase which they themselves prefer. Wherever possible, I talked to individual Chinese men and women – in aeroplanes, trains, boats, restaurants (this is the new 'open' China) – and I found that there is a degree of public understanding of the way in which the individual's desires and behaviour relate to the common good that is unthinkable in most western societies. Perhaps this is a reflection of 6000 years of social organization in China – at the city, town, village and family level – rather than the role of the Chinese Communist party or the organs of state. Perhaps it 's an illustration of the way in which the tools of communication, information and education can be used to get a particular message across on a massive scale where the medium itself is receptive. Perhaps it has to do with the efforts that have been made to ensure that safe, effective and simple ways of contraception are available to the half-billion people who require them. Whatever the cause, to describe China's family planning programme as 'organized coercion' is about as far-fetched an accusation as I have ever heard.

Wherein, then, might coercion lie? People talk glibly about 'coercive abortion' and 'widespread female infanticide' – and of course these are headline-making phrases. But they are far from the reality.

Take abortion. China has in the full and legitimate exercise of national sovereignty legalized abortion. It is by no means the only country to have done so. Indeed, the liberalization of the laws restricting abortion has, on the whole, been one of the hallmarks of the progressive modernization of different societies. Given that abortion is legal, it is not surprising that it is used as a method of birth control in the event of an unwanted pregnancy. It is infinitely preferable that safe, clean and legal methods of abortion should be used in such cases rather than dangerous back-street practices.

It is true that the number of abortions which occurs in China each year is large. In 1984, for example, there were about 18 million births and nine million abortions. Given the degree of social organization both at home and at the workplace (as one family-planning worker explained it to me: 'we know immediately if one of the women is pregnant because they don't ask for their Tampax!'), it is likely that most of these abortions took place at an early stage of pregnancy. In any extent, I saw no evidence that abortion was being coerced or imposed. The abortions that do occur take place in the context where a particular social group has accepted a certain target level of fertility and where individuals are fully cognizant of the advantages accruing both to themselves and to the group if the target levels are achieved.

Over a period of time, and provided that the family-planning programme is maintained with a continuous momentum, the number of abortions is likely to drop. Meanwhile, the sensible thing seems to be to put this into its historical perspective. There have probably always been large numbers of abortions in China (legal or illegal), just as there are large numbers of abortions (legal or illegal) in most other countries of the world including the United States. If the 'right-to-lifers' and other pressure groups are really concerned about the problem then they should direct their efforts to ensuring that the United Nations increases rather than diminishes its population activities in China, since the antidote to abortion in all-known or imaginable situations is safe, cheap and effective family planning.

Another 'canard' is the notion that infanticide, especially female infanticide, is rampant. This particular story appears to owe its origin to a report by a researcher on the China desk at the US Bureau of the Census, who pointed out that according to the result of the manual tabulations of the 1982 census in China, the sex ratio among the newborns was 108.47 male to 100 female. This was then compared to the world norm and the conclusion drawn that there had been a loss of 232,000 baby girls in 1981 alone!

The reality is that the sex ratio of newborns varies from country to country and region to region. In 1977 the sex ratio at birth (males for each 100 females) in Malawi was 90.71, while in Iraq it was 109.62. In 1980 it was 99.76 in Luxembourg, while it was as high as 118.23 in West Samoa. It is absurd to adduce widespread infanticide as an explanation of these differences and specially absurd to do so in the context of modern China where great efforts have been made to reform archaic attitudes, including the outlawing of infanticide.[8] For example, Article 49 of the National Constitution explicitly states that 'children are protected by the State and maltreatment of old people, women and children is prohibited'. Article 15 of the Marriage Law reads 'Infanticide by drowning and any other actions causing serious harm to an infant are prohibited' (including, presumably all other forms of infanticide).

In his report on the Sixth Five-Year Plan, Premier Zhao Ziyang said:

> The whole society should resolutely condemn the criminal activities of female infanticide and maltreatment of the mothers. The judicial departments should resolutely punish the offenders according to law.

The Chinese authorities do not deny that there may have been isolated cases of infanticide, particularly in certain backward rural regions ('a few villages in the lower reaches of Huaihe River') but all those to whom I spoke left me in no doubt that this is a serious crime and should be punished as such. The notion that infanticide is promoted or condemned by the State as a method of population control is frankly not one that can be given any credence.

Modern China is what it is precisely because it has made an attempt to get away from the old vicious practices. To adopt them now (infanticide in particular) would be tantamount to a denial of the Chinese revolution and all that it stands for.

Having healthy babies

The third prong in the Chinese strategy for implementing national population policy is 'having healthy babies'. China's infant mortality rate (1981) was 34.68 per 1,000 (35.56 for males, 33.72 for females).

These are figures which can be compared with those obtaining in western industrialized countries, rather than the developing Third World. In recent years, unremitting efforts have been made to promote hospital-based midwifery. In fact about 92.7 per cent of women at delivery are assisted by trained midwives. Not only has the infant mortality rate declined; so too has the maternal mortality rate – to 0.5 per thousand in 1982.

Overall, the mortality rate has declined drastically since 1949, when it stood at around 25 per thousand. In 1952, according to surveys in selected regions, the average mortality rate dropped to 17 per thousand. In 1965 it fell to 9.6 per thousand and in 1981 it further declined to 6.36 per thousand.

The life expectancy has also grown. In 'old China', the average life-span was 35 years. In 1967, it rose to 59, and in 1980 it reached 69, nearly double the life expectancy of pre-Liberation times.

We are talking in short of a revolution in health care – a revolution which has not only been good in its own context (good health being of absolute value) but which has also contributed dramatically towards improving the climate in which successful family-planning programmes can take place.

Chapter 50 of the Seventh Five-Year Plan sets out China's objectives in the field of public health:

1. We shall continue to promote preventive medicine and health education. By 1990 safe drinking water will be available for 80 per cent of the rural population and over 85 per cent of the total population will have received inoculations against major diseases.

2. We shall build more key hospitals. During the period of the Plan we shall increase the number of hospital beds by 400,000. The State will allocate funds to build 16 general hospitals, each specializing in one or more branches of medicine, and two modern hospitals with advanced equipment and techniques.

3. We shall develop traditional Chinese medicine, especially by establishing centres for research in Chinese pharmacology. We shall increase the number of institutions, hospitals and hospital beds for traditional Chinese medicine, so that most cities and counties will have a hospital or clinic where it is practised.

4. We shall train more professional health workers. During the period of the Plan, their number will increase by 770,000 of which 560,000 will be doctors trained in both traditional Chinese and Western medicine.

5. We shall step up medical research, concentrating on key projects for the study of the cause, prevention and treatment of common illnesses.

6. We shall establish a state system of food and drug administration.

As noted earlier, UNFPA is contributing in a modest way to these improvements in the health services (see Table 11.1). And other international organizations, such as the World Health Organization and the World Bank, are even more directly involved. No one to my knowledge has yet suggested that these basic health activities have a coercive character, though they certainly make an important contribution to China's ability to achieve its population goals.

What will be the eventual outcome of the continuing dispute between the United States and UNFPA over China's population policy? Though the present US Ambassador to China, Mr Winston Lord, is reputed to believe that this is an issue which has been blown up out of proportion, and that the United States has other far more important business to do with China, the informed opinions of foreign service diplomats reporting from the field do not always, or necessarily, prevail in Washington (Senator Jesse Helms, now the minority leader on the Senate's powerful Foreign Relations Committee, originally opposed the nomination of Mr Lord to China asserting that Mr Lord had not taken a sufficiently vigorous stand against China's birth control policies).

But there are other straws in the wind. Shortly before my own visit to China at the end of 1986, a US Congressional delegation visited the country, invited by China's People's Congress. Members of the delegation discussed environmental as well as demographic issues and some of them, it is said, expressed considerable interest in China's reliable rocket launchers as a possible means of boosting America's satellites into space. Out of such strange juxtapositions, major policy 'voltefaces' have been known to occur.

Nor can one ignore the impact of recent events, such as the change in the composition of the US Congress following the November 1986 elections and the difficulties faced by President Reagan's Administration over the 'arms for Iran' affair.

But is is far too early to say that this particular problem will quickly disappear. As Rafael Salas wrote in an article published in the *New York Times* on 13 December, 1986.

The United States' vision and support helped launch the United Nations population assistance programme 17 years ago. Some of today's controversies will fade, but the need for global efforts to address population problems will never be more urgent or more timely. Population programmes can be made more effective with full participation by the United States.

Table 11.3. *Population of China (1984)*

Region	Population	Region	Population	Region	Population
Beijing	9,230,687	Anhui	49,665,724	Yunnan	32,553,817
Tianjin	7,764,141	Fujian[a]	25,931,106	Tibet	1,892,393
Hebei	53,005,875	Jiangxi	33,184,827	Shaanxi	28,904,423
Shanxi	25,291,389	Shandong	74,419,054	Gansu	19,569,261
Inner Mongolia	19,274,279	Henan	74,422,739	Qinghai	3,895,706
Liaoning	35,721,693	Hubei	47,804,150	Ningxia	3,895,578
Jilin	22,560,053	Hunan	54,008,851	Xinjiang	13,081,681
Heilongjiang	32,665,546	Guangdong[b]	59,299,220	Taiwan	18,270,749
Shanghai	11,859,748	Guangxi	36,420,960	Hongkong	
Jiangsu	60,521,114	Sichuan	99,713,310	and Macao	5,378,627
Zhejiang	38,884,603	Guizhou	28,552,997	Servicemen	
				and women	4,238,210

Notes: *a* This figure includes 57,847 people on the Jinmen and Mazu islands of Fujian Province.
b Figures were not available at the time of publication for the Dongsha and Xisha islands of Guangdong Province.

Source: China facts and figures – population. Foreign Languages Press, Beijing, 1984.

The demographic situation in China today

What is the demographic situation in China today? Is China's population likely to stay below the figure of 1200 million which the Chinese have fixed as their goal for the year 2000? What relaxations might there be in the 'one couple, one child policy' without prejudicing the overall targets?

According to China's 1982 Population Census, China had a population of 1,031,882,511 on 1 July, 1982. Of this figure, 1,008,175,288 lived in the 29 mainland provinces, autonomous regions and municipalities directly under the Central Government (including those serving in the army). 18,328,596 (calculated according to data released by the Taiwan authorities) lived in Taiwan Province and the Jinnen and Mazu islands of Fujian Province and 5,378,627 (calculated according to data released by the authorities of Hong Kong and Macao) are Chinese people in Hong Kong or Macao. (See Table 11.3.)

The most populous administrative region is Sichuan Province with nearly 100 million people. The Tibet Autonomous Region is the least populous, with 1.9 million people.

China's 1982 population density was 107 people per square kilometre, as compared with the figure of 74 determined by the 1964 Census.

Population growth between 1949 and 1982

Chinese officials and academics to whom I spoke in the course of my visit explained that many of the demographic challenges confronting the country today reflect previous periods in recent Chinese history – population 'peaks' or 'baby booms' – whose impact is still being felt. They use colourful images to describe the situation, for example, that of the boa-constrictor which has swallowed several large meals and where the lumps can still be seen as the slow process of digestion takes place.

The first such peak occurred in the period 1950 to 1957. Though Dean Acheson, the US Secretary of State at the time, ascribed the start of the Chinese revolution to the excessive growth of population and the insufficiency of food, Mao Tse-tung criticized the idea of population determinism in his paper 'The Insolvency of the Idealist Conception of History' in which he presented his famous thesis: *Revolution plus Production will solve China's food problem.*

Influenced no doubt by the thoughts of Chairman Mao, China's population increased from 541.67 million to 646.53 million during the period 1950 to 1957, or an average of 13.11 million each year with an annual growth rate of 2.2 per cent.

The first peak was followed by a valley – the period between 1958 and 1961 – where China's population increased by only 3.02 million a year, with a yearly average growth rate of 0.5 per cent. However, a second peak occurred between 1962 and 1973, covering the period of the Great Leap forward and the long, dark night of the Cultural Revolution when organized family planning came virtually to a halt throughout the country. (I have consulted the extensive notes I made during my earlier trip to China in 1975 and find no references to family planning though we visited what seemed to be at the time an endless succession of communes, factories and centres of medicine, both traditional and 'western'.)

During the period 1962–73, China's population grew from 658.59 million to 891.43 million, showing an average increase per year of 19.40 million, with an annual growth rate of 2.6 per cent. Though this second peak was once again followed by a valley as the organization of a nationwide family-planning programme was successfully attempted (the average yearly growth-rate between 1974 and 1982 dropped to 1.5 per cent), China is today confronting the prospect of a third peak in births, the consequence of that earlier 'bulge', which represents as great a demographic challenge as any that country has faced so far.

This challenge is all the more daunting in that it comes at a time when China is itself undergoing a structural and economic revolution which in its way is probably as significant and as profound as that which occurred in 1949. The introduction of the 'four modernizations', the opening up of China to modern technology, the absorption of foreign ideas and influences (in the special economic zone of Shenzhen all the television aerials point towards Hong Kong – a neat symbol of a growing trend affecting the country as a whole) – all this will certainly have an impact on China's ability to control its population through organized family planning in the manner of the past. Economic and financial incentives and disincentives of the kind described in Chapter 8 may be less effective than they have been in previous years thanks to the general increase in prosperity that is now occurring in China. The introduction of 'free markets', for example, in which farmers and villagers can sell their produce and retain the proceeds for themselves has, I noticed, created an air of bustle and energy, of entrepreneurial vigour which was totally absent on my previous visit. The family-planning programme's system of rewards and penalties will certainly have to take account of the rise in the earning and spending power of many Chinese people. This will apply as much to family-planning workers (earning 30 yuan a month where they might earn 300 yuan selling chickens and pigs) as to the average 'target couple'.

It is already apparent that the family-planning programme is least effective in the most prosperous provinces. There the attractions of the 'incremental' child (perhaps a second child in the city, perhaps a third or even fourth child in the countryside) may outweigh the anticipated penalties, whether of a social or economic nature. Thus paradoxically it is the considerable economic achievements of the new China which may pose possibly the biggest threat to the continued success of the family-planning programme. Over the Sixth Five-Year Plan period (1980-5), the per capita income of rural residents went up by 13.7 per cent annually and that of urban workers and other employees and their families by 6.9 per cent annually. It is clear that the consumption level of both urban and rural people has been raised rapidly, with notable changes in the consumption pattern. Diets have improved, clothing has become more varied (I have only to compare my 1986 photographs with those I took 11 years ago); the sales of durable consumer goods – especially TV sets, washing machines, radio-cassette recorders and refrigerators and other household electrical appliances – have grown rapidly. Housing conditions, though still restricted, have certainly improved. During the Sixth Five-Year Plan period, according to official statistics, more than 630 million square metres of floor space were built in cities and towns and 3.2 billion square metres in the rural areas. Lack of living space has always been a potent factor in limiting people's desire for large families. That constraint may no longer be as powerful as it was.

According to the classic theories of demographic transition, the rise in living standards should, in time (once the kinks in the demand curve have been ironed out) lead to falls in fertility. On this argument, the Chinese authorities could perhaps afford to take a relaxed view of the present situation. Unfortunately, given the size and profile of China's current population, given in particular the still present consequences of the 'baby boom' of the 1960s and 1970s, China cannot afford the luxury of experimenting with theoretical approaches to its demographic problems. Time is not on China's side. If the target of more than 1.2 billion by the year 2000 is to be achieved, the family planning programme has to be pursued with unrelenting vigour.

The need is all the more acute if the environmental impact of population pressure in China is considered. As one travels through the country it is impossible not to be aware of just how stretched already are China's environmental resources. Statistically speaking, China disposes of one-third of the world average as far as territory per capita is concerned, the same figure applies to the availability of farm land. China has only one-quarter of the world average for per capita supply of water and one-ninth for forests.

Wildlife and habitat is under continuous and growing pressure. The ultimate threat to the giant panda, the world-wide symbol of conservation, for example, is not so much the availability of the panda's staple food – the arrow bamboo – but the sheer pressure of human populations on the animal's habitat and the disruption of the overall ecology which this is causing.

The problems of air pollution and water pollution are already acute in many places. Deforestation and desertification are growing threats. Though some important steps have been taken (for example, the planting of the 'Great Green Wall' of trees in the country's northern provinces against the encroaching desert, and as a counter to sandstorms – the 'yellow dragons' – and erosion), much remains to be achieved. The present Chinese leadership appears to recognize that any slackening in the nation's efforts to curb population growth will make these environmental questions – which are intimately linked to the viability of China's economic and social structures – still harder to resolve.

On June 5, 1986 – World Environment Day (so proclaimed because it was on that day that the first United Nations Conference on the Human Environment was opened in Stockholm in 1972) – China announced a

306

comprehensive programme of environmental protection for implementation over the next five years. Ye Rutang, China's Minister of Urban and Rural Construction and Environmental Protection, indicated that, in addition to making major efforts to control pollution from new and existing plants, his Ministry would devote special attention to preserving the ecological balance and in this context he referred in particular to the need to control 'the sharp growth of the human population[9]'.

So how far has China proceeded along the difficult path towards zero population growth? I had the opportunity in Beijing and Xian to meet with some of China's foremost demographers. In Beijing, Professor Liu Zheng, Director of Population Research at the People's University of China, and Professor Wu Cangping, the Deputy Director, explained the present situation as they saw it. In Xian, Professor Jiang Zhenghua, Head of the Population Research Institute at Xian Jiaotong University, continued my education. Table 11.4, given me by Professor Jiang in Xian, demonstrates, in the most graphic manner possible, the extent of the achievement in reducing birth- and death-rates in China over the last 30 years or so. (The adjustments for under-reporting result from the need to take into account situations where for some reason actual registrations of births and deaths fail to give an accurate picture of these vital events. For example, Professor Jiang indicated that the massive under-reporting of births in 1961 coincided with the new emphasis on population policy and family planning following the early baby boom. Under-reporting of births of similar magnitude, and for apparently similar reasons, occurred in 1976 as the national family-planning programme resumed after the shock of the cultural revolution. In both cases, the data suggest that parents concealed the births of 'supernumerary' children. Professor Jiang had also noted an increase in the number of 'twins' being registered, including twins of palpably different ages! As far as the under-reporting of deaths is concerned, Professor Jiang observed that in a society where allocations of food, particularly grain, and housing have been based on those present in a household, it is not surprising that some under-reporting of death occurs. He had heard of an occasion where a pig had actually been registered as a member of a household! But under-reporting of both births and deaths was on the whole diminishing.)

It can be seen from the Table that the (adjusted) birth-rate has fallen from a high point of 46.23 in 1963 to around 19 per thousand by 1980. Today it stands at about 17 per thousand.

The present annual growth rate of China's population is 1.2 per cent a year. The hope is to reduce that to 1 per cent by 1995 and to zero growth by 2020 or 2030.

Table 11.4. *The birth- and death-rates in China (adjusted for under-reporting)*

Year	Birth-rate (%)			Death-rate (%)		
	Year book	Adjusted	Under-reported rate (%)	Year book	Adjusted	Under-reported rate (%)
1953	37.00	39.56	6.47	14.00	20.70	32.37
1954	37.97	39.39	3.60	13.18	23.78	44.58
1955	32.62	37.32	12.59	12.28	22.54	45.52
1956	31.90	35.92	11.19	11.40	21.52	47.03
1957	34.03	36.84	7.63	10.80	20.53	47.39
1958	29.22	31.77	8.03	11.98	20.06	40.28
1959	24.78	27.86	11.06	14.59	26.91	45.78
1960	20.86	24.24	13.94	25.43	31.58	19.47
1961	18.02	25.03	28.01	14.24	24.38	41.59
1962	37.01	39.65	6.66	10.02	17.83	43.80
1963	43.37	46.23	6.19	10.54	16.35	38.59
1964	39.14	43.63	10.29	11.50[1]	14.93	22.97
1965	37.88	39.51	4.13	9.50	13.04	27.15
1966	35.05	36.54	4.08	8.83	11.62	24.01
1967	33.96	34.85	2.55	8.43	10.40	18.94
1968	35.59	37.78	5.80	0.21	9.91	17.15
1969	34.11	37.50	9.04	8.03	9.54	15.83
1970	33.43	35.84	6.72	7.60	8.80	13.64
1971	30.65	33.75	9.19	7.32	8.23	11.06
1972	29.77	31.51	5.52	7.61	7.68	0.91
1973	27.93	29.95	6.74	7.04	7.54	6.63
1974	24.82	27.25	8.92	7.34	7.50	2.13
1975	23.01	24.64	6.62	7.32	7.43	1.48
1976	19.91	22.84	12.83	7.25	7.38	1.76
1977	18.93	21.40	11.54	6.87	7.22	4.85
1978	18.25	21.20	13.92	6.25	6.93	9.81
1979	17.82	20.49	13.03	6.21	6.74	7.86
1980	18.21[2]	18.91	3.70	6.34	6.46	1.86

Note: [1] The population census in 1964 corrected the death registration data. Since then, the under-reporting rates tend to be reduced.

[2] Since 1980, the published data was compared with data from other sources, so that the under-reporting rates go down again.

Source: Professor Jiang Zhenghua, Population Research Institute, Xian Jiaotong University.

The total fertility rate (TFR) is today around 2.2. That rate will have to come down further if the official target of no more than 1.2 billion in the year 2000 is to be achieved. Professor Jiang, who disposes of sophisticated computer equipment acquired with the help of UNFPA, estimates that a TFR of 1.73 or 1.74 would – allowing for projected levels of per capita income – result in a population of 1.26 billion in the year 2000, or, in other words, an overshoot of the targeted figure by some 60 million. In the Chinese context, 60 million may seem neither here nor there. Yet 60 million is approximately the population of a fairly large West European country (Britain or France or West Germany). An extra 60 million by the year 2000 may mean an extra 200 million by the middle or end of the next century. So these somewhat technical terms – total reproduction rate, net reproduction rate and so on — are vital in every sense. Instead of reaching zero population growth in the year 2020 or 2030 (with a total population of around 1.4 billion), the date at which a stationary population is ultimately achieved would be pushed back into the more distant future and the 'final' total would be that much larger.

The Chinese authorities are keenly aware of the dangers involved in any relaxation of the family planning programme. At the end of September 1986, in a series of newspaper articles and circulars to local Communist Party leaders, the authorities launched a new campaign to strengthen enforcement of population policies in the rural areas where nearly 800 million Chinese live. Beijing's municipal Communist Party Committee sent an open letter to all party members in the countryside around the capital, urging them to marry late, to delay the decision to become parents and to stick to the limit of one child to each family. The party cadres were then told to try to ensure that others around them do likewise.

"The peasants' life has been greatly improved', said the Committee. 'However, if there is no efficient birth control, further increases in the standard of living will be restrained by population increases.'

Similar letters have been sent out by party officials in other parts of China. On September 25, 1986, the sixth anniversary of the formal adoption of China's 'one child, one family' policy, the official nationwide Chinese publication Health News warned in an editorial that the one-child limitation is a 'long-range strategic principle policy'.

Inevitably, there is a degree of ambivalence in the current situation. China wishes to reach its proclaimed goals of demographic policy which means that further reductions in fertility rates have to be realized. At the same time, recent economic achievements and the spirit of the reforms introduced by Deng Xiaoping and his colleagues, are seen as arguments in favour of a certain relaxation in the approach to birth-control. In an interview with the *Chinese Daily* published on 6 December 1985, Mr Wang Wei, Chairman of the State Family-Planning Commission, said that the one-child policy, implemented since 1979, would continue for most couples, with the aim of limiting annual population growth to about 1.2 per cent. But the government would gradually relax the rule to allow parents in special circumstances to have two children.

'On the one hand we are facing a new baby boom which will last more than ten years. On the other, we are relaxing our policy;' Mr Wang was quoted as saying. He said that people in parts of Shandong, Guangdong, Zhejiang and Guangxi provinces could now have one more child if their first-born was a girl. Couples living in remote or mountainous areas, or on

islands, and those in hazardous occupations, are also allowed two children, as are parents who were themselves only children.[10]

This then is the tight-rope along which China must walk for the
foreseeable future. Will the country manage to keep its balance? Too tough
a line, in spite of the proclaimed 'voluntariness of the masses' may set up a
reaction as happened in India in the days of the sterilization drive. As I
write these words (2 January, 1987) the news is full of student unrest in
China – in Shanghai, Beijing and other centres. Those who protest today
about the 'lack of democracy' in general terms may quickly seize on family
planning policy as a useful stick to beat a dog.

On the other hand, any further relaxation of the 'one couple, one child'
principle (for example, a general easing off in the rural areas where the
vast bulk of China's population still lives) would effectively negate China's
demographic goals. In that case, not only would China's achievements in
reducing fertility begin to look much less spectacular, but so too, inevitably, would the global picture, since China represents a fifth part of
mankind. Today, the world's population growth rate stands at 2.1 per
cent, an awesome enough figure in all conscience but one which denotes,
as I have indicated elsewhere, a substantial decline in global fertility. If,
however, we leave China out of the calculations, then we find that the
total population of the remainder of the world (i.e. the World *minus* China)
is growing at the rate of 2.7 per cent annually. Seen from this perspective,
it is clear that, globally as well as nationally, what happens in China over
the next few decades is of critical importance. If China succeeds, perhaps
the rest of the world will follow. But if China fails, after having demonstrated an unprecedented level of political commitment to population
policy, and after having devoted so many human and material resources to
family planning, we may ask: what hope is there after all for the large
populous nations of the Third World who, taken together, account for the
vast bulk of humankind?

Can the Chinese experience be repeated in other countries?

The third question I had in mind in setting off for China at the end of 1986
was whether or not the Chinese success in bringing down birth-rates could
be emulated in other countries. In this case, the United Nations might have
an additional role to play: as the vehicle or conduit through which lessons
from China (Chinese 'know-how') could be made available to a wider
audience. Already new patterns of technical assistance are developing as
far as population is concerned (and of course in other areas as well), with
experts *from* Third World countries providing advice *to* Third World
countries. China could provide a powerful impetus to this process.

Clearly there are some elements in the Chinese experience which are unrepeatable. China's 6000 years of history are unique and specific to China. I had the privilege of seeing the vast terracotta army of warriors which guards the tomb of the first Qin Emperor outside Xian. It is a sight that brings home to the visitor the extraordinary fact that China was a unified nation as long ago as 200 BC and, give or take a few episodes of varying duration, has more or less remained united ever since. Dynasty has succeeded dynasty, but on the whole the integrity of the country has survived.

The internal cohesion of China has benefited from nature's great arteries of communication such as the Yellow and Yangzi rivers and these have been supplemented by road and rail and, latterly, by a comprehensive, though sometimes idiosyncratic, network of internal flights. As noted earlier, the Han nationality predominates to a very large extent and this ethnic homogeneity has itself perhaps facilitated action in the field of family planning (racial or tribal rivalries usually have a negative effect on the smooth running of family-planning programmes).

Probably the structures established as a consequence of the Chinese revolution in 1949 have played their part as well, though most qualified Sinologists take the view that, even without the Chinese Communist party, there would exist a degree of political and social cohesion sufficient to permit, amongst other things, the effective operation of a family-planning programme which includes, if it is not wholly determined by, a system of rewards and penalties.

All this said, it is certain that some features of the Chinese system are indeed 'exportable' in the sense that they could be usefully copied in other parts of the world. I have already mentioned the emphasis on women's rights and on the basic health structure including maternal and child health/family planning. Of equal relevance is the importance attached in successive Five-Year Plans to educational reforms and improvements. Chapters 28 to 31 of the Seventh Five-Year Plan (1986–90) deal respectively with Elementary Education, Vocational and Technical Education, regular Higher Education and Adult Education. There is no doubting the commitment of the Chinese Government to this sphere. Total enrolment in regular colleges and universities reached 1.7 million in 1985, up from 1.4 million in 1980. Some initial successes have been achieved in restructuring middle school education. There has been rapid growth in vocational and technical school education, and good progress has been made towards universal elementary education.

These programmes – in the field of women's rights, public health and education – are the vital underpinnings of successful population and family planning policies. Add to these the element of economic dynamism,

311

as exemplified by growth in per capita income, which is so clearly present in China today; add, still further, a well-organized family-planning system based on safe, efficient and reliable contraception (but without eschewing legal abortion as a last resort) and you have, I submit, a pattern of achievement which could, and should, be successfully repeated *mutatis mutandis* in those areas of the world where men and women are not yet able to plan their families or otherwise control their fertility and where, at the macroeconomic level, population growth is outstripping resources – whether social, economic or environmental.

In the last analysis, what matters is not whether China is or is not a Communist State or whether the country is or is not run by the Communist party. It is the nature and the pattern of the development which is important and that is something, I believe, which can, and should, serve as an inspiration to nations and peoples who have chosen to follow other political paths.

12

Postscript and conclusions

I started work on this book in August 1984, soon after returning from the International Conference on Population held in Mexico City earlier that month. Because the scope of the project was already large, and because all books of this kind must have a cut-off date, I decided that I would try not to deal with events arising *post-Mexico*. Thus the detailed account of the involvement of the United Nations with World Population ends as the final gavel came down on 14 August, 1984, in that conference hall in the Tlatelolco Centre, Mexico City.

In the event, it proved impossible to stick rigidly to the self-imposed limit. For example, though the outlines of the US–UN controversy over China were already apparent in 1984, the story has evolved over the last years and Chapter 11 deals with these latest developments. There have been other important developments which need mentioning if only in summary form.

Fertility declines and ageing

Most of this book has been concerned with world population *growth* because that is the main problem – the rocket taking off and accelerating towards the stratosphere; much of the United Nations' activities have been taken up with charting the course of this unprecedented phenomenon as well as, in the later part of the period covered by this account, trying to mitigate its impact. I doubt whether the donor nations of the world would be putting up $140 million annually if UNFPA tomorrow announced that it would no longer be concerned with the problems of high fertility and had no intention of financing any more family planning in the Third World.

Yet it has to be said that in recent years, and particularly since the Mexico Conference, the problems of falling birth-rates and ageing populations have come increasingly to the fore in certain parts of the world.

313

The cover story in *Newsweek's* edition of 15 December, 1986, was entitled: 'Europe's Baby Bust: how it will affect employment, education, social security and defence'. The magazine reported that the French Government had, in November 1986, announced a new and dramatic programme to encourage larger families; it would pay mothers who give birth to a third or fourth child a 'temporary maternal salary' for three years. In Britain, Prime Minister Thatcher had begun to cut back on university subsidies. In Belgium, the Government was laying off high-school teachers. Starting in 1989, West German draftees would be required to serve 18 months in the Bundeswehr, rather than the 15 months that had been standard for decades. In East Germany young parents now received no-interest housing loans and part of the principal was 'forgiven' for each new child a couple produced[1].

Newsweek suggested that all these seemingly unrelated developments had the same cause: 'a demographic revolution that is unprecedented in European history'. More young Europeans than ever were *not* getting married. Those who did marry were doing so later and having fewer children, and a significant number of two-career couples were deciding against starting families at all. As a result the continent's population would begin to decline in the 1990s.

West German demographer Rolf Benkert, co-ordinator of a recent demographic study for the Council of Europe (the total population of whose 21 nations now stands at 400 million) was reported as saying that if the decline continued at the current rate, there would be only half as many Europeans in 2086 as there are now[2].

West Germany now had the lowest birth-rate – 1.3 children per woman – in its recorded history. In England, fertility had fallen by a third and marriage rates by 40 per cent in the past 14 years. Even Italy, despite its overwhelmingly Catholic population, would soon start to lose population if present trends continued. The only countries in Western Europe that were maintaining birth-rates sufficient to keep their populations steady were 'tiny Ireland and underdeveloped Greece'.

The report cited French Prime Minister Jacques Chirac as saying 'In demographic terms, Europe is vanishing,' as well as the warning of Gaston Thorn, the former Prime Minister of Luxembourg and former President of the EEC Commission, that 'Europe is committing collective suicide'.

This is not the place for a discussion of the causes of this new phenomenon. Sociologists and politicians will come to their own, possibly different, conclusions. Christine Wattelar of the Catholic University of Louvain in Belgium, for instance, believes that: 'Children are no longer perceived as an investment in the future. They are seen as an extra expense and the only return they offer is an emotional one.' Michel Debré, a former French Prime Minister, puts the case even more strongly: 'We have destroyed marriage and the family as social values. We have erected greed and self-indulgence as our idols'[3].

Nor is this the place for an evaluation of the consequences of the downturn in fertility or for making predictions or projections of future population trends. Once again we encounter a wide diversity of opinions. Some observers believe that the decline in Europe's birthrate will have severe social consequences (particularly as far as society's ability to care for the increasing proportion of elderly people is concerned.) Others see the problems as being of a transitional nature, to be rectified once a new demographic equilibrium has been established. Indeed, they anticipate positive benefits (for example a reduction in the pressures on the environment) from a return to the smaller populations of the past. Similarly there is no agreement as to how long the downward trend is likely to continue. Professor William Brass, for example, who heads the Centre for Population Studies at the London School of Hygiene and Tropical Medicine, argues that the natural tendency for populations, at least in England, is to move up or down periodically, then veer back toward stability[4].

It is clear that these demographic and social questions are of interest and concern not only at the national level but also to the United Nations and its system of agencies. International concern for the aged, for example, was acknowledged by countries as early as 1948 in the Universal Declaration of Human Rights. In 1973, the General Assembly recommended that governments develop programmes for the welfare, health and protection of older people. UNFPA was directed 'to continue to provide financial support in the field of ageing' and assisted with the preparations for the World Assembly on Ageing, held in Vienna, Austria, in July 1982.

Present areas of concern for UNFPA and other bodies within the United Nations system include:

basic data collection

continuing the work already done in the collection, analyses and projections of data on the aged. (Older persons, aged 60 and above, in 1975 constituted 15.0 per cent of the population of developed nations, a figure that will increase to 18 per cent by the year 2000);

research

Continuing research on the implications of a country's changing age structure for labour supply and for social services; research on the social and economic consequences of rural-to-urban migration and the impli-

315

cations for the older populations of such migration, research on measures to maximize the contributions of the elderly to socio-economic development and inter-country research on changes in age structure and their implications for economic and social development;

support communication

Including dissemination of research findings and training methodologies, information on legislative policies as well as other governmental policy and programme information[5].

As one example of this range of activity, a regional meeting on Population and Development was being organized in February 1987 in Budapest, Hungary by the United Nations Economic Commission for Europe (ECE) with the support of UNFPA. It was envisaged that the meeting would provide a forum for the exchange of information on population trends, problems and policies, as well as research findings and their utilization.

Looking ahead, we must expect this type of activity to become of increasing importance to the United Nations. Nor is concern likely to be confined to the developed industrialized world. Indeed, the very successes which are achieved in reducing fertility in the developing world give rise to new problems connected with the age-structure of populations and the shape of the population profile.

Already in China, for example, I noted some concern for the long-term consequences of the rapid fertility declines that have been achieved in recent years. Professor Wu Cangping pointed out that, in the year 2040, 20 per cent of the population would consist of old people. Given that the number of dependants at the other end of the pyramid is steadily falling (in China today the proportion of the population below 15 is 30 per cent as compared with 50 per cent and higher in many other developing countries), the situation may not appear to be very alarming. Still, it is a nice example of the way in which, over the next decades, we may expect a further evolution in national and international perceptions of the population problem and, hence, in the orientation and emphasis of United Nations activities in this area.

AIDS

One other issue which has burst into international prominence over the last two or three years is AIDS, the so-called 'Acquired Immune Deficiency Syndrome'. It is not clear at the present time whether AIDS will have a positive or negative effect on family-planning programmes.

A positive impact might result from increased publicity for, and use of, condoms and other protective methods of contraception, if such use were either more effective than the methods currently practised or represented 'additional' couples protected. On the other hand, a negative impact might result if the 'moral backlash' which is beginning to be felt (a backlash which though aimed in general at the sexual mores of the 1960s and 1970s encompasses also the 'pill' and other manifestations of the liberal approach to life) had the effect of weakening public and political support for family-planning programmes.

My personal opinion is that population and family-planning programmes will indeed, in one way or another, feel the effect of the 'moral backlash' in areas that go beyond the abortion issue (which I have referred to in Chapter 11), and that it would be as well for the United Nations to be ready to take evasive or defensive action.

Role of the non-governmental organizations

One of the more interesting recent developments is the growing importance of non-governmental organizations in the field of population and family planning. In part, this is simply a reflection of the larger trend towards 'privatization' of the international aid effort. There is a widespread feeling, exemplified most dramatically by the outpourings of charitable relief during the drought and famine which affected so many African countries in the early 1980s, that private agencies – sometimes associated with international NGOs like OXFAM and the Red Cross, sometimes not – can 'deliver' assistance better than official government-to-government relations.

As noted in earlier chapters, UNFPA has been unusual in that, almost from the start of its operations, it has both supported and worked with the non-governmental sector. This partnership is likely to be of increasing importance, not only in those countries where the level of official commitment to population and family-planning programmes is low, but also in countries where for one reason or another the NGOs are well placed to bring the services to the people who need them.

The 'doyen' of NGOs working in the population field is the International Union for the Scientific Study of Population (IUSSP) which is dedicated exclusively to research in all aspects of demography and its application to public policy. The Union was founded in Paris in 1928, following the first World Population Conference held in Geneva in 1927. As Julia Henderson, herself a former senior UN official and former Secretary-General of IPPF, points out:[6]

From the inception of the United Nations Population Commission by the Economic and Social Council in 1946 and the establishment of the Population Division of the Secretariat under the direction of Professor Frank Notestein, the relationships between the UN Secretariat and the IUSSP were close and fruitful. Most of the senior professional staff of the Population Division were members of IUSSP, and its research papers prepared by members for IUSSP seminars, workshops, and general assemblies or international conferences were frequently of direct benefit to the work of the Population Commission.

At a working level, UNFPA's relationships with IPPF have been of the closest. Sir David Owen, former co-administrator of the UNDP, was appointed Secretary-General of IPPF in 1968 while the Fund was still in its embryonic stage. Though he sadly died shortly thereafter, Julia Henderson succeeded him and, both under her and under the subsequent leadership of Carl Wahren, formerly of SIDA, and Pradman Weerakoon of Sri Lanka, strong day-to-day links between IPPF and UNFPA have been built up.

As Julia Henderson comments:[7]

UNFPA encouraged Governments to cooperate with voluntary agencies including FPAs affiliated with IPPF and, in a number of countries, provided financial assistance through the Government to the FPA. For its part, IPPF strongly encouraged its affiliates to work closely with ministers of health, education and labour by demonstrating the most effective approaches to providing education and services. In 1981, IPPF co-sponsored with UNFPA and the Population Council a seminal conference in Jakarta resulting in important recommendations for the direction of 'family planning in the eighties'[8].

Apart from IUSSP and IPPF, the Population Council, the Ford and Rockefeller Foundations, and the Pathfinder Fund who have long been involved in providing assistance for population and family-planning activities, there is a growing range of national and international NGOs who have developed, or are developing, an interest or proven competence in the field. The United Nations has been able from time to time to help these bodies with their work. At the same time, the collaboration has been mutual and, where successes have been achieved, much of the credit has been due to joint effort.

In 1985, for example, $14.4 million, or 10.2 per cent of total project allocations was channelled through NGOs. In Africa, the national family-planning or child-spacing programmes of Swaziland and Tanzania are both executed by the International Planned Parenthood Federation (IPPF). The Centre for Development and Population Activities has provided managerial and technical training in maternal and child health and family planning to a number of African countries.

Table 12.1. *UNFPA assistance by executing agency*

Executing agency	Expenditures for 1984	Allocations for 1985
UNESCO	4.5	5.2
ILO	3.8	5.1
FAO	1.4	1.6
UNDP	–	0.5
Regional Commissions	5.8	5.4
UNICEF	1.4	1.6
WHO	15.2	20.3
UNFPA	15.8	14.4
United Nations	11.2	12.2
Non-governmental organizations	8.0	10.2
Governments (directly executed)	32.9	23.5

In Asia, the Programme for the Introduction and Adaptation of Contraceptive Technology (PIACT) is executing several large-scale projects on contraceptive production in China and in Vietnam. The Australian University has provided technical support to the UNFPA funded programme in Indonesia. The Japanese Organization for International Co-operation in Family Planning (JOICFP) and IPPF have been jointly executing projects in support of family planning integrated with parasite control and nutrition services in several Asian countries, as well as in Africa and Latin America. In Latin America, the Family of the Americas Foundation received substantial UNFPA funding in partial support of the third Congress, to discuss issues concerning family life, including natural family planning. The International Organization for Chemical Sciences in Development, IUSSP, JOICFP, the Population Council, the Population Crisis Committee and PIACT are among the NGOs receiving major UNFPA support for programme, scientific and informational activities. This is a trend which is bound to continue in the future. It represents one of the most distinctive (and desirable) characteristics of the Fund's mode of operations.

Urbanization

A follow-up to the Rome Conference on Population and the Urban Future which was held in Rome in 1980 (see Chapter 9) took place in Barcelona between 19–22 May, 1986. The International Conference on Population and the Urban Future was convened by the United Nations Fund for Population Activities, and co-sponsored by Spanish national, regional and local authorities, including the Metropolitan Corporation of Barcelona which hosted the meeting, the United Nations Centre for Human Settlements (HABITAT) and the International Union of Local Authorities (IULA). As on the previous occasion, the Conference was attended by decision-makers – in this case mayors from cities which will have four million or more inhabitants by the year 2000, and national, city and urban planners from around the world. At the end of the Conference, delegates from the 58 cities and 29 countries represented at the Conference unanimously approved a Declaration which reaffirmed the objectives and recommendations of the Rome Declaration while stressing that 'the emergence of mega-cities in the developing countries has exceeded any past experience'.

Urban life has become essential to the social nature of the world. Cities are part of a nation and policies intended for them should be integrated into national plans and programmes[9].

The Barcelona Declaration reaffirmed:

the need for the formulation of comprehensive national population policies, policies for balanced development and policies to improve the quality of life in the urban areas as essential components of any strategy to deal with the complex problems associated with rapid urban growth.

While I was in China I had the chance to meet with some Chinese delegates who had themselves attended the Barcelona Conference (as indeed had the UNFPA representative in Beijing, Mr Aprodisio Laquian, himself a sociologist of distinction specializing in urban affairs). Altogether, representatives from ten Chinese cities came to Spain for the meeting – Beijing, Chengdu, Chongqing, Guangzhou, Harbin, Nanjing, Shanghai, Shanyang, Tianjin, Wuhan, Xian[10] and Zibo. Each of these ten cities would exceed 4 million inhabitants by the end of the century. Yet I learned that, on the basis of that sole criterion, many other Chinese cities would have qualified to send delegates to Barcelona. It was an image which brought home to me clearly the implications of that rather ponderous word 'urbanization'.

There is no doubt that the problems of cities, especially of megacities, and the associated issues of migration both within and between countries will grow in importance. The links between urbanization, migration and high levels of fertility are evident though, as more than one delegate to the Barcelona Conference pointed out, not all the problems of large cities or of uncontrolled immigration can be put down to a lack of family planning.

Precisely what the role of United Nations bodies could, or should, be in this area is perhaps less clear. The World Bank is now heavily involved in urban programmes particularly those involving water supply and sanitation. But it is not likely that other bodies within the United Nations will ever have either the mandate or the resources to respond in a similar way. The Barcelona Declaration urged UNFPA, together with other concerned international organizations, to 'promote the collection and publication of comparative data on urban population trends and structures and problems relating to population dynamics' and to 'undertake and support workshops, seminars and other training programmes to enhance technical knowledge and expertise toward the solution of urban problems'.

This seems to me to be pitching it about right.

Population and politics

As mentioned in Chapter 9, the International Conference of Parliamentarians on Population and Development was held in Colombo, Sri Lanka, in August 1979. This Conference which I attended both as a Parliamentarian and as a Rapporteur was a fine example of the 'outreach' of one particular United Nations body, namely UNFPA, towards a political constituency whose support would be vital for its long-term success. The Fund's political activity ('lobbying' is too unsubtle a word) has continued to be of importance. A Global Committee of Parliamentarians on Population and development has been formed consisting of parliamentary leaders, individual former heads of government and experts from different sectors with the aim of:

> stimulating world opinion leaders to study population and development as they relate to global issues and to serve as a forum for the exchange of ideas and information;
>
> to encourage the formation of as many national parliamentary groups on population and development as possible and to work with regional parliamentary groups on population and development;
>
> to identify potential projects that would support national or regional parliamentary activities and provide seed money for their implementation.

Following the Colombo Conference of August 1979[11], which was co-sponsored by UNFPA and the Inter-Parliamentary Union (IPU), various regional and sub-regional parliamentary conferences – with varying forms of assistance from UNFPA – were held. Examples are the African Conference in Nairobi (1981), the Asian Conference in Beijing (1981), the Latin American and Caribbean Conference in Brasilia (1982), the European Conference in Strasbourg (1982), the Asian Conference in New Delhi (1984), the Caribbean Conference in Barbados (1984), and the Nordic meeting in Copenhagen (1985).

UNFPA's concern to involve parliamentarians in its work and the support it has given to, and received from, bodies like the Global Committee on Parliamentarians, on Population and Development, or – at the regional level – the Asian Forum of Parliamentarians on Population and Development, and the Inter-American Parliamentary Group on Population and Development, has been an essential factor in building and retaining political commitment for United Nations work in the population field.

Most recently, a European Parliamentarians' Forum on Child Survival, Women and Population was held in The Hague, Netherlands, on 12 and 13 February, 1986. Parliamentarians from 16 European countries participated in the Forum, as well as parliamentarians and 'policy-makers' from eight developing countries. The Forum's main topic was the development of 'Integrated Strategies' through which the links between programmes involving reductions in infant mortality, improvements in women's health and population policy could be more firmly established. In a background paper presented to the Conference UNICEF pointed out that:

> about 40 per cent of all children under five in developing countries, some 125 million children, are stunted from chronic protein-energy malnutrition;
>
> over 20 per cent of all infants born in developing countries, some 17 million annually, are low birth-weight infants, most of whom reflect inadequate maternal health and nutrition;
>
> half of all women of child-bearing age in developing countries, some 220 million, have nutritional anaemias.

UNICEF argued that through the application of low-cost relevant technologies emphasizing mass communications and social mobilization, combined with efforts to improve female literacy and enhance family planning, a major reduction in infant and early childhood mortality and morbidity – directly linked to improved nutritional status – could be rapidly brought about.

> The confidence gained by parents in seeing their children survive and thrive as a result of their efforts is likely to be the most persuasive incentive for, and in many sometimes a necessary prerequisite to, widespread choices for family planning and reduction of fertility rates[12].

As James P. Grant, the Executive Director of the United Nations Children's Fund, put it in his speech to the Forum:

> Halving the infant and child death rate can be expected to greatly accelerate the drop in fertility rates from those now projected and, in fact, could be the most important new intervention in the last 15 years of this century towards reducing population rates.... If all the world had the infant and child death rates

of Sri Lanka, 7 million fewer children would be dying each year. And if all the world had the birth rates of Sri Lanka, 35 million fewer babies would be born each year.

The importance of getting this kind of message across before an audience of parliamentarians, who in the end will have to vote the funds for population and development programmes, can hardly be over-estimated.

Similarly, an approach to the international secretariat of the four big political movements (Socialist, Conservative, Liberal and Christian Democrat) bore fruit in June 1986 when a meeting held in Vienna's old Imperial Palace (which I had the pleasure of attending) resulted in a solemn declaration on Population, Development and Peace which will, no doubt, serve many useful purposes both now and in the future. On this particular occasion, the skill of Jyoti Singh, UNFPA's Director of Public Information, in nursing agreement to the final text was much in evidence.

But in most of these affairs it is the arrival not the journey that matters. The United Nations can now flourish a few short but not insignificant paragraphs as representing a consensus among those present, and in the rarefied world of international organizations there are few higher achievements. Meanwhile, the agony (and sometimes the tedium) of the process is buried and forgotten with the transcript of the proceedings.

The fact that the Communist Party, the world's fifth great 'international' was not present in Vienna in June 1986 at the Hofburg meeting was regrettable but, in the political circumstances prevailing, probably inevitable. Though countries with Communist regimes – China, Cuba, the Eastern European bloc – are in the forefront of those who have managed to reduce their fertility and population growth (in some cases even achieving negative rates) Marxist dogma will never tolerate any overt manifestations of 'Malthusianism' or 'anti-natalism', such as could detract from the basic doctrine that revolution will solve the problems of production and, by implication, reproduction. Today, as was the case when the United Nations first entered the field, the Communist nations tend to practise fertility control rather than preach it.

Religion

If the United Nations has made a considerable *percée* in influencing the political milieu, the same can hardly be said as far as the world's great religions are concerned. Though Mr Salas has met the Pope, that encounter and other contacts have not so far produced any visible switch of position by the Vatican whose official statements on the subject of population policy, contraception and abortion have been recorded at several points in this narrative. The truth of the matter is that on the whole the religious leaders of the world, and most notably Pope John-Paul II, have failed to grasp the meaning of demographic realities or, if they have understood the relevance of the statistics, have resolutely decided to ignore them on the ground, presumably, that they have to deal with eternal verities.

Seminars, it is true, have been held (sometimes under UN auspices or with UN support) on topics such as 'Islam and Family Planning'. 'Muftis' are reported to have discovered 'fatwas' that seem, if not to encourage contraception, then at least to condone it. There are even priests in the Roman Catholic Church, such as Arthur MacCormack, who have made desperate attempts over the years to bridge seemingly unbridgeable gaps between dogma and sanity – and, of course, the effort must go on. But, at the moment, the prospect of major breakthroughs in attitude, at least as far as Islam and Catholicism are concerned, seems dim.

Perhaps the likeliest area for a beach-head to be established against the wall of religious opposition is on the environmental front. As a Council member of the United Kingdom branch of the World Wildlife Fund I was invited (with my wife) to attend the 25th Anniversary celebrations of WWF which were held in Assisi in September 1986. The theme of the meeting was 'how the world's great religions – Islam, Judaism, Buddhism, Hinduism and Christianity – can work together with the ecological movement'. The high point of the ceremonies came at a 'multifaith service' in the marvellous Basilica of San Francesco in Assisi decorated with Giotto's famous frescoes, including, of course, that lively and lovely rendering of St Francis preaching to the birds.

While the congregation was being seated that sunny morning, a procession led by His Royal Highness, the Duke of Edinburgh, set forth from the *Sacro Convento* beside the Basilica heralded by the Assisi trumpeters. Swiss Alpine horns then sounded to symbolize the call to the Ceremony and to the 'new alliance' between religion and conservation.

At the door of the Basilica, the procession was challenged by a Maori warrior 'on behalf of the indigenous peoples and cultures of the world'. His Royal Highness accepted the challenge on behalf of all the representatives present.

The multifaith service itself represented, among other things, a triumph of textual research by those good souls who were determined to prove on this occasion that religion was the friend, not the enemy, of ecology. Whereas the Genesis which I remembered spoke of 'subduing the earth and having dominion over it' and of 'bruising the serpent's head', WWF's religious advisers had located passages in the scriptures which if not overtly 'environmental' in character were at least guardedly neutral.

324

The high point of the ceremony came when six giant banners were borne in procession into the Church. Five of them carried the symbols of the five great religions: the Cross, the Star and Crescent, the Prayer Wheel, the Menora, the Hindu hieroglyph. The sixth in a breathtaking display of 'chutzpah' by WWF depicted the giant panda, the world-wide symbol of conservation.

At the Conference which preceded the 'multi-faith ceremony', very little was said by any of the speakers or participants about the crucial link between religion and ecology in the area of population policy and, specifically, about the negative impact of most religious teaching as far as contraception (and abortion) is concerned. The Duke of Edinburgh whose record of outspokenness on the demographic issue (as on other issues) is well-known referred to the question of population growth and its impact on the environment. Sir Peter Scott, who received the Gold Medal of the World Wildlife Fund on the occasion of the 25th Anniversary Celebrations, asked the question 'Is there any possibility that the leaders of the world's great religions can include, in their teaching, a recognition of the dangers to Planet Earth of an ever-increasing human population?' But, as Mrs Frances Dennis, Director of Public Affairs and Information for IPPF reported, 'there was no sustained attempt to bring population issues into the public platform[13].

However, these are early days. Can the United Nations, in particular UNFPA, step in where pandas fear to tread? Can a dialogue with the world's 'great' religions, and even the 'minor' ones (serving presumably lesser Gods), be mounted on population issues? It will certainly not be easy. Though attitudes are changing, they are not always changing in the right direction. Questions of contraception, sterilization and abortion seem to excite political and public opinion as much, and possibly more, than most other issues. According to a survey recently published by the Alan Guttmacher Institute, the large majority of the world's people live in areas where abortion is legal at least for health reasons, and the recent trend has been towards further liberalization of laws. Yet there are real anomalies and archaisms to be found even in so-called advanced western societies. In Ireland, until recently, contraception was permitted only within the framework of marriage and even then the degree of tolerance was more apparent than real since (a) the import of contraceptives was illegal, while (b) no contraceptives were manufactured domestically![14]

Law and population

More generally, there is still enormous scope for improvement in the framework of laws having a bearing on fertility and population, such as those relating to maternal and child health, to family planning, abortion, sterilization and to the status of women. A comprehensive review published in November 1984 by the Population Information Program of Johns Hopkins University evaluated on a world-wide basis the laws and policies affecting fertility over the decades 1974–84. Though the review identified several areas of progress (for example, the repeal of laws banning the advertising or distribution of contraceptives in former French West African colonies), it also recognized that much had still to be achieved[15].

Voluntary sterilization is illegal under statute, ministry regulations, or decree in Burma, Chile, Iran, Peru, Saudi Arabia, and Somalia, and its legal status is unclear in most French-speaking African countries, as well as some countries of Europe and Latin America. Less than 1 per cent of the world's population lives in the seven countries that, according to the 1983 UN Monitoring Report, limit access to modern methods of fertility regulation. (These seven countries are Chad, Ivory Coast, Malawi, Laos, Kampuchea, Saudi Arabia and – not surprisingly – the Holy See.) Yet there are 32 countries – accounting for a further 7 per cent of the world's population – which, though they place no restrictions on family planning, provide no financial support. Nor is it clear to what extent the passage of legislation concerning family planning has actually improved the situation in practice, as opposed to theoretically, in some of the other countries which make up the remainder of the world.

As far as the status of women is concerned, and the whole raft of legal measures which could, and should, be adopted in this field, the review makes it clear that there is still a long way to go. The authors point out, for example, that the impact of laws on age at marriage can be diluted by lack of enforcement and by legal exceptions. India, for example, has found it difficult to enforce the law because the marriage registration system is limited. Sri Lankans of Islamic faith are exempt from the law and may ignore the minimum age requirements of 16 for women and 18 for men. In Indonesia, among other countries, children may marry before reaching the legal minimum age if they have parental consent.

Polygyny – a man's right to take another wife – can lower the status of women and affect their economic welfare. Where religious teachings allow polygyny, however, as in Islamic countries, abolishing the practice is difficult and controversial because it may be thought anti-religious. Among Islamic countries, Tunisia has prohibited polygyny. In 1976, Malaysia abolished polygyny but only for non-Muslims.

This whole field of law and population – which has been of concern to the United Nations, and in particular to UNFPA, from the early days[16] – is of major importance and is likely to remain so. Though an adequate legal framework is not usually a sufficient condition for successful population programmes, it is certainly a necessary one.

A better mousetrap

When Mr McNamara, in the speech he gave to the Board of Governors of the World Bank on 30 September, 1968, committed the Bank 'to join others in programmes of research to determine the most effective methods of family planning'[17], he puts his finger on an area of activity which was – and would remain – of central importance. The search for better, safer methods of contraception is a vital part of the world-wide efforts to promote population policy and family planning. (The granting of the United Nations Population Award in 1984 to Dr Sheldon Segal, Director of Population Sciences at the Rockefeller Foundation, New York, in a special ceremony which took place during the Mexico Population Conference is a clear illustration of this. Mr Segal received the UN prize jointly with Mrs Carmen Miro, Director of CELADE.) Moreover, this is a field in which the United Nations, particularly through the World Health Organization, has played a leading role. WHO's Special Programme on Research, Development and Research Training in Human Reproduction has for the last 15 years acted as the main instrument for conducting, promoting, coordinating and evaluating international research and development related to fertility regulation and family planning.

The contributors to the Special Programme include not only concerned governments, but also large groups of concerned citizens of more than 100 Member States of the United Nations – thousands of physicians, laboratory scientists, research fellows, technicians, midwives, nurses, auxiliary personnel, secretaries and clerks working many hours and sometimes under difficult conditions to contribute at the grass root level to the success of a global effort. Another group of contributors is represented by the 200,000 volunteer subjects, citizens of many countries throughout the world.

Writing in the July 1986 issue of *Contraception*[18] Egon Dicsfaluzy summarized the achievements of WHO's Special Programme on Human Reproduction in the field of fertility control as follows:

> The Programme has developed and brought to the stage of clinical testing a variety of new chemical entities for improved injectable and implantable contraception; it developed, tested and submitted for registration a new vaginal delivery system, providing long-term contraception with a minimum of steroid load. In large-scale multicentre trials the Programme established significantly improved regimens for both injectable and oral contraceptive preparations and –

for the first time – evaluated the short- and long-term safety and efficacy of such preparations in various developing country settings.

In comparative trials involving more than 15,000 volunteers, the Programme has established which prostaglandin derivative, dose regimen, formulation and route of administration is the most suitable in different clinical situations. It developed improved and safe procedures for the medical termination of first and second trimester gestation, generated a large body of clinical pharmacological data for registration of several products and negotiated agreements with three manufacturers for the supply of their products for distribution in the public sector at concessionary prices.

The Programme has also conducted multicentre studies with intrauterine devices, providing more than 500,000 women–months of experience. As a result of these studies, inert (plain) plastic devices are being replaced by copper-releasing devices. One of these has been widely used by the Programme (almost 150,000 woman–months of experience) with excellent results. The Programme has also established that – in contradistinction to insertion after second trimester abortion – insertion following first trimester termination of gestation is as safe and effective as after interval insertion.

The Programme has developed an almost totally synthetic birth control vaccine, and brought it to the stage of clinical testing, after obtaining permission from both the Food and Drug Administration (FDA) in the USA and the Australian Drug Regulatory Authority.

A network of collaborating centres, predominantly in developing countries, collected, extracted and evaluated in animal tests some 500 plant species with alleged antifertility effects, identified by an intensive literature search. Several new chemical entities possessing antifertility activity in rodents have been isolated and some of them synthesized for non-human primate studies.

Multicentre clinical studies were conducted with the aim of assessing the feasibility of using progestogen–androgen combinations as male antifertility agents. These studies revealed the necessity of developing much longer acting androgens than those available today. A series of novel testosterone testers have been synthesized and patented. A single injection of one of these was shown to maintain physiological testosterone levels in castrated male rhesus monkeys for several months.

In addition to research on the medical and physiological aspects of fertility control, the Programme has investigated the psychosocial and pharmacological aspects; has provided extensive research training to scientists through a global network of clinical research centres, and funded a grand total of $25 million worth of equipment and supplies for centres in the developing countries.

WHO is not, of course, the only institution to be active in this area. The development of new contraceptive methods remains a major priority of the Population Council, the New York – based body first established in 1952 at the initiative of John D. Rockefeller 3rd. The Council runs an International Committee for Contraceptive Research whose current projects include long-acting sub-dermal implants releasing progestins, a vaginal ring releasing progestin and estradiol, a long-acting progestin-releasing intra-uterine device, a pregnancy vaccine, improved barrier methods, and analogues of luteinizing hormone releasing hormone for inhibition of ovulation in women and inhibition of spermatogenesis in men.

A considerable number of North American universities and medical institutions, as well as foundations such as the Ford and Rockefeller Foundations, also work on these problems, and support for biomedical research in fertility regulation is provided by several of the bilateral donors, e.g. USAID, SIDA, ODA, CIDA, and the Federal Republic of Germany[19].

Will all these efforts eventually result in better methods of contraception, methods which are safe, simple, cheap and effective and which can be used, by men or women, the world over? And, if such methods are found, will this in any way alter or transform the world's demographic prospects?

These questions are hard to answer. If we look back over the last 20 or 30 years, there have been several promising developments – the discovery of the contraceptive pill, the development of the IUD – which were heralded by some at the time as 'breakthroughs' which would revolution-ize fertility control. Yet, over time, almost all approaches to birth control have proved to have their drawbacks, whether these stem from unantici-pated side-effects, from social inhibitions or from psychological reserva-tions on the part of the users. Today, liability suits against manufacturers – one aspect of 'consumer rights' – look like having a marked, perhaps crippling effect on the willingness of industry to develop and market new devices, or even to continue the production of existing ones, such as the pill and IUD.

These liability suits are generally filed in the rich industrialized coun-tries, such as the United States, where alternatives are available, though they may not be so convenient. But their real impact could be felt in the developing world where the disappearance of contraceptive methods based on, for example, the pill and the IUD, could represent a real setback for population and family-planning programmes.

We must therefore be wary of false dawns, of technological 'break-throughs' (reversible sterilization? 'morning-after' pills?) which may in the end prove to be nothing of the kind. Nevertheless, these caveats recorded, it is clear that the search for better contraceptives must go on. In April 1968, David Bell, a former Administrator of USAID, said: 'the first and foremost requirement for more effective family-planning programmes around the world is more research to find simpler and cheaper means for preventing conception'. And Robert McNamara, in his May 1969 speech at Notre Dame University, Indiana, commented: 'Hundreds of millions for death control. Scarcely one per cent of that amount for fertility control.'

Twenty years later, these remarks are still relevant. There are always multiple demands on medical research funds. Today with the 'cure' for cancer still stubbornly lurking somewhere just beyond the horizon, and the widespread panic over AIDS, birth-control will find it harder than ever to compete with death-control in the continual struggle to secure adequate funding.

Conclusions

As a layman privileged to look in from the outside at an effort which now spans 40 years, I draw the following conclusions:

1. The United Nations and its system of agencies has over the last 40 years made a serious effort to come to grips with the problems of population growth. It has created institutions, in particular the United Nations Fund for Population Activities, which have proved capable of effectively delivering assistance in the field of population and family planning to countries which have requested such assistance. In this manner the UN has contributed to the goals of successive development decades and to the fulfilment of its own primary mandate, the maintenance of world peace.

2. The problems of population growth in the developing world are by no means resolved. There have been successes in bringing down birthrates, notably in China, but unremitting efforts are needed at national and international level if progress is to be maintained. The present dispute between the United States and the United Nations over China is not helpful and should be resolved – in the UN's (and China's) favour – as soon as possible.

3. The difficulties associated with population and family-planning policies and programmes – whether religious, political or social – remain great. There can be no slackening in the attempts being made to expound to a wide variety of audiences the causes and the consequences of rapid population growth and the need for action.

4. Though world population growth has been the main subject of this book, other problems within the population field – such as ageing, migration and urbanization – deserve attention; but this should not in my view lead to any major reallocation of programme resources.

5. We should, however, expect to see some further developments within the existing framework of policies, particularly the attempt to match population and family-planning programmes with other programmes aiming at improvements in maternal and child health (such as nutrition) and in the status of women (such as female education). These programmes not only have a value in themselves; they also appear to be an effective way of achieving (sometimes rapid) falls in birth-rates.

Annex A

UN General Assembly Resolution: 1838 (XVII)
Population growth and economic development
of 18 December 1962

The General Assembly,

Considering that rapid economic and social progress in the developing countries is dependent not least upon the ability of these countries to provide their peoples with education, a fair standard of living and the possibility for productive work,

Considering further that economic development and population growth are closely interrelated,

Recognizing that the health and welfare of the family are of paramount importance, not only for obvious humanitarian reasons, but also with regard to economic development and social progress, and that the health and welfare of the family require special attention in areas with a relatively high rate of population growth,

Recognizing further that it is the responsibility of each Government to decide on its own policies and devise its own programmes of action for dealing with the problems of population and economic and social progress,

Reminding States Members of the United Nations and members of the specialized agencies that, according to recent census results, the effective population increase during the last decade has been particularly great in many of the low-income less developed countries,

Reminding Member States that in formulating their economic and social policies it is useful to take into account the latest relevant facts on the interrelationship of population growth and economic and social development, and that the forthcoming World Population Conference and the Asian Population Conference might throw new light on the importance of this problem, especially for the developing countries,

Recalling its resolution 1217 (XII) of 14 December 1957, in which the General Assembly, *inter alia,* invited Member States, particularly the developing countries, to follow as closely as possible the interrelationship of economic changes and population changes, and requested the Secretary-General to ensure the co-ordination of the activities of the United Nations in the demographic and economic fields,

Recalling Economic and Social Council resolution 820 B (XXXI) of 28 April 1961 which contains provisions for intensifying efforts to ensure international co-operation in the evaluation, analysis and utilization of population census results and related data, particularly in the less developed countries, and in which the Council requested the Secretary-General to explore the possibilities of increasing technical assistance funds for assistance to Governments requesting it in preparing permanent programmes of demographic research,

Recognizing that further studies and research are necessary to fill the gaps in the present knowledge of the causes and consequences of demographic trends, particularly in the less developed countries,

Recognizing also that removals of large national groups to other countries may give rise to ethnic, political, emotional and economic difficulties,

1. *Notes with appreciation* the report of the Secretary-General on measures proposed for the United Nations Development Decade in which he refers, *inter alia*, to the interrelationship of population growth and economic and social development;

2. *Express its appreciation* of the work on population problems which has up to now been carried out under the guidance of the Population Commission;

3. *Requests* the Secretary-General to conduct an inquiry among the Governments of States Members of the United Nations and members of the specialized agencies concerning the particular problems confronting them as a result of the reciprocal action of economic development and population changes;

4. *Recommends* that the Economic and Social Council, in co-operation with the specialized agencies, the regional economic commissions and the Population Commission, and taking into account the results of the inquiry referred to in paragraph 3 above, should intensify its studies and research on the interrelationships of population growth and economic and social development, with particular reference to the needs of the developing countries for investment in health and educational facilities within the framework of their general development programmes;

5. *Further recommends* that the Economic and Social Council should report on its findings to the General Assembly not later than at its nineteenth session;

6. *Endorses* the view of the Population Commission that the United Nations should encourage and assist Governments, especially those of the less developed countries, in obtaining basic data and in carrying out essential studies of the demographic aspects, as well as other aspects, of their economic and social development problems;

7. *Recommends* that the second World Population Conference should pay special attention to the interrelationship of population growth and economic and social development, particularly in the less developed countries, and that efforts should be made to obtain the fullest possible participation in the Conference by experts from such countries.

1197th plenary meeting
18 December 1962

Annex B

UN General Assembly Resolution: 2211 (XXI)
Population growth and economic development
of 17 December 1966

The General Assembly,

Recalling its resolution 1838 (XVII) of 18 December 1962 on population growth and economic development and Economic and Social Council resolution 933 C (XXXV) of 5 April 1963 on the intensification of demographic studies, research and training, 1048 (XXXVII) of 15 August 1964 on population growth and economic and social development and 1084 (XXXIX) of 30 July 1965 on work programmes and priorities in the field of population,

Recalling World Health Authority resolutions WHA 18.49 of 21 May 1965 and WHA 19.43 of 20 May 1966 on the health aspects of world population,

Taking note of resolution 3.252 adopted on 29 November 1966 by the General Conference of the United Nations Educational, Scientific and Cultural Organization at its fourteenth session, and of paragraphs 842–844 of the programme for 1967–1968 of that organization on the subject of education and information related to population growth,

Recalling the inquiry conducted by the Secretary-General among Governments on problems resulting from the interaction of economic growth and population change, and his report thereon, which reflected a wide variety of population problems,

Commending the Economic and Social Council and the Secretary-General for convening the World Population Conference, held at Belgrade from 30 August to 10 September 1965, in which a large number of specialists in demography and related fields from developing countries were able to participate,

Taking note of the summary of the highlights of the World Population Conference,

Noting the steps taken, by the organizations of the United Nations system which are concerned, to co-ordinate their work in the field of population,

Concerned at the growing food shortage in the developing countries, which is due in many cases to a decline in the production of food-stuffs relative to population growth,

Recognizing the need for further study of the implications of the growth, structure and geographical distribution of population for economic and social development, including national health, nutrition, education and social welfare programmes carried out at all levels of government activity,

Believing that demographic problems require the consideration of economic, social, cultural, psychological and health factors in their proper perspective,

Recognizing the sovereignty of nations in formulating and promoting their own population policies, with due regard to the principle that the size of the family should be according to the free choice of each individual family,

1. *Invites* the Economic and Social Council, the Population Commission, the regional economic commissions, the United Nations Economic and Social Office in Beirut and the specialized agencies concerned to study the proceedings of the 1965 World Population Conference when pursuing their activities in the field of population;

2. *Notes with satisfaction* the decision of the World Health Organization to include in its programme of activities the study of the health aspects of human reproduction and the provision of advisory services, upon request, within its responsibilities under World Health Assembly resolution WHA 19.43, and the decision of the United Nations Educational, Scientific and Cultural Organization to stimulate and provide assistance towards scientific studies concerning the relations between the development of education and evolution of population;

3. *Requests* the Secretary-General:

(a) To pursue, within the limits of available resources, the implementation of the work programme covering training, research information and advisory services in the field of population in the light of the recommendations of the Population Commission contained in the report on its thirteenth session, as endorsed by the Economic and Social Council in its resolution 1084 (XXXIX), and of the considerations set forth in the preamble of the present resolution;

(b) To continue his consultations with the specialized agencies concerned, in order to ensure that the activities of the United Nations system of organizations in the field of population are effectively co-ordinated;

(c) To present to the Population Commission at its fourteenth session, as envisaged in Economic and Social Council resolution 1084 (XXXIX), proposals with regard to the priorities of work over periods of two and five years, within the framework of the long-range programme of work in the field of population;

4. *Calls upon* the Economic and Social Council, the Population Commission, the regional economic commissions, the United Nations Economic and Social Office in Beirut and the specialized agencies concerned to assist, when requested, in further developing and strengthening national and regional facilities for training, research, information and advisory services in the field of population, bearing in mind the different character of population problems in each country and region and the needs arising therefrom.

1497th plenary meeting
17 December 1966

Notes

Introduction

1. Published by Chatto & Windus for Sussex University Press, 1973.
2. Published in *The Global Partnership: International Agencies and Economic Development*, edited by Richard N. Gardner and Max F. Millikan, Frederick A. Praeger, New York, 1968.
3. Other references for the material cited in the Introduction are to be found in the individual Chapters and in the relevant Notes.
4. Population and Development Series No. 2, World Bank Staff Working Paper No. 677.

1. The rise of concern

1. According to John D. Durand, a former head of the Population Division within the Secretariat of the United Nations, the most comprehensive and detailed series of population estimates for the world, region by region, since the beginning of the Christian era is that given in Colin Clark's: *Population Growth and Land Use* (New York: St Martin's Press, 1968); see article by John D. Durand entitled 'Historical Estimates of World Population: an evaluation', published in *Population and Development Review*, Vol. 3, No. 3, September 1977, pp. 253–69. Clark composed his series by selecting estimates from the works of many authors and filling in some of his own. Table 1.1 shows Clark's estimates for selected dates between AD 14 and 1900, recast into a classification of 15 regional segments. The series is completed with 1975 estimates from the United Nations *Demographic Yearbook* and embellished with Durand's own grading – on a scale of A to D – of the reliability of these estimates.
2. Symonds & Carder – published by Chatto & Windus for Sussex University Press, 1973.
3. Symonds & Carder– op. cit., p. 4.
4. Symonds & Carder – op. cit., p. 13.
5. Albert Thomas, Director of the International Labour Organization, was a socialist and gave much more support than Sir Eric Drummond to the World Population Conference of 1927.
6. Symonds & Carder op. cit., p. 28.
7. Symonds & Carder op. cit., p. 44.
8. Published in the *Global Partnership*, edited by Richard N. Gardner & Max F. Millikan, Praeger, New York 1968 pp. 345.
9. See J. Boyd-Orr, *The White Man's Dilemma*, London, 1953, pp. 71–81, quoted by Symonds & Carder, op. cit., p. 55.
10. Symonds & Carder op. cit., p. 61.

11. Symonds & Carder op. cit., p. 65.
12. The long-term success of malaria eradication programmes remains, of course, to be evaluated. Substantial occurrences of malaria are reported in certain regions, particularly on the Indian sub-continent, and the emergence of 'DDT-resistant' strains of mosquito.
13. Gardner & Millikan, op. cit., p. 345.
14. Symonds & Carder, op. cit., p. 86.
15. Symonds & Carder op. cit., p. 87.

2. The breakthrough in the United Nations

1. G A Resolution 1710 (XVI) of December 19, 1961.
2. G A Resolution 1711 (XVI) of December 19, 1961.
3. Gardner & Millikan, op. cit., p. 19.
4. Symonds & Carder, op. cit., p. 95 and Gardner & Millikan, op. cit., p. 346.
5. Stanley P. Johnson, *Life Without Birth*; Little, Brown, 1970, p. 188.
6. Stanley P. Johnson, op. cit., p. 240.
7. See Muramatsu, Minoru; *Japan's Experience in Family Planning, Tokyo*: Family-Planning Federation of Japan, 1967.
8. Gardner & Millikan, op. cit., pp. 349 and 350, also Symonds & Carder, op. cit., pp. 118–22.
9. Symonds & Carder, op. cit., p. 135.
10. Report of the Asian Population Conference and Selected Papers: New Delhi, India, December 1963. UN Publication Sales Number 65.II.F.11.
11. *ECLA Annual Report 1965–1966*, Supplement 4; UN Doc. E/4181, 1966.
12. Symonds & Carder, op. cit., p. 138.
13. Resolution 1048 (XXXVII), or of ECOSOC 37th Session, 1964, Supplement No. 1, p. 13.
14. See Professor James Avery Joyce's study for the Law and Population Program of the Fletcher School of Law and Diplomacy at Tufts University: 'A Study of the Capacity of the United Nations System – Family Planning and Population Control – revised typescript, September 1970. In UNFPA archives.
15. Symonds & Carder, op, cit., p. 145.
16. These were: Colombia, Finland, India, Republic of Korea, Malaysia, Morocco, Nepal, Singapore, Sweden, Tunisia, United Arab Republic and Yugoslavia.
17. *Population Newsletter*, No. 1, April 1968.
18. Chaired by Professor Richard Gardner, its members included former President of the World Bank, Eugene R. Black; General William H. Draper; and John D Rockefeller 3rd.
19. See Gardner & Millikan op. cit., p. 361.
20. UN Press Release, ECOSOC, SG/SM/51, July 11, 1967.
21. Gardner & Millikan, op. cit., p. 361.
22. See *Population Newsletter* No. 4, issued by the Population Division of the Department of Economic and Social Affairs, United Nations. The Statement was issued on December 10, 1967, on the occasion of Human Rights Day. The Secretary-General welcomed on additional 18 signatories (at Head of State level) to the Declaration on Population and Human Rights which had been promulgated exactly a year earlier. See p. 24, and Note 2.16. The additional signatories were: Australia, Barbados, Denmark, Dominican Republic, Ghana, Indonesia, Iran, Japan, Jordan, Netherlands, New Zealand, Norway, Pakistan,

Philippines, Thailand, Trinidad and Tobago, United Kingdom and the United States.

23. See p. 24.
24. Symonds & Carder, op. cit., p. 179.
25. ECOSOC Resolution 1347 (XLV) on Population and its relation to economic and social development, adopted at the 1556th Plenary meeting on 30 July 1968.
26. Stanley P. Johnson, op. cit., pp. 17 ff.
27. First issued by the UN in 1950, *"Determinants and Consequences"* was regarded as one of the most influential of United Nations publications on demography and, as much as any other single work, had helped to establish the intellectual basis for action.
28. E/CN 6/497.
29. The text of the Nairobi Forward-Looking Strategies for the Advancement of Women was adopted by consensus by the World Conference to Review and Appraise the Achievements of the United Nations Decade for Women, which was held at Nairobi from 15 to 27 July 1985. Paragraph 156 of that document states: 'The ability of women to control their own fertility forms an important basis for the enjoyment of other rights...'.

3. The role of the agencies

1. See p. 27.
2. WHO's mandate to work on the health aspects of human reproduction, of family planning and of population dynamics, was set out in World Health Assembly Resolutions 18.49 of 2 May 1965, 19.43 of 20 May 1966, 20.41 of 25 May 1967, 21.43 of 23 May 1968 and 22.23 of 23 July 1969.
3. Resolution 1.241 adopted by the General Conference of UNESCO at its 15th session November 1968.
4. See p. 23.
5. See p. 26.

4. Four reports

1. See pp. 24 ff.
2. Symonds & Carder, op. cit., p. 189.
3. Report on the United Nations Trust Fund for population activities and the role of the United Nations in Population Action Programmes. UN Doc ST/SOA/SER.R.10
4. The Commission was subsequently established under the chairmanship of John D. Rockefeller 3rd, and reported on March 27, 1972. In his covering letter to the President and Congress, Mr Rockefeller wrote: 'After two years of concentrated effort, we have concluded that, in the long run, no substantial benefits will result from further growth of the Nation's population, rather that the gradual stabilization of our population through voluntary means would contribute significantly to the Nation's ability to solve its problems. We have looked for, and have not found, any convincing economic argument for continued population growth. The health of our country does not depend on it, nor does the vitality of business nor the welfare of the average person.
5. See Note 9.10.
6. *Venture*: Vol. 22, No. 1, published by the Fabian Society in January 1970.

7. *Study of the Capacity of the United Nations Development System.* UN Doc. DP/5, 1969.
8. Symonds & Carder, op. cit., p. 192.

5.   UNFPA: the early days

1. UN Press Release SG/SM/1055 of 14 January 1969.
2. Informal panel discussion at UN headquarters, 22 December 1967, cited by Joyce, op. cit., Chapter 4.
3. See p. 49 ff.
4. Rafael M. Salas. *People: An International Choice,* published by Pergamon Press, Oxford 1976, p. 97.
5. Salas, op. cit., especially Chapter 6.
6. Salas, op. cit., p. 18.
7. Salas, op. cit., p. 25.
8. Salas, op. cit., p. 29.
9. See pp. 68 ff.
10. Salas, op. cit., p. 31.
11. Salas, op. cit., p. 33.
12. Salas, op. cit., p. 32.
13. *Population Newsletter,* No. 10 of March 1970.
14. Salas, op. cit., p. 32.
15. G A Resolution 2815 (XXVI) of 14 December 1971.
16. Salas, op. cit., p. 61.
17. See p. 72.
18. Salas, op. cit., p. 64.
19. Salas, op. cit., p. 69.
20. Salas, op. cit., p. 69.
21. See pp. 220 ff.
22. See pp. 80 ff.
23. UN Sales No. E71 II A 12 – ST/ECA/18
24. First Report to the Governing Council by the Executive Director of UNFPA, 15th Session of UNDP Governing Council, United Nations, 29 January, 1973.
25. Salas, op. cit., p. 69.

6.   The World Population Conference, Bucharest, 1974

1. *Only One Earth* was the title of the book which was commissioned by the United Nations before the Stockholm Conference, written by Barbara Ward and Rene Dubos, and published in many languages. (W. Norton, 1972).
2. See p. 23 and Note 2.16.
3. ECOSOC Resolution 1672 (LII).
4. E/CN/9/245.
5. Paragraph 91 of the Report of the Population Commission's 16th Session. E/5090; E/CN.9/263.
6. Salas, op. cit., p. 101.
7. ECOSOC Resolution 1672G (LII).
8. E/CN.9/292 add.1, 27 August, 1973.
9. Economic and Social Council, official records: 56th Session, Supplement No. 3, E/5444: E/Cn.9/296.

10. E/conf.60.7.
11. A/Res/3201/S-VI.
12. Report of the United Nations World Population Conference 1974, E/Conf. 60/19.
13. See Jason L. Finkle & Barbara B. Crane: *The Politics of Bucharest, Population and Development Review,* September 1975.
14. China returned to the attack when its delegates told the First Committee, meeting to consider population and social and economic development, that the Third World had great opportunities for development if the countries built themselves up through self-reliance and independence.

    'All pessimistic views are groundless. The future of mankind is infinitely bright.'

    This engaging turn of phrase, as well as others to be found in the Chinese statement, was later picked up in the revised WPPA – paragraph 14a in particular, where we read: 'Of all things in the world, people are the most precious. Man's knowledge and ability to master himself and his environment will continue to grow. Mankind's future can be made infinitely bright.'
15. Finkle & Crane, op. cit., p. 102.
16. As far as abortion was concerned, the debate in the Working Group centred around a paragraph in the draft Plan in the section of the Recommendations for Action dealing with morbidity and mortality. Paragraph 22 called for national and international efforts to achieve, *inter alia,* 'reduction of involuntary sterility, subfecundity, defective births and illegal abortions'. The Working Group rejected by 49 votes to 11, with 11 absentions, an amendment to replace the word 'illegal' by the word 'induced', and also rejected by 46 votes to 11, with 10 absentions, a further amendment to replace the world 'abortion' by the word 'miscarriage'. The Working Group finally adopted the paragraph as proposed in the Draft Plan by 65 votes to none with 5 abstentions (see paragraph 24 of WPPA).

7. The World Population Plan of Action

1. Issue of 26 August, 1974. *Planet* was produced by a consortium of non-governmental organizations which included the Population Council and IPPF.
2. Report of the United Nations World Population Conference 1974, E/Conf.60/19.
3. Full voting list is given in E/Conf.60/19.
4. The corresponding paragraph in the draft Plan was 89.
5. Finkel & Crane, op. cit.
6. *Planet,* issue of 28 August 1974 published Bucharest.
7. See pp. 83 ff.
8. Salas, op. cit., p. 103.
9. Salas, op. cit., p. 109.
10. UN Doc. no. E/5444, E/CN.9/296.

8. Falling birth-rates

1. ST.ESA.SER.A/85, Department of International Economic Affairs, Population Studies no. 85, United Nations, New York 1984.

2. See pp. 24 ff.
3. *Population: The UNFPA Experience*, edited by Nafis Sadik, New York University Press, New York and London 1984: pp. 31, 51 and 52.
4. Article on China by Katherine Ch'iu Lyle & John S. Aird in the *International Encylopaedia of Population* (IEP).
5. Lyle & Aird, op. cit.
6. Article by Liu Zheng, published in *Populi*, Vol. No. 3, 1981.
7. Salas, op. cit., p. 94.
8. World Bank, World Development Report 1984, pp. 106 and following.
9. Jan.–Feb. 1977 issue of *Development Forum*, United Nations, Geneva.
10. Ronald Freedman & Bernard Berelson, *Studies in Family Planning*, January 1976.
11. UNFPA 1984 Annual Report.
12. See Chapter 10.
13. Report on the Family-Planning Programme in India, UN Doc. TAU/IND/48.
14. See p. 76.
15. See p. 74 ff.
16. The UN's Rapporteur was Professor Richard Symonds who had prepared the important report on the role of the United Nations Trust Fund for population activities, see p 48.
17. Sadik op. cit., pp. 40, 41.
18. *India Today*, June 30, 1986.
19. Sadik, op. cit., pp. 42 and 43.
20. Sadik, op. cit., p. 43.
21. Sri Lanka, Population Profile No. 13, UNFPA, undated.
22. The World Fertility Survey was founded in 1972 as a project of the International Statistical Institute. Its main objective was described as 'carrying out nationally representative, internationally comparable, and scientifically designed and conducted surveys of human fertility behaviour.' Forty-two developing and 20 developed countries participated, representing 39 per cent of the world's population. By the end of June 1984, UNFPA funding to the operations of the central organization of WFS had reached $15 million.
23. *Population Newsletter* No. 12, March 1971, pp. 6 and 7.
24. World Bank, World Development Report 1984 pp. 173 ff.
25. Sadik, op. cit., p. 34.
26. Article by J. Mayone Stycos on Latin American demography, *International Encyclopaedia of Population* p. 405.
27. Sadik op. cit., p. 51.
28. Stycos, op. cit.
29. Sadik, op. cit., p. 54.
30. *World Watch* paper No. 8, October 1976, World Watch Institute, Washington.
31. Sadik, op. cit., p. 61.
32. Col/73/P03/1980 – UNFPA.
33. Article on Brazil by Moreira, da Silva and McLaughlin in *IEP*, p. 70.
34. See Chapter 6.
35. World Bank, World Development Report 1984, p. 170.
36. UNFPA 1980 Annual Report.
38. IEP p. 477 article by Karol J. Krotki.
39. Abdel-Rahim Omran. *Population in the Arab World, Problems and Prospects*, published by Croom Helm Ltd, London. 1980. p. 54.
40. Krotki, op. cit.
41. Omran, op. cit., p. 77.

42. Omran, op. cit., p. 98.
43. Population Profile No. 17, UNFPA, undated.
44. Sadik op. cit., p. 79.
45. Issue of 2–8 August, 1986.
46. Evaluation report – family planning and population educational programme in Tunisia, submitted to UNDP Governing Council.
47. Sadik op. cit., p. 71.
48. Sadik op. cit., p. 85.
49. World Bank Paper entitled 'Population Growth and Policies in Sub-Saharan Africa', 1986.
50. Published by World Bank, Washington.
51. 'A Review of Current and Planned Activities in the Population Field', World Bank, 1986.
53. E/Conf.76/PC/10.

9.   *Evolving perceptions*

1. See, for example, the summary given in the Pearson Report on International Development.
2. Published by the National Academy of Sciences, Washington, DC, USA.
3. Book of that title published by Club of Rome in 1972. Earth Island, London. Co-authors, Donella H. Meadows, Dennis L. Meadows, Jorgen Randers, William H. Behrens III.
4. Population and the Urban Future, Report of the International Conference, UNFPA, 1980.
5. The Brandt Commission on Population – *Population and Development* Review, 1980.
6. Pergamon Press, 1980.
7. Published by the International Union for the Conservation of Nature and Natural Resources, 1196 Gland, Switzerland.
8. Perspectives, published by UNFPA 1984.
9. See Para 12 of the Report of the International Conference on Population, 1984 UN Doc E/CONF.76/19.
10. See pp. 49 ff.
11. *Earthscan – Environment and Conflicts*, November 1984, IIED, London.
12. See Nazli Choucri, *Multidisciplinary Perspectives on Population and Conflict*, Syracuse, 1984; also *Population and Conflict* by the same author, UNFPA, New York, 1983.
13. Gardner & Millikan, op. cit., p. 361.

10.   *The International Conference on Population, 1984*

1. 1982/42
2. *News Mexico 84*, 7 August 1984.
3. Report of the International Conference on Population 1984 E/Conf/INF 1976/19.
4. *Populi*, Vol II, No. 4, 1984; article by Leon Tabah.
5. August 5, 1984.
6. August 5, 1984.

7. Tabah, op. cit.
8. *News Mexico*, 9 August 1984.
9. Attempts to strengthen the references to 'natural methods of family planning' beyond what was already in the draft recommendations failed. Fred Zai, who chaired the Main committee, comments in his article in *Populi* Vol. II No. 4 1984.

   When insistence was made in Mexico that specific mention be given to so-called 'natural' methods of family planning, I found myself suspended between the political need to be impartial and my professional judgement as a medical doctor, that these methods are ineffective and likely to prove detrimental to family planning programmes. The reference to 'natural' methods will strengthen the position of those who are against technical means of contraception and will divert resources into an approach whose present record is one of failure.

10. E/Conf.76/5, 6 June 1984.
11. See p. 117. Also Paragraph 17 of the World Population Plan of Action, contained in the Report of the United Nations World Population Conference, 1974, E/CONF.60/19.
12. E/Conf.76/19, Paragraphs 43 and 44.
13. *Populi*, Vol. 2, No. 4, 1984.
14. The Population Division of the Department of International Economic and Social Affairs of the United Nations Secretariat, in January 1985 published a collection of speeches given by governmental delegates to the Mexico City Conference under the title 'The Debate on The Review and Appraisal of the World Population Plan of Action'.
15. Alma-Ata 1978, Report of the International Conference on Primary Health Care, WHO Geneva 1978.
16. *News Mexico*, 8 August 1984.
17. *Populi*, Vol. 12, No. 4, 1985.

11. China, the United States and the United Nations

1. *Hong Kong Standard*, 29 August, 1986.
2. *China Daily*, 21 November, 1986.
3. Xinhua, 17 November, 1986.
4. Article by Rafael Salas in *New York Times* entitled 'the UN Population Fund needs the US', 13 December, 1986.
5. *China Facts and Figures: Population.* Foreign Languages Press, Beijing 1984.
6. *China Facts and Figures: Women, Marriage and the Family.* Undated. Foreign Languages Press, Beijing.
7. *A Brief Introduction to China's Population Situation and Policy.* State Family Planning Commission, People's Republic of China.
8. In old China, the female/male ratio was much higher. Census records taken during the reign of Emperor Xuantong (1909–11) of the Qing Dynasty which were published in 1912 showed the ratio to be 100:121.06 (166 million females to 202 million males). In later census records between 1932 and 1939, the ratio became 100:112.17. The first national population census of New China taken in 1953 showed a ratio of 100:107.5 which fell to 100:105.5 in the second national population census taken in 1964.
9. *China Daily*, 6 June, 1986
10. *International Herald Tribune*, 9 October, 1986.

12. Postscript and Conclusions

1. *Newsweek*, December 15th, 1986.
2. *China Daily*, December 6th, 1986.
3. *Newsweek*, December 15th, 1986.
4. Ibid.
5. Ageing – A matter of International Concern, Statement by Rafael M. Salas, Executive Director, UNFPA, to the World Assembly on ageing, Vienna, Austria, 27 July, 1982. *UNFPA's Speech Series no. 78*.
6. Julia Henderson, *Populi*, Vol. 12, no. 4, 1985.
7. Ibid. *Report of the International Conference on Family Planning in the 80s* held in Jakarta, Indonesia, 26–30 April, 1981, has been published by IPPF.
8. *Report of the International Conference on Population and the Urban Future*, 1986. UNFPA, New York, 1986.
9. Ibid.
10. The population of Xian exceeded 1.6 million at the time of the Qin dynasty.
11. See page 235.
12. *Report of the European Parlimentarians 'Forum on Child Survival, Women and Population Integrated Strategies'*, The Hague, Netherlands, 1986.
13. IPPF. Open File, 10 October, 1986.
14. *Induced Abortion: A World review*, 1986, 6th Edition; by Christopher Tietze and Stanley K. Henshaw. Alan Guttmacher Institute, USA, 1986.
15. *Population Reports. Series E*, No. 7, November 1984. 'Law and Policy'. Published by Population Information Program, Johns Hopkins University, Baltimore, Maryland 21205, USA.
16. One early project supported by UNFPA was that on Law and Population, directed by Luke Lee of Tufts University in the United States.
17. See page 40.
18. *Contraception*, July 1986, Vol. 34, No. 1. Published by GERON X INC, Box 1108, LOS ALTOS, California, 94023-1108 USA.
19. 'Population Programmes and Projects': Vol. 1; *Guide to Sources of International Population Assistance*, UNFPA, New York.

Subject index

Italic numbers refer to the Figures.
Bold numbers refer to the Tables.

Name Index